W0377437

Gateway

Das neue *Gateway* wurde für Bildungsgänge entwickelt, die zum Mittleren Bildung schluss führen (Berufsgrundschuljahre, Berufsfachschulen der verschiedenen Ausrichtungen, Berufsaufbauschulen). Am Ende werden die sprachlichen Kompetenzen des Niveaus B1 des Gemeinsamen Europäischen Referenzrahmens erreicht.

Gateway zeichnet sich durch eine leicht zu bewältigende Progression, Klarheit und Benutzerfreundlichkeit sowie motivierende berufsbezogene und zielgruppengerechte Themen aus; gleichermaßen bewährte und aktuelle Methoden gewährleisten gründliches, erfolgreiches Lernen. Die Lernenden werden dort abgeholt, wo sie mit ihrem Vorwissen stehen, und sicher zum Ziel geführt.

Aufbau des Schülerbuchs

Das erste Jahr des Lehrgangs besteht aus einem Vorkurs sowie den *Units* 1–8, das zweite aus den *Units* 9–17. Jedes Jahr schließt mit einer kurzen Wiederholungseinheit *(Revision)*. Das Material folgt dem Doppelseitenprinzip und gestaltet die Unterrichtsarbeit so klar und einfach. Die kommunikative Funktion jeder Übung ist durch Buchstaben deutlich gekennzeichnet: [R]ezeption, [P]roduktion, [I]nteraktion und [M]ediation (Sprachmittlung)

Jede *Unit* besteht aus vier bzw. fünf Doppelseiten:

- **Focus** stimmt auf die Grammatik und die Sprachmittel der *Unit* ein. Dabei werden manche Regeln vorgegeben, andere wiederum stellen die Lernenden selbständig auf.
- **Practice** übt und festigt die zuvor auf Deutsch zusammengefasste Grammatik und kann im Unterricht und/oder zu Hause erarbeitet werden. Die Schülerinnen und Schüler lernen Formen und Regeln sicher zu verwenden.
- In **Reading and listening** wenden die Schülerinnen und Schüler die Grammatik und die Sprachmittel, die sie sich angeeignet haben, frei und in z. T. neuen Situationen an. Unterschiedlichste Übungstypen trainieren das Lese- und Hörverstehen und bereiten systematisch auf Klassenarbeiten und Prüfungen vor. Vertiefende Übungen und Tests finden sich im Workbook inklusive Schüler-Audio-CD zur Schulung des Hörverstehens.
- **Gateway to work** richtet sich an Lernende aller Berufsfelder und vermittelt die sprachlichen Fertigkeiten, die beim Einstieg in die Berufswelt benötigt werden: u. a. Telefonieren, Kommunikation mit Muttersprachlern und auf Geschäftsreisen sowie Wegbeschreibungen.
- **At work** ab *Unit* 8 behandelt die sprachlichen Mittel, die in den verschiedenen Berufsfeldern, Wirtschaft und Verwaltung, Hauswirtschaft, Sozialpädagogik und Gesundheit sowie Technik, benötigt werden; berufsspezifische Fähigkeiten, wie z. B. das Schreiben eines Geschäftsbriefs, der Umgang mit Kunden einer Werkstatt, das Verstehen eines Koch-/Backrezepts, werden gezielt geschult.

Immer wieder weisen die Kategorien *Tips and tricks* und *Culture tips* auf typische Fehler deutschsprachiger Lerner sowie auf den kulturellen Hintergrund des Englischen hin. *Projects* regen immer wieder zur Internetrecherche an.

Das Schülerbuch wird u.a. ergänzt durch einen umfangreichen Anhang. Die Ausklappseiten vorne und hinten bieten geografische Karten, nützliche Redemittel, eine Übersicht der Zeiten und der englischen Satzstellung sowie die unregelmäßigen Verben.

Zusammenfassung

Das neue *Gateway* ist ein Lehrwerk, das Schülerinnen und Schüler motiviert, intensiv zu lernen, und sie bestens auf Klassenarbeiten, Prüfungen und Beruf vorbereitet.
Wir wünschen Ihnen gutes und erfolgreiches Arbeiten mit unserem Lehrwerk!

Autor und Redaktion

Inhaltsverzeichnis

YEAR TWO

Anhang

Vorkurs

A Excuse me. Do you speak English?

[R] **1 Listen and answer the questions.**

1 This is a big, international airport. What's its name?
2 How many flights are there every day at this airport?
3 There are thousands of passengers here every day. Where are they from?
4 What's the international language at a big airport like this?

[R] **2 Signs are very important at an airport. Can you match these signs with the German and English words and phrases?**

A B C D E F

G H I J K L

Abflug	**Toilets**
Ankunft	**Buses**
Toiletten	**Information**
Treffpunkt	**Departures**
Passkontrolle	**Baby change**
Wickelraum	**Shopping**
Restaurant	**Meeting point**
Café	**Bank**
Information	**Arrivals**
Busse	**Passport control**
Einkaufen	**Café**
Bank	**Restaurant**

[R] **3 Listen.**
Here are two people in a café at the airport today.
Where are they from?

Kim	Excuse me. Do you speak English?
Elke	Hmm. A bit.
Kim	Is this seat free?
Elke	Yeah, sure.
Kim	Hi. My name's Kim.
Elke	Hi. I'm Elke.
Kim	Where are you from, Elke?
Elke	I'm from Dortmund, here in Germany. Where are you from?
Kim	I'm from Boston in the USA.

Example: Elke is from …

[I] **4 Read the dialogue with a partner.**

[I] **5 This is Steve from London. You're in the café at the airport with Steve.**
Make a dialogue with a partner. Take it in turns to be Steve.

Steve	Excuse me. Do you speak English?
You	…
Steve	Is this seat free?
You	…
Steve	Thanks. Hi. My name's Steve.
You	…
Steve	Where are you from, (name)?
You	…
Steve	I'm from London in England.

[I] **6 Say 'hi' to the people in your class.**

Hi. I'm …

Hello. My name's …

▶ TIPS AND TRICKS

Wenn Sie etwas nicht verstehen, fragen Sie:

Excuse me. What does … mean?

How do you say … in English?

[R] **7** **Where are these European teenagers from? Match the people and the countries.**

My name's Katarina.
I'm 15 years old.
I'm from Athens in …

We're from Vienna in … We're 17 years old and our names are Liesl and Frank.

Hi! I'm Michel. I'm from Paris in…
I'm 19 years old.

Hi! My name's Metin.
I'm from Istanbul in …
I'm 15.

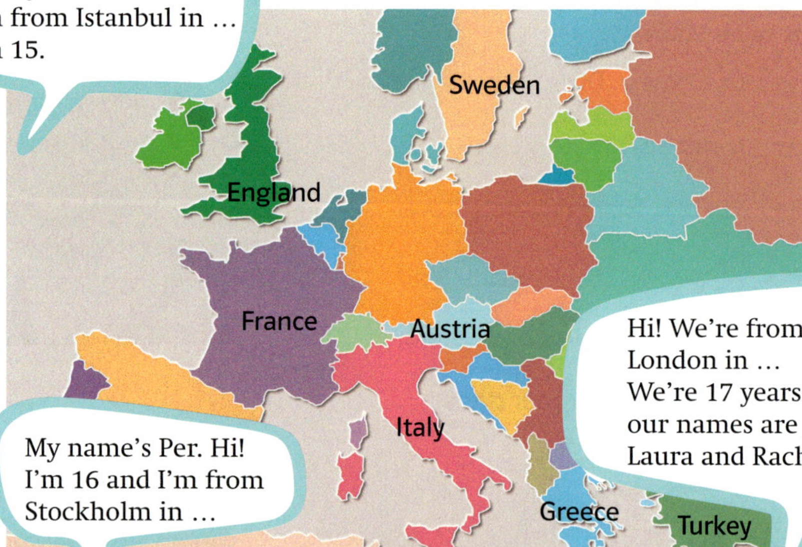

Hi! We're from London in …
We're 17 years old and our names are Jason, Laura and Rachel.

Buongiorno! I'm Anita from Rome in …
I'm 18 years old.

My name's Per. Hi!
I'm 16 and I'm from Stockholm in …

[I] **8 Ask a student in your class.**
Where's Per from? – He's …
Where are Liesl and Frank from? – They're …
How old is/are …? – …

Where's Katarina from?

She's from …

[I] **9 What are their names? Ask around the class again.**
She's from Rome. – Her name's …
He's from Istanbul. – His name's …
They're from Vienna. – Their names are …
He's/She's/They're 17 years old. – …

[P] **10 Complete the sentences with my, his, her, its, our, your or their.**
1 Hello! My name's Elke. I'm from Germany. What's … name? – I'm Steve.
2 Hi! … names are Liesl and Frank. We're from Austria.
3 … names are Liesl and Frank. They're from Austria.
4 That boy over there. What's … name?
5 That girl over there. What's … name?
6 This is Dusseldorf airport. … full name is: Dusseldorf International Airport

[P] **11 Give the sentences again with the full forms of to be.**
Example: I'm from Dusseldorf. → I am from Dusseldorf.
1 This is Dusseldorf airport. It's in North Rhine Westphalia in Germany.
2 Her name's Laura and she's 18 years old.
3 Are they from England? Yes, they're from London.

Now give these sentences again with the short forms.
Example: I am from Dortmund. → I'm from Dortmund.
1 Where is Per from? He is from Stockholm in Sweden.
2 Our names are Liesl and Frank. We are from Vienna.

[I] **12 Introduce your partner to the class.**
1 Copy and fill in this form for you.
2 Interview a partner:
What's your name? How old are you? Where are you from?
3 Introduce your partner to the class:
This is … (S)he's … years old and (s)he's from …

Name ______________
Age ______________
Hometown ______________

GRAMMAR SPOT: Das Verb to be

To be	Kurzform	Frageform	Personal- und Possessivpronomen	
I am	I'm	am I?	I	my
he is she is it is	he's she's it's	is he? is she? is it?	he she it	his her its
we are you are they are	we're you're they're	are we? are you? are they?	we you they	our your their

B Have you got a mobile?

[R] **1** This is Julia. She's also at Dusseldorf airport today. Julia has got an older brother in London, and she is on her way to England for a holiday. Julia has got a small bag for the flight – her handluggage.
What has she got in her bag? Find the things 1–9.

mobile • water • photos • magazine • money • tissues • MP3 player • sweets • make-up

1

2

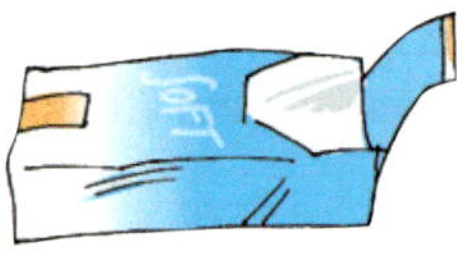

3

4

5

6

7

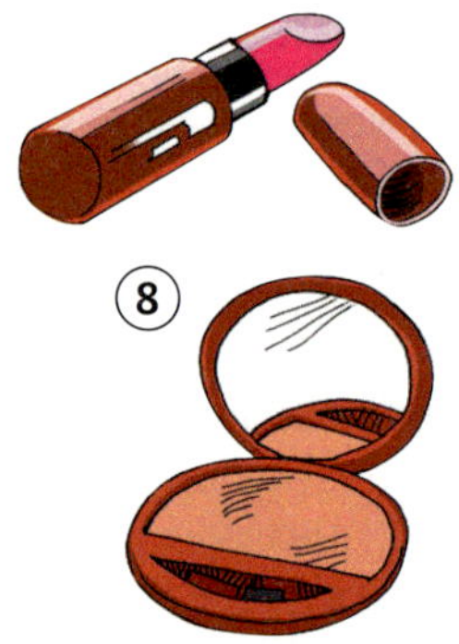
8

9

[P] **2** **Which things in Julia's bag can you count 1, 2, 3 . . . ?**
Which things can't you count? Make three lists.

countable things		uncountable things
● a/an	●● some (einige)	some (etwas)
mobile …	sweets …	water …

[P] **3** **Make sentences about Julia.**
In her bag, Julia has got a mobile. She's got some …

[P] **4** **Close your book! Can you remember what Julia has got in her bag?**
She's got a …, some …, some …

[R] **5** **Find the countable things in this list.**

1 water
2 coffee
3 cup of coffee
4 book
5 butter
6 chocolate
7 coke
8 can of coke
9 sandwich
10 ruler
11 calculator
12 dictionary
13 pen
14 pencil
15 fruit juice
16 bread
17 cheese
18 milk

[P] **6** **Say it in English.**

1 etwas Wasser
2 etwas Kaffee
3 eine Tasse Kaffee
4 „Zwei Kaffees, bitte."
5 einige Bücher
6 ein Apfel
7 etwas Schokolade
8 eine Dose Cola
9 etwas Cola
10 ein Wörterbuch

GRAMMAR SPOT: Zählbare und nicht zählbare Substantive

zählbar	**nicht zählbar**
Wir sagen a/an: a mobile, an MP3 player	Wir können nicht sagen: ~~a~~ water, ~~a~~ money
Zählbare Wörter haben eine Mehrzahl: sweets, tissues	Nicht zählbare Wörter haben keine Mehrzahl water~~s~~, make-up~~s~~
	A bottle of …, a kilo of … Wir zählen Mengen von nicht zählbaren Substantiven so: a bottle of water, a kilo of butter 'Two coffees, please.' Wenn man Getränke bestellt, sagt man "two coffees" (= two cups of coffee).

Some
Some wird mit zählbaren und nicht zählbaren Substantiven verwendet:
some sweets (ein paar Süßigkeiten),
some water (etwas Wasser)

▶ **TIPS AND TRICKS**

a can of coke,
a bar of chocolate,
a loaf of bread,
a tin of tomatoes,
a carton of milk

[I/P] **7 What have you got in your schoolbag?**

a **Look at the things on pages 10–11. Choose five and put them in your schoolbag.**
b **Now work with a partner. What has (s)he got in her/his schoolbag? Ask questions. Like this …**

Have you got any water?

Have you got a mobile in your bag?

Have you got any pencils?

Yes, I have.

No, I haven't.

b **Make three sentences about your partner.**
(Name) has got a … but (s)he hasn't got a …
(S)he's got some … but she hasn't got any … **(countable things)**
(S)he's got some … but she hasn't got any … **(uncountable thing)**

[I] **8 What have you got with you in class today?**
Tell the class two things that you've got and one thing that you haven't got.
Today I've got … and …
I haven't got …

[P/I] **9 What have you got in your room at home?**
Write a list for you, then ask a partner.

GRAMMAR SPOT: Das Verb to have got

to have got	Kurzform	Verneinung	Frageform
I have got	I've got	I haven't got	have I got?
he/she/it has got	he's/she's/it's got	he/she/it hasn't got	has he/she/it got?
we have got you have got they have got	we've got you've got they've got	we haven't got you haven't got they haven't got	have we got? have you got? have they got?

Some und any
In Fragen und bei Verneinungen verwendet man any statt some:

Have you got any CDs?

Yes, I've got some CDs,
but I haven't got any DVDs.

P] **10** **Answer the questions about the pictures. Can you see a rule about How much ...? and How many ...?**
(Tip: think of 'countable' and 'uncountable' things).

1 How much coke is there in the bottle?
– There's about ...
2 How many planes are there? – There are ...

P] **11** **Now complete these questions with much or many and give the answers.**

Example: How much coke is there in a full 2-litre bottle?
– Two litres!

1 How ... chocolate is there in a 200-gram bar?
2 How ... days are there in a week?
3 How ... weeks are there in a year?
4 How ... money have you got with you today?

[I] **12** **Choose one of the questions below (or think of your own question).**
Find the answer to the question and tell the class.

How many people are there in class with ...
- black (brown/red/blond) hair?
- brown (blue/grey/green) eyes?
- a T-shirt?
- a bag?
- jeans?
- trainers?
- a mobile?
- an email address?
- a brother or sister?
- a bike/moped/car?

In our class today, there are ... people with ...

Metin has got black hair, brown eyes, a blue top, a bag → and jeans.

GRAMMAR SPOT: How much/How many • There is/There are

How much ...? How many ...?	There is ... There are ...
How much wird verwendet, um nach nicht zählbaren Dingen zu fragen. Mit how many fragt man nach zählbaren Dingen.	There is wird mit Wörtern in der Einzahl verwendet, there are mit Wörtern in der Mehrzahl.
How much water? How many people?	There's one teacher. There are 20 students.

C At an airport

[R] **1** **Read and put photos A–F in the correct order for the text.**

Last call for flight ...

A

B

C

D

When passengers arrive at an airport, they normally look first at the flight information monitors. All the information about their flight is on these big TV screens – the flight number, the time of the flight, and the number of a check-in desk for the flight. At the check-in desk, a check-in agent checks the passengers' tickets and takes their luggage. She (or he) also gives the passengers a boarding pass. On it is their seat number on the plane and the gate number for the flight. At an airport, all the planes depart from different gates, so this gate number is very important.

Passengers normally arrive at an airport about an hour before their flight, so now after the check in, they have got time to relax. They drink a cup of coffee, or eat in a restaurant, or perhaps buy things in the shops at the airport.

About 30 minutes before their flight, passengers begin to go to their plane – but first, there is a security check. Staff at the airport check the passengers' handluggage and their clothes. Now passengers go to the gate – the gates have all got numbers like A84 or B12.

When it is time for the flight, passengers board the plane, find their seat, and the plane takes off – destination Europe, Asia, Africa or America!

E

F

[R] **2** **Find a sentence in the text to go with each photo.**

[M] **3** **A German friend wants to fly to London next week. It's her first flight. Answer her questions in German.**

1 Wie lange vor dem Abflug kommen die Passagiere normalerweise am Flughafen an?
2 Ich weiß, dass ich einchecken muss, wenn ich am Flughafen ankomme, aber wie finde ich heraus, an welchen Schalter ich gehen muss?
3 Woher weiß ich, von welchem Gate mein Flugzeug abfliegt?
4 Kann ich ein Geschenk kaufen, bevor ich abfliege?
5 Wie lange vor dem Abflug sollte ich zum Gate gehen?
6 Ich habe von den Sicherheitskontrollen gehört. Was passiert dabei?
7 Wenn ich ins Flugzeug steige, wo sitze ich?

[R] **4 Read about the 24-hour clock, then match the clocks A–F and the times 1–6.**

We can say times like this.

half past seven
(in the morning)

ten to five
(in the afternoon)

But at an airport, we normally use the 24-hour clock.

1 six forty-five
2 fourteen fifteen
3 seventeen thirty
4 eleven am
5 ten twenty-five
6 eleven oh five

A 17:30

B 11.00

C 11:05

D 06:45

E 10:25

F 14:15

[I] **5 Here's a flight information monitor at an international airport, but some things are missing. Work with a partner. Ask questions to find the missing information. (Partner B: look now at page 208).**

What time's the flight to …?
– It's at …

What's the flight number of the flight to …?
– It's …

What's the check-in desk for …
– It's …

What's the destination of flight number …/the flight at …?
– It's …

DEPARTURES

Flight		To	Time	Check in
AZ	459	ROME	?	A27
?		MUNICH	09:20	A4
MNB	1224	ANTALYA	09:25	?
LH	438	CHICAGO	?	B6
?		ZURICH	09:40	C18
IB	3521	MADRID	?	A12
KL	1845	?	10:00	B16
BA	935	LONDON	10:05	?

/P] **6 Look at this boarding pass. What names, numbers, days, dates, times and abbreviations can you find on it?**

BORDKARTE **BOARDING PASS**

PASSENGER'S NAME FISCHER/KARIN FRAU
FROM DUESSELDORF DUS
TO LONDON-HEATHROW LHR

FLIGHT NUMBER EA4147 **DAY** M **DATE** 24JAN **TIME** 16:35

SEAT 12F **GATE** A17 ***EUROPEAN AIRLINES***

D We work at the airport

[R/P] **1 Listen to Selda and Jürgen, then complete the sentences.**

There are thousands of passengers at Dusseldorf airport, but 13,000 people work there, too. Here are two people with jobs at the airport.

Hello. My name's Selda Yildirim and I work in an office at Dusseldorf airport. I'm a secretary. I live in Krefeld, about 20 kilometres from Dusseldorf. I travel to work every day by car.

Hi. I'm Jürgen Ehlers and I'm a shop assistant. I work in a shop at Dusseldorf airport. I live in the centre of Dusseldorf and I travel to work every day by S-Bahn.

Example: Selda is a secretary.
1 She … in an office at Dusseldorf airport.
2 Jürgen is … shop assistant.
3 He … in a … at the airport.
4 Selda … to work every day … car.
5 Jürgen … to work every day …
6 Jürgen … in the … of Dusseldorf.
7 Selda lives …
8 Selda works at Dusseldorf airport and Jürgen works at Dusseldorf airport. They both … at Dusseldorf airport.

▶ TIPS AND TRICKS

I'm a secretary.
I'm ~~a~~ secretary.

He's a shop assistant.
He's ~~a~~ shop assistant.

I go to work …
by bus/train/car.
on foot.

[P] **2 Make questions about Selda and Jürgen, then give the answers.**

Example: Where does Selda work? ➔ She works in an office at Dusseldorf airport.

1 Where/Selda/live?
2 How/she/travel to work?
3 Where/Jürgen/work?
4 How/he/travel to work?
5 Where/he/live?
6 Where/Selda and Jürgen/work?

[I] **3 Tell the class.**

Do you have a job?
Where do you live?
How do you travel to college?

GRAMMAR SPOT: Das simple present

Aussagesatz		Fragen im simple present			
I	work	Where	do	I	work?
he she it	works		does	he she it	
we you they	work		do	we you they	

R/P] **4** **Here are Bernd and Nadja. Listen then answer the questions.**

Trainees at the airport

Bernd and Nadja are trainees at Dusseldorf airport. They work in one of the big hangars. They learn about planes and help the engineers. They work at the airport on Mondays, Tuesdays and Wednesdays, and they go to college in Dusseldorf on Thursdays and Fridays.

Nadja's full name is Nadja Kotomina. Her mum and dad are from Russia, but they live in Germany now and Nadja is German. Bernd's parents are German, and Bernd is German, of course.

Nadja lives in a flat in Dusseldorf with her mum and dad. She travels to work every day by S-Bahn. Bernd has got a car. It's a very old car, but it's a car! So he travels to the airport every day by car. He lives in Solingen, about 10 kilometres from Dusseldorf, with his mum and his sister Sabine.

1 Where do Bernd and Nadja work?
2 What do they do there?
3 When do they work at the airport?
4 Where are Nadja's parents from?
5 Where do they live now?
6 Is Nadja Russian or German?
7 Is Bernd Russian or German?
8 Where does Nadja live and how does she travel to the airport?
9 Where does Bernd live and how does he travel to the airport?

[I] **5** **Work with a partner. Write an interview with Nadja or Bernd.**
Partner A: you're Nadja (or Bernd).
Partner B: you're a reporter for young-europe.com, an Internet e-zine for European teenagers. This week, your website has got some interviews with young people at work in different European countries.

Partner B: Thanks very much for this interview.
Partner A: You're welcome. How can I help?
Partner B: I've got some questions about your job. Is that OK?
Partner A: Sure.
Partner B: OK. Where do you work?

[R] **6 Listen and find the missing words and phrases.**

Remember Jason, Laura and Rachel from page 8? They live in England and they go to college in London. They're students on a **(1)** ... This week, their **(2)** ... is at Dusseldorf airport. They've got a project. It's to interview people at the airport and to take **(3)** ... They're with the man below at the moment.

Jason	Hi. I'm Jason and this is Laura and Rachel.
Dirk	Hi. Nice to meet you. I'm Dirk.
Jason	**(4)** ... for this interview.
Dirk	You're welcome. How can I help?
Laura	We've got some questions about your job. Is that OK?
Dirk	**(5)**...
Laura	OK. Where do you work?
Dirk	At Airport City. It's a big business park near Dusseldorf airport with a conference centre and a hotel.
Laura	Do you work at the conference centre?
Dirk	No, I work at the hotel. I'm **(6)**...
Rachel	When do you work? What's a typical day?
Dirk	Well, it depends. The hotel is open 24 hours. Sometimes I work in the morning, sometimes in the afternoon and evening, and sometimes **(7)**...
Jason	What do you do when you're at work?
Dirk	I welcome guests, **(8)** ..., I help people when they've got a problem – lots of things.
Laura	Do you speak English in your job?
Dirk	Oh yes, every day. Our guests are from all over the world.
Jason	Do you like your job?
Dirk	**(9)** ...! It's great.

a thanks very much
b photos
c I answer the phone
d a receptionist
e at night
f class
g sure
h media studies course
i of course

[I] **7 Read the conversation in a small group.**

[R/P] **8 True or false? Correct the false sentences.**

Example: Dirk works in Dusseldorf. → True.

1 He works in Karstadt. → No! He doesn't work in Karstadt. He ...
2 He works at the conference centre at Airport City.
3 Sometimes he works at night.
4 He sleeps when he's at work.
5 He doesn't speak English in his job.

[P] **9** **These sentences about Jason, Laura and Rachel are all false. Correct them.**

Example: Jason, Laura and Rachel live in New York. **(London)**

→ They don't live in New York. They live in London.

1 Jason, Laura and Rachel go to college in Germany. **(England)**
2 They go to college on Mondays and Tuesdays. **(every day from Monday to Friday)**
3 They travel to college by plane. **(underground)**
4 They speak German every day. **(English)**
5 They hate their college. **(like)**

[P] **10** **Now correct these sentences about Laura.**

1 Laura goes to college in Germany. → Laura doesn't … She …
2 She lives in Tokyo.
3 She goes to college on Sundays.
4 She travels to college by taxi.
5 She speaks Russian every day.

[P] **11** **Which sentences are true for you? If a sentence is false, give a true sentence.**

1 I live in the USA.
2 I like lemonade.
3 I hate pop music.
4 I travel to college every day by S-Bahn.
5 I work in a shop at the weekend.
6 I live in a large city.
7 I live in a flat.
8 We speak Chinese in our English lessons at college.

[P] **12** **Write a short text (about 100 words) about you, your English class and your college. Here are some questions to help you.**

1 What's your name?
2 How old are you?
3 Where do you go to college?
4 What's the name of your college?
5 How old is your college – is it old or modern?
6 How many people are there in your English class?
7 How many boys are there, and how many girls?
8 What's your English teacher's name?
9 What days of the week do you go to college?
10 What days do you learn English?

GRAMMAR SPOT: Das simple present: Verneinung

I	don't	
he / she / it	doesn't	work
we / you / they	don't	

13 **Test yourself!**
What do you remember from this introduction to your book? Find out!
Try this 10-minute test. Just choose the correct answer a, b or c.

Question	a	b	c
1 Hi. My name's Zeynep. What's … name? – I'm Erich.	my	her	your
2 Where … you from, Erich? – I'm from Cologne, in Germany.	are	is	am
3 This is Maria. … from Greece.	He's	They're	She's
4 Emma … got a mobile in her bag.	have	haves	has
5 What … you got in your bag?	have	haves	has
6 In my bag I've got …	a books	some books	some book
7 Has our teacher got … books in her bag?	any	some	a
8 Yes, she's got … English books in her bag.	any	some	a
9 How … students … in your class?	much … is there	many … are there	many … is there
10 This is Jenny.	She's a secretary.	She's secretary.	She's an secretary.
11 She … in an office.	work	works	is work
12 Hi. We're Marina and Hans. We … in a shop in the centre of the city.	work	works	are work
13 We travel to work every day … bus.	with	in	by
14 Where … ?	do you work?	does you work?	work you?
15 Where … ?	does Artur works	does Artur work	works Artur
16 Hello. I'm Barbara. – Hi, Barbara. …	Nice to meet you.	Nice you to meet.	Nice to you meet.
17 I like coke but I … milk.	like not	likes not	don't like
18 We … German in our English lessons.	doesn't speak	don't speak	speak not
19 What's your … name?	teachers	teacher's	teacher
20 … Mr Schiller.	Its	It's	It's is

Main course

Unit 1 A day in my life

Dan

Jennie

Dave

Carol

Laura

Justin

[P/I] **1 Work in teams.**
Make a list of things that you do in a typical day.
Which team can find the most activities?

I get up …
I have breakfast …
…

[P] **2 The six teenagers above are friends at a college in England.**
How often do they do these things – sometimes, often or never?
What do you think? Tell the class your answers.
Dave … listens to music.
Dan … goes to a fitness club.
Jennie … does her homework in the park.
Justin is … late for college.
Carol … has pizza for supper.
Laura … tidies her room.

I think (Dave)
… sometimes …
… often …
… never …

[R/P] **3 Sometimes, often and never are adverbs. Where do we put them in a sentence? Look at the sentences in exercise 2 and complete the rule below with before or after.**
We put adverbs like sometimes, often and never … main verbs (listen, go etc.) but … the verb to be.

▶ TIPS AND TRICKS
I often listen to music.
I often ~~hear~~ music.

[P] **4 Make a sentence about YOU with sometimes, often or never and tell the class.**

[P] **5** **Jennie is one of the six friends. She's on a Health and Social Care course at the college. Read her typical day aloud. Use the 12-hour clock. (Times, dates and numbers: Klappumschlag A.)**

	Jennie usually gets up at half past seven. She has her breakfast, then she has a shower, and then she takes the bus to college.
	Like all school pupils and college students in England, Jennie has lessons all day. Her first lesson begins at …
	At … she goes into town with her friends for lunch. Her lessons begin again at half past one.
	The last lesson of the day finishes at a quarter to five in the afternoon and Jennie normally gets home at about … She has a snack and watches TV for a while, then she does her homework.
	Supper is always at half past seven. After supper, Jennie finishes her homework, plays on the computer, or reads a book. She goes to bed at …

[P] **6** **What things does Jennie do in the morning (before midday), in the afternoon (from midday to 6 o'clock), in the evening (after 6 o'clock)?**

[R/P] **7** **Find the verbs and the expressions.**

a **After he, she and it, we put an -s or -es on the verb (listens, goes). Look at pages 22–23. What verbs can you find where we put -es? Can you find a verb that ends in -ies?**

b **Look at Jennie's day. Can you find four expressions with to have?**

▶ TIPS AND TRICKS

I usually watch TV in the evenings.

I usually ~~see~~ TV.

[I] **8** **Work in a group and talk about your typical day. Who gets up earliest in your group? Who goes to bed very late? What do you usually do in the evenings?**

GRAMMAR SPOT: Das simple present (einfache Gegenwart)

Adverbs of frequency

- Das simple present wird häufig zusammen mit Wörtern wie often, sometimes, always, und normally (Häufigkeitsadverbien) verwendet, um regelmäßige oder wiederholte Handlungen auszudrücken.
- Die Adverbien stehen **vor** einem Vollverb, aber **nach** dem Verb to be.
  I usually get up at seven o'clock.
  I'm never late for college.

Schreibweise

Bei der 3. Person Einzahl (he/she/it) wird ein -s oder -es an das Verb angehängt. Verben, die auf einen Konsonanten -y enden (to tidy), erhalten die Endung -ies.

Zeitangaben mit at, on und in

in the morning/evening/afternoon
on Monday(s)
at 6 o'clock/night/the weekend

→ Grammar summary, page 196

[P] **1** **Jon is an American high school student. Here are some things that Jon does in a typical week. Give the correct forms of the verbs. Use the simple present. Be careful of spellings!**

Jon **(1)** goes **(go)** to high school five days a week, from Monday to Friday. He sometimes **(2)** … **(take)** the bus to school, but when the weather is nice, he normally **(3)** … **(bike)**. Jon **(4)** … **(study)** a lot. He **(5)** … **(want)** to be a doctor. He **(6)** … **(work)** hard in lessons and every day in the evenings he **(7)** … **(do)** homework. Jon also **(8)** … **(relax)**, though. After his homework, he **(9)** … **(listen)** to music or **(10)** … **(watch)** TV, and two evenings a week he **(11)** … **(go)** to a fitness club. Jon is busy at the weekends.
On Saturdays, he **(12)** … **(have)** a part-time job as a waiter in a restaurant. He also **(13)** … **(help)** his dad. He **(14)** … **(work)** in the garden, **(15)** … **(tidy)** the garage, and **(16)** … **(wash)** the car.

[P] **2** **Make sentences about Jon with the adverb in brackets.**

Example: Jon helps his dad. **(often)** → Jon often helps his dad.

1 He bikes to school in the mornings. **(usually)**
2 He is late for lessons! **(never)**
3 Jon goes to a fitness club on Tuesdays and Thursdays. **(always)**
4 He is busy at the weekends. **(always)**
5 He tidies the garage at the weekends. **(often)**
6 Jon likes his high school, but he's happy when it's Friday. **(always)**

[P] **3** **Give the missing forms in the table.**

to have			**to have got**		
statements	questions	negatives	statements	questions	negatives
I have	**(2)** ▪ I have?	I don't have	**(5)** ▪	have I got?	I **(7)** ▪ got
he/she/it **(1)** ▪	does he/ she/it have?	he/she/it **(4)** ▪ have	he's/she's/ it's got	**(6)** ▪ he/ she/it got?	he/she/it **(8)** ▪ got
we/you/ they have	**(3)** ▪ we/you/ they have?	we/you/they don't have	we've/you've/ they've got	have we/ you/they got?	we/you/they **(9)** ▪ got

[P] **4** **Give these sentences again with to have.**

Example: I've got some books in my bag. → I have some books in my bag.

1 Jennie has got a brother.
2 Jon hasn't got a brother.
3 Have you got a brother?
4 No, I haven't got a brother.
5 Has Jon got a sister?
6 Yes, he's got two sisters.

[P] **5 Now give these sentences again with to have got.**

1 Jon has two sisters, but he doesn't have a brother.
2 Jennie has a brother, but she doesn't have a sister.

[P] **6 Expressions with to have. Complete the conversation with the missing words and phrases.**

A What time do you usually get up?
B About 8 o'clock.
A What do you do then?
B Well, I have **(1)** … in the bathroom, then I have **(2)** …
A What do you normally have **(3)** …?
B I normally have **(4)** …
A What's a typical day for you after that?
B OK. Well, I'm a college student, so I have **(5)** … from 9 o'clock to about 4 o'clock in the afternoon. Then I come home, have **(6)** … – toast or something like that – and do my homework until about seven. We always have **(7)** … at seven. Then I watch TV and go to bed at about eleven.

cereal and a cup of tea
supper
breakfast
a snack
a shower
for breakfast
lessons

[P] **7 In, on or at? Complete the sentences.**

1 I normally get up … half past seven.
2 I have lunch … about one o'clock.
3 In Britain, we always have lessons … the afternoon.
4 Jon's first lesson … Monday morning is maths.
5 … the evening, I usually listen to music, watch TV, or play on the computer.
6 What do you usually do … the weekend?
7 … Saturdays, I normally go to town with my friends, and … Sundays I always sleep until about midday.

R/P] **8 Look back at pages 22–24 and collect words under these headings. Then add three more words to each list.**

College and school	Food and meals	Free time
homework	breakfast	to watch TV

[P] **9 The marked words are the answers. What are the questions?**

* Example: Jennie lives **in Oxford**. **(where?)** → Where does Jennie live?

1 Jennie gets up at **7.30**. **(when?)**
2 She has breakfast at **8.00**. **(when?)**
3 She travels to college **by bus**. **(how?)**
4 She goes **into town** for lunch. **(where?)**
5 She has **a snack** when she gets home. **(what)**
6 She finishes her homework **after supper**. **(when?)**
7 She reads a book **in her bedroom**. **(…?)**
8 She goes to bed **at half past ten**. **(…?)**

[P] **10 Write 50–100 words about your typical day. Begin like this:**

* → On a typical day, I normally get up at …

[R] **1** **The website young-europe.com has a careers page where you can read about and listen to 'A Day in the Life of ...' people with different jobs. Listen to Emma and Rob and answer the questions below.**

HOME | CAREERS | **A DAY IN THE LIFE OF ...**

Emma Wells: radio DJ

I usually get up at about 10 o'clock, have breakfast (always toast and about three cups of black coffee!), then I listen to music. Music companies send me a lot of new releases and I listen to these (with more coffee) until about midday or 1 o'clock. In the afternoon, I often go into town – I go shopping or perhaps meet a friend. I go to the studio at about 6 o'clock. My show is from 10 o'clock in the evening to 1 o'clock in the morning. Before the show, I prepare all my music and at about 8 o'clock I have supper in the canteen. When my show finishes, I take a taxi home and go to bed.

Listen to Emma

Rob Taylor: footballer

My club is a typical town football club. We play in the national league and in Europe, but I'm not a megastar and I'm certainly not rich! In fact, I have two jobs. In the morning, I'm a postman. I get up at 4 am and work from 5 am until about midday. When I get home, I have lunch then I sleep for a couple of hours. In the evening and at the weekend, I'm a footballer. Our matches are on Saturdays but we have training every evening, Monday to Friday, from 7 o'clock to 10 o'clock. After training, I sometimes go for a drink with my friends in the team. Then I go home and go to bed.

Listen to Rob

1 What does Emma have for breakfast?
2 What does she do then until about midday or 1 o'clock?
3 What does she often do in the afternoon?
4 When is her radio show?
5 What does she do before the show?
6 How does she travel home after the show?

1 Where does Rob's club play?
2 What's Rob's job in the morning?
3 What does he do in the afternoon?
4 What's his job in the evening and at the weekend?
5 When does he have training?
6 What does he sometimes do after training?

[P] **2** **Who's this – Emma or Rob? Say the sentences with the names. Then make four more sentences about Emma and Rob.**

1 Emma gets up at 10 am.
2 ... gets up at 4 am.
3 ... sleeps for a couple of hours in the afternoon.
4 ... sometimes meets a friend in town in the afternoon.
5 ... drinks a lot of coffee.
6 ... certainly isn't rich.
7 ... has supper at 8 o'clock.
8 ... sometimes goes for a drink with friends in the evening.
9 ... works at night.
10 ... has only one job.

[R] **3 Find words in the texts that complete these sentences.**

1 A postman brings letters to your flat.
2 A … plays music on the radio.
3 A … plays football.
4 EMI and Sony are music …
5 When you buy things in shops you go …
6 There are eleven people in a football …
7 Rob sleeps for about two hours. He sleeps for a … of hours.
8 A restaurant at a factory, an office, a college etc. is a …
9 A very, very famous footballer, film star, singer etc. is a …
10 A special room at a radio station. Emma works in a room like this. It's called a …

[R] **4 Find words and phrases in the texts that have the opposite meaning.**

Example: to get up → to go to bed

1 to begin
2 old
3 poor
4 before
5 (at) exactly (6 o'clock)

[I] **5 What do you think about Emma's job? And Rob's job(s)?**

I think Rob's/Emma's job is good because …

I think Rob's/Emma's job isn't so good because …

[P/I] **6 Choose one of the projects.**

1 The website young-europe.com wants to have 'A Day in the Life of …' a German college student. Write a text like Emma's or Rob's about YOU for the website.

2 Do you have a favourite footballer? singer? musician? film star? What do you know about her or him? Can you answer these questions and then write a short text?

- How old is (s)he?
- Where's (s)he from? (Germany, the USA?)
- What's her/his job?
- Is (s)he a megastar?
- Where does (s)he live?
- What's the name of her/his team/band/latest release/ latest film?

ICH KANN JETZT …

- über meinen Tagesablauf sprechen und schreiben,
- Fragen zum Alltag stellen,
- einen einfachen Text über den beruflichen Alltag lesen und dazu meine Meinung äußern,
- in Englisch mit dem Internet (etwas) umgehen.

[R] **1** **Can you match the jobs and the job descriptions?**

The A ... to Z of jobs

From architect to zoo worker,
there are hundreds of different jobs in the big world of work.

	Job		Job description
1	an architect	a	designs clothes
2	a bank employee	b	works in a kitchen
3	a bricklayer	c	cuts hair
4	a chef	d	works in a hospital
5	a driver	e	repairs cars
6	a fashion designer	f	designs buildings
7	a fitness trainer	g	sells a company's products
8	a hairdresser	h	protects people, catches criminals etc.
9	an IT technician	i	installs and repairs water pipes etc.
10	a journalist	j	builds houses and flats
11	a (car) mechanic	k	helps people with family problems etc.
12	a nurse	l	looks after animals
13	a plumber	m	works in a fitness club
14	a police officer	n	works in a school or college
15	a sales representative	o	works in a bank
16	a secretary	p	installs and repairs telephones, cables etc.
17	a social worker	q	works for a newspaper or a magazine
18	a teacher	r	works in an office
19	a telecom technician	s	drives a lorry, a bus, a taxi etc.
20	a zoo worker	t	repairs and programs computers

[R/P] **2** **Match the English and the German verbs, then make sentences.**

to work • to build • to design • to repair • to install • to drive • to help • to cut • to look after • to sell • to protect • to catch	reparieren • bauen • verkaufen • installieren • entwerfen • arbeiten • sich kümmern um • fangen • helfen • schneiden • beschützen • fahren

Example: A bank employee works in a bank.

P/I] **3 Answer the questions about these jobs. Then make more questions and ask another student in your class.**

Example: What does an architect do? → He or she designs buildings.

1 Where does a bank employee work? → He or she works in …
2 What does a fashion designer do?
3 Where does a nurse work?
4 Where does a teacher work?
5 What does a social worker do?

▶ TIPS AND TRICKS

My boss is Herr Meyer.

Never:
My ~~chef~~ is Herr Meyer.

chef = Küchenchef

[I] **4 Work with a partner.**

Partner B: Choose one of the jobs on page 28.
Partner A: Ask questions and find your partner's job.

Do you design clothes?

No, I'm not a fashion designer.

Do you work in a school?

No, I'm not a teacher.

Do you repair cars?

Yes, I'm a mechanic!

/P] **5 Listen to Martin.**
Which one of the jobs on page 28 does he have? Now listen again. True or not true? Correct the false sentences.

1 In the photo, Martin is at work.
2 He works five days a week.
3 He sometimes works from 3 o'clock in the afternoon to 9 o'clock in the evening.
4 He has about ten clients.
5 His clients are young men and women.
6 One of his clients at the moment is a dancer.
7 Martin helps his clients with tips about a healthy lifestyle.
8 He works in a zoo.

[M] **6 A friend of yours is interested in Martin's job as a career. But she can't understand English very well. Write a short summary for her in German.**

[P] **7 What do you want to be? Is your job on the list on page 28? Can you say your job in English and give a sentence about it?**

I want to be a …

A … works/looks after/builds/repairs …

ICH KANN JETZT …

- einige Berufe nennen und beschreiben,
- Fragen über Berufe stellen,
- jemandem helfen einen gesprochenen Text auf Englisch zu verstehen.

Unit 2 Stay in touch!

[P/I] **1 How do you stay in touch with your friends? Do you have a mobile phone? Do you chat to friends on your computer? Do you send holiday postcards?**

[R] **2 Read about Marco and answer the questions.**

Marco lives in Germany. He's a student on a computer course at a vocational college in Cologne. In the evenings, at home, he often chats to his friends on his computer. He's even got some Internet friends in different countries. Right now, it's 8 o'clock on Wednesday evening. Marco is sitting on the floor of his room. He's looking at a picture message on his mobile. The message is from Matt in the States. Matt is a high school student in Denver, Colorado and he's one of Marco's Internet friends.

1 Where does Marco live?
2 What course is Marco on at his college?
3 What does he often do in the evenings?
4 In the picture, it's 8 o'clock on Wednesday evening. What's Marco doing?

▶ TIPS AND TRICKS

In the USA it's a **cell (phone)**.

In the UK it's a **mobile (phone)**.

But it's **never** a ~~handy~~!

[P] **3 What are you doing right now? Where are you sitting? Are you looking at a picture message on a mobile? What language are you speaking at the moment?**

[P] **4 Complete this table.**

The present continuous		
I	▪	sitting in a classroom.
he/she	▪	speaking English.
we/you/they	▪	looking at a message.

5 Read about Matt and answer the questions.

The great thing about Denver – where Matt lives – is that it's at the foot of the Rocky Mountains. In the spring and autumn, it's warm and sunny in the city, but in a couple of hours you can be in the mountains. There it's snowy and you can ski or snowboard. Classes from Matt's high school often go to the mountains on class trips. Matt is spending five days this week in the Rockies with his class and their teacher, Mr Kowalski. They're staying at a youth hostel, and Matt is having a 'gr8' time.

1 What's the great thing about Denver?
2 What do classes from Matt's high school often do?
3 What's Matt doing this week?
4 Is he having a good time?

[P] **6 Make sentences about Matt.**

1 Here are some things that Matt normally does when he's at high school. Can you think of more things that he does in a typical week?

He travels to school every day by bus.

He quarrels with his sister!

He meets his friends in town for a pizza.

He sleeps in his room at home.

2 Matt isn't doing these things this week – he's on a class trip in the Rockies. Make sentences about him like this:
Example: He isn't travelling to school every day by bus. He isn't …
3 What is Matt doing this week? What's he doing in the picture, for example?
Example: He's sleeping at the youth hostel. He's …

Denver is at the foot of the Rocky Mountains

CULTURE TIPS:
COUNTRIES WHERE THEY SPEAK ENGLISH

It's good to know these countries. There are maps of the USA and the UK at the front and back of your book.

GRAMMAR SPOT: Das present continuous und das simple present

Das present continuous wird mit dem Verb to be und dem Vollverb + -ing gebildet.

• Das present continuous wird für Handlungen verwendet, die:	
– im Moment stattfinden,	Marco is sitting in his room.
– auf einen gegenwärtigen Zeitraum begrenzt sind.	Matt isn't having lessons this week.
• Das simple present wird für regelmäßige Handlungen/ Gewohnheiten verwendet.	Matt often goes to the mountains.

→ Grammar summary, page 197

[R] **1 Maria is also a high school student in the States. She often gets picture messages from her friends. Match the messages 1–4 and the pictures A–D.**

1

2

3

4

C

D

[P] **2 Find these words and expressions in the messages above and write the messages in full. Remember to use capital letters!**

great
see you
are
do you want to?
for
later

[P] **3 Make sentences about the people in exercise 1. Can you make eight sentences?**

Example: Katherine is having a great time at a party.

Katherine Haley Ben Adam Brittney Hannah	is are	having cooking wearing jogging shopping dancing smiling buying	a hat. jogging clothes. a pizza. a T-shirt. a great time. at a party. in the park. in town.

[R/P] **4 Look at exercise 3. True or false? Correct the false sentences.**

1 Haley is buying a hat. True.
2 Katherine is dancing in the park. No! She isn't ...
3 Ben and Adam are wearing jogging clothes.
4 They're cooking.
5 Brittney and Maria are shopping.
6 Haley is jogging.
7 Ben and Adam are smiling.

[P] **5 Complete the sentences with the simple present or the present continuous.**

1 Jenna lives **(live)** in the USA. She's a high school student.
2 She … **(go)** to a high school in Los Angeles.
3 Jenna … **(see)** her friends every day at school.
4 But after school she always … **(chat)** to them again on the Internet with instant messages. Her screen name is 'cyberkid77'.
5 She … **(chat)** to her friend Tina ('chats_a_lot') at the moment.
6 Jenna and Tina often … **(talk)** about boys when they're together.
7 They … **(talk)** about a boy right now. His name's Josh and he's new in their class.
8 Josh often … **(chat)** to his friends on the Internet, too.
9 Perhaps he … **(chat)** to a friend right now.
10 Perhaps he … **(write)** a message to a friend at the moment that 'Jenna is COOOOOOL!'

☺ cyberkid77

chats_a_lot: What do you think of the new guy in our class?
cyberkid77: Josh?
chats_a_lot: Yeah.
cyberkid77: He's CoooooooL! ♥

R/P] **6 Which sentences are true about YOU?**

1 I often wear jeans.
2 I'm wearing jeans at the moment.
3 I often have English lessons.
4 I'm having an English lesson now.
5 I do homework.
6 I'm doing homework.
7 I speak German.
8 I'm speaking German.
9 I phone my friends.
10 I'm phoning a friend.
11 I watch TV.
12 I'm watching TV.

[P] **7 Write four sentences yourself about things you often/always/sometimes do and four sentences about things you're doing right now.**

[P] **8 Complete the sentences with in, on or at.**

1 Marco is a student … a vocational college … Cologne.
2 He's sitting … the floor of his room … home.
3 Matt is … a class trip at the moment. He's staying … a youth hostel … the Rockies.
4 Katherine is having a great time … Tony's party.
5 Haley is shopping … town.
6 Jenna lives … the USA.
7 She sees her friends every day … school.
8 But she also chats to them every day … the Internet.

[P] **9 Imagine that you are on holiday. Write a postcard (30–40 words) to a friend in**
* **England. Here are some useful phrases:**

Dear (name) • I'm having a great time (in) • I'm spending (5) days in … •
I'm camping/staying at a hotel (with) … • The weather is … •
The great thing about … is that you can … • Give my love to … •
See you soon • Lots of love/Best wishes/Love and kisses (your name)

[R] **1 Read about Mary and look at the questionnaire.**
Mary Ford lives in Chicago. She works for a market research company and is doing a survey about cell phones.

a Find the English for these words and phrases in Mary's questionnaire.

Kollegen • SMS • Spiele • Fotos machen • typisch • auswählen • das Wichtigste • Größe • sieht gut aus • effizient und leicht zu bedienen • Was sind Sie von Beruf?

b Mary is talking to a man and she's writing his answers on the questionnaire. Some answers are already on the questionnaire. Can you find the missing answers? Listen.

1 Do you have a cell phone?
yes ☒ no ☐

2 Which of these do you do with your phone?

	yes	no
phone friends, family, colleagues etc.?	☒	☐
send text messages?	☒	☐
send picture or video messages?	☐	☒
play games?	☐	☒
take photos?	☒	☐

3 In a typical week:
how many minutes do you normally talk on your phone?
☐ 0-30 ☒ 30-60 ☐ 60-120 ☐ 120-240 ☐ 240+
how many text messages do you send?
☐ 0-10 ☐ 10-20 ☐ 20-50 ☐ 50-100 ☐ 100+
how many pictures or video messages do you send?
☐ 0-10 ☐ 10-20 ☐ 20-50 ☐ 50-100 ☐ 100+

4 When you choose a new phone, which one thing is the most important for you?
☐ it's a good size (not too big or too small)
☐ it looks good
☐ it's efficient and easy to use
☐ you can play good games on it
☐ the camera is good

5 How old are you?

6 What's your occupation?

▶ **TIPS AND TRICKS**

I take photos with my mobile.

Never:
I ~~make~~ photos with my mobile.

R/P] **2 True or not true? Correct the false sentences.**

1 The man in the interview with Mary is a high school teacher.
2 He's 43 years old.
3 He phones friends, family, colleagues etc. and he sends text messages, but he doesn't send picture or video messages.
4 He plays games on his cell phone but he doesn't take pictures.
5 In a typical week, he normally talks for between 30 and 60 minutes on his phone.
6 He sends between 20 and 50 text messages.
7 When he chooses a new phone, the most important thing for him is that it looks good.

[R] **3 Mary is talking to a teenager now. Listen and answer the questions.**

1 Which things does (or doesn't) she do with her phone?
2 In a typical week, how many minutes does she normally talk on her phone?
3 How many text messages does she send?
4 How many pictures or video messages does she send?
5 What is the most important thing for her when she chooses a new phone?
6 What is the teenager's occupation?
7 How old is she?

[I] **4 Talk in class.**

1 Are you like the man in Mary's interview or are you like the teenager? How do you use your phone? What's the most important thing for you when you choose a new phone?
2 Teenagers and parents don't always agree about mobile phones! Look at this picture. Where are the people? What time of day do you think it is? What's happening? What's the girl doing? What are her mum and dad doing? Do you think there is a problem?

P/I] **5 Choose one of the projects.**

1 Do a survey in your class about mobile phones. You can think of new questions. For example, do you listen to music on your phone? Do you use the Internet or watch TV on your mobile?
2 Visit the website of a mobile phone company and get information about a new phone. Then tell the class.

ICH KANN JETZT …

- über Sachen sprechen, die ich regelmäßig tue, und sagen, was ich gerade mache,
- über moderne Kommunikationsmittel (Internet, Handys) sprechen und schreiben,
- einfache Mitteilungen verstehen und verfassen,
- typische Fragen in einer Umfrage verstehen und beantworten.

[R] **1 Christa Merten works as a receptionist at the Hotel zur Post. She often speaks English on the phone and so she has a list of phrases. Here's Christa's list. Match the correct English and German phrases.**

English telephone phrases

1 Christa Merten speaking. How can I help you?
2 Can I take your name, please?
3 How do you spell that, please?
4 When would you like the room?
5 a single room
6 a double room
7 That's fine.
8 I'm sorry, but we're fully booked then.
9 May I take a credit card number?
10 What's the expiry date?
11 Thank you for calling the Hotel zur Post.
12 We look forward to seeing you (soon).

a Ab wann brauchen Sie das Zimmer?
b Das ist in Ordnung.
c Danke, dass Sie sich für das Hotel zur Post entschieden haben.
d Wie schreibt man das?
e Sie sprechen mit Christa Merten. Wie kann ich Ihnen behilflich sein?
f ein Einzelzimmer
g ein Doppelzimmer
h Wie lautet Ihre Kreditkartennummer?
i Wie ist Ihr Name?
j Wir freuen uns, Sie bald begrüßen zu dürfen.
k Es tut mir Leid, aber zu diesem Zeitpunkt sind wir restlos ausgebucht.
l Wie lautet das Ablaufdatum?

[R] **2 Christa is talking on the phone to someone from England.**
Use Christa's list and find the missing phrases. Then listen and check.

Christa Hotel zur Post. Sie sprechen mit Christa Merten. Wie kann ich Ihnen behilflich sein?
Man Do you speak English, please?
Christa Of course. Christa Merten speaking. **(1)** …?
Man Oh great, thanks very much. I'd like to book a room, please.
Christa Certainly. **(2)** …?
Man Yes, it's Ogilvie. John Ogilvie.
Christa How do you spell that, please?
Man O-G-I-L-V-I-E.
Christa Thank you, Mr Ogilvie. **(3)** …?
Man For two nights, from 15 to 17 November.
Christa Is that a single or **(4)** …?
Man A single room, please.
Christa Yes, that's fine. **(5)** …? That just confirms the booking.
Man Yes. It's an American Express Card, number 7166 8883 2190 0557.
Christa And the expiry date?
Man Er, 6/2009.
Christa OK. I've got all that. Thank you for calling the Hotel zur Post, Mr Ogilvie. **(6)** …
Man Thanks very much. Bye.
Christa Goodbye.

[P/I] **3** **Complete these sentences about the conversation. Then practise the conversation with a partner.**

1 The caller's name is John … and he's from …
2 He … German.
3 He wants to arrive at the Hotel zur Post on …
4 He wants to leave again on … That's … nights at the hotel.
5 He would like a … room.
6 He's got an … card. The … date of the card is June 2009.

[I] **4** **Now YOU. Work with a partner. Take it in turns to be an English businessman or woman and Christa.**

Partner A: You are the caller. Think of an English name and decide what you want: dates, room etc. You need a credit card, too!

Partner B: You are Christa. Copy the form and fill in the information for your partner.

HOTEL ZUR POST ANMELDEFORMULAR

Name des Gastes: ______________________

Aufenthalt: von ______________ bis __________

Einzelzimmer ☐ Doppelzimmer ☐

Anzahl der Übernachtungen: ________

Kreditkartennummer: ☐☐☐☐ ☐☐☐☐ ☐☐☐☐ ☐☐☐☐

Ablaufdatum: ☐☐ 20☐☐

☐ Visa ☐ American Express ☐ Master Card

▶ **TIPS AND TRICKS**

Wenn Sie etwas nicht verstehen können, fragen Sie: Sorry, could you repeat that, please?

CULTURE TIPS:
BE POLITE

British and American people are very polite.
Notice phrases like:
"May I take your credit card number?" and how often people say 'please' and 'thank you'. You'll learn much more about this later.

[M] **5** **A German friend wants to book a room in a hotel in England. His English is not very good and you help him to prepare for the phone call. He has notes of what he wants.**
Help your friend: make a list in German and English of useful phrases for him when he phones the hotel.

Name: Gerhard Ippendorf
Einzelzimmer
Aufenthalt: 2 Übernachtungen, 28. bis 30. März
Kreditkarte (Visa) 0049 7123 7124 8888
(Ablaufdatum 1/2010)

ICH KANN JETZT …

- ein Hotelzimmer auf Englisch reservieren,
- jemandem mit wenig Englischkenntnissen helfen, ein Hotelzimmer zu buchen.

Unit 3 What's your favourite food?

[P/I] **1** **Is there one thing that you really LOVE eating? Is there one that you hate? Tell the class.**

[R] **2** **Match the words and the pictures.**

1 apple juice
2 bananas
3 biscuits
4 bread
5 burger and fries
6 carrots
7 chocolate
8 coffee
9 coke
10 kiwis
11 milk
12 mixed salad
13 oranges
14 peas
15 pizza
16 sausage with curry sauce
17 spaghetti
18 strawberries

[I] **3** **Talk about the food and the drinks in the pictures.**

Which of the kinds of food and the drinks in the pictures …

1 do we often call 'fast food'?
2 are vegetables?
3 are kinds of fruit?
4 are usually a main meal, or part of a main meal?
5 are snacks that you can eat between meals?
6 are from other countries, but are now popular in Germany?

[R] **4 Read about these three British teenagers and answer the questions.**

1 Where do the three girls live? How big is the city?
2 Where do they always go on Saturday afternoons?
3 Where do they eat and drink?
4 Who likes: **a** burgers? **b** salad? **c** chips?
5 What drink do all the girls like?

▶ **TIPS AND TRICKS**
WOULD YOU LIKE A CHIP?

	Pommes	Chips
UK	Chips	Crisps
USA	Fries	Chips

Sharmila, Amy and Michelle are best friends. They live in Birmingham, the biggest city in England after London. On Saturday afternoons, the three girls always go to town together. There are lots of cafés and fast food restaurants and they always eat and drink something. Sharmila's grandma and grandad are originally from India. At home, her mum cooks delicious curries, but when Sharmila is in town, she loves chips! She thinks that they are even nicer than curry. Amy (the girl on the mobile) likes chips, too, but she prefers burgers. Her favourite is cheeseburgers. Michelle tries to be healthy, so she usually just has a salad. They all love drinking milkshakes. Their favourite is chocolate.

[P] **5 Complete the sentences about the girls with words from the table.**

adjective	comparative	superlative
nice	nicer	(the) nicest
healthy	healthier	(the) healthiest
delicious	more delicious	(the) most delicious
good	better	(the) best

1 Sharmila's mum cooks … curries, but in town Sharmila loves chips. She thinks that they're even … than curry.
2 Amy thinks that chips are nice, but she prefers burgers. She thinks they're … than chips.
3 Amy's favourite burgers are cheeseburgers. She thinks they're the … of all.
4 Michelle tries to be healthy and she usually just has a salad. She thinks that salad is … than chips and burgers.
5 All three girls like milkshakes. They think that strawberry and vanilla are delicious, but the … milkshake of all is chocolate. It's their favourite.
6 Sharmila, Amy and Michelle aren't just good friends, they're … friends.

[I] **6 Talk in class.**

1 What are your favourite things to eat and drink when you are in town?
2 Are there lots of fast food restaurants where you live? Which is the best?

GRAMMAR SPOT: Die Steigerung des Adjektivs

Kurze Adjektive und Adjektive mit -y am Ende bilden Komparativ und Superlativ mit -er/est:

Burgers are nicer than chips, but pizza is the nicest food of all.

Für längere Adjektive wird more/most verwendet:

Strawberries are more delicious than oranges, but I think kiwis are the most delicious fruit of all.

Unregelmäßig:

good/better/best

→ Grammar summary, page 197

[R/I] **1** **Ben's Burgers is an international chain of American burger restaurants. Here's the menu at one of their restaurants in Birmingham. Look at the menu and give the prices. Partner A ask questions, Partner B look at the menu. (Numbers: Klappumschlag A.)**

1 a burger?
2 a Monsterburger?
3 a portion of chicken nuggets?
4 a milkshake?
5 a chicken salad?
6 an ice cream?
7 a medium portion of fries?
8 a large coke?

A
How much is ...?

B
It's ...

[P] **2** **Copy and complete the table. Then use the words in the sentences. (There is sometimes more than one answer.)**

1 The cheeseburgers are big, but the Monsterburger is even bigger. It's the ... thing on the menu.
2 A medium portion of fries is ... than a small portion of fries.
3 A cheeseburger is £1.49. It's ... than a chickenburger but it's ... than a burger.
4 A fishburger with a small portion of fries and a milkshake is ... a chicken burger with a medium portion of fries and a large coke.
5 I think that milkshakes are ... than coke.

adjective	comparative	superlative
cheap	▪	(the) ▪
nice	▪	(the) ▪
big	▪	(the) ▪
healthy	▪	(the) ▪
delicious	▪	(the) ▪
expensive	▪	(the) ▪

▶ TIPS AND TRICKS
Nicer than ...
Never: Nicer ~~as~~...

[P] **3** **Now write five more sentences. Use the adjectives from the table.**

[R/P] **4**

ICE CREAM is one of the most popular kinds of food all over the world. The biggest consumers of ice cream in the world aren't, in fact, the Americans (they're number two), but the New Zealanders. Per person per year, they eat about 26 litres. The Germans eat only 3.8 litres and are number eleven on the list. The biggest consumers in Europe are the Swiss at 14.4 litres. So what kinds of ice cream do we like? In Europe and the USA the most popular flavour is vanilla. About 33 per cent of all the ice cream that we eat is vanilla ice cream. Next is chocolate (19%), then nut, cookie and caramel flavours (7%), then Neapolitan (5%) – that's three flavours together – and finally strawberry (4%). For us, ice cream is always sweet, but this isn't always true in Asia. In India, for example, you can buy chilli ice cream. The Japanese eat some of the most exotic (and for us some of the strangest) ice creams. There you can buy garlic, potato, tomato and even chicken ice cream!

True or not true? Correct the false sentences.

1 The biggest consumers of ice cream in the world are the Americans.
2 The Swiss are bigger consumers of ice cream than the Germans.
3 In Europe and the USA, strawberry ice cream is more popular than chocolate ice cream.
4 The most popular flavour in Europe and the USA is vanilla.
5 In Asia, people often eat ice cream that isn't sweet.
6 People in India eat some of the strangest ice creams.
7 You can buy chicken ice cream in Japan.

[P] **5** **A customer is buying a meal at Ben's Burgers. Read the conversation, then write a conversation for YOU at Ben's Burgers. (C = customer, A = assistant)**

A Hi. What can I get for you?
C I'd like a cheeseburger and a medium portion of fries, please.
A Would you like a drink with that?
C Yes, a coke, please.
A Regular or large?
C Regular, please.
A Would you like a dessert?
C No, thanks.
A That comes to three pounds seventy-eight, please. …
Here you are. Enjoy your meal.
C Thanks.

[R] **6** **All these kinds of food and drinks are on pages 38–41. What are they?**

1 GERRUB → burger
2 DALSA
3 CCHENKI
4 LAKHEMSKI
5 LAVALIN ECI ARCME
6 DOTUN
7 PLEPA UCIEJ
8 THEGATIPS

[P] **7** **Translate into English.**

* 1 Was ist dein Lieblingsessen?
2 Berlin ist die größte Stadt in Deutschland.
3 Ich denke, Schokolade ist sogar besser als Kekse.
4 Ich mag Milkshakes, aber ich trinke lieber Apfelsaft.
5 Ich möchte bitte einen Cheeseburger und eine Coke.

[R] **1 Read the article about fast food from a British teenage magazine and answer these questions.**

1 What does Dr. Aziz say? Choose the best statement below.
 a Fast food is very good for you. Eat it every day.
 b Too much fast food is bad for you. Don't eat it too often.
 c Fast food is bad for you. Never eat it.
2 What is the most important rule about food generally?

Stay healthy with Dr. Aziz

This week …
Is fast food bad for you?

Hello there. Yes, this week it's the big question! We all like burgers, pizza and other kinds of fast food, but you often read that they're unhealthy. So, what's the truth? Is fast food bad for you?

What's in a burger?

Let's look first at a typical burger meal. You're in town, you're hungry (OK, **very** hungry!) so you buy a double burger with cheese, a large portion of fries and a large soda drink. What do they contain? You know about calories, right? OK. Here we go …

Food/drink	Calories
Burger	1,000
Fries	500
Soda	300
	Total: 1,800

Is that bad?

It isn't terrible! The meal doesn't have any fresh vegetables (only a small portion of salad), and that isn't so good. Also, there's a lot of sugar in the soda drink. That's bad for your teeth, of course. But our bodies need calories. The problem is, that the meal contains almost **all** the calories that you need for one day (about 2,000). In other words, if you eat this meal too often, you will very soon be overweight!

What can I do?

The most important rule about food is: enjoy what you eat! So have a burger sometimes, but not every day. Even better, when you're in town, try a salad. A lot of fast food restaurants sell chicken salads and they're delicious (and only contain around 300 calories). Drink a bottle of water or orange juice instead of a soda. And say 'no' to fries.

Until next week.
Stay healthy!

Dr Aziz

[R] **2 Complete the sentences with information from the article.**

1 We need about … calories for one day.
2 A double burger with cheese, a large fries and a large soda contain … calories.
3 The meal contains a small portion of salad but it doesn't have any … That isn't so …
4 There's a lot of … in the soda and that's bad for your …
5 If you have the double burger, fries and soda too often, you will soon be …
6 A lot of fast food restaurants sell chicken salads. They're delicious and they contain only … calories.
7 A bottle of water or … is better for you than a soda.

[R] **3 Find words or phrases in the article that have the same meaning:**

1 not healthy
2 big
3 little
4 peas, carrots, potatoes etc.
5 we could also say
6 fat
7 about, approximately
8 drink A and don't drink B

[P] **4 Give the comparative and superlative forms of the adjectives.**

Example: important → more important → the …

1 healthy
2 delicious
3 good
4 bad

[I] **5 Talk in class.**

1 Do you agree with Dr Aziz? Is fast food OK (but not too often)?
2 Do you try to be healthy? Do you think that it's important? What tips have you got for a healthy life? Talk about:
   a food,
   b sport and exercise,
   c watching TV or using a computer.

[P/I] **6 Choose one of the projects.**

1 "What's your favourite food?" Do a survey in class. First, make a list of five or six things that you all like to eat. Then put them in order (1 = the nicest). At the end you can make a pie chart.

2 Find out on the Internet about British or American food. If you can, find a recipe in English. Perhaps you can cook the dish at home.

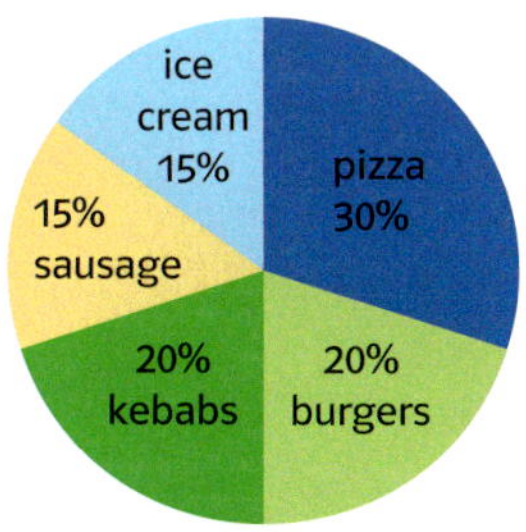

ICH KANN JETZT …

- Dinge vergleichen und sagen, welche billiger, besser, größer etc. sind,
- beliebte alltägliche Speisen und Getränke benennen und darüber sprechen und schreiben,
- meine Meinung in einer einfachen Diskussion äußern – z. B. über gesundes Leben.

3 What's your favourite food?

Looking after visitors to a company

[R] 1 Listen and answer the questions.

Saskia and Daniel are apprentices at a company in Germany. It makes furniture. It also has a factory in England, and this week, two English apprentices, Kate and Andy, are visiting Germany. It's lunchtime and Saskia, Daniel, Kate and Andy are in the works canteen. They're looking at the menu …

Daniel: So, what would you like to eat? Today there's tomato soup, a big salad, … how do you say 'Schwein' in English, Saskia?
Saskia: Pork.
Daniel: Ah yes. Pork with chips and a salad, a small salad. Then 'Bratwurst', that's sausage with potatoes.
Saskia: Potato salad.
Daniel: Yes, potato salad.
Andy: I know 'Eis', that's ice cream.
Daniel: Ja, yes, mixed ice cream. And, I don't know how to say 'Apfelstrudel' in English.
Kate: We call it apple strudel.
Daniel: OK! Apple strudel with …
Kate: Vanilla sauce. Hmm, that all looks nice. I'd like the sausage with potato salad and the ice cream.
Daniel: And what about you, Andy?
Andy: Yes, for me the salad, the big salad … can I have chips with that, too?
Daniel: Yes, sure.
Andy: Great. And the apple strudel.
Daniel: OK. Let's get our food.

TAGESMENU

Tomatencremesuppe
~
Großer Salatteller
~
Schweineschnitzel „Wiener Art" mit Pommes frites und gem. Salat
Bratwurst mit Kartoffelsalat
~
Gemischtes Eis
Apfelstrudel mit Vanillesoße

1 What product does Saskia and Daniel's company make?
2 Where are Kate and Andy from? What are they doing this week?
3 Where are the four apprentices at the moment? What are they doing?
4 What does Kate choose for her lunch?
5 What would Andy like to eat?

[R] 2 Find these phrases in the conversation in English.

Was möchtest du essen?

Ich möchte …

Ich weiß nicht, wie man … auf Englisch sagt.

Und du?

Holen wir unser Essen.

R/I] **3 Work with a partner. Match the German and English food words. Then listen and check your answers.**

1 Schwein
2 Rind
3 Lamm
4 Hähnchen
5 Pute
6 Wurst
7 Schinken
8 Fisch
9 Suppe
10 Salat
11 Tomate
12 Spargel
13 Champignons
14 Karotten
15 Erbsen
16 Zwiebeln
17 Kartoffeln
18 Pommes frites
19 Reis
20 Nudeln
21 Käse
22 Ei
23 (Schlag)sahne
24 (Obst)torte
25 Eis
26 Soße, Sauce

a (whipped) cream
b cheese
c ice cream
d sauce
e sausage
f beef
g soup
h onions
i tomato
j asparagus
k egg
l (fruit) tart
m lamb
n noodles
o ham
p peas
q potatoes
r turkey
s mushrooms
t carrots
u rice
v fish
w chicken
x salad
y pork
z chips

[I] **4 Ask your partner for the English words.**
Partner B close your book when you know the words.

Example:

Partner A: What's 'Schwein' in English? What are 'Karotten'?
Partner B: It's/they're …
Partner A: How do you say 'Pommes frites' in English?
Partner B: You say 'chips'.

M] **5 Some English apprentices are visiting your company in Germany. Some of you are looking after them. It's lunchtime, and you are in the canteen.**
Work in a group of 3–4 students. Take the parts of the German apprentices and the English visitors. Explain the menu to them, and then find out what they would like to eat.

TAGESMENÜ

Erbsensuppe mit Wursteinlage
Französische Zwiebelsuppe mit Käse überbacken

~

Großer Salatteller

~

Jägerschnitzel vom Schweinerücken mit Champignons in Rahmsoße, dazu Pommes frites und Salat
Hähnchenbrustfilet mit Salzkartoffeln und Salat
Currywurst mit Reis

~

Obsttorte mit Schlagsahne
Vanilleeis mit heißer Schokoladensoße

ICH KANN JETZT …

- helfen, Englisch sprechende Besucher in Deutschland zu betreuen,
- eine typische deutsche Speisekarte in Englisch erklären,
- mehr alltägliche Lebensmittel in Englisch benennen.

Unit 4 Famous people

[P/I] **1** **Who is your favourite film star, singer, musician or sportsperson?**
Can you name a famous businessperson, author or scientist?
What do you know about these people?

[R] **2** **Every week, the teenage magazine COOL has a biography of a famous person.**
This week it's the film star Julia Roberts. Look at her details and answer the questions.

Julia Roberts

Date of birth: 27 October 1967

Real name: Julie Fiona Roberts

Eyes: Brown

Hair: Dark blonde

Family: Married to cameraman Danny Moder. Two children (twins), a girl Hazel, and a boy Phinnaeus (born 2004)

Birthplace: USA

Occupation: Actress

Star sign: Scorpio

Height: 5 feet 9 inches (1m 75)

Residence(s): A ranch in New Mexico and a flat in New York

1 What's Julia's real name?
2 Where does she live?
3 Is she married?
4 What colour eyes does she have?
5 What colour hair does she have?
6 Does she have any children?
7 How tall is she?
8 What's her star sign?

[R] **3** **Now read the second part of the article.**

Julie Fiona Roberts was born in the small town of Smyrna, near Atlanta, Georgia, on 27 October 1967. Her father was a vacuum cleaner salesman and her mother worked as a secretary. Julie loved animals, and she wanted first to be a vet, but then in 1984 her brother Eric (an actor in Hollywood) arranged a small part in a movie for Julie and her career as a film star began. She changed her name to 'Julia' because there was already an actress called Julie Roberts. Julia's first successful film was Mystic Pizza in 1988. Lots of people fell in love with this new, young actress and her big smile. But her really big breakthrough came in 1990 when she appeared with Richard Gere in the movie Pretty Woman. Julia became famous overnight. In 2000, Julia starred in a movie about the life of a real person – Erin Brockovich. Julia was brilliant in the movie and she won an Oscar that year for Best Actress (and she earned $20 million!). Julia is still making fantastic films today and is the highest-paid actress in Hollywood.

P/I] **4** **Two English friends, Lisa and Kelly, are talking about film stars. Lisa is asking Kelly questions about Julia Roberts. Kelly saw the article in COOL yesterday, so she knows all the answers! Complete what Kelly says, then read the conversation with a partner.**

Lisa Where was Julia born?
Kelly **(1)** ...
Lisa Did she want to be an actress when she was small?
Kelly No, she didn't want to be an actress at all. She wanted **(2)** ...
Lisa So when did her career as a film star begin?
Kelly In **(3)** ... Her brother Eric arranged a small part in a film for her.
Lisa Her name was Julie then, wasn't it? Why did she change her name?
Kelly **(4)** ...
Lisa Oh, I see. So what was her first successful film?
Kelly It was a movie called **(5)** ... But her big breakthrough came in **(6)** ...
Lisa What did she do then?
Kelly **(7)** ...
Lisa Did she win an Oscar for that movie?
Kelly No, she didn't, but she won one for her next big film **(8)** ...
Lisa Oh, yes. She was brilliant in that!
Kelly And she became very rich!
Lisa How much did she earn?
Kelly **(9)** ... She's **(10)** ... in Hollywood.

▶ **TIPS AND TRICKS: FALSE FRIENDS**

I ~~became a sausage~~!
= Ich wurde eine Wurst!

to become = werden
bekommen = to get

GRAMMAR SPOT: Das simple past

• Wir verwenden das simple past, um über Ereignisse in der Vergangenheit zu sprechen, die jetzt abgeschlossen sind.	I you he/she/it we you they	lived worked began
• Wir bilden Fragen und Negativsätze mit did/didn't: Where did you live when you were small? Julia didn't live in New York when she was small.		

→ Grammar summary, page 198

[P] **1 Make sentences about Chuck's day yesterday. Use the simple past. (Be careful: some verbs are irregular!)**

This is Chuck (and his assistant Jeff). Chuck works in Hollywood. He isn't a famous actor but everybody there knows him because he's a brilliant cameraman. Chuck does the same things every day.

Example: He gets up at about 6 o'clock.
→ He got up at 6 o'clock yesterday.

1 He goes to the studio at about 8 o'clock.
2 He works on the set.
3 He talks to the film director.
4 He meets a lot of famous film stars.
5 After work he runs five kilometres.
6 In the evenings he usually eats in a restaurant with other movie people.
7 He goes home at about midnight.
8 He sleeps.

[P] **2 On the left are the answers to some questions about Chuck's day. What are the questions?**

Example: **(At 6 o'clock)** → When did Chuck get up yesterday?

1 **(In his garden)** Where … he … his breakfast?
2 **(At 8 o'clock)** When … he … to the studio?
3 **(On the set)** Where … he …?
4 **(The director)** Who … he … to?
5 **(A lot of famous film stars)** Who …?
6 **(Five kilometres)** How many …?
7 **(In a restaurant)** Where …?
8 **(At midnight)** When …?

[P] **3 Chuck doesn't normally work on Sundays. He didn't work last Sunday, and he didn't do the usual things. Give sentences like this:**

Example: He got up at 6 o'clock last Sunday. **(10 o'clock)**
→ No! He didn't get up at 6 o'clock. He got up at 10 o'clock.

1 He went to the studio. **(go to the beach with his family)**
2 He talked to the movie director. **(talk to his wife and kids)**
3 He met a lot of film stars. **(meet his neighbours and friends)**
4 Eat in a restaurant. **(eat at home)**

[P] **4 Say the years aloud, then complete the sentences for YOU. (Numbers: Klappumschlag A.)**

a	1967	f	2001
b	1984	g	2006
c	1990	h	2010
d	1999	i	2020
e	2000		

1 I was born in …
2 I started school in …
3 I started my college course in …

▶ TIPS AND TRICKS

I was born in 1989.

Never:
~~I was born 1989.~~
~~I am born in 1989.~~

[P] **5** **Here's an article from COOL magazine about another famous person – but the verbs are all in the simple present. Give the verbs again in the simple past.**

What do you know about Robbie?

ROBERT PETER WILLIAMS **(1) is** was born in the north of England on 13 February 1974. When Robert **(2) is** two years old, his mum and dad **(3) separate** and young Robbie **(4) grows up** with his mum and his sister Sally. Robbie **(5) is** a terrible pupil and he **(6) leaves** school when he **(7) is** 16. He **(8) works** first as a salesman. Then, in 1991 he **(9) joins** the band Take That. From 1991–1995, the band **(10) sell** 15 million singles and it **(11) has** eight number 1 hits, but Robbie **(12) leaves** the band in 1995 and he **(13) begins** his solo career. He **(14) is** very wild for the first year! He **(15) drinks** a lot and he **(16) takes** drugs, and his first songs **(17) aren't** very successful. But then in 1997, he **(18) releases** 'Angels'. It **(19) is** an enormous hit. Today, Robbie is one of the most famous musicians, singers and songwriters alive. He lives in London.

R/P] **6** **Answer the questions about Robbie. Give whole sentences.**

1 Where was he born?
2 When was he born?
3 What was his first job?
4 What did he do in 1991?
5 How many number 1 hits did the band have?
6 What did Robbie begin in 1995?
7 What happened for the first year?
8 What single did he release in 1997?
9 Where does he live today?

[P] **7** **All the sentences below about Robbie are false! Can you correct them?**

1 Robbie's parents separated when he was ten.
→ No, they didn't separate when he was ten. They …
2 He was a brilliant pupil at school.
3 He left school when he was 18.
4 Take That sold 5 million singles.
5 Robbie's first solo songs were very successful.
6 Today, Robbie lives in New York.

[R] **8** **Find the missing words and phrases on pages 46–49.**

1 Julia Roberts is an … **(Schauspielerin)**.
2 When she was small, she wanted to be a … **(Tierärztin)**.
3 She … **(wurde)** famous overnight when she appeared in the movie Pretty Woman.
4 She was … **(ausgezeichnet)** in the movie Erin Brockovich.
5 Chuck met his … **(Nachbarn)** last Sunday.
6 Robbie Williams … **(wuchs auf)** with his mum and his sister Sally.
7 He … **(trat/bei)** the band Take That in 1991.
8 Robbie is one of the most famous musicians, singers and … **(Liedermacher)** alive.

[P] **9** **What did you do last weekend? Write a short text (30–50 words). Write some things**
* **that you did and some things that you didn't do.**

→ I got up …
I had breakfast …
I didn't have lessons at college!
I …

[R] **1** **Read about this famous businessperson.**

The richest man in the world

Around 85 per cent of all computers in the world use Microsoft software. So it isn't a surprise perhaps that this man is the richest man in the world. He's the founder and the boss of Microsoft, Bill Gates.

The story of Microsoft

WILLIAM ('BILL') GATES was born in Seattle in the north-west of the USA, on 15 October 1955. Even as a kid he loved computers and he wrote his first software when he was 13. After school, Bill became a student at Harvard, one of the most famous universities in the States. His father was a lawyer, and Bill wanted first to be a lawyer, too. But computers were more interesting. In his second year, he met an old school friend, Paul Allen, and together they developed a programming language called BASIC. Bill left university and he and Paul founded the Microsoft software company. That was in 1975.

In 1981, IBM – the world's biggest computer company – produced the first 'home computer'. Bill and Paul produced the software for IBM. The home computer revolution began. IBM sold millions of PCs – and Bill and Paul earned millions of dollars. Paul became ill in 1983 and left Microsoft. Bill worked hard alone and in 1987 he produced the first version of Microsoft Windows. When he released Windows 95 in August 1995, it sold seven million copies in the first six weeks! Microsoft became the world's biggest software company almost overnight.

Bill Gates the person

So what kind of person is the world's richest man? Well, he lives here, in this house near Seattle. (Microsoft's head office is not far away in the town of Redmond.) The house cost $53 million and has a cinema (with a popcorn machine!), a fitness centre, a library, a swimming pool, offices, a guest house and an underground garage. Bill lives here with his wife Melinda and their three children. For the boss of one of the world's biggest companies, he's a very shy man. He's also very generous and he gives away hundreds of millions of dollars every year.

[R] **2** **Answer the questions.**

1 Here are some important years in Bill Gates' life. What happened in each year? 1955 • 1975 • 1981 • 1987 • 1995
2 What was the name of the old school friend who founded Microsoft with Bill? When did he leave the company? Why?
3 How much did Bill's house cost? Where is it? Where can Bill watch movies at home?
4 Is Bill married? Does he have any children?
5 Find two words that describe Bill as a person.

[R] 3 Complete the sentences with information from the text.

1 Around 85 per cent of all computers in the world use …
2 It isn't a surprise that Bill Gates is the …
3 Bill wrote his first software when …
4 At university, Bill wanted first to be …
5 In Bill's second year at Harvard, he and Paul wrote a programming language called …
6 Bill left Harvard and he and Paul …
7 IBM sold millions of its home computers and Bill and Paul earned …
8 When Bill released Windows 95, Microsoft became …

> ▶ **TIPS AND TRICKS**
> Bill gates founded Microsoft.
> to found/founded = gründen
> to find/found = finden

[R/P] 4 True or not true? Correct the false sentences.

1 Bill's father was a doctor.
2 Bill and Paul produced the software for IBM's first home computers.
3 Bill and Paul produced the first version of Windows together in 1987.
4 Bill released Windows 95 in June 1995.
5 Microsoft's head office is in Seattle.
6 Bill's wife is called Melinda.
7 Bill gives away thousands of dollars every year.

[R] 5 Find the word or words in the text.

1 Another word for a child is a …
2 A place where people study. Harvard is a … in the USA.
3 You use this when you program a computer. BASIC is a …
4 American money. Bill and Paul earned millions of … from their software for IBM.
5 Bill's house is not far from Seattle. It's … Seattle.
6 A place where you find lots of books.
7 Bill's house has a … His friends can sleep here when they visit him.
8 If you give away lots of money, you are a … person.

[P] 6 Make notes, then close your book and give a talk about Bill Gates.

Early life	Harvard	Microsoft and IBM	Microsoft Windows	Bill Gates the person
Seattle				

[I] 7 Talk in class.

1 What do you think of Bill Gates' house? Do you like it? Do you think it's a big house for the richest man in the world?
2 Bill Gates has a normal life with his family, but people often have problems (with drugs, for example) when they become rich and famous. Do you know a famous person like this? Why do you think this happens?

[P/I] 8 Choose one of the projects.

1 Look on the Internet and find out about a famous person (or band). Write a biography like the one of Julia Roberts on page 47. (Tip: lots of famous people have fansites).
2 You often find quizzes about film stars, singers etc. on the Internet and in magazines. Choose a famous person and write a quiz for the other people in your class.

> **ICH KANN JETZT …**
> • über Ereignisse in der Vergangenheit sprechen und schreiben,
> • über einige bekannte britische und amerikanische Persönlichkeiten erzählen,
> • einen ziemlich langen englischen Text lesen und verstehen.

[R] **1** **Jane Miller is a secretary in a fitness club in England. This is the office where Jane works every day. Can you find these fifteen things in the picture?**

desk • computer keyboard • printer • plant • office chair • computer mouse • filing cabinet • calendar • some letters • computer screen • telephone • radiator • window • notice board • cuddly toy

[R] **2** **Jane does lots of different jobs. She answers the phone, writes emails and letters, and looks after the finances. She also keeps records of the club's members. Look at the personal details of a typical member. Answer the questions. (Numbers: Klappumschlag A.)**

1 What town does Jonathan live in?
2 What's his house number?
3 What's his post code?
4 What's his email address?
5 What's the area code of his home telephone number?
6 What's his mobile number?

Full name: Jonathan Michael Green
Address: 21 Church Street
BANBURY
Oxfordshire
OX17 2BX
Home telephone: 01295-256134
Mobile: 07786-559229
Email: j.green@hotmail.com

▶ TIPS AND TRICKS

What's your address?

Never: ~~adress~~

[R] **3** **When new members join the club, Jane puts their personal details on to her computer. She's talking to a new member now. Listen and note down Susan's details on a separate sheet of paper.**

NEW MEMBER	Start date: 17.02.07
Full name	Susan Elizabeth James
Date of birth	
Address	
Home telephone	
Mobile	
Email	
Height	
Weight	
Membership Number	1156

Save Edit Delete

[M] **4** **You're an apprentice with a company in Germany. As part of your training, you and three others are spending three months in Banbury. You all want to join Jane's fitness club. One of your group doesn't speak English, so you're helping him/her today to join.**
Work in groups of three. First listen to exercise 3 again, then take parts.

Partner A: Sie möchten Mitglied werden, aber Sie sprechen kein Englisch. Denken Sie sich eine Adresse, Telefonnummer etc. in Banbury aus.

Partner B: You are Jane. Ask the two students their personal details. You don't speak German.

Partner C: You are helping. Translate Jane's questions for your friend. Then translate the answers into English for Jane.

CULTURE TIPS:
ADDRESSES

Look at the address again on page 52. What important differences can you find between addresses in Britain and Germany?

ICH KANN JETZT ...

- Gegenstände in einem Büro benennen,
- Adressen, auch E-Mail-Adressen und Telefonnummern, in Englisch sagen,
- persönliche Angaben machen und verstehen,
- jemandem mit wenig Englischkenntnissen helfen, persönliche Angaben zu machen.

Unit 5 Where I live

[P/I] **1** **Look at these two pages. What country are they about? What do you know about this country? Can you name a town? A famous person? An animal?**

[R] **2** **Read about Nick Johnson.**

Hi! I'm Nick Johnson and I'm from Australia. I live in Sydney, in the south-east of the country. Most big towns in Australia are on the coast. Sydney is, too. It's the oldest and the biggest town in Australia but it isn't the capital. That's Canberra.

This is my dad. Mum and Dad immigrated to Australia from England in 1985, so they have lived here for over 20 years. Dad is in the garden of our house. He's cooking a barbecue right now. It's a great house. We have lived here since 1991.

Here are some kids at my school. Australia is a warm country in the summer – that's December, January and February for us – and we always sit outside in the breaks. It's a secondary school and I have been here for five years. I'm in my final year now. Next year, I want to study at a vocational school here in Sydney and to become an electrician.

[R] **3** **Complete these sentences about Australia and Nick.**

1 The capital of Australia is …
2 Australia is about the same size as …
3 The population is …
4 The summer months in Australia are …
5 Most big towns in Australia are …
6 Nick lives in …
7 His parents immigrated to Australia in …
8 Next year, Nick wants …

AUSTRALIA: QUICK FACTS

- Population: 20 million
- Capital: Canberra
- Size: About the same as the USA
- Average temperatures (Sydney):
  summer 26°
  winter 17°

[P] **4** **Look at this diagram, then complete the sentences below.**

Example:

Nick's mum and dad immigrated to Australia in 1985.

a They have lived in Australia since 1985.
b They have lived there for over 20 years.

1 Nick's mum and dad bought their house in Sydney in 1991.
   a They have lived in the house … 1991.
   b They have lived in the house … over 15 years.
2 Nick has been at his school … five years.
   a He started at the school in … (year? Work it out!).
   b He … … there … … (year?)

[I] **5** **Ask a partner, then tell the class your partner's answers.**

1 How long have you lived in the town where you live now?
   → I've …
2 How long have you lived in the flat or house where you live now?
3 How long have you been a student at our college?
4 When did you arrive at college this morning?
5 How long have you been here today?

Bernd/Martina has lived …

GRAMMAR SPOT: Das present perfect mit since und for

I have he has she has it has we have you have they have	I've he's she's it's we've you've they've	lived been	Wir verwenden das present perfect mit since oder for, um die Frage „How long …?" zu beantworten. Wir verwenden since für einen Zeitpunkt und for für einen Zeitraum.

→ Grammar summary, page 199

[P] **1 Complete the sentences with the correct form of to have.**

Example: How long have you lived in Sydney, Nick?
1 I was born here and I'm 16. I ... lived here for 16 years.
2 How long ... Nick lived in Sydney?
3 He ... lived here for 16 years.
4 Nick's parents ... lived in Australia since 1985.
5 This is the Sydney Opera House. It ... been here since 1973.

▶ TIPS AND TRICKS

I have lived here since 1995.

Never:
I ~~live~~ here since 1995.

[P] **2 For or since? Complete the sentences in this text.**

A short history of Australia

The Aborigines of Australia

The oldest inhabitants of Australia are called Aborigines. They are like the Native Americans in the USA. The first Aborigines arrived in Australia about 5,000 BC. So they've lived in Australia (1) ... about 7,000 years! Today, one person in a hundred in Australia is an Aborigine.

Captain Cook

Europeans have lived in Australia (2) ... 1770, when an Englishman, Captain Cook, landed at Botany Bay, near Sydney. That's why Sydney is the oldest and biggest town in Australia, and why Australians speak English! The first English people were criminals from prisons in London.

Australia today

Today, people from all over the world live in Australia. It's a very 'multicultural' country. Kamala (on the left) and Sumio (on the right) are two pupils from Nick's school. Kamala has lived in Sydney (3) ... 2001, when her family came here from India. Sumio's family is Japanese. They have lived in Australia (4) ... about 15 years. Kamala and Sumio are Asian. About seven people in a hundred in Australia today are Asian.

R/P] **3 Answer these questions about the history of Australia. Use full sentences. Be careful of the tenses!**

Example: How long have Aborigines lived in Australia? → They've …

1 When did the first Aborigines arrive in Australia?
2 How long have Europeans lived in Australia?
3 Where did Captain Cook land?
4 Who were the first English people in Australia?
5 Who are Kamala and Sumio?
6 Where do they live?
7 When did Kamala and her family come to Sydney?
8 How long have Sumio and his family lived in Australia?
9 How many people in Australia today are Asian?

[P] **4 Look at the words and phrases below, then complete the sentences about Australia.**

1 Canberra, the capital, is in the … of Australia.
2 Perth is in the … of Australia.
3 The biggest town in the … of Australia is Darwin.
4 The most important rainforest is in … Australia.
5 A lot of the country in … Australia is desert. Only Aborigines can live here.
6 The biggest rock in the world is Ayers Rock. It's in … Australia.
7 The only big town in the … of Australia is Alice Springs. It's near Ayers Rock.

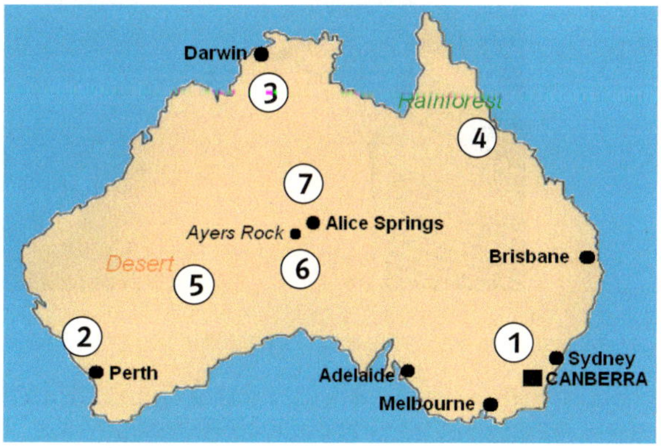

Sydney is in the south-east of Australia. It's in south-eastern Australia.

- in the north/south/east/west/south-east/north-west of …
- in northern/southern/eastern/western/south-eastern/north-western …
- in the centre of … in central …

R/P] **5 Complete these sentences with words from pages 54–57. Then find six more new words in this unit that you think are important. Compare your list with a partner's.**

1 Nick's parents … to Australia in 1985. **(wanderten nach Australien ein).**
2 The … of Australia is 20 million. **(Bevölkerung)**
3 The original… of Australia were the Aborigenes. **(Einwohner)**
4 Australia is a very … country. **(multikulturell)**

[P] **6 Translate into English.**

1 Nick wohnt seit 16 Jahren in Australien.
2 Kamala wohnt seit 2001 in Australien.
3 Wie lange wohnt ihr schon in eurer neuen Wohnung?
4 Wir wohnen seit drei Monaten in unserer neuen Wohnung.
5 Sydney ist die größte Stadt in Australien.
6 Adelaide ist im Süden des Landes.

[R] **1 Listen and find the missing information.**

Across the outback

Australians call them 'road trains'. These monster trucks travel across Australia from north to south, east to west. They carry things like rocks, cattle and oil and are Australia's most important means of freight transport.

Jack Smith is a 'truckie' – a road train driver. Here's an interview with Jack.

Interviewer	Hi, Jack, and thanks for the interview.
Jack	G'day! No problem!
Interviewer	How long have you been a road train driver?
Jack	A truckie? For about **(1)** … years.
Interviewer	And where in Australia do you drive?
Jack	I drive all over the country, but I work for a company in Perth, and I drive mostly in **(2)** … Australia.
Interviewer	How are the roads where you drive?
Jack	Well, most big Australian towns are **(3)** … We call central Australia the 'outback', and it's pretty empty. In the desert, the roads aren't really roads at all, just tracks.
Interviewer	How big is a road train, Jack?
Jack	Big! My road train is **(4)** … metres long and it weighs about **(5)** … tonnes. It's got 62 wheels! And it's fast. When you drive a road train, you start and you don't stop. I normally travel at about **(6)** …, maybe **(7)** … kilometres an hour. When I want to stop, it takes **(8)** …!
Interviewer	How long are your journeys?
Jack	Normally, about **(9)** …
Interviewer	Where do you eat and sleep?
Jack	Well, there are little restaurants and motels on the road, but my truck has got a **(10)** …, a fridge, a cooker and a **(11)** … I usually sleep **(12)** …
Interviewer	Jack, thanks very much.
Jack	You're welcome!

[R] **2 Copy and complete the notes on the right with information about Jack.**

[R/P] **3 True or not true? Correct the false sentences.**

1 Jack has been a truckie for 10 years.
2 He drives mostly in the east of Australia.
3 The roads in the desert are often not very good.
4 When Jack wants to stop in his truck, it takes 200 metres.
5 His truck has got a bed, a fridge, a cooker and a cinema with a popcorn machine.

Name: Jack Smith
Job: ...
How long: ...
Company: ...
Drives mostly: ...
Size of his road train: ...
Journeys are normally: ...
Normally sleeps: ...

[R] **4 Find phrases in the text that have the same meaning.**

Example: I drive **everywhere** in the country. → all over

1 I'm **an employee of** a company in Perth.
2 **Our name for** central Australia is 'the outback'.
3 **What's the size of** a road train?
4 I normally travel at about 100, **perhaps** 110 kilometres an hour.
5 **You can find** little restaurants and motels on the road.

[R] **5 Find these words in the interview.**

Example: A very hot place where there's a lot of sand and there isn't any rain. → a desert

1 The Australian word for central Australia.
2 The Australian word for a road train driver.
3 A thousand metres.
4 A place where you eat.
5 Your food stays cold in this.
6 An Australian word for 'hello'.
7 You find these things on a car, a truck etc. They're round.
8 A thousand kilogrammes.

ICH KANN JETZT ...

- auf Englisch sagen, wie lange ich etwas gemacht habe,
- einige wichtige Orte in Australien nennen und Informationen über das Land und seine Geschichte geben,
- einem längeren Interview mit einer Person zuhören und Einzelheiten verstehen.

[I] **6 Talk in class.**

1 What do you think about Jack's job? Is it interesting? Boring? Exciting? A bit lonely?
2 Imagine a day in Jack's life. What do you think he does?

[P/I] **7 Choose one of the projects.**

1 **Make a poster about Germany. Draw a map and show the most important towns. Give some 'quick facts'. What's the capital? How big is the country? What's the population?**
2 **Do you know another country? Write about it. Find some pictures if you can.**
3 **There are some good websites about Australia. Look on the Internet and find out about:**
   a **famous Australians (Nicole Kidman and Mel Gibson are Australian),**
   b **sport in Australia,**
   c **Australian animals (kangaroos etc.),**
   d **Aborigines in Australia.**

CULTURE TIPS:
ENGLISH AROUND THE WORLD

People in countries where they speak English (Britain, the USA, Australia etc.) speak 99% the same language, but they all have some special words and of course they have different accents.

[R] **1** **Henni Bach is a German lorry driver. He delivers his company's products all over Europe, and today he's in this town in the east of England. Look at the street map and find these things:**

Stadtmitte • Busbahnhof • Supermarkt • Autobahn • Park • Parkhaus • Gewerbegebiet • Bahnhof • Kino

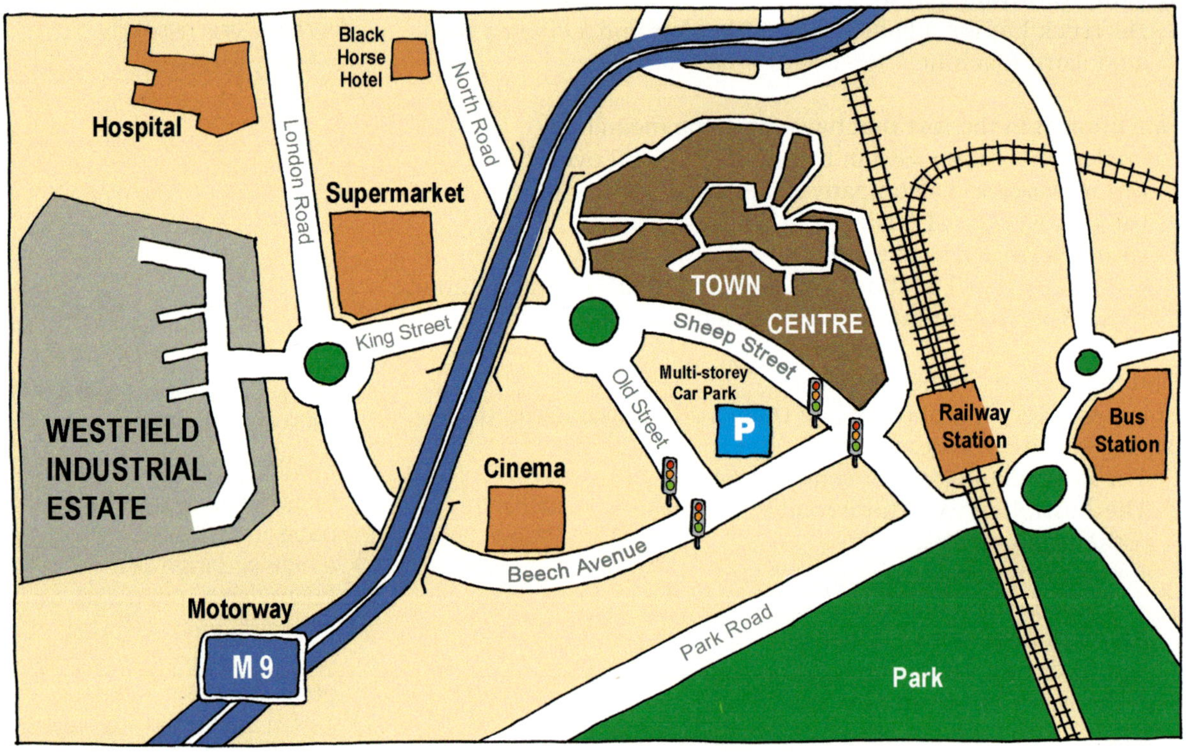

[R] **2** **Henni is in his lorry in Park Road and he wants to go to the Westfield Industrial Estate. He's asking a woman for help. Listen and follow the directions on the street map. Then read the dialogue with a partner.**

Henni Excuse me. I'm looking for the Westfield Industrial Estate. Can you help, please?

Woman The Westfield Industrial Estate? Hmm, yes. Go straight up here and take the first left. That's Sheep Street. At the traffic lights, turn left again into Beech Avenue.

Henni Beech ...?

Woman Avenue. Go along Beech Avenue, past the cinema, under the motorway bridge, until you come to a roundabout. Turn left there and the industrial estate is in front of you.

Henni Great. So, straight up here, take the first left, then turn left again, along Beech Avenue, and turn left at the roundabout.

Woman That's right.

Henni Thanks very much.

Woman You're welcome.

CULTURE TIPS:
EXCUSE ME

'Excuse me' is a very useful phrase when you want to ask for help – about direction, for example.

[R] **3** **The woman in Park Road is giving directions to three different places in the town (from Park Road). What are the places? Listen and write the names.**

[M] **4** **An English tourist in a German town can't find a street, and he/she can't understand directions in German.**
Work in a group of three. Look at the map. You are in front of the Tourist Information Office. Give the directions in English.
The tourist wants to go to:

1 Theaterstraße
2 Burgstraße
3 Friedrichstraße
4 Domgasse
5 Schuhstraße

Partner A (tourist):
Good morning.
I'm looking for …

Partner B:
Gehen Sie geradeaus und nehmen Sie die erste rechts …

Partner C:
Go straight on and then take the first right …

GIVING DIRECTIONS

Excuse me.
I'm looking for …

Thanks very much!

Go straight up/along …	Gehen Sie geradeaus.
Take the first left.	Nehmen Sie die erste links.
Take the second right.	Nehmen Sie die zweite rechts.
Turn left/right.	Biegen Sie links/rechts ab.
Go straight on.	Gehen Sie immer geradeaus.
Go past/under …	Gehen Sie … vorbei/ unter …
At the traffic lights …	An der Ampel …
At the roundabout …	Am Verkehrskreisel …
… is in front of you.	… ist vor Ihnen.
… is on the left/ on the right.	… ist auf der linken/ rechten Seite.

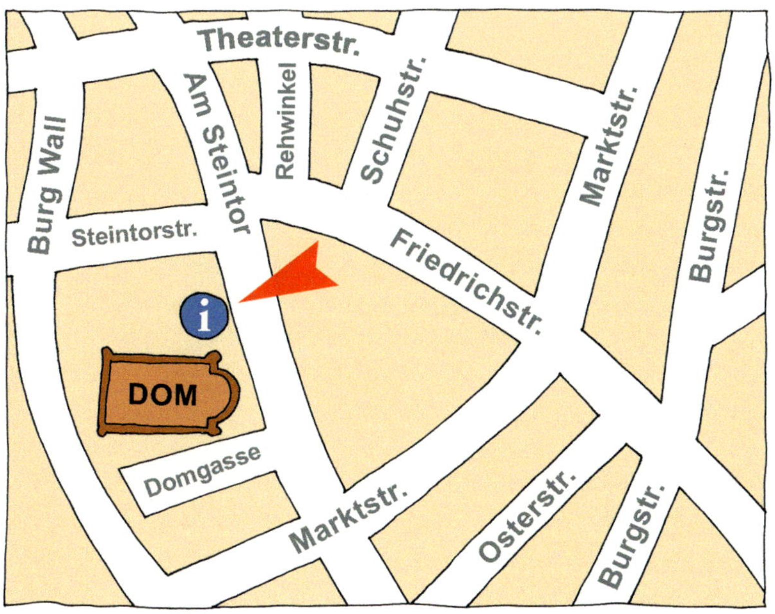

ICH KANN JETZT …

- Gebäude und Orte in einer Stadt in Englisch benennen,
- Richtungsanweisungen geben und verstehen,
- einer Englisch sprechenden Person in einer deutschen Stadt helfen, sich zu orientieren.

Unit 6 Have you ever …?

[P/I] **1 What did you do last weekend? Was it fun? Boring? Exciting? Unusual? Just normal for a weekend? Tell the class.**

▶ TIPS AND TRICKS

It was fun. = Es machte Spaß.

It was funny. = Es war lustig.

[R] **2 Read about Glenn and answer the questions.**

Last weekend Glenn Hart did something very exciting. Glenn is a high school student in Miami, Florida, and on Saturday afternoon he made a bungee jump. It was his first jump. It was certainly fun, but it was also terrifying!

1 Where does Glenn live?
2 What did he do last weekend?
3 Was it just normal for a weekend?
4 Do you think that Glenn wants to make another bungee jump?

[I/P] **3 What about you? Talk in class.**

1 Have you ever seen a bungee jump? Have you ever made a bungee jump?

Yes, I have.

No, I haven't.

No, never.

2 Tell the class.
→ I saw/made a bungee jump last year. It was in Dusseldorf/in a park/on TV …
3 What do you think? Are people who make bungee jumps crazy? Or do you think the idea is exciting?

[R] **4 Read about these two British teenagers and answer the questions.**

Allison and Vicky also had a great weekend last weekend. Allison loves all sports, but her favourite sport is football and she plays in her school girls' team. Last Saturday afternoon, they played in a competition – and they won. It was a fantastic feeling and Allison was very happy.

Vicky lives in London and last Saturday evening she went to a rock festival. She saw all her favourite bands and singers. It was amazing and she had a really great time.

1 Who …?
 a … went to a rock festival?
 b … played in a sports competition?
 c … was 'very happy'?
 d … had a 'great time'?

2 What …?
 a … was 'amazing'?
 b … was 'fantastic'?

3 When …?
 … did Allison and Vicky do the things in the pictures?

▶ **TIPS AND TRICKS**

Have you ever been to a rock concert?

= Have you ever gone to a rock concert?

[I] **5 Tell the class.**

1 Have you ever been to a rock festival or a rock concert?
2 Have you ever seen your favourite band or singer live on stage?
3 Have you ever played in a sports team?
4 Have you ever played in a sports competition?
5 Have you ever won a sports competition?

[P/I] **6 Who has done what in your class? On a piece of paper, write your name and one special thing that you have done. Then give the paper to your teacher. Your teacher asks questions. Guess who the person is.**

I have run in a marathon.

I have lived in another country.

Who has run in a marathon in our class?

GRAMMAR SPOT: Das simple past und present perfect	
Simple past	**Present perfect**
Um von Ereignissen aus der Vergangenheit zu erzählen (wann, wo usw.), benutzt man das simple past:	Das present perfect wird ohne Zeitangabe benutzt, um auszudrücken, ob bzw. dass wir etwas schon mal gemacht haben:
Last weekend I went to a rock concert. I flew on a plane last year. I flew to Greece. It was great.	Have you (ever) been to England? – Yes, I have./No, I haven't. I've seen Robbie Williams live.

→ Grammar summary, page 199

[R/P] **1 Read about Alan, his family and their holidays, and answer the questions.**

Alan, his sister Jessica, and their mum and dad live in England. They aren't rich, but they love holidays. They save their money and then when they can, they go somewhere really interesting.

Disneyland, Florida 1997
It was fun!

Cairo, Egypt 2000
Hot! The pyramids were fascinating!

New York 2002
Hated it! Hot, noisy, chaotic!

Kenya 2004
Amazing! The animals were wonderful!

Japan 2007
Beautiful! Fascinating!

1 On the world map, you can see some really nice places for a holiday. Look at the list of Alan's family's holidays and answer the questions.
Example: Has Alan ever been to New York? → Yes, he has.
a Has he ever been to Moscow? → No, he …
b Have Alan, his sister and his mum and dad ever been to Disneyland in Florida?
c Have they ever been to the Taj Mahal in India?
d Have they ever been to Sydney in Australia?
e Has Alan ever been to Egypt?
f Has he ever seen the pyramids?

2 Look at the list of holidays again and answer these questions. Give whole sentences.
Example: When did Alan go to Disneyland in Florida?
→ He went there in 1997.
a When did he go to Kenya?
b When did Alan, Jessica and their mum and dad go to Japan?
c What did they see in Cairo?
d What did they see in Kenya?
e What did they think of Disneyland? → It was …
f What did they think of Kenya? And Japan?
g What did they think of New York?

R/P] **2 Read about Lynn Hill and answer the questions. Use the present perfect or the simple past in your answers.**

Extreme sports

Some people like really exciting and dangerous sports. One of these 'extreme sports' is rock climbing and the woman in the picture, Lynn Hill from America, is one of the most famous rock climbers in the world. She has climbed lots of the most difficult rocks in the world. She has won over 30 international competitions against the world's best rock climbers. And she is the only person who has ever climbed this rock in a day. It's over 1 km high, and it's in the beautiful Yosemite National Park in California. Lynn began at midnight on 20 September 1994. She climbed all that day and she reached the top after 23 hours. It was the most exciting – and probably the most dangerous – day of her life.

1 Where is the rock which Lynn climbed?
2 When did she climb it?
3 What time did she begin that day and what time did she finish?
4 Has Lynn ever climbed other difficult rocks?
5 Has she ever won any competitions?

[P] **3 Complete the sentences with words from the table. (There is sometimes more than one answer.)**

1 Rock climbing is an exciting and sometimes dangerous sport.
2 We were very excited when we won the sports competition.
3 The rock concert was absolutely …
4 I was … when my friend suddenly left college and got a job.
5 Are you … in football? – Hmm. I think it's OK, but not fantastic.
6 I love articles in magazines about other countries. I think life in other countries is …
7 Pete and I saw that new Zombies movie last week. The movie was … and we were …!
8 Do you like heavy metal music? – I think it's … I went to a heavy metal concert last month and I was totally …

-ing

amazing erstaunlich
boring langweilig
exciting aufregend
fascinating faszinierend
interesting interessant
terrifying erschreckend

-ed

amazed erstaunt
(to be) bored gelangweilt
excited aufgeregt
fascinated fasziniert
interested (in) interessiert (an)
terrified erschreckt

[P] **4 Write a short text with the title: 'My most interesting friend'.**

* 1 Who is your most interesting friend?
2 What things has (s)he done in her/his life?
3 What was the most interesting thing of all? What happened?

[R] **1** **Here's a web page from an e-zine for apprentices in the UK. Read this true story about Tim White and answer the questions.**

News > apprentices' stories > Tim White

Have you ever been in a movie? Tim has!

Tim White is an engineering apprentice at Northern Air Services, a helicopter company in the north of England. The company charters helicopters, that's to say, people can hire its helicopters – for a day, a week or whatever. As an apprentice, Tim is learning to service and repair helicopters. He really likes the work and the company, but one day last month, his job became extra exciting …

Click to hear Tim's story

1 Where does Tim work?
2 What's the company's business?
3 Where's the firm based?
4 What's Tim learning to do as an apprentice at the firm?
5 What happened one day last month?

[R] **2** **Listen to Tim's story and choose the correct answers a, b or c.**

1 Last month … hired a helicopter from Tim's company.
a a big oil company
b an advertising company
c a film company

2 The star of the film was …
a Brad Pitt.
b Matt Damon.
c Leonardo DiCaprio.

3 The film director and the filmstar arrived at
a 8 o'clock.
b 9 o'clock.
c 10 o'clock.

4 In the first scene, the filmstar … very fast across the airport.
a ran
b flew in a helicopter
c drove a car

5 There was a big problem at midday because …
a they didn't have a helicopter for the next scene.
b a man with a machine gun killed the filmstar.
c the actor in the helicopter wasn't there.

6 Tim became …
a the guy in the helicopter.
b the pilot of the helicopter.
c the filmstar.

7 They gave Tim …
a a baseball cap.
b a machine gun.
c an old jacket.

8 The pilot flew down near to the car and … fired the machine gun.
a Tim
b a guy from the film company
c the filmstar in the car below

9 When the helicopter landed, the filmstar said …
a "Congratulations, Tim!"
b "Good work, Tim!"
c "It was fantastic."

[R] **3 Find the words on page 66.**

1 A person who flies a helicopter. → a pilot
2 The most important or famous actor in a film.
3 A (young) person who is learning to do a job.
4 A person who directs a film.
5 You fly a helicopter but you … a car.
6 Something that baseball players wear on their head.
7 A gun that you fire very fast.
8 Another word for 'a firm'.
9 Another word for 'a film'.

[R] **4 Find expressions on page 66 that have the opposite meaning.**

1 south → north
2 boring
3 next month
4 small
5 to leave (a place)
6 slowly
7 to take off (a plane etc.)
8 above

[P] **5 Give the missing verb forms, then complete the sentences.**

be	was	been	fly	flew	flown
become	▪	▪	give	▪	▪
drive	▪	▪	say	▪	▪
fire	▪	▪	take	▪	▪

1 Tim's job … extra exciting last month.
2 The star of the film … Brad Pitt.
3 In the first scene, Brad … very fast across the airport.
4 They … Tim a machine gun, and the helicopter … off.
5 Tim … above the airport and … the gun.
6 When the helicopter landed, the film director … "Congratulations!".
7 What about you? Have you ever … in a helicopter?
8 Have you ever … a car?
9 Have you ever … in a movie?

[P] **6 Listen to Tim's story again, then write or tell the story yourself.**

[I] **7 Tell the class.**
What about you? Have you ever worked in a company?
Have you ever had a part-time job?
Do you have a story about the company or the people there?

P/I] **8 Choose one of the projects.**

1 **Bungee jumping and rock climbing are two extreme sports. But there are others, like BMX, skateboarding, surfing and skydiving. Find out more about an extreme sport and give a short talk to the class. Find some pictures on the Internet.**
2 **Do a survey in your class and write about the results.**
- **Where have people been to on holiday?**
- **What's the most popular place for holidays in your class?**

ICH KANN JETZT …
- über meine Erlebnisse und die von Anderen sprechen und schreiben,
- Erlebnisse beschreiben,
- einer längeren Erzählung zuhören, sie verstehen und besprechen.

[R] **1** **Leo Besold is the telephone receptionist at Schuhmann Architects in Germany. His company designs buildings worldwide and so Leo often speaks English on the phone. Here are two conversations. Listen and find the missing phrases A–F.**

Conversation 1

Leo	Schuhmann Architects, guten Tag.
Woman	Oh, hi. Could I speak to Mr Waldmann, please?
Leo	**(1)** …
Woman	It's Diane Smith. I'm the English project engineer on the new museum project in London.
Leo	One moment, please, Ms Smith. **(2)** …

Conversation 2

Leo	Schuhmann Architects, guten Tag.
Man	Do you speak English, please?
Leo	Certainly. My name's Leo Besold. **(3)** …
Man	Thanks. Could I speak to Ms Henneke, please?
Leo	I'm sorry, but she isn't in the office at the moment. **(4)** …
Man	Yes, OK.
Leo	Who's calling please?
Man	It's Fredrik Olsson. I'm the Swedish project manager on a project in Stockholm.
Leo	Thanks, Mr Olsson. **(5)** …
Man	Yes, she does.
Leo	**(6)** …
Man	Thanks. Bye.
Leo	You're welcome. Goodbye.

How may I help you? **(A)**
Who's calling, please? **(B)**
I'll tell her as soon as she comes into the office. **(C)**
Does Ms Henneke have your number? **(D)**
Can she call you back this afternoon? **(E)**
I'm putting you through now. **(F)**

[I/P] **2** **Read the dialogue with a partner. Look again at the missing phrases A–F. How would you say these things in German?**

[R/I] **3 These two telephone conversations are not in the correct order. Read them correctly with a partner. The first speaker is always the telephone receptionist at ABC Ltd.**

Conversation 1

a This is Mr Brown.
b Good morning. Could I speak to Ms Jones, please?
c One moment, Mr Brown. I'm putting you through now.
d ABC Ltd. Good morning. (1)
e Who's calling, please?

Conversation 2

a Yes, thanks. My name is Carol Wilson and my number is 01676 744553.
b Good morning. Could I speak to Mr Robertson, please?
d ABC Ltd. Good morning.
e Thank you Ms Wilson. I'll tell Mr Robertson as soon as he comes into the office.
f I'm sorry, but he isn't in the office today. Can he call you back tomorrow?

[M] **4 You work as a secretary in a company in Germany. Your boss Frau Grone isn't in the office today. She'll be back tomorrow morning. An important English customer phones.**

a Make a telephone conversation. Invent names and other details.
Partner A: you are the secretary.
Partner B: you are the caller.

b Then write a note in German for your boss.

Secretary (Partner A)	Customer (Partner B)
Melden Sie sich. →	Fragen Sie, ob A Englisch spricht. ←
Antworten Sie ‚ja' und fragen Sie, wie Sie behilflich sein können. →	Sie hätten gern mit Frau Grone gesprochen. ←
Es tut Ihnen Leid, aber Frau Grone ist heute nicht im Haus. Ob sie Partner B morgen früh zurückrufen darf? →	Ja, das wäre nett. ←
Bitten Sie B um seinen/ihren Namen. →	Geben Sie Ihren Namen durch und erklären Sie, wer Sie sind. ←
Fragen Sie, ob Frau Grone Bs Telefonnummer hat. →	Antworten Sie ‚nein' und geben Sie Ihre Handynummer durch. ←
Bedanken Sie sich und erklären Sie, dass Sie Frau Grone Bescheid sagen, sobald sie ins Büro kommt. →	Bedanken Sie sich und verabschieden Sie sich.

CULTURE TIPS:
ENDING A PHONE CALL

There isn't a special English word on the telephone for 'auf Wiederhören'.
We just say: 'Goodbye'

ICH KANN JETZT …

- eine englischsprachige Firma anrufen und mich durchstellen lassen.

Unit 7 The Internet

[P/I] **1 When did you last use the Internet? What did you do?**

[I/R] **2 Talk about the questions below, then read the text and check your answers.**

1 What do you think? How many people in the world today use the Internet?
2 What are the top five languages on the Internet? Which one is the top language of all?
3 When did the World Wide Web begin: 1960? 1970? 1980? 1990? 2000?

This is an Internet café in Costa Rica in Central America. From here a teenager – just like you – can read a newspaper in London, send an email to the President of the USA, buy a bicycle on eBay, chat in Spanish to friends in Spain, download the latest hit music for an MP3, and play online games against YOU here in Germany. We can do all these things because with the Internet we are part of a global village. Worldwide, 900 million people now use the Internet – one person in every seven. As you can imagine, English is the top language – 33 per cent of Net users speak English. Next is Chinese (13 per cent), then Japanese (7.5 per cent), and then Spanish (6.5 per cent). German (6 per cent) is number five on the list. And the really amazing thing is that we have had the World Wide Web only since about 1990!

[R] **3 In the USA over 90 per cent of teenagers are online. Read what these American teenagers say.**

Jessica: I use the Internet a lot because I can download quickly all the latest hits.

Emily: My family like the Internet because you can buy things really cheaply on eBay.

Sarah: I like the Internet because I can chat easily to my friends. I use Instant Messenger all the time.

Rachel: I use the Internet for my homework. I can get information very fast – it's great.

1 Why does Rachel like the Internet?
2 Why does Sarah like the Internet? What does she use all the time?
3 Why do Emily and Jessica like the Internet?

[P] **4 Look at the examples then choose the correct adjective or adverb. Find one word to complete number 6.**

Example:
a My new mobile was cheap. – I bought it cheaply on eBay.
b Google is very fast! – You can get information very fast.

1 Emails are **quick/quickly**.
2 Emails arrive **quick/quickly**.
3 You can often buy things **cheap/cheaply** on the Internet.
4 Was your MP3 player expensive? – No, it was really **cheap/cheaply**.
5 Adjectives and adverbs are **easy/easily**. I can understand them **easy/easily**.
6 Otto is crazy – he drives very … He has a … car.

▶ **TIPS AND TRICKS**

There is a lot of **information** on the Internet.

There ~~are~~ a lot of information~~s~~ on the Internet.

P/I] **5 Technology changes very quickly. In 1969, Neil Armstrong walked on the moon. What other things do you think you could or couldn't do in 1969? (Answers page 210.)**

1 surf the World Wide Web
2 send emails
3 watch colour TV
4 buy a mobile phone
5 buy a pocket calculator

You could …

You couldn't …

[I] **6 What do you think? Are computers and the Internet amazing, interesting or just boring?**

GRAMMAR SPOT

Can	Adverbien	You = 'man'
Can/can't bleibt in allen Personen unverändert. Das simple past ist could/couldn't.	Adverbien sagen wie etwas passiert: I read the book quickly. Die meisten Adverbien enden mit -ly. Einige sind mit dem Adjektiv identisch: fast – fast	You couldn't buy a mobile phone in 1969.

→ Grammar summary, page 200

[R/P] **1 What things can and can't you do on these websites? Match the verbs and the expressions. Then make sentences.**

I think you can buy mobiles on the handy site.

You can't listen to music on the handy site.

buy • download • book • listen to • read • search for	books • a flight • antivirus software • music • ringtones • everything! • mobiles

easyJet.com Come on, let's fly!

AntiVir®

amazon.de and you're done.

Google™

iTunes

handy.de

[P] **2 Can you remember when you were ten years old? Which things below could and couldn't you personally do then? Make sentences that are true for YOU.**

1 swim
2 ride a bike
3 use a computer
4 speak English
5 speak German
6 repair things
7 cook
8 write an email

I could swim. I couldn't ride a bike. I …

CULTURE TIPS: REMEMBER

Never say 'handy' for a mobile phone! The word 'handy' in English means 'praktisch, gelegen (kommen)'.

[P] **3 Joss is an American teenager. How does he use the Internet? Give the adverbs.**

Example: Joss uses the Internet every day. He's a **regular** user. He uses the Internet *regularly*.

1 He's a high school student and he uses the Internet a lot for his homework. It's **quick** and **easy** to find information on the Net. He finds information … and … on the Net.
2 Joss has lots of friends and he's always **happy** when he can chat to them online. He chats … with his friends online.
3 Joss often listens to music when he uses his computer, but he doesn't like **loud** music. He doesn't play his music …
4 He prefers **quiet** music. He plays his music …
5 Joss uses Hotmail for his emails. He likes emails. Letters are **slow** but emails are **fast**. Letters arrive … but emails arrive …
6 Joss could already use a computer when he was a little kid. He's very **good** on the computer. He uses computers …

[P] **4 Adjective or adverb? Choose the correct forms.**

Meet the inventor of the World Wide Web

The Internet began in 1965, but at first it was only for the US military. It wasn't today's World Wide Web for everyone. That began later, and the inventor was this English scientist, Sir Tim Berners-Lee.

In 1980, Sir Tim was a scientist at CERN, the atomic research centre in Switzerland. He had hundreds of documents on his computer, and he wanted a system to find things **(1) easy/easily**. He invented HTML (HyperText Markup Language), a **(2) simple/simply** computer language where you can put links in documents (this is a link!). It worked really **(3) good/well** and soon colleagues at CERN also had Sir Tim's system on their computers. The problem was, they couldn't send documents from one computer to another. Sir Tim invented an **(4) easy/easily** method. He gave it the **(5) horrible/horribly** name HTTP (HyperText Transfer Protocol!), but it also worked **(6) wonderful/wonderfully** and with it, everyone at CERN could now send documents **(7) quick/quickly** and **(8) safe/safely** over the old Internet. Sir Tim developed his system **(9) careful/carefully** for the next five or six years and in 1991 he opened the World Wide Web to the world. The system was

absolutely free – Sir Tim has never earned any money from his invention. Today, he lives **(10) happy/happily** in America and is a teacher at the MIT (Massachusetts Institute for Technology), the USA's top technical university.

[P] **5 Complete the sentences with words from the box and is or are.**

1 My eyes are brown. What colour is your hair? – It's brown, too.
2 You know a lot of English. Your … of English … very good!
3 … your new … Levi's? – No, they're Wranglers.
4 You can get facts about everything on the Internet. There … a lot of … on the Internet.
5 I want to cut this paper. Where … the …? – They're here. Here you are.
6 Those black … nice. They go well with your jacket. – Thanks!
7 No … … good … (Keine Nachrichten sind gute Nachrichten.)
8 I can't read this book. Where … my …?

Singular in English	
hair	Haare
information	Informationen
knowledge	Kenntnisse
news	Nachrichten
Plural in English	
glasses/spectacles	eine Brille
jeans	eine Jeans
trousers	eine Hose
scissors	eine Schere

[P] **6** * **You are in an Internet chat room. The language is English and people are talking about their favourite websites. You can see part of the conversation below. Write a short message (about 30 words) yourself. Invent a screen name!**

surfer101	My favourite site is iTunes. I visit it all the time. I think it's great that you can download all the latest hits quickly. They've got more than a million tracks!
(YOU) …	

[R] **1** **When we buy and sell things on the Internet, it's called e-commerce.
Below, Michael is buying a new computer game online. Match the four stages in the diagram and the short texts A–D. Then listen and check.**

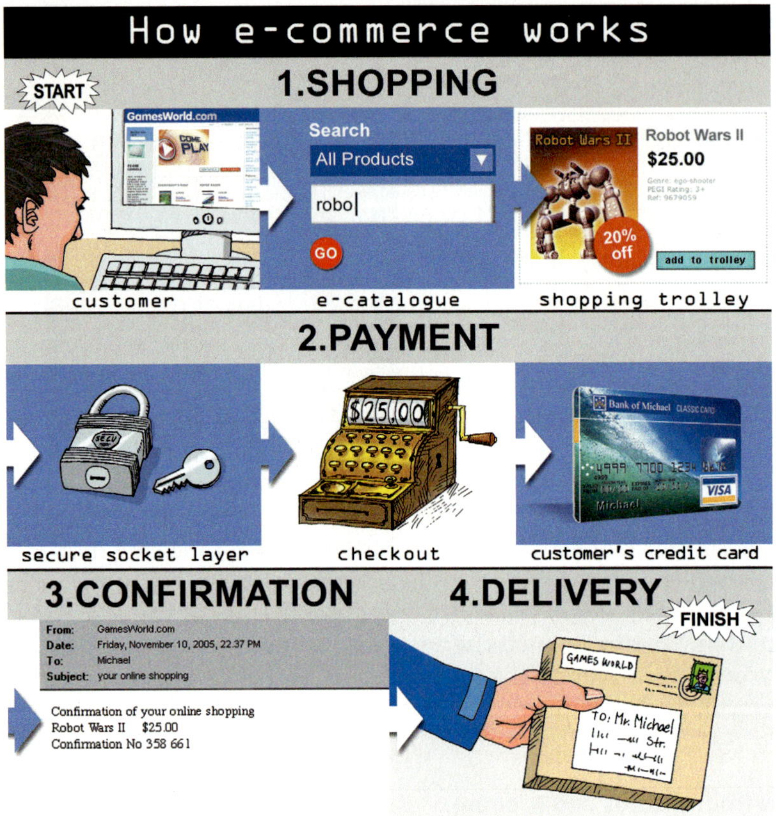

A So that Michael knows that everything is OK, Games World now sends him a quick email. It confirms that he has bought Robot Wars II.

B When you shop online, it's important that you can buy things safely – that no one can steal your credit card number, for example. Like all good e-commerce companies, Games World uses a 'secure socket layer' (SSL). That means that all the customer's information is encrypted. Michael logs on, then goes to the checkout with his game. He types in his credit card number, and Games World takes the money immediately from his account.

C Michael wants to buy a new computer game, so he goes to his favourite online games store, Games World. There, he can browse easily through an e-catalogue and search for products. He finds his game (Robot Wars II). Great! It's on special offer at the moment and there's 20% off! He puts the game quickly in his shopping trolley.

D Three days later, the postperson delivers a small package to Michael's house. Fantastic! It's his game! Now he can play Robot Wars II happily on his Playstation.

[R] **2 Choose the correct answer a, b or c.**

1 In the diagram, Michael is buying a new computer game …
a in a store in town.
b online.
c on eBay.

2 At the moment, the game is …
a more expensive than usual.
b the normal price.
c cheaper than usual.

3 Michael can buy the game safely on Games World because the company uses …
a a checkout.
b a secure socket layer.
c shopping trolleys.

4 At the checkout, Michael types in …
a his credit card number.
b his dad's credit card number.
c his favourite website.

5 So that Michael knows that everything is OK, the company sends him …
a a payment.
b a delivery.
c a confirmation.

6 Michael's game arrives …
a the next day.
b after three days.
c after a week.

[R/P] **3 True, false or 'don't know'? Correct the false sentences.**

1 Michael's favourite online games store is Games World.
2 He buys games online every week.
3 At the moment, Robot Wars II costs $30.00.
4 You can't buy products safely at Games World.
5 When Michael buys the game, Games World sends him a letter.
6 Michael is very happy when he gets the game. Now he can play it on his XBox.

[R] **4 Find the words in the text.**

Example: A person who buys something is a customer.

1 Another word for a 'shop' is a … Games World is an …
2 When a product is cheaper than usual we say that it's on …
3 When you shop online, you first put things in your …, then you go to the … This is where you pay.
4 Finally, if all goes well, the postperson … your product.

[M] **5 A German-speaking friend wants to buy something online from a website in Britain. Write a short text in German to help. Begin like this:**

Die Produkte befinden sich in einem 'e-catalogue', also eKatalog. 'Search' heißt 'Suche'. Da gibt man Produkte ein und klickt einfach auf 'Go' (wir sagen 'los') …

[P/I] **6 Choose one of the projects.**

1 We use a lot of English words in German when we talk about computers and the Internet – 'chatten' and 'downloaden', for example. Work in a group and make a list. How many words like this can you find?

2 Do a survey in your class about the Internet. How many hours a week do you spend online? What are the favourite websites? Do you go online at home or at college? How often do you visit an Internet café (cyber café). Do you visit chat rooms? … ?

ICH KANN JETZT …

- über das Internet sprechen und schreiben,
- sagen wie ich etwas mache (**quickly**, **easily** usw.),
- ein einfaches Diagramm auf Englisch verstehen und besprechen,
- einen englischen Text auf Deutsch erklären.

[R] **1 Look quickly at this home page of an American e-commerce company.**

1 What's the name of the company? What American state do you think it is in?
2 What products does it sell? Can you buy the products online?
3 What can you do if you often buy from the company? Why is this an advantage?

[R/I] **2 There's a lot of information on the website about the company itself, its products etc. The buttons below are links to the different pages. Use the information below and ask and answer questions about the buttons.**

How do you find information about the company?

You click on the 'About us' button.

1 Information about the Montana Bread company – when it began, how big it is etc.
2 An e-catalogue of the company's products. You can see the products here and buy online.
3 News about the company. New products, for example.
4 A page for children: 'fun facts' about bread, competitions etc.
5 An email address for the company (usually something like: info@montanabread.com). You can write directly to the company if you have a question or a problem.
6 A basic introduction to the company and a login for regular customers.

[R] **3 Candy Laville is an American web designer – in fact, she designed the Montana Bread website. She's talking now about how to design a website. Listen and find the missing expressions.**

web pages • easy to find • extremely good • easy to navigate • exit • downloads quickly • easy to read • search engine • information

Candy Laville, web designer

"There are hundreds of thousands of websites on the Internet, so it's really important that your website is not just good, but (1) extremely good! What's an extremely good website? Well, I have four golden rules. One, it's (2) … on the web. You need a good name for your company, a name that people can find easily with a (3) … The best names often say already what you can buy – Montana Bread, for example. Rule number two is: the website is (4) … Good websites are simple. Don't use too many colours, and don't put too much (5) … on a page. People read very quickly on the Internet. Rule number three: the website is (6) … What does that mean? It means that you can go from one part of the website to another part quickly and easily. Organise your (7) … clearly, and use good, clear buttons. And my final rule is: a good website (8) … Flash animation and lots of pictures are nice, but often the home page then downloads very slowly. On the Internet, people don't like to wait! After four or five seconds they (9) … your website and look at the next one! Those are my four golden rules!"

[M] **4 A German friend is very interested in web design and wants to know about Candy's four golden rules. Give her ideas in German.**

P/I] **5 Now YOU. Work in a group. Design a website, then show your ideas to the class. You can choose one of these companies, or think of a company yourselves.**

ICH KANN JETZT …

- eine Website auf Englisch verstehen und erklären,
- Anderen sagen, wie man eine Website benutzt,
- mit Anderen diskutieren und meine Ideen darstellen.

Unit 8 Career plans

[P/I] **1 Have you ever met teenagers from other countries? When and where? Tell the class.**

[R] **2 Read the text and the conversation and answer these questions.**
a Where are these teenagers at the moment? What countries are they from?
b What are they doing right now in this picture?

Niku (on the left), Judyta, Nola, Ulrik and Marina are all students at vocational colleges in different European countries. They are on a 'working holiday' on a farm in England. They are talking about their plans for the future.

Marina What course are you on at your college in Poland, Judyta?

Judyta A nursing course.

Marina What are you going to do when you finish the course?

Judyta I'm going to come to England and I'm going to work in an English hospital for a couple of years. Then I'm going to go back to Poland and I'm going to work as a nurse there. What course are you on?

Marina I'm on a business course. I've got one more year, then I'm going to look for a job in a company in Germany. What about you, Niku? What are your plans?

Niku I'm learning to be a bricklayer. When I finish my apprenticeship in Romania, I'm going to get a job with a construction company.

Ulrik Me too – that is, I'm going to get a job with a construction company. I'm learning to be an electrician at my college in Denmark.

Marina So that leaves you, Nola. What are you going to do after college?

Nola Me? Well, I'm going to find a rich man and I'm going to get married and I'm going to have lots of kids! No, seriously. I'm at an agricultural college in Ireland and I'm going to look for a job on a farm.

P/I] **3** **What are the teenagers' plans? Complete the sentences with the names, then ask a partner questions.**

Example: Marina is going to look for a job in a company in Germany.
1 … is going to work in an English hospital for a couple of years.
2 … is going to get a job as an electrician with a construction company.
3 … is going to look for a job on a farm.
4 … is going to look for a job as a bricklayer with a construction company.

→ What's Nola going to do when she finishes her course?
– She's going to …

R/I] **4** **The friends think that their lives will be very different when they have a job. Which ideas below do you think are positive and which are negative? Make two lists with a partner.**

a) I think it will be exciting.

b) I think it will be a bit frightening.

c) It will be great to earn money.

d) Great! No more class tests!

e) We won't get so many holidays.

f) There will be strict rules. We won't be able to be late in the mornings.

▶ **TIPS AND TRICKS**

I have a job as **a** bricklayer.
= Ich habe eine Stelle als Maurer.

[I] **5** **What do you think? Do you agree with the teenagers' ideas about the world of work? Do you have other ideas about how your life will be different? Talk in class.**

GRAMMAR SPOT: Going to-Future und Futur mit will

Going to wird verwendet, um über Pläne und Vorhaben zu sprechen: When I finish college, I'm going to look for a job.	Will/won't werden verwendet, um Vorhersagen und Vermutungen auszudrücken: The world of work will be exciting – and we won't have class tests!

→ Grammar summary, page 200

[R/P] **1 The eight teenagers below are all students on different courses at an FE college in England. They are talking about their plans for the future. Match the students and their plans (a–h), then write two sentences about each person.**

→ Anthony is on an electronics course. After college, he's going to …

Danielle:
travel & tourism

Brendan:
catering

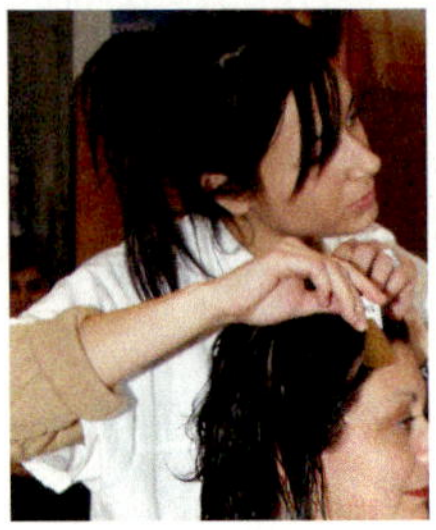
Melissa:
hairdressing

John:
construction

Kevin:
motor mechanics

Penny:
art & design

Kristen:
health & social care

Anthony:
electronics

a) I'm going to work for an electronics company.

b) I'm going to look for a job with a building firm.

c) I'm going to look for a job at a travel agent's.

d) I'm going to get a job in a restaurant.

e) I'm going to work in a nursery with small children.

f) I'm going to get a job in a hairdressing salon.

g) I'm going to repair cars in my dad's garage.

h) I'm going to work in an advertising company.

[R/P] **2 True or not true? Correct the false sentences.**

Example: Anthony is going to work for an electronics company. → True.

1 Brendan is going to get a job in a hairdressing salon.
→ No! Brendan isn't going to get a job in a hairdressing salon. He's …
2 Melissa is going to get a job at a travel agent's.
3 John is going to look for a job with a building firm.
4 Kristen is going to work in a restaurant.
5 Kevin is going to repair cars in his dad's garage.

:/P] **3** **Next month, Sarah will start her first job! It will be at a garden centre in the town where she lives in England. Answer the questions about her job below in full sentences. Use the short forms of will when possible.**

Acorn Garden Centre

Working hours: Mon–Sat, 8 am–5 pm

Lunch break: 1 pm–2 pm (free meal in garden centre restaurant)

Duties: Serve customers, check stock, water plants

Boss: Mr Holland

Wages: £950 a month

Uniform: red apron, grey and white T-shirt

1 Which days of the week will Sarah work?
→ She'll work Monday to Saturday.
2 What time will she start work in the mornings?
3 When will she finish work?
4 Will she wear a uniform?
5 What things will she do every day?
6 How much will she earn?
7 Who will her boss be?
8 Will she have a lunch break?
9 Where will she be able to eat at lunchtime?
10 How much will the meal cost?

[P] **4** **Complete the sentences with the right prepositions.**

Example: A person who works in a nursery looks after children.

1 What job are you going to look … when you finish your college course?
2 What does 'catering' mean?
– Look the word … in your dictionary!
3 Are you looking … your new job next week?
– Yes, I'm … to it very much.
4 Look … the pictures. What are the people doing?

to look after auf jmdn. achten, jmdn. betreuen
to look at anschauen
to look for suchen nach
to look forward to sich auf etw. freuen
to look up nachschlagen

[P] **5** **There are two spelling mistakes in each of the following sentences. Correct them.**

1 Rihgt now, the students are talking about there plans for the future.
2 Ulrik is lerning to be an elektrician.
3 Where does Sarah life? – She lives in england.
4 Which idees below do you think are positiv?

[P] **6** **Write an email to a friend in England about YOU (80–100 words).**

* **Write about these things:**

your college – your course – your plans after your course – your ideas about the world of work

[R] **1 Here's a page from a website. Look at the pictures and the headlines and read through the text once.**

1 What's the name of the website?
2 What do you think Mark Newton often writes about on the website?
3 What is he giving tips about this week? How many tips are there?
4 What real person is telling a story? Will the story will be about a good or bad experience?

young-europe.com > Homepage > Careers > Tips

Career Tips with Mark Newton

This week …

Some Do's and Don'ts for your first day at work

Great! You got the job! And now next Monday morning you'll be at work! Excited? Nervous? Probably both.
Don't worry. Here are five tips to help you through your first day at work.

1 Don't be late!

Get up, have a good breakfast, and leave the house early. You'll soon know the journey to work, but this is your first day. Maybe the bus will be late. Maybe the traffic will be bad. If your job starts at 8:30, then be there at 8:00!

2 Wear the right clothes!

Jeans and trainers were OK at college, but life in the world of work will be different. Will your job be in an office? Then be smart. Will you be in a workshop or on a construction site? OK, then remember that there will be strict rules. If the rules say: 'Wear a hard hat', then wear a hard hat.

3 Ask!

Lots of things will be new for you – not just on your first day, but for the first week or even month. That's OK. You can't learn everything immediately. Ask! That way you won't make mistakes – and people like helping.

4 Listen!

Remember that the people at work have been there longer than you. You won't be popular if you say things like: "At college I learned a much better method than that!" Or: "That's really stupid!" Maybe your ideas are good – but listen first. You can make suggestions later.

5 Be positive!

Don't forget that you'll be in your new job for a year, two years, maybe more. And you'll be with your colleagues every day. Be positive and friendly. Smile. People will remember their first impressions of you.

Some first days at work aren't, well, brilliant …

"I'll never forget my first day at work!"

Click to hear Kim's story

R/P] **2** **Listen to Kim's story. What happened?**
Tell the story in your own words.

[R/I] **3** **Mark Newton talks about do's and don'ts – things that are good to do and things that are bad. Work with a partner and make two lists.**

DO's	DON'Ts
Leave the house early!	Don't be late!

[R] **4** **Complete the sentences with information from the text.**

1 One reason why it's a good idea to leave the house early on your first day is that …
2 The right clothes are important. For example, in an office, …
3 There will be lots of things at first that you don't know, so …
4 When you start work, listen first. You can …
5 People will remember their first impressions of you, so it's a good idea to …

[R] **5** **Complete Kim's story with expressions from the list.**

Kim wanted to take (1) the bus to work. She was a bit late so she ran to (2) … . (3) … a big BMW came round the corner very fast. It almost (4) … Kim. Kim shouted: (5) "…" at the driver of the car. When Kim arrived at work, she found that the driver of the car was (6) … Things are (7) … now, but the first week was a bit (8) … !

fine • her new boss • hit • the bus stop • difficult • You stupid idiot! • suddenly • the bus

[R] **6** **Find words or phrases on the webpage that have the same meaning.**

1 suggestions, good ideas
2 a little frightened
3 perhaps
4 clean and attractive (clothes)
5 don't forget
6 seven days
7 people won't like you very much
8 a first idea or feeling (about a person, for example)
9 wonderful, very successful, very clever

I/P] **7** **A friend is at secondary school at the moment but is going to come to your college next year. Give her/him some tips. What are the most important do's and don'ts for successful college life? Make a list in class.**

P/I] **8** **Choose one of the projects.**

1 **Visit the website of a British FE (Further Education) college and find out about its courses, student life there, and other facts. Just put 'fe colleges uk' into your search engine and follow the links. Then give a short report to the class about a college.**
2 **The world of work today is very international. Do you think that one day you will work in an English-speaking country? Why (not)? Do a survey in your class, then talk about the results.**

ICH KANN JETZT …

- über meine Pläne und Absichten sprechen und sie aufschreiben,
- meine Meinung zu zukünftigen Ereignissen äußern,
- mehrere Kurse in der Berufsbildung auf Englisch nennen,
- mit Websites auf Englisch besser umgehen.

[R] **1 Read the short text about Harald and listen to the two conversations.**

1 Why is Harald in London this week?
2 Who is he talking to in the first conversation? What two questions does the man ask Harald?
3 Who is Harald talking to in the second conversation? What two questions does this person ask?

Harald Schulte is a mechanic in a large car repair workshop in Germany. This week, he's on a training course in London. It's the first evening of the course and people are meeting for the first time …

Mr Watts	How do you do. I'm George Watts. I'm the organiser of the course this week.
Harald	Pleased to meet you, Mr Watts. I'm Harald Schulte from Germany.
Mr Watts	Did you fly over from Germany today, Mr Schulte?
Harald	Yes, I flew over this afternoon.
Mr Watts	And how was your flight?
Harald	Fine, thanks.
Mr Watts	Good. Well, I'll see you during the week. Enjoy the course.
Harald	Thanks very much.

Luke	Hi, can I introduce myself? I'm Luke.
Harald	Hi Luke. I'm Harald.
Luke	Where are you from, Harald?
Harald	I'm from a place called Wiesbaden in Germany. What about you?
Luke	I'm from here in England.
Harald	From London?
Luke	No, from Newcastle. It's a big town in the north-east. Is this your first visit to England?
Harald	No, not quite. I was …

[R/P] **2 Find and complete the English phrases in the conversations. What are they in German?**

1 How … … do.
2 … to … you.
3 Can I … … ?
4 How was … … ?
5 … … … from?
6 What … you?
7 Is this … … … … England?

- Guten Tag.
- Es freut mich Sie kennen zu lernen.
- Darf ich mich vorstellen?
- Wie war Ihr Flug?
- Wo kommen Sie her?
- Und Sie?
- Ist das Ihr erster Besuch in England?

[I] **3 Listen again, then practise the conversations with a partner.**

[R] **4** **Here's a web page about meeting British and American people. Read the page and the Culture Tips, then complete the sentences.**

MEETING BRITISH AND AMERICAN PEOPLE

Saying 'hello'

British and American people are usually very friendly. When you meet a younger person or a colleague for the first time, you can normally just say "Hi (or Hello). Can I introduce myself? I'm …" and you shake hands. Younger people often use first names straight away, or say after a couple of minutes "Please call me Mike/Jennie". You can answer "And I'm Christa/Jörg".

When you meet older or important people (bosses etc.) it's best to be a bit more formal. The normal phrase is "How do you do". This just means **guten Tag**, and you answer "How do you do" or "Pleased to meet you". DON'T say "I'm fine, thanks". In these formal situations, use family names (Ms Smith/Mr Jones).

Small talk

One important thing when you meet new people is 'small talk'. That means friendly conversation about simple, everyday things. Small talk is important for British and American people. They don't like serious conversation too quickly!

Some good questions are:
Where are you from? • How was your journey/your flight?
Is this your first visit to (Germany)? • What's your job?

1 First names or family names? When you meet a younger person or a colleague, it's OK to use …, but with an older or important person, it's best to use …
2 Younger British and American people use first names very quickly. After a couple of minutes they often say "Please, call me (Mike/Jennie)." You can answer "…".
3 Remember that "How do you do" just means … in German. The answer is "…" or "…". Not "…"!
4 When you talk about simple, everyday things with new people it's called … and it's very important for British and American people.
5 When you meet a British or American woman for the first time, it's best to call her … (not Mrs or Miss).

CULTURE TIPS:
MR, MRS, MS OR MISS?

Mr is easy – we use it for all men. **Mrs** is for married women, **Miss** for unmarried women, but in the world of work today, most women prefer **Ms**, which is for all women.
When you meet British or American women, use **Ms** first.

[I] **5** **You are all on an international training course. Make conversations. You can invent names, jobs and companies. Your teacher is the organiser of the course – so be formal with her or him.**

ICH KANN JETZT …

- Leute auf Englisch begrüßen und angemessen ansprechen,
- Small talk auf Englisch machen.

[R] **1 Read about Inge.**

Inge Wegener works for a big German company called Aqua. It's based in Stuttgart and it makes showers. Inge is German, but she lives and works in Birmingham in England. She's Aqua's sales representative in Britain. Here are some things that Inge often does in her job:

- She visits new (and old) customers and sells Aqua's products. Many of Inge's customers are big department stores like Marks & Spencer, Debenhams and British Homestores.
- She attends trade fairs.
- At the end of every month, she attends a sales meeting in Stuttgart for all the Aqua sales representatives from around Europe.

[R/P] **2 This is Inge's diary for next week. True or false? Correct the false statements.**

Example: On Monday morning, she's visiting a customer (Debenhams) in Birmingham. → True.

1 She's visiting Marks & Spencer at 4.30 on Monday afternoon. → No, she isn't …
2 She's visiting two customers in London on Tuesday.
3 On Wednesday, she's attending a trade fair all day in London.
4 She's attending a sales meeting in Stuttgart all day on Friday.
5 She's flying to Stuttgart on Thursday morning.
6 She's flying back to Birmingham on Friday afternoon.
7 She isn't working on Sunday.

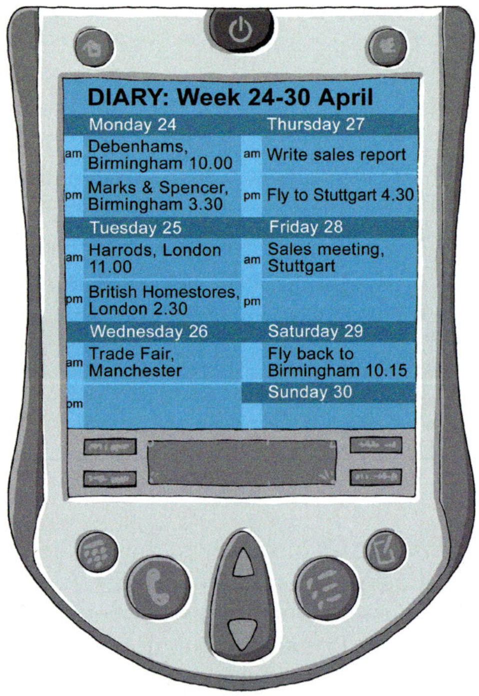

[I] **3 Ask and answer questions about Inge's diary with a partner.**

What's Inge doing on Monday (morning)?
→ She's …
When is she attending/visiting/flying/writing …?
→ She's …

GRAMMAR SPOT: Das present continuous mit zukünftiger Bedeutung

Das present continuous wird auch verwendet, um für die Zukunft fest geplante Handlungen auszudrücken:

I'm meeting Ms James next week. (Ich treffe Frau James nächste Woche.)

Präpositionen mit Zeitangaben:

at 10.00
in the morning/afternoon
on Monday
on Tuesday afternoon

R/I] **4 The week after next, Inge wants to visit a customer in Oxford. She's phoning the store manager, Jeffrey Taylor. Listen and find the missing phrases. Then practise the dialogue with a partner.**

I'm free • I can't make • This is • I look forward to seeing you then • that looks fine • I'm busy • How about Wednesday • Is that possible

Jeffrey Jeffrey Taylor speaking.
Inge Good morning, Mr Taylor. **(1)** … Inge Wegener from Aqua Showers.
Jeffrey Oh, hello, Ms Wegener. How can I help you?
Inge I'd like to visit you the week after next, that's the week of the first to the sixth of May. **(2)** … ?
Jeffrey Just a minute, I'll look at my diary. OK. I'm afraid **(3)** … all day on Monday and Tuesday. **(4)** … ?
Inge I'm visiting a customer in London in the morning, but **(5)** … in the afternoon.
Jeffrey Hmm. I'm afraid **(6)** … Wednesday afternoon.
Inge How about Thursday morning?
Jeffrey Yes, **(7)** … Is 10 o'clock OK for you?
Inge Yes, 10 o'clock is fine.
Jeffrey Great. **(8)** …
Inge Thanks very much. Yes, I look forward to seeing you, too. Bye now.

[I] **5 Now YOU.**
Partner A: you are Inge.
Partner B: you are a store manager at a department store in England.
a Write your diaries for one week. Put in activities for Monday to Friday, but leave two mornings and two afternoons free.
b Now make a telephone conversation. Use the phrases below. Can you find a time when you are both free?

Good morning/afternoon. Guten Morgen/Tag.
This is … Hier spricht …
I'd like to visit you … Ich möchte Sie besuchen …
Is that possible? Ist das möglich?
Is that convenient? Passt Ihnen das?
I'm afraid I'm busy … Ich bin leider beschäftigt …
I'm afraid I can't make … Das schaffe ich leider nicht …
I'm visiting/attending … Ich besuche/nehme an … teil.
How about … ? Wie wäre … ?
Is 9.30 OK for you? Ist 9.30 für Sie in Ordnung?
Yes, that's fine. Ja, das ist in Ordnung.
I look forward to meeting you. Ich freue mich darauf Sie kennen zu lernen.

ICH KANN JETZT …
- über Termine sprechen,
- Termine telefonisch ausmachen.

Revision (1)

1 **Read about Kelly on her website and answer the questions below.**

Hi! I'm Kelly!
Welcome to my website!

My name's Kelly Richards and I live in Bristol in the west of England. I'm a student at an FE college (that's college of further education). I'm on a 2-year Media Studies course. These guys are my friends – Will, Hannah and Josh. In this photo, we're all standing in front of our college.

1 What's Kelly's full name?
2 Where does she live?
3 What course is she on at college?
4 Who are the four people in the photo?
5 What are they all doing at the moment in the photo?

Simple present and present continuous

Kelly lives in England.
Right now (in this photo) she's standing in front of her college.

When do we use the **simple present** and the **present continuous**? Can you give a rule?

2 **Read more about Kelly and answer the questions again.**

I live in this typical English house in Bristol with my mum and dad and my sister Marie. I wasn't born in Bristol. I was born in London and mum and dad moved to Bristol when I was 10. So I've lived here for seven years. Bristol is OK, but London was COOOOL! I want to work there when I finish college!

1 Where was Kelly born?
2 When did her mum and dad move to Bristol?
3 How long has Kelly lived in Bristol?
4 How does Kelly describe her house?
5 Which town does she prefer – London or Bristol?

Simple past and present perfect

Kelly was born in London. She moved to Bristol when she was 10.
She has lived in Bristol for seven years/ since she was 10.

When do we use the **simple past** and the **present perfect** in these sentences? What's the difference between **for** and **since**?

3 **Read about Kelly's favourite things and her visit to New York. Say if the sentences below are true or not true. (Correct the false sentences.)**

Favourite ...	... is OK	☺ I like ...	♥ I LOVE ...
food	pizza	curry	fish and chips
movie star	Nicole Kidman	Matt Damon	Johnny Depp
hobby	reading	going to the cinema	being with friends

The coolest place in the world!

Have you ever been to New York? I have! It was totally AMAZING. We saw the Statue of Liberty, Fifth Avenue, Central Park ... and we went up the Empire State Building. I want to go again!

1 Kelly thinks pizza is OK, but curry is tastier.
2 She thinks Matt Damon is better than Johnny Depp.
3 She thinks reading is OK but being with friends is more interesting, and the most interesting thing of all is going to the cinema.
4 Kelly has never been to New York.
5 She thought it was the coolest place in the world.

Adjectives

Which **adjectives** (short? long?) do we compare with -er/-est and which with more/most?

Have you ever ... ?

When do we use the **present perfect** with ever? Give two examples.

4 **Kelly is talking about her plans after college and her ideas about work. Complete with going to or will.**

Kelly Richards – camerawoman!

At college I'm training to be a camerawoman and when I finish I (1) 'm going to look for a job with a movie company. I think it (2) ... be great! I think (I hope!) I (3) ... be a good camerawoman. My teachers say that I learn quickly and that I work very well. Then – my BIG plan! – I (4) ... go to Hollywood. America here I come!

5 **Look at the two sentences in exercise 4 above from: 'I think (I hope!) ...' to '... that I work very well'. Can you find one adjective and two adverbs?**

6 **Now YOU. Write 100–150 words about you – where you live, your favourite things, plans for the future etc.**

Going to and will

When do we use going to and when do we use will to talk about the future?

Adjectives and adverbs

We use **adjectives** to talk about people and things. How do we use **adverbs**?

Unit 9 Love at first sight

A

B

C

D

[P/I] **1 What is 'love at first sight'? Do you believe that it happens in real life?**

[R] **2 We sometimes meet the boy or girl of our dreams in the strangest places. Match the pictures and the texts.**

1
Patrick was standing in the shopping mall when he saw Sophie for the first time. Suddenly, she became the only girl in the mall.

2
Zoe was at the cinema when she met her boyfriend Dylan. She was eating popcorn, when suddenly the boy in the next seat put his hand in the bag and took some!

3
It was the first day of a new year at high school and Nicole was putting books in her locker, when suddenly Antonio opened the locker next to Nicole's.

4
Carlos met his girlfriend Anita in a café. He was working as a waiter, when suddenly the most beautiful girl in the world came in with her friend and sat down at one of the tables.

▶ TIPS AND TRICKS

Carlos/Carla is my **friend.**
= ein(e) Freund(in) von mir

Carlos/Carla is my **boyfriend/ girlfriend.**
= mein Freund/ meine Freundin

[P] **3 Look at the diagram and the example, then complete the sentences about Carlos, Patrick and Zoe.**

1 Patrick **(stand)** was standing in the shopping mall, when he **(see)** … Sophie for the first time.
2 Zoe **(eat)** … popcorn at the cinema, when suddenly the boy in the next seat **(put)** … his hand in the bag and took some.
3 Carlos **(work)** … as a waiter in a café, when suddenly the most beautiful girl in the world **(come)** … in with a friend and **(sit)** … down at one of the tables.

Nicole was putting books in her locker.
↑
Antonio opened the next locker.

[P] **4 All the sentences below are false. Correct them.**

1 Patrick was playing football when he first saw Sophie.
→ No, he wasn't … He was …
2 Carlos was sitting in a maths lesson when he saw Anita for the first time.
3 Zoe and Nicole were jogging in the park when they met their boyfriends.

[P] **5 Look at the example below, then make sentences again about Carlos, Patrick and Zoe with while.**

Example: Nicole first met Antonio while she was putting books in her locker.
1 Carlos first saw Anita …
2 Patrick met …
3 Zoe …

[P/I] **6 This is Miranda and her boyfriend Jackson. What do you think? How did they first meet? Make a short text and tell the class. Use when or while.**

→ I think that Miranda was … when she …
I think that Miranda met Jackson while …

GRAMMAR SPOT: Das past continuous (Verlaufsform der Vergangenheit)

Das past continuous wird für eine Handlung verwendet, die schon im Gange war, als eine andere Handlung einsetzte.

Für die zweite Handlung wird das simple past verwendet.
I was watching a movie, when a beautiful girl sat down next to me.
A beautiful girl sat down next to me while I was watching a movie.

I	was(n't)	doing
he/she/it	was(n't)	doing
we/you/they	were(n't)	doing

→ Grammar summary, page 201

[P] **1** **What are the missing forms in the table?**

Past continuous		
I	(1)	watching a movie at the cinema.
he/she/it	was	
we/you/they	(2)	

[P] **2** **Yesterday evening Jason went to a party. What was everybody doing when he arrived? Complete the sentences with the expressions below.**

Example: When Jason arrived at the party, …
→ the DJ was playing music.

1 Alice and Ed …
2 Jeff and Anne …
3 Sue and Pippa …
4 Steve …
5 Harry and Luke …
6 Daisy and Max …
7 Megan …

to dance (together) • to chat (together) • to sit (together) • to hold hands • to tell a joke • to laugh • to get food (from the buffet) • to play music • to take a photo (with a mobile)

[P] **3** **Give the sentences again with while.**

Example: I was watching TV when the telephone rang.
→ The telephone rang while I was watching TV.

1 I was sitting in an English lesson when my girlfriend texted me on my mobile.
2 Tim was doing his homework when I arrived at his flat.
3 Mary was jogging in the park when she saw her best friend with her boyfriend!
4 We were waiting outside the classroom when our teacher arrived.
5 I was walking to college when it started raining.
6 Laura was surfing the Internet when she 'met' her boyfriend.

[P] **4** **Complete the text with the past continuous or the simple past.**

The date that almost went wrong

Last Saturday evening, Joe and Sally arranged to meet at the cinema at 8 o'clock. Unfortunately, there were two cinemas, the ABC and the Odeon and when Sally **(1)** arrived **(arrive)** at the ABC, Joe **(2)** … **(wait)** at the Odeon. After about five minutes at the ABC, Sally thought: "Oh dear! I bet Joe is at the Odeon." Unfortunately, Joe thought: "Oh dear! I bet Sally is at the ABC." Joe ran to the ABC and Sally ran to the Odeon. So this time, when Sally **(3)** … **(arrive)** at the Odeon, Joe **(4)** … **(wait)** at the ABC. And Joe **(5)** … **(arrive)** at the ABC while Sally **(6)** … **(wait)** at the Odeon. After about five minutes again, Sally phoned Joe on her mobile. "Where are you, Joe?" she asked. "I'm here," answered Joe. When she **(7)** … **(turn)** round, Joe **(8)** … **(stand)** just behind her!

[P] **5** **Complete the sentences with the correct object pronouns.**

Example: Where did Lara meet her boyfriend Sam? – She met him at a disco.

1 Where did Tony meet his girlfriend Rachel? – He met … on a holiday in Spain.
2 Did you see Karen and Jennie yesterday? – Yes, I saw … in town.
3 Where did you put my mobile? – I put … in your bedroom.
4 Can you help …? We're looking for the Odeon cinema. – Sure. Go up here and it's on the left.
5 Do you love …, Anne? – Yes, I love … very much, Jeff!

I	me
he	him
she	her
it	it
we	us
you	you
they	them

[P] **6** **There are two spelling mistakes in each sentence. Correct them.**

1 Do you beleive in love at first sihgt?
2 I think that my girlfreind is the most beautifull girl in the world.
3 Megan was taking fotos with her mobil.
4 Were was Sally when Joe arrivd at the Odeon?
5 We arranged to go to the cinema together on saturday, but unfortunatly I forgot!

[P] **7** **Write out this short text with CAPITAL letters where necessary.**
*

last year when i was on holiday …

in the usa, i met a wonderful girl called amber. she was a student at an american high school in denver, colorado. we wrote lots of letters and sent lots of emails but, of course, i never saw her. then last saturday she came to germany. i met her at the airport in dusseldorf on saturday evening and we took the bus to my house here in neuss. my mum cooked a big meal and my dad told lots of stupid jokes. they liked amber very much. then on sunday we visited the city. we saw the rhine, had a burger in mcdonald's, and then we saw a movie (in english) with julia roberts. these days together with amber are the happiest days of my life!

[P/I] **1** **Look at the picture below. What do you think is happening? Where are the people? Is the girl in the red T-shirt happy? Why (not)? Do you know a word to describe people when they feel like this?**

[R] **2** **Read the story Dancing in the Rain.**

DANCING IN THE RAIN

IT WAS the end of the year at college, and the disco was on the big lawn outside the main building. Britta and her friend Steffi arrived at about 8 o'clock. It was a warm summer evening.

"Now", said Steffi to Britta. "Nico is over there with his friends, next to the stage and the sound system. Just go up to him, smile, and say: 'Nico, would you like to dance?' OK?"

Britta was very nervous. Nico was the nicest boy in her year! But Steffi was her best friend, and she always gave good advice. "OK", said Britta. "Here goes!"

Britta walked across the grass towards the stage. And then she stopped, her mouth open. Oh, no! There was Nico, but he was talking to another girl! And she looked fantastic. Lots of make-up, an expensive hair style, and a very sexy dress. She was flirting with Nico and he was holding her in his arms. Britta felt so jealous that she almost cried.

Suddenly, Britta felt a raindrop on her face. In a couple of minutes, the rain started falling ... and Britta started laughing. The girl's make-up and hair were all over her face. She looked terrible. The girl stamped her foot and ran towards the college building.

Nico had a problem, too. The sound system was expensive and in the rain it was getting very wet. Britta went up to Nico and said: "Can I help? We can put the speakers in that classroom over there." "Great." said Nico. "Thanks." For about ten minutes, Britta worked with Nico and his friends. They carried the speakers, amplifier and other sound equipment into the college – and the rain got heavier and heavier. Finally, the equipment was safe. Nico's friends left, and Britta and Nico were alone together.

"Thanks again", said Nico. He looked at Britta while she was standing there. She was really pretty! And she was so kind and helpful. She had a beautiful smile, too. "Britta", he said. "Would you like to dance?"

He put his arms round her and they danced, very slowly, in the rain.

R/P] **3 Answer the questions with full sentences.**

1 What time did Britta and Steffi arrive at the college disco?
2 What advice did Steffi give to Britta? (Give Steffi's words.)
3 Why was Britta very nervous?
4 What was happening when Britta saw Nico? How did Britta feel about this?
5 Why did Britta start laughing?
6 How did Britta help Nico?
7 Did the story have a happy ending? What happened?

R/P] **4 True, false or not in the text? Correct the false sentences.**

1 The college disco was on the big lawn outside the main building.
2 Nico was the oldest boy in Britta's year at college.
3 When Britta saw Nico he was talking to a girl called Jutta.
4 It started raining and the girl ran towards the college building with Nico.
5 Britta, Nico and his friends put the sound system in a classroom in the college.
6 Nico's friends left, then Nico and Britta danced together in the rain.
7 After a couple of minutes, he kissed her.

[R] **5 Find the words and phrases in the text.**

Example: the biggest building (of a college, for example) → the main building

1 a little frightened
2 you put this on your face to look more beautiful (lipstick, for example)
3 speakers and amplifiers are two parts of a ...
4 there weren't any other people there – they were ... together
5 a ... person has a nice personality, likes to help friends etc.
6 the opposite of 'quickly'

[I] **6 Discuss in class.**

1 Did you like this story? Why (not)? Did you find it romantic? Silly? Sexist? Interesting? Boring?
2 Girls: what is important for you when you see a boy? What do you find attractive? Boys: what's important for you when see a girl? What do you find attractive?
Use the expressions below.

to be good-looking (boys) • to be beautiful/pretty (girls) • to be tall/slim/sporty • to have a nice figure (girls) • to wear great clothes • to have nice eyes • to be kind • to be friendly • to have a nice personality • to be funny • to be intelligent • to like the same things as you • to be honest • to have a car/money

P/I] **7 Choose one of the projects.**

1 Work with a partner or in a group. Write a short story and read your story to the class. It can be a true story or a story that you think of yourselves.
2 Do a survey in class. What is important for boys and girls about girls and boys? Do boys have different ideas from girls? Make a questionnaire, then talk about the results. Use your discussion from exercise 6 (2).

ICH KANN JETZT ...

- über die Beziehungen zwischen Mädchen und Jungen reden und schreiben,
- kompliziertere Sätze in der Vergangenheit bilden,
- eine typische Kurzgeschichte lesen, verstehen und besprechen.

[R] **1 Read the short text about Lena and Heinz and the conversation below then answer these questions.**

1 Where are Lena and Heinz from?
2 What are they doing this week?
3 Who is Mrs Wilson?
4 When did Lena and Heinz fly to England?
5 Where are they staying while they are in England?
6 What does Mrs Wilson offer Lena and Heinz when they are in her office?
7 What question does Heinz have at the end of the conversation?

Lena Rostova and Heinz Röhl are from Ulm in Germany. They are training to be nursery school teachers at college and this week they're visiting a nursery school in England.

Ann Lena? Heinz? Hello, I'm Ann Wilson, the head teacher.
Lena How do you do, Ms Wilson.
Heinz Pleased to meet you, Ms Wilson.
Ann How was your flight yesterday?
Lena It was fine, thank you.
Ann And is your bed and breakfast OK?
Heinz Oh, yes. It's great, thanks. We had a really big breakfast this morning!
Ann That's good. Well, my office is on the first floor. Would you like to come this way?
...
So, please come in. Would you like a cup of tea or coffee?
Lena A cup of coffee would be very nice, thank you.
Heinz Yes, for me, too, please. And could I use your toilet, please, Ms Wilson?
Ann Of course. The toilets are just outside, along the corridor on the right. And please, call me Ann.
Heinz Thank you, er, Ann.

[R/I] **2 Listen then practise the conversation in a small group.**

[I] **3** **Now YOU. Look at the phrases and the Culture Tips, then role-play the conversation with a partner. Invent details yourselves.**
Partner A: you work in a school, a company or factory in your town in Germany and today you are meeting a visitor from England.
Partner B: you are the visitor.

Meeting a visitor
Hello./How do you do. I'm …
(Hello./How do you do./Pleased to meet you.)
Small talk
How was your flight/journey?
Is your hotel OK?
Did you find us OK this morning?
(Fine, thanks. No problem.)
My office is …
My office/the conference room is on the first floor/just over there …
Would you like to come this way/follow me?
Please, come in./Please, take a seat.
Polite offers
Would you like a cup of tea/coffee?
(A cup of coffee would be very nice, please.)
Polite requests
Could I use your toilet/telephone, please?
(Of course./Certainly.)

CULTURE TIPS: BE POLITE

British and American people are very polite! Here are some good tips:

Please and thank you:
These words are very important. Use them often!

Polite offers:
Would you like a cup of tea?
Would you like some lunch?

Polite requests:
Could I use your toilet, please? (Not I ~~want~~ to …)

ICH KANN JETZT …
- eine Besucherin/einen Besucher begrüßen und mich um sie/ihn kümmern,
- etwas höflich anbieten,
- und höflich um etwas bitten.

[M] **4** **Your boss wants to learn about the Culture Tips above but doesn't speak English. Give the ideas in German in your own words.**

[R] **1 Match the parts of the body and the pictures.**

ankle • arm • chest • ear • elbow • eyes • face • finger • foot • hair • hand • head • knee • leg • mouth • nose • shoulder • stomach ('tummy') • teeth • toe

[P] **2 Complete these sentences with words for parts of the body.**

1 Karina has blue eyes and blond …
2 You have five … on your hand and five … on your foot.
3 You put your shoes on your …
4 You bite an apple with your … They are white.
5 When you eat food, it goes into your …
6 Your … is in the middle of your face. You smell things with it.
7 When you speak or laugh, you move your …
8 You have two … but cats and dogs have four.
9 You put a hat on your …
10 People often carry a bag on their …
11 When you're listening to music, you're using your …
12 You have knees so that you can bend your legs. You have … so that you can bend your arms.

▶ **TIPS AND TRICKS: SINGULAR AND PLURAL WORDS**

one foot ➔ two feet

one tooth ➔ two teeth

Remember that **hair** is singular in English:

She has blond hair.

She has blond ~~hairs.~~

[R] **3 The children below don't feel well. Can you match the pictures A–F and the problems 1–6?**

1 I've got a headache. ➔ D
2 I've twisted my ankle.
3 I've cut my finger.
4 I feel sick.
5 I've hurt my knee.
6 I've got a cold.

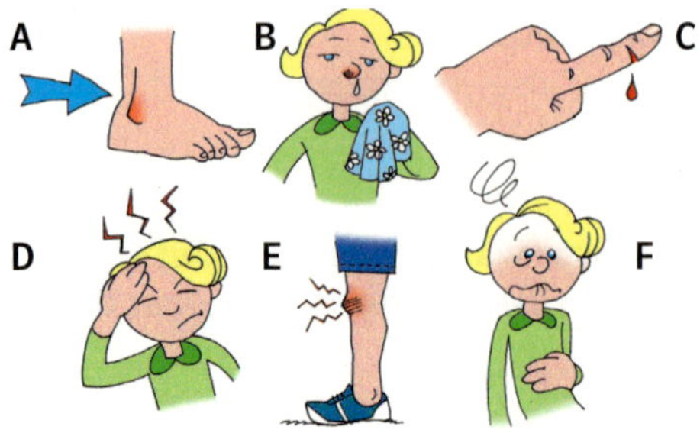

1/P] **4** **What's the best thing to do in the situations in exercise 3? Discuss the problems in groups then tell the class your ideas.**

Useful expressions:
to take a tablet (an aspirin/a paracetamol) • to put a plaster on (a wound) • to rest • to lie down • to go to bed • to stay warm • to drink (lots of) water • to put ice on something • to bandage (something) • to wash (something)

We think that the best thing to do is to go to bed.

[R] **5** **Debbie Morris is a primary school teacher in Wales. She's talking about her job and her school. Listen and choose the correct answer.**

1 Debbie has been a teacher at the school for …
a 5 years. b 10 years. c 15 years.

2 She teaches the pupils in the … year.
a first b second c third

3 There are … boys and girls in her class.
a 20 b 25 c 30

4 In England and Wales, children start primary school when they are … years old and leave when they are … years old.
a 5 / 10 b 6 / 11 c 5 / 11

5 The school day begins at 9.00 and finishes at …
a 2.15. b 2.45. c 3.15.

6 At lunchtime, the children usually eat …
a sandwiches. b a hot meal. c sweets.

7 In all schools in England and Wales the pupils also get … from the school.
a a drink b fruit c bread

8 As in most schools in the UK, the pupils at Debbie's school wear …
a a uniform. b hats. c jeans.

9 One reason why Debbie is always busy at school is because there are …
a lessons on Saturday. b too many children. c clubs.

JOB PROFILE:
PRIMARY SCHOOL TEACHER

Name: Debbie Morris
School: Long Park Primary School
Town: Cardiff, Wales

[I] **6** **How are primary schools in Britain and Germany different? How are they the same? Talk in class.**

ICH KANN JETZT …
- Körperteile benennen und über einfache Krankheiten reden,
- britische und deutsche Grundschulen vergleichen.

Unit 10 Living together

[P/I] **1 'Germany' is a country and 'German' is a nationality. How many nationalities can you name in one minute?**

[R] **2 Read about Asha.**

Asha is the girl in the middle in this picture. She's with her 'little' sister Lalima (she's standing on the right in the photo), and her older cousin Padmini. Asha lives in Nottingham in England. Today, Asha is at a festival. It takes place in Nottingham every summer and it's for all the Asian people in the town. Asha is a 'British Asian'. British Asians have parents or grandparents from India, Pakistan or Bangladesh. Asha's grandparents immigrated to England from India in the 1960s. Asha loves the festival. There are lots of stalls. They sell delicious food, jewellery, clothes and other things. And best of all for Asha, there are some Asian singers. They are singing all her favourite pop songs today.

> ▶ TIPS AND TRICKS
>
> The girls are **in** this photo/picture.
>
> … ~~on~~ this photo/picture.

[P] **3 Look at the two example sentences, then make more sentences with who or which.**

→ Asha is the girl who is in the middle in the photo.
→ She's at a festival which takes place every summer.

1 Lalima is the girl		is for all the Asian people in the town.
2 Padmini is the girl		is standing on the left in the picture.
3 Nottingham is a town		is standing on the right in the picture.
4 Asha is at a festival	who	are singing Asha's favourite songs.
5 British Asians are people	which	sell food, jewellery and clothes.
6 There are stalls at the festival		have (grand)parents from South Asia.
7 There are some Asian singers		is in England.

[R] **4 Read what Asha says about her life as a British Asian.**

A British Asian

"Hi! You know that my name's Asha and that I'm a British Asian. For me it means that I live in two worlds – I'm Asian and I'm British. I think that's great! For example, in the picture you can see my dad and my grandma (she lives with us). The people who I see at home are Asian. The language which I speak at home is Asian, too. It's called Hindi.

But I'm also a student at a college here in Nottingham and in the other picture you can see my three best friends. The people who I meet at college are mostly British. And, of course, the language which I speak there is English."

[P] **5 Look at the phrases in blue in the text and the examples below. Give two more sentences about Asha.**

The people who Asha sees at home are Asian.
→ The people Asha sees at home are Asian.
The language which she speaks at home is Hindi.
→ The language she speaks at home is Hindi.

[P] **6 Which Asian or British things does Asha like best? Look at the table and make sentences.**

Example: The food she likes best is Asian food.

	Asian	British
Food	✓	
Music	✓	
Films		✓
Magazines		✓
Language	Hindi	English ✓
Clothes	✓	

[P] **7 Make sentences that are true for YOU.**

1 The language I speak at my college is …
2 The music I like best is …
3 The TV programme I like best is …
4 The people I meet at college are …
5 The food I eat most often at home is …
6 The subject I like best at college is …

GRAMMAR SPOT: Relativsätze

In Relativsätzen wird bei Personen who und bei Sachen which verwendet:

A girl who lives in England …
A festival which takes place every year …

Wenn who oder which Objekt des Relativsatzes sind, kann man sie weglassen:

The people (who) I meet at college …
The food (which) I like best …

→ Grammar summary, page 201

[R/P] **1** **Read the text, look at the map and the nationalities, then complete the sentences about the three teenagers.**

Multicultural Britain

Britain is a very multicultural society. About 6.5 per cent of people are from an ethnic minority – that's about one person in every fifteen. Today, most young people from ethnic minorities were born in Britain, and so they are British. Their parents or grandparents usually came to Britain in the 1950s or 60s. Most came from three areas – the Caribbean Islands, South Asia (India, Pakistan or Bangladesh), or China. Here are three young people who all live in Britain.

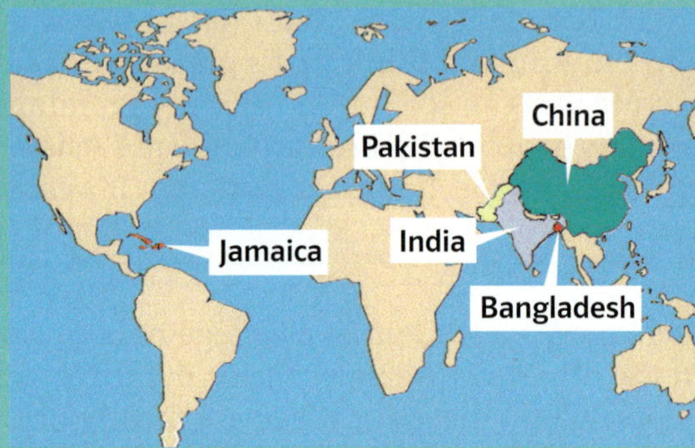

Chris

Imran

Lin

1 Chris's grandparents came from the Island of Jamaica. People who come from Jamaica are called …
2 Imran's grandparents came to England from Pakistan. People … come from Pakistan are called …
3 Lin Chang's grandma and grandad came from China. People … come from China are called …

▶ TIPS AND TRICKS: NATIONALITIES

Asia	Asian
Bangladesh	Bangladeshi
China	Chinese
India	Indian
Jamaica	Jamaican
Pakistan	Pakistani

[P] **2** **Write three more sentences about nationalities.**
→ People who come from …

[P] **3** **Can you complete these sentences with the names of the correct continents?**
Example: China is a country which is in Asia.
1 Britain is a country … is in …
2 Pakistan, India and Bangladesh are countries … are in …
3 Sydney is a town … is in …
4 Jamaica is an island … is between … and …

Africa • Antarctica • Asia • Australia • Europe • North America • South America

R/P] **4** **Read about the Notting Hill Carnival, then make sentences from the table. (There is sometimes more than one answer.)**

The Notting Hill Carnival

Notting Hill is a part of London, near the centre of the city. In the 1960s, it was the part where most of London's black people lived – the first immigrants from the Caribbean Islands. In 1964 they started a festival: the Notting Hill Carnival. The first carnival was very small, but today around two million people come to dance, listen to the bands, and have a great time. And there are lots of white faces in the crowd, too. The carnival is in August and lasts three days. People say that it's the biggest street party in the world.

The people The clothes The music The food The dancers The atmosphere	the bands people you	wear at the carnival are fantastic! feel at the carnival is amazing! can buy and eat in the streets is delicious. meet at the carnival are of all different races and colours. play is very, very loud! see at the carnival have a lot of energy.

→ The people you meet at the carnival …

[P] **5** **Choose four sentences from your answers in exercise 4 and write them again with who or which.**

→ The people who you meet at the carnival …

[P] **6** **Complete the sentences with the correct prepositions.**

Example: The person you can see in this picture is my dad.

1 Asha is the girl who is … the middle, and her sister is the girl who is … the right.
2 Lin Chang's grandma and grandad came … England … China.
3 Is Tom … home today? – No, he isn't. He's … the Notting Hill Carnival … London.
4 The carnival is fantastic. People sing and dance … the streets. It's the biggest street party … the world.

at • in • on • to • from

[M] **7** **A friend wants to know about the different nationalities who live in Britain. Read exercise 1 again and tell him or her in German about the situation.**

[P] **8** * **An American friend wants to know about a festival in Germany (Karneval, for example). Write an email. Write about 80–100 words.**

[R] **1** Read this web page.

Moving to Britain

Bibi, Salima, Parvin and Seeta are four young British Pakistanis. They are now the third generation of their families who have lived here. For them Britain is home – in fact, Parvin and Seeta have never been to Pakistan. But life in Britain was very different for their parents and grandparents. Here we look at those early days when the first immigrants from South Asia arrived in Britain.

The first people from India and Pakistan began arriving in Britain in the 1950s and 60s. A few were doctors and other qualified professionals, but most were poor people who just wanted a new and better life in Britain. Men almost always came first. They usually found jobs in factories or perhaps as cleaners.

After a couple of years, the wives followed their husbands to Britain. Sometimes they came with small babies, or babies were born here, and so a second generation began to grow up. The lives of these first new, young British Asians varied very much, from family to family and place to place. Some found it easy to integrate and to be 'British'. For others, there was an enormous contrast between life at home (where mum and dad couldn't speak English) and life at school, and they sometimes felt that they were people who were 'between two worlds'. And sadly, in some big towns, there was prejudice against Asian people.

Despite all the problems and difficulties, however, the second generation grew up, learned English and got jobs, this time as nurses, doctors, teachers, electricians, secretaries. In the 60s and 70s, young British Asians were very often more successful at school and college than their white friends!

Today it is their children who are the third generation – people like Bibi, Salima, Parvin and Seeta. People who feel that Britain is home.

Bibi's grandma's stories
Bibi has some stories about her grandma.

Click here to listen.

P/I] **2** **Make notes about the text. Begin like this. Then talk about the most important information in the text.**

THREE GENERATIONS
The first generation of Asians in Britain were people who ...
The second generation were people who ...
The third generation are now people who ...

R/P] **3** **True or not true? Correct the false sentences.**

1 Bibi, Salima, Parvin and Seeta have all been to Pakistan.
2 Most people who arrived in Britain from Pakistan in the 1950s and 60s were doctors and other qualified professionals.
3 The first generation of people often got jobs in factories or as cleaners.
4 All the young people of the second generation found it easy to integrate and to be British.
5 Despite all the problems, the second generation of people were successful and got good jobs.
6 People like Bibi, Salima, Parvin and Seeta often feel that they are 'between two worlds'.

[R] **4** **Look in the text and find the words.**

1 to immigrate **(noun)** → an immigrant
2 life **(verb)** → to …
3 sad **(adverb)** → …
4 to succeed **(adjective)** → …

R/P] **5** **Listen to Bibi's stories about her grandma.**
Make notes about these things, then tell the stories in your own words.

1 When Grandma arrived: …
2 Her journey to England: …
3 The weather: …
4 Shopping: …
5 People in the town: …
6 Grandma's first day at work: …

[I] **6** **Talk about the questions below in class.**

1 For some young British Asians of the second generation, there was a big contrast between life at home and life at school. Give examples: the language they spoke at home; the food they ate at home; the clothes …
2 Why do you think young British Asians in the 1960s and 70s were often more successful at school and college than their white friends?

P/I] **7** **Choose one of the projects.**

1 **Use the Internet to find out more about the Notting Hill Carnival. Find and download a picture you like, then write a short text to describe the scene, the people etc.**
2 **'Bollywood' (Bombay + Hollywood) is the name for the Indian film industry. It makes hundreds of films every year which are popular with Asian people all around the world. Find out about Bollywood and give a short talk.**

ICH KANN JETZT …

- Personen und Sachen mit **who** und **which** näher beschreiben,
- über ethnische Minderheiten in Großbritannien sprechen und schreiben,
- einen längeren Sachtext lesen, verstehen und besprechen.

[R/P] **1 Look at the bar chart, then complete and say the sentences.**
In Britain today, around 6.5 per cent of people – 3.7 million – are from an ethnic minority. The bar chart below shows the percentages of ethnic people.

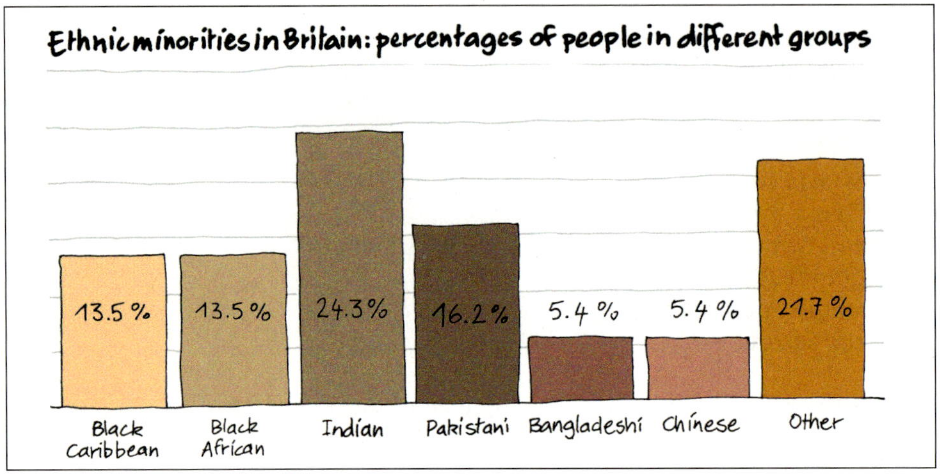

Example: Thirteen point five per cent of ethnic people in Britain today are Black Caribbean.
1 … are Black African.
2 … are Indian.
3 Sixteen point two per cent are …
4 Five point four per cent are … and another … are Chinese.
5 There is also a group which is called 'Other'. … of ethnic people are in this group.

[I] **2 Ask and answer questions with a partner.**
Example: What percentage of ethnic people are Black African?
– 13.5 per cent (are Black African).

[R/P] **3 True or not true? Correct the false sentences. (Look at the Grammar Spot.)**
Example: There are more Black Caribbean people in Britain than Chinese people. → True.
1 There are more Chinese people than Pakistani people. → No, there are fewer …
2 There are fewer Indian people than Bangladeshi people.
3 The two ethnic groups which have the most people are the Bangladeshi and the Chinese groups.
4 The group which has the fewest people is the Indian group.

[P] **4 Write a true sentence about the bar chart and read your sentence to the class.**

GRAMMAR SPOT: Zählbare Sachen vergleichen

Wir vergleichen zählbare Sachen (z. B. Menschen) mit more, the most, fewer und the fewest.	the most more (than) ↑ ↓ fewer (than) the fewest

▶ TIPS AND TRICKS

Six **point** five per cent of people …

Six ~~comma~~ five per cent of people …

[R] **5 Look at this second bar chart and answer the questions.**

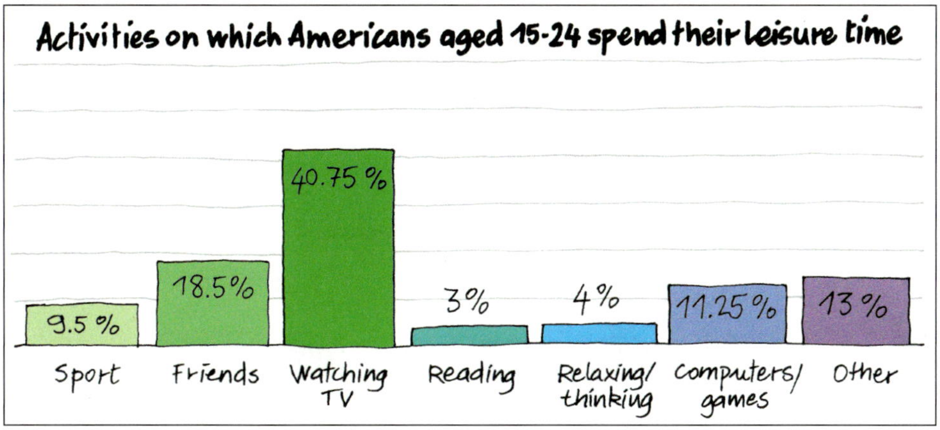

1 What does the bar chart show? Give some examples.
2 What percentage of their leisure time do young Americans spend on sport?
3 What percentage of their time do they spend on computers and computer games?
4 What about watching TV, friends and reading? What percentages of their time do they spend on these activities?

[P] **6 Look at the Grammar Spot below and complete the sentences below with more, the most, less or the least.**

1 Young Americans aged 15–24 spend more time on computers and games than on sport.
2 But they spend … time on computers and games than on their friends.
3 They spend … time on relaxing or thinking than on reading.
4 They spend … time on reading than on relaxing or thinking.
5 The activity on which they spend … time is watching TV.
6 And the activity on which they spend … time is reading.

I/P] **7 Now YOU. Choose one of the topics below and do a survey in your class. Make a bar chart with the results and write a short text to describe the chart.**

1 Leisure time:
How much leisure time do you have?
What activities do you spend time on?
2 Part time jobs:
Do you have one? Which jobs are the most popular?
3 Travel to and from college:
How do you travel? How much time do you spend on travel?
4 Mobile phones:
Do you have one? How do you use it?
5 The Internet:
How much time do you spend on the Internet? What do you do online?
6 Opinions:
What do you think about: smoking, your town, music, sport, famous people etc?

GRAMMAR SPOT: Nicht zählbare Sachen vergleichen

Wir vergleichen nicht zählbare Sachen (z. B. die Zeit) mit more, the most, less und the least.	the most more (than) ↑ ↓ less (than) the least

ICH KANN JETZT …
- über Prozentzahlen sprechen und schreiben,
- ein Balkendiagramm auf Englisch beschreiben.

[R] **1** **Read about how you say dimensions in English.**

Dimensions

In the world of work, we often talk about the dimensions of things. Here are three things – a box, a scooter and a plastic pipe.

high, wide, deep

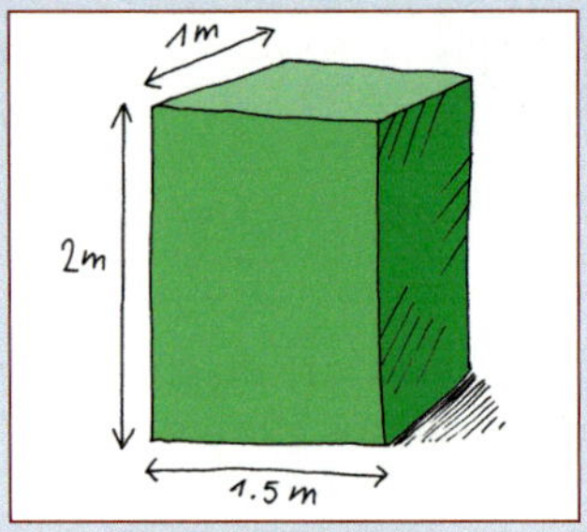

How high is the box?
– It's two metres high.

How wide is it?
– It's one point five metres wide.

How deep is it?
– It's one metre deep.

The box is two metres high by one point five metres wide by one metre deep.

long, heavy

How long is the scooter?
– It's one point seven six metres long.

How heavy is the scooter?/ How much does the scooter weigh?
– It weighs ninety-five kilogrammes.

across

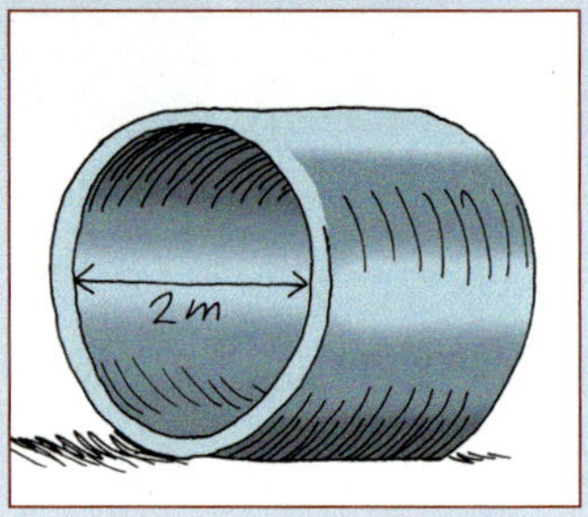

What's the diameter of the pipe?
– It's two metres across.

height, width, length

Here are the dimensions of the three things again:

The height of the box is two metres. The width is one point five metres. The depth is one metre.

The length of the scooter is one point seven six metres. The weight is ninety-five kilogrammes.

The diameter of the pipe is two centimetres.

[P] **2** **Complete the sentences.**

1 How high is the box? – It's 2 m …
2 How … is the box? – It's 1.5 m …
3 And how … is it? – It's 1 m …
4 So the box is 2 m high … 1.5 m wide … 1 m deep. – Yes, that's right.
5 The … of the box is 2 m, the … is 1.5 m and the … is 1 m.
6 How … is the scooter? – It's 1.76 m … The … is 1.76 m.
7 How much does the scooter … ? It … 95 kg. The … is 95 kg.
8 And what's the … of the pipe? The … of the pipe is 2 cm. It's 2 cm …

[R] **3** **Erica is phoning Steve about the dimensions of a laser printer and its cable. Listen and find the missing dimensions 1–5.**

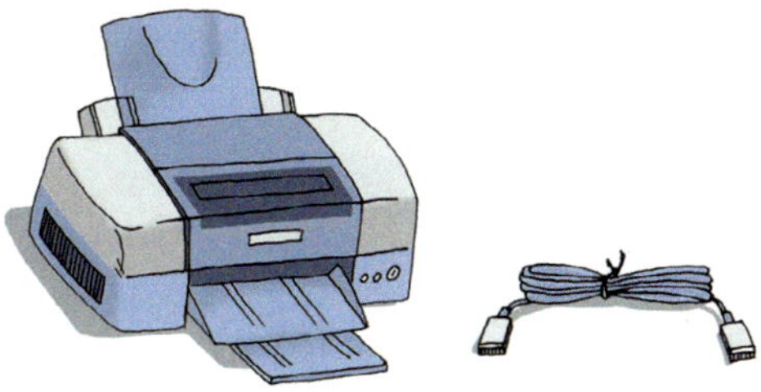

DIMENSIONS	
Printer	
Height:	41 cm
Width:	**(1)**
Depth:	**(2)**
Weight:	**(3)**
Cable	
Length:	**(4)**
Diameter:	**(5)**

[I] **4** **Below are two real, but crazy inventions. Work with a partner.**
Partner A: look at the information about the inventions on this page.
Ask your partner about the details and dimensions of invention B.
Answer his or her questions about invention A.
Partner B: look at page 208–209.

A The Ski Fan

You ski down, then with the ski fan, you ski back up! Easy! A great new invention. It consists of a two parts: a motor (a) and a fan (b).

DIMENSIONS

Part A
Height: 91 cm
Width: 52.5 cm
Depth: 27.5 cm
Weight: 17 kg

Part B
Diameter: 1.45 m

B

DIMENSIONS

Part A
Height: ...
Width: ...
Length: ...
Weight: ...

Part B
Length: ...

CULTURE TIPS: MEASUREMENTS (GB/USA)

Britain now uses centimetres, metres, litres etc. just like Germany (But: distances are still in miles on roadsigns).
In the USA people still use the old measurements (feet, inches, pounds etc.).

TIPS AND TRICKS

The height is 91 centimetre**s**.

It weighs 17 kilogramme**s**.

I live 2 kilometre**s** from college.

Don't forget the s!

ICH KANN JETZT ...

- nach Maßangaben fragen und sie vermitteln.

Unit 11 Teenage life

WIN AN iPOD!

Competition!

Take a break!

Magazine for Europe's teenagers £2.50

- 'Must-see' movies – the top 10 movies that you have to see!
- Stay safe online
  Our do's and don'ts for Internet chat rooms
- Around Europe. This week: learning to drive in the UK
- Brother of rock star Phil Winton tells us: "I don't want to be famous!"
- Camera? Sun cream? The things you mustn't forget to take on holiday! What's your list?
- CAREER SPOT You needn't be a guy to do a technical job! How the world of work is changing.

Plus! Letters, fashion tips, sports news and MUCH MORE!

[P/I] **1 Do you ever read magazines? What's your favourite magazine? Why?**

[R] **2 Look at the front cover of this magazine and find:**

1 some tips about the Internet
2 something about holidays
3 something about films
4 an article about jobs
5 some facts about a European country
6 a prize you can win in a competition

▶ TIPS AND TRICKS

The first prize is an iPod.
The price of the magazine is £2.50.

[R] **3** **Read this article from Take a break! about learning to drive in Britain. Then copy and complete the table below with phrases from the text.**

Learning to drive in Britain

It's that great day when you have your driving licence! And for Karen in Britain, that means that she can finally take the L-plates off her car …

Quick facts
You must be 17 to learn to drive in Britain. For your driving test, you must first pass a theory test, then drive on the road for about 30 minutes with an examiner. But you needn't go to a driving school in Britain. Most young people have some lessons at a school, but you can learn (or practise) with mum or dad or with a friend with a licence. You just have to put red L-plates on your car to show that you're a 'learner driver'.

So how do Karen (and her dad) feel today?

The good things

I don't have to ask my dad every day: "Can you give me a lift to town?"

I don't have to get wet and cold when I go to college!

The bad thing

I have to buy petrol and pay for car insurance.

Karen's dad

Karen mustn't think that because she has her driving licence she can now drive perfectly. You have to drive for a while to get experience.

müssen	dürfen nicht	brauchen nicht/müssen nicht
You must be 17.	■	■

[R] **4** **Look at the magazine cover again. Can you find more sentences with must, have to, mustn't, don't have to or needn't? Translate the sentences into German.**

GRAMMAR SPOT: Modale Hilfsverben

You must/have to see these movies.	Sie müssen …
You mustn't forget your camera.	Sie dürfen nicht …
I don't have to/needn't ask my dad for lifts now.	Ich muss nicht/brauche nicht mehr …

→ Grammar summary, page 202

[R/P] **1 Read the article and then complete the sentences below with must or mustn't.**

Stay safe online

Chat rooms are a great way to meet people and to make friends around the world. BUT you must follow some basic rules when you're online. Here are our DO's and DON'Ts …

DO's	DON'Ts
■ invent and use a screen name when you visit chat rooms	■ use your real name online
■ keep your personal information private	■ give your address, email address or phone number
■ be careful about downloads	■ download files from people you don't know
■ be very careful about people who you meet online	■ meet people who you don't know offline
■ remember your 'netiquette' and be polite!	■ insult other people in the chat room or SHOUT when you write

Example: The article says that you mustn't give your address or phone number.

1 You … keep your personal information private.
2 You … be careful about downloads.
3 You … download files from people you don't know.
4 You … invent a screen name for chat rooms. You … use your real name online.
5 When you write with CAPITAL LETTERS, people say that you're 'shouting'. You … do this in a chat room.
6 You … be very careful about people who you meet in a chat room. You … arrange to meet a person from a chat room offline.

[R/P] **2 Read the article 'I don't want to be famous!' on the next page and answer these questions. Use full sentences.**

1 What is Phil Winton's occupation and what does Ashley want to be when he leaves college?
2 How often does Ashley go to Phil's concerts?
3 Does Ashley want to be a rock star like his brother?
4 Which of the two brothers has to be away from home for months?
5 Which of the two brothers doesn't have to be away from home for months?
6 Which of the two brothers doesn't have to live most of his life in hotels?
7 Which of the two brothers can't go shopping like you and me?
8 Which of the two brothers needn't worry about photographers?
9 Which of the two brothers has to sing in front of thousands of people?
10 Does Ashley have to sing in front of thousands of people?

I don't want to be famous!

Take a break! talked to Ashley Winton from London in England, brother of the famous rock star Phil Winton.

TAB Hi Ashley! Do you go to your brother's concerts?

Ashley Sure. All the time. I love his music. I get lots of free tickets for me and my friends. And I meet other famous bands and singers when I'm with Phil.

TAB Do you want to be a rock star, too?

Ashley No way! I'm a college student and I want to be a nurse.

TAB But your brother has a great life. He's rich and he travels a lot. You don't want that?

Ashley The life of a rock star looks fantastic. But Phil has to be away from home for months, so he can't see his friends and his family. In fact, he has to live most of his life in hotel rooms. He can't just go shopping or get a burger like you and me. He has to worry about photographers all the time. And he has to sing almost every night in front of thousands of people. No thanks! I like my life. I like my friends and my family. I like being 'ordinary'. I don't want to be famous!

[P] **3 Complete the sentences with words from the table.**

		-ful		-less	
beauty	Schönheit	**beautiful**	schön	■	■
care	Sorgfalt	**careful**	sorgfältig	**careless**	achtlos
help	Hilfe	**helpful**	hilfreich	**helpless**	hilflos
stress	Stress	**stressful**	stressig	■	■
success	Erfolg	**successful**	erfolgreich	■	■
to use	nutzen	**useful**	nützlich	**useless**	nutzlos

Example: Thanks very much for the tips. They helped me a lot.
They were very helpful.

1 You made lots of mistakes in your last class test.
You were very …
2 There's a lot of stress when you're a rock star.
The life of a rock star is very …
3 Be very … when you visit chat rooms.
You must follow some basic rules.
4 My car broke down at night and there was no one to help me.
I was …

▶ TIPS AND TRICKS

useful	usefu~~ll~~
helpful	helpfu~~ll~~
beautiful	beautifu~~ll~~

[P] **4 An American friend wants to know about the rules at your college.**
*** Write an email (80–100 words). Think about these things:**

- What days of the week must you go to college? What days needn't you go?
- What things do you have to do? (For example, come to lessons regularly.)
- What things mustn't you do? (For example, smoke or use mobiles in class.)

[I] **1** **Here are the four most popular traditional apprenticeships for girls and for boys in Germany. But which are which? And which is the most popular of all in each group? Talk in a small group and decide. (Answers on page 210.)**

shop assistant	(car) mechanic	doctor's assistant	electronic technician
plumber	office clerk	painter and decorator	dentist's assistant

[R] **2** **Read the short text then listen to the interview.**

This week, **Take a break!** has an article called 'You needn't be a guy to do a technical job'. It is about girls who are training for jobs which are not traditional girls' jobs. Last week, a reporter from the magazine interviewed some apprentices around Europe for the article. This is the interview with Nicola from England.

TAB What career are you training for, Nicola?

Nicola I'm training to be an industrial electrician.

TAB Why did you choose that job?

Nicola When I was a kid, I always loved repairing things. And at school, my favourite subject was maths. So this is a pretty natural job for me.

TAB What did your friends and your parents say about your career choice?

Nicola The boys in my class at school were a bit sceptical! Some of them said: "You won't do it!" But my parents were great. They supported me a hundred per cent.

TAB Are you the only girl apprentice in your firm?

Nicola At the moment, yes. There are five boys and me.

TAB How did the other apprentices react to you?

Nicola We were all new together. That made a bond between us. We quickly became good friends.

TAB What about the older people in the firm?

Nicola One or two sometimes make stupid comments! If you're a girl and you choose this job, then you must expect that. And you must learn to give as good as you get!

[R] **3** **Complete the sentences with information from the text.**

1 Nicola chose her job because …
2 When Nicola chose her job, the boys in her class at school were … but her parents …
3 Nicola is good friends with …
4 The older people in Nicola's firm sometimes … but she says that you must …

[R] **4 Now here is an interview with Marlies. Listen and choose the correct answers.**

1 Marlies is from …
a Germany. b the Netherlands. c France.

2 She is training to be a …
a plumber. b artist. c painter and decorator.

3 At school, her favourite subject was …
a art. b maths. c geography.

4 In her last year at school, Marlies visited …
a England. b a factory in her town. c some firms in her town.

5 Her friends and her parents …
a were sceptical at first. b saw immediately that it was the right job for her. c told Marlies: "You mustn't do that!"

6 Sometimes the men in her firm …
a are critical. b make stupid comments. c want to help her.

7 Marlies thinks that there aren't more girls in her job because …
a girls aren't strong enough. b girls think: "I can't do that". c guys laugh at them.

[R] **5 Look at these two pages and find the English for:**

skeptisch • kritisch • blöde Bemerkungen • Berufswahl • jmdn. unterstützen • sofort • Band (Freundschaft) • etw. erwarten • Lieblingsfach

[P] **6 Choose one of the two girls and write a short profile. Listen again if necessary. Begin like this:**
→ (Name) is from (country). She is training to be a … She chose that job because …

[I] **7 Discuss in class.**
1 Why do you think that boys and girls often choose 'traditional' jobs?
2 Do you agree with Marlies that "girls can do everything that guys do"?

[P/I] **8 Choose one of the projects.**
1 There are some teenage magazines in English on the Internet. Find an article which you think is interesting and tell the class about it.
2 Write a class magazine in English. Include interviews, quizzes, articles, tips etc.

ICH KANN JETZT …

- Sachen, die man muss/nicht muss bzw. nicht darf beschreiben,
- eine typische Zeitschrift für englischsprachige Teenagers lesen, verstehen und besprechen,
- ein Interview verstehen und in einem kurzen Text zusammenfassen.

[R] **1** **We often want to get more information about something – from an advertisement in a newspaper, for example. The quickest way to do this is often by phone. Listen to Mike who saw this advertisement. Which phrase does he use – A or B?**

Man – The Bikeshop. Jeff speaking.
Mike – Oh, hi. **(1)** … about the advertisement in the paper this morning. Is the sale still on?
Man – Yes, it's on all week. It ends on Sunday.
Mike – Great! **(2)** … the bikes you have in the sale?
Man – Sure. We've got all sorts of bikes – BMX, mountain bikes, road bikes. Are you interested in anything in particular?
Mike – Yes, **(3)** …
Man – Oh right, OK. We've got about 30 at the moment in the sale.
Mike – What makes do you have?
Man – Trax, Bergen and Sunrider.
Mike – **(4)** … do you have on Sunrider bikes?
Man – Just a minute. We have the new Sunrider 20X at 30 per cent off.
Mike – That sounds great. And the sale is on until Sunday, you said?
Man – That's right. But hurry. We're selling the bikes fast!
Mike – OK, **(5)** …
Man – You're welcome.
Mike – Great. Bye.

A	B
I'm calling	I'm ringing
Could you tell me a bit about	Could you give me an idea of
BMX bikes	mountain bikes
What sort of offers	What sort of reductions
Thanks a lot for your help	See you

[I] **2** **Practise the dialogue with a partner. Take it in turns to be Mike.**

[R] **3 Choose the best answer to these questions.**

1 Is your sale still on?
  a It started on Monday.
  b Yes, it's on until Sunday.
  c Hurry!

2 Could you tell me a bit about your products?
  a How can I help?
  b That's right.
  c Sure.

3 What sort of reductions do you have on the products?
  a There's up to 50% off all the products.
  b We have all sorts of products.
  c You're welcome.

4 Are you interested in anything in particular?
  a That sounds great.
  b Yes, mobile phones.
  c Thanks a lot for your help.

[I] **4 Make telephone conversations with a partner. The ad below was in a newspaper this morning. Work with a partner and phone the computer shop for details. Use the useful phrases below.**

Partner A: You are a sales assistant in the shop. Look now at page 209.
Partner B: You're phoning about the ad. Here's your list of questions.

Is the sale still on?
PCs? Laptops? Handhelds?
What makes? offers? prices?
Opening hours of the shop?

Telephone enquiries: useful phrases
I'm ringing/calling/phoning about …
… your advertisement in the newspaper/ on TV/on the Internet.
Could you tell me a bit about/give me an idea of/give me some details of/give me some information about …?
How much is it/are they?
What makes do you have?
Do you have any special offers at the moment?
What sorts of offers/reductions/deals do you have on …?
How long is your sale on for?/When are you open?/When can I come in to buy …?
Can I buy online?
Thanks a lot/Thanks very much (for your help).

ICH KANN JETZT …
- einfache Informationen über Produkte usw. per Telefon einholen.

[R] **1 Read about Nikki and look at the catalogue.**
Nikki Moss works in the sales department of a big telecoms firm in the UK. In Nikki's company, employees can work in the company's office, or they can work from home. Nikki is going to work from home. At the moment she is buying things for her home office and she has a catalogue from a company called Planet Office. Here are some items from the catalogue.

Desk

SPECIAL OFFER! £150

ED 1478

Office chair

£99

Available in blue, grey and red

AX 5153

Filing cabinet

£120

Available in grey, green and white

UV 9786

Lamp

£45

OY 2121

Clock

£20

EI 3326

Bookcase

£60

AM 9091

Waste bin

£5

Also available in blue or red

RA 8451

Cuddly toy

£20

QT 7741

[I] **2 Nikki has £450. Which things above do you think she should order from the catalogue? Talk in a small group, then tell the class your ideas.**
→ We think that the most important things are …
… and … are not so important.
We think that Nikki should buy …
That comes to …

[R/P] **3** **Nikki is phoning Planet Office with her order. Listen and find the missing information, then use it and other information from the dialogue to complete the order form below.**

Woman Planet Office. Kelly speaking. How can I help you?
Nikki I'd like to order some items from your catalogue, please.
Woman Certainly. Can I take your name, please?
Nikki Yes, It's Moss, M-O-double S.
Woman And your address, Ms Moss?
Nikki …
Woman Thank you. So, what would you like to order?
Nikki The desk, please. The catalogue number is ED 1478.
Woman That's on special offer at the moment, so it's only £150. Anything else?
Nikki Yes, the office chair, catalogue number …
Woman The chair is available in blue, grey or red. Which colour would you prefer?
Nikki Blue, please.
Woman OK. One chair, in blue. Anything else, Ms Moss?
Nikki No, that's all.
Woman That comes to £249, then. How would you like to pay?
Nikki By credit card.
Woman Could you give me your credit card number, please?
Nikki It's a Visa card, …
Woman Fine. Thank you very much. We'll deliver your order in about seven days.
Nikki Thanks. Bye now.
Woman Goodbye, Ms Moss. And thank you again for your order.

Planet Office

Telephone Order
ORDER NO. 2539

ITEM	CAT. NO.	QUANTITY	PRICE	TOTAL
Desk	ED 1478	1	£ 150	£ 150
Office chair (blue)	(1)	(2)	(3)	(4)
				£ 249

Ms Moss
(5)
BS5 3KK

PAYMENT
~~Cheque~~
Credit card

(6) ☐☐☐☐ ☐☐☐☐ 7 1 7 8 ☐☐☐☐

[I] **4** **Make telephone conversations with a partner. Copy Planet Office's telephone order form, then take it in turns to be a person in the sales department at Planet Office and a customer. Think of items, quantities, colours, your address etc. yourself.**

ICH KANN JETZT …

- eine einfache telefonische Bestellung aufgeben,
- eine telefonische Bestellung aufnehmen und ein Bestellformular ausfüllen.

Unit 12 Famous companies

[P/I] **1 Work in a small group. How many famous companies do you know? You have one minute to write them down. Are they American, Japanese, German, ... ?**

[R] **2 Read the text below and find the answers to these questions.**

1 What are Ben and Jerry's full names?
2 Where is Vermont, and why is it a good place to make ice cream?
3 When did the Ben & Jerry Company start selling ice cream in Germany?

Two hippies and milk from Vermont

In the north-east of the USA, between New York and the border with Canada, is the part of the country which is called New England. One of the six small states here is Vermont. The cows here produce milk which is particularly creamy. In 1977, two 'hippy' friends from New York – Ben Cohen and Jerry Greenfield – moved to the town of Burlington, Vermont, and decided to start a business. They were 26 years old. Together they had $8,000. They borrowed $4,000 more from the bank, paid $5 for a quick course in how to make ice cream, and on 5 May 1978, they began selling 'Ben & Jerry's Homemade Ice Cream' from an old gas station in the middle of town. It was an instant success. People liked eating the delicious ice cream, and Ben and Jerry loved inventing new flavours with crazy names. The business grew quickly and in 1985, they opened a factory. In 1994, they started selling ice cream in the UK, then in 1996 in Belgium, Luxembourg and the Netherlands, in 1998 in France and Japan, and in 2002 in Germany. Today, although Ben & Jerry's is a big international company, the two guys still want to have fun with their business. Jerry says about work: "If it isn't fun, why do it?".

R/P] **3 Finish these sentences with information from the text, then complete the table.**

1 In 1977, two 'hippy' friends from New York moved to Vermont and decided …
2 They borrowed some money from the bank, and on 5 May 1978, they began …
3 It was an instant success. People liked …
4 Ben and Jerry also loved …
5 After the business had grown very quickly, they opened a factory, and in 1994 they started …
6 Today, Ben & Jerry's is a big international company, but the two guys still want …

Verb + -ing form		Verb + infinitive	
begin	doing	■	to do
like		■	
■			
■			

[P] **4 Make sentences about YOU with verbs from the table.**

→ I like/love …
I started/began …
One day, I want …

R/P] **5 Here are some events from the history of the company. Decide which one happened first, then make a sentence with after.**

Example: Ben and Jerry decided to start a business. (1)
They borrowed $4,000 from the bank. (2)
→ After they had decided to start a business, they borrowed $4,000 from the bank.

1 They began selling ice cream.
They paid $5 for a quick course.
2 They sold their ice cream from an old gas station for a while.
They opened a factory.
3 They started selling their ice cream in the Netherlands.
They started selling their ice cream in the UK.

New England

GRAMMAR SPOT:

Verb + -ing Form/Infinitiv

Nach einigen Verben steht die -ing Form, nach anderen der Infinitiv:

I like/love eating ice cream.
I want to go to the USA one day.

Das past perfect

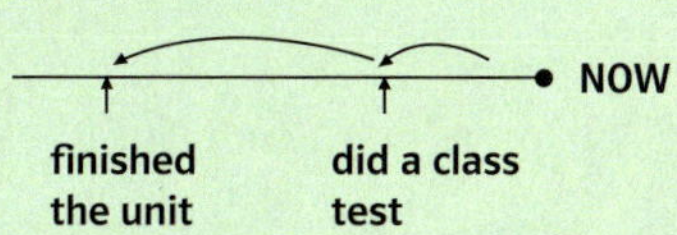

After we had finished the unit, we did a class test.

▶ TIPS AND TRICKS

companies — compan~~ys~~
hippies — hipp~~ys~~
countries — countr~~ys~~

→ Grammar summary, page 202

[P] **1** **Two English friends, David and Paul, are on holiday in the USA. David wrote this email to a friend in Germany. Complete it with the infinitive or the -ing form of the verbs.**

To: steinebach_ulrich@hotmail.com
Subject: Having a great time in the States!

Hi Uli!

Hope you're well and that college is still going OK.

Paul and I are having a great time in the States! We only decided (1) to come (come) about a month ago. We managed (2) ... (get) two cheap flights to Boston, and here we are! We're driving around the north-east in a hire car, from Boston down through New York and Philadelphia to Washington DC (then back again to Boston). This is my first trip to the USA and I really love (3) ... (see) all the famous places.

Yesterday, we visited the Harley-Davidson factory in York, Pennsylvania (about 150 kilometres from Philadelphia). That's where they manufacture the 'Fat Boy' bikes, the ones the cops all ride – 550 kilos, five gears, and a top speed of 190 kph! Did you know that Harley-Davidson started (4) ... (make) motor cycles back in 1903? A guy called William Harley and two brothers, Arthur and Walter Davidson, began (5) ... (build) the first bikes in their garden shed. That was in Milwaukee (near Chicago) and the company headquarters and main factory are still there. Man, Harley-Davidsons are SO coooooool! I can't afford (6) ... (buy) one now, but one day I want (7) ... (have) one. You look at a bike and you can imagine (8) ... (ride) along a long, open road! I took lots of photos at the factory, and I promise (9) ... (send) you some when I'm back in England.

OK, must go. Tomorrow, we plan (10) ... (drive) to Washington DC.

Hope (11) ... (see) you soon.

Paul

▶ TIPS AND TRICKS

You **drive** a car but you **ride** a (motor) bike.

[P] **2** **Read how these famous companies began, then complete the sentences. In each sentence, one verb is in the simple past, the other in the past perfect.**

NOKIA	• The Nokia company started in the town of Nokia, Finland, in 1865. It sold wood products to the paper industry. • In 1912, it also began making electric cables. • It started making mobile phones in 1987.
	• In 1974, a young computer wizard called Steve Jobs was a student in the USA. To earn some money, he worked on an apple farm. • In 1976, he founded a computer company and wanted to find a name for it. He remembered the farm and called the company Apple Computers.
THE BODY SHOP	• Anita Roddick is a famous English businesswoman. In 1976, her husband left England to travel for a year around the States. • While he was in the States, Anita opened a small shop and sold environmentally friendly soaps and other products. She called the shop The Body Shop.

Example: The Nokia company started **(start)** making mobile phones in 1987, but before that it had sold **(sold)** wood products and cables.

1 Steve jobs … **(call)** his company Apple Computers because as a student he … **(work)** on an apple farm.
2 Anita Roddick … **(open)** her shop after her husband … **(leave)** England to travel round the States for a year.
3 Anita … **(open)** her shop because her husband … **(leave)** England.
4 The Nokia company only … **(start)** selling mobile phones after it … **(sell)** wood products and cables.
5 Steve Jobs … **(found)** a computer company in 1976, but before that he … **(be)** a student.
6 After Anita's husband … **(leave)** England, she … **(open)** a shop.
7 Because he … **(work)** on an apple farm as a student, Steve … **(call)** his company Apple Computers.

[P] **3** **Translate the missing parts of the sentences.**

* 1 Zwei Freunde aus New York entschlossen sich, ein Unternehmen zu gründen.
In 1977, two friends from New York decided … a company.
2 Sie fingen an, Eis zu verkaufen.
They … ice cream.
3 Nachdem das Geschäft gewachsen war, eröffneten sie 1985 eine Fabrik.
After the business … and in 1985 they … a factory.
4 Nachdem Paul die Fabrik besucht hatte, wollte er eine Harley-Davidson kaufen.
After Paul … the factory, … a Harley-Davidson.

[R/P] **1** **Read this article about Sony and suggest headings for the paragraphs 1–3.**

The story of Sony

When Masaru Ibuka and Akio Morita founded their company in 1946, nobody had ever heard the expression 'Made in Japan'. Today, their company is a global leader in electronics.

(1) …

In 1946, the Japanese capital, Tokyo, lay in ruins after the war. In the city, there was water and electricity, but people were very poor and many didn't have proper homes. Two young men lived here. Their names were Masaru Ibuka, an engineer, and Akio Morita, a physicist. They had met and had worked together during the war. Now they met again and decided to found a company together. They planned to repair all the electrical equipment – radios and so on – which people had and which was often broken. They called their company Tokyo Tsushin Kogyo, the 'Tokyo Telecommunications Engineering' company. They couldn't afford to open a workshop, so they used a room over a department store. The company employed seven people. Parts were also very difficult to get, and often they bought things on the black market.

(2) …

Despite all the problems, the company grew. Masaru and Akio managed to find a building for a proper workshop. The two men also loved inventing things, and Masaru had lots of good ideas. One was a cheap electrical rice pot. Unfortunately, it wasn't very successful because it often burned the rice! Then, in the early 1950s, he travelled to the USA. There, the Bell telephone laboratory had just invented the transistor. Masaru immediately saw that with transistors he could make small, portable radios. In August 1955, the company started selling its first radios. People wanted to buy them all over the world and the company became famous. But its name was a problem, and in 1957 Masaru and Akio decided to change it to Sony.

(3) …

Many other famous products followed, including the Walkman in 1979, and the first PlayStation in 1995. Today, Sony is one of the biggest and most successful electronics firms in the world. Mr Ibuka died in 1997 and Mr Morita in 1999.

[R/P] **2 True or not true? Correct the false sentences.**

1 Masaru Ibuka and Akio Morita met for the first time in Tokyo in 1946.
2 The first name for their company was Tokyo Tsushin Kogyo.
3 Masaru's first invention, a rice pot, was an instant success.
4 Masaru learned about transistors when he visited the USA in 1955.
5 He used the transistors to make portable video recorders.
6 Masaru and Akio changed the name of their company to Sony in 1975.
7 Masaru and Akio died in 1999.

[R] **3 Find phrases in the text which mean the same.**

1 they didn't have enough money (to)
2 hard to get
3 although there were lots of problems
4 he went to
5 they produced many other products after that

[R] **4 Find words in the text which mean the opposite.**

1 to break
2 sold
3 became smaller
4 fortunately
5 slowly, after a while
6 stopped

[P] **5 Make a summary of the text in about 50–80 words. Here are some helpful phrases which you can use in your summary.**

→ In this text the reader learns that …
The first paragraph tells us that …
In the second paragraph we read/learn that …
The last paragraph is about …
In the text it (also) says that …
For example, …
Finally, we learn/read that …

▶ **TIPS AND TRICKS**

- the text tells us that …
  ~~the text says us that~~
- In the text it says that …
  ~~In the text it stands that~~

[I] **6 Talk in class.**

1 Why do you think that people start companies? Is it just to earn money?
2 Today, large, famous companies are 'global'. What does this mean? Why are so many companies today global?

[P/I] **7 Choose one of the projects.**

1 **Find out about a company (perhaps one in the town where you live) and give a short talk to the class.**
2 **Work in a small group. Imagine that you want to start a company. What will be your business? Find a name for your company and design a logo.**

ICH KANN JETZT …

- besser über Ereignisse in der Vergangenheit sprechen,
- manche Ausdrücke + Verb benutzen,
- über einige weltbekannte Unternehmen sprechen und schreiben.

[R] **1 Read about Sarah and look at the two emails. Find these words and expressions in English.**

Raststätte • Kette • Zentrale • Personalchef • Posteingang • von • an • Betreff • Bitte schicken Sie mir • aktuell • Personal/Belegschaft • beste Wünsche • Kopie (an) • Als Anlage erhalten Sie • Sagen Sie mir Bescheid, wenn Sie weitere Fragen haben • mit herzlichen Grüßen

Sarah King works at a motorway service station in England. It is called Motostop, and it is one of a chain of Motostop service stations around the UK. Sarah is the manager's secretary. Motostop's head office is in London, and every day Sarah corresponds with people at the head office by email. She has an email from the company's personnel manager this morning. And she has written a reply.

Inbox

From: d.tate@motostop.net **To:** s.king@motostop.net
Subject: restaurant staff list

Dear Sarah

Could you please send me an up-to-date list of all the staff who work in the restaurant (full-time and part-time)?

Many thanks!

Best wishes
Don

New message

To: d.tate@motostop.net
Cc:
Subject: restaurant staff list
Attach: restaurant_staff.doc (50 KB)

Dear Don

Thanks for your email. I'm attaching a full list of all our restaurant staff.
Please let me know if you have any further questions.

Kind regards
Sarah

[R] **2** **The emails 1–3 below are from Sarah or to Sarah from people at Motostop's head office. Find the correct replies A, B or C and give the missing names.**

Hello Sarah

Hope you're well. Could you send me last month's sales figures for your shops, please? Thanks!

Best wishes
Anna 1

Dear …

Thanks for your email. An engineer will be with you tomorrow morning. Please let me know if I can help further.

Kind regards,
… A

Hi Sarah

How are things? Do you have the phone number of that nice hotel (Rose Hotel?) near your service station? I want to stay there next month.

Kind regards, Jake 2

Hello …

Hectic! Good to hear from you. It's called the White Rose Hotel and the phone number is 01765 817294. Let me know if I can help further.

All the best, … B

Dear John

We're having a problem with our security cameras. Could you send an engineer asap? Thanks in advance.

All the best
Sarah 3

Hello …

I'm fine, thanks. Hope you are too. Here are the sales figures which you wanted. Let me know if you have any further questions.

Best wishes
… C

P/1] **3** **Partner A: you are Sarah.**
Partner B: you work at Motostop's head office.
Write an email and give it to your partner, then write a reply to your partner's email. Think of ideas yourself for the emails. Use the phrases below.

Beginning your email
Dear …/Hi …/Hello …
Hope you're well/How are things?
Requests
Could you (please) send (me) …?
Do you have …?
(Many) thanks/Thanks in advance

Replying
I'm attaching …
Here is/Here are the … which you wanted.
(Please) let me know if you have any further questions/if I can help further.
Ending your email
Best wishes/Kind regards/All the best

CULTURE TIPS: EMAILS

At work in Britain or the USA, emails are often short and informal. People who often correspond normally use first names – even bosses.

ICH KANN JETZT …

- kurze E-Mails schreiben und E-Mails entsprechend beantworten.

[R] **1** **Read about Jamie Oliver and answer the questions.**

Jamie Oliver

Jamie Oliver is a famous English chef. He has a restaurant in London, he writes great cookbooks, and he is often on TV. A few years ago, he made some programmes about food in English schools – and how unhealthy it often was!

Jamie grew up in a small town in the east of England. His mum and dad had a pub. In England, pubs almost always serve hot food. As a kid Jamie loved cooking and helping in the kitchen. He wasn't a very good pupil at school – in fact, he was very bad! – but after school he became a student at a college in London and learned to cook. His teachers saw that he was fantastic, and after college he got jobs with some famous chefs in London. One of these chefs had a show on TV – and that was how Jamie became a TV star himself.

Jamie believes that good food is simple, fresh and healthy, but also very tasty. He also thinks that traditional English food is great. He is right. It is just a stereotype that English food is bad!

1 Where did Jamie grow up?
2 Where and when did he first cook?
3 Where did he go to college?
4 How did he become famous? Explain!
5 What does the text say about English food? What does Jamie think is 'good food'?

[R] **2** **On the next page are two simple, healthy recipes, just as Jamie likes them. Find the expressions in the recipes which match the German expressions below.**

golden, goldfarben • Zubereitung • Teelöffel • rühren • Esslöffel • braten • schneiden • kochendes Salzwasser • Zutaten • Mischung • erhitzen • köcheln lassen • Mehl • kochen • verrühren • geschält und gehackt • vermischen • weich • hinzufügen • bestäuben • tauchen

[R] **3** **In which of the two recipes do you do these things?**

1 first fry some onions until they are soft
2 cut some potatoes into chips
3 simmer a sauce for 15 minutes
4 use balsamic vinegar
5 boil something for 4 minutes
6 fry something for about 5 minutes
7 add pepper and salt at the end

Tomato pasta

Serves 4

Ingredients

1 onion, peeled and chopped
2 cloves of garlic, peeled and chopped
100ml of olive oil
1 teaspoon of dried oregano
½ a dried chilli, chopped
800g of good quality tinned tomatoes
3 tablespoons of balsamic vinegar
1 teaspoon of sugar
a handful of fresh basil
200g of pasta

Method

1. Fry the onions, garlic, oregano and chilli in the olive oil for about 5 minutes until the onions are soft.
2. Add the tomatoes and simmer for 15 minutes.
3. Add the balsamic vinegar and sugar and stir until you have a sauce.
4. Meanwhile, cook the pasta for 8 minutes in boiling salted water.
5. Mix together the cooked pasta and the sauce. Add pepper, salt and the fresh basil.
6. Enjoy!

Fish and chips

Serves 4

Ingredients

2l oil
2 large potatoes, cut into chips
3 teaspoons of baking powder
250g of white flour
285ml of beer
4 pieces of white fish

Method

1. Heat the oil to around 190°.
2. Beat together the flour, baking powder and the beer until the mixture is thick and creamy.
3. Dust the fish with a little extra flour and pepper and salt. Dip it into the flour and beer mixture, then fry it in the oil for around 4 minutes until golden. Take it out of the oil and keep it warm in the oven.
4. Cook the chips in boiling salted water for 4 minutes. Dry them and fry in the oil until golden.

[I] **4 Talk in class.**
The text about Jamie Oliver says that it is 'a stereotype that English food is bad'. What does this mean? What do you think of English food? Have you ever eaten it?

ICH KANN JETZT …
- ein englisches Kochrezept verstehen (ggf. mit Hilfe eines Wörterbuches).

Unit 13 Destination Canada

[P/I] **1** **Have you ever been late – for a train, a plane, an interview, an important test at college? When? What happened? How did you feel?**

[R] **2** **Read about Louis and answer the questions.**

Louis Santiago is at New York's JFK Airport. He is on the way to Vancouver in Canada for an important business meeting early tomorrow morning. There is just one problem. Louis is late! This is the last flight from JFK to Vancouver today. It leaves in fifteen minutes. And Louis must check in in the next five minutes. If Louis reaches the check-in desk in time, he will catch his plane. But if he doesn't reach the desk, he will miss his plane!

1 Where is Louis this afternoon? Why is he there?
2 What must he do in the next five minutes?
3 What will happen if he doesn't do that?

[P] **3** **Complete these sentences about Louis with will or the simple present.**

1 If Louis reaches **(reach)** the check-in desk in five minutes, he ... **(catch)** his plane.
2 If he ... **(catch)** his plane, he ... **(be)** in Vancouver for his meeting.
3 But if he ... **(not/reach)** the desk quickly, he ... **(miss)** his plane.
4 And he ... **(not/be)** in Vancouver for the meeting if he misses his plane!

GRAMMAR SPOT: If-Sätze Typ 1

Wir bilden If-Sätze Typ 1 mit if + dem simple present und will. Wir benutzen sie, um über konkrete Situationen zu sprechen, die wir eventuell für erfüllbar halten.

if	simple present	will
If	Louis reaches the check-in desk,	he will catch his plane.

R/I] **4** **Look at the pictures and facts about Canada below. Which facts did you know? Are there any facts which you find surprising? Where is Vancouver? (That's where Louis is going to.)**

P/I] **5** **Imagine YOU are visiting Canada. What would you like to see there? Ask a partner, then tell the class.**

Where would you go if you visited Canada?

If I visited Canada, I would go to northern Canada. I'd like to see polar bears!

→ Bernd/Martina would go to northern Canada if they visited Canada. They'd like to see polar bears.

GRAMMAR SPOT: If-Sätze Typ 2

	if	simple past	would
Wir bilden If-Sätze Typ 2 mit if + simple past und would ('d). Wir benutzen sie, um über imaginäre Situationen zu sprechen.	If	I went to Canada,	I would (I'd) visit Montreal.

→ Grammar summary, page 203

[R/P] **1** **Continue this conversation with the correct forms of the verbs. Use if-sentences type 1.**

Jack and Holly from England want to go on holiday to Montreal next summer, and they're looking on the Internet for hotels. They like two hotels and can't decide which is better …

Hotel Saint-Pierre **

Small, family hotel, 27 rooms, 2 minutes on foot from the old port of Montreal, cafés and restaurants, 20 minutes on foot from the city centre

Price per night: single CAN$85, double CAN$100

Facilities: bath/shower, TV and Internet

Meals: breakfast in your room is included in the price

Parking: there is no car park at the hotel but there is a public car park nearby (CAN$5 per day)

Hotel Royal ***

Large, modern hotel with 180 rooms, 5 minutes on foot from the city centre and shops

Price per night: single CAN$120, double CAN$150

Facilities: bath/shower, TV, Internet, fitness centre, swimming pool

Meals: the hotel has an excellent restaurant. Breakfast in the restaurant is included in the price

Parking: free in the hotel car park

Jack: How much will it cost if we stay at the Hotel Saint-Pierre?
Holly: A double room will cost a hundred Canadian dollars per night.
Jack: And how much will it cost if we stay at the Royal?
Holly: A hundred and fifty.
Jack: So if we (1) stay (stay) at the Saint-Pierre, it (2) … (be) cheaper.
Holly: Sure, but we (3) … (be) nearer to the city centre if we (4) … (stay) at the Royal.
Jack: And if we (5) … (stay) at the Saint-Pierre, we (6) … (be) nearer to the old port and all those great cafés and restaurants. I think that will be much nicer.
Holly: OK, but remember that we want to hire a car, and there (7) … (not/be) a car park if we (8) … (choose) the Saint-Pierre. If we (9) … (choose) the Royal, we (10) … (get) free parking.

Montreal – one of Canada's 'French' cities

[P] **2 Complete the magazine article with the correct forms of the verbs. Use if-sentences type 2.**

If you were a Canadian teenager …!

Of course, if you were a teenager in Canada you would speak English – or if you lived in the province of Quebec, you would speak French. But there **(1)** would be **(be)** lots of other differences if you **(2)** were **(be)** Canadian too. What about music, for example? Well, you **(3)** … still … **(love)** listening to music if you **(4)** … **(be)** a Canadian teenager. But if you **(5)** … **(live)** in Canada, you **(6)** … **(listen)** mainly to Canadian bands and singers. Some Canadian singers have become famous in Europe, by the way. Avril Lavigne is from Canada.

Ice hockey is Canada's national sport. If you were a sports fan, you'd love it here!

College? Yes, there are vocational colleges in Canada just like in Europe, but if you **(7)** … **(go)** to a college in Canada it **(8)** … **(be)** called a 'community college', and if you **(9)** … **(be)** a student there, maybe you **(10)** … **(have to)** pay for your courses. Many Canadian schools and colleges are private. What about sport? Canadians love sport, and if you **(11)** … **(be)** a Canadian sports fan, you **(12)** … **(love)** ice hockey. It is the Canadian national sport in winter (in summer it is baseball or basketball).

But perhaps the thing which is most different in Canada is that it is just so big! If you **(13)** … **(live)** there and if you **(14)** … **(want)** to visit another city, you **(15)** … **(fly)**. Car journeys are just too long! And if you **(16)** … **(live)** in northern Canada, then in many places you **(17)** … **(fly)** to college at the beginning of term – and you **(18)** … **(fly)** home again at the end of term.

[P] **3 There are two spelling mistakes in each sentence. Find and correct them.**

1 If I visited Kanada, I would go to toronto.
2 My flight to Vancouver leafes in fife minutes!
3 Why are you runing – becuase I'm late!
4 Many schools and collegs in Canada are privat.
5 At this hotel, all rooms have a bad or a shower, and breakfast is included in the preis.

[P] **4 Give the sentences again with the full forms of the verbs.**

* Example: I'd like to visit Canada. → I would like to visit Canada.

1 If we're late, we'll miss our plane.
2 If Louis doesn't run, he'll miss his plane, too.
3 There won't be a car park if we stay at this hotel.
4 If Harry didn't talk so much in class, he'd learn more.

▶ **TIPS AND TRICKS**

Would benützen wir nie zweimal:

If I **visited** Canada, I would go to the Rockies.

If I ~~would visit~~ Canada, I would go to the Rockies.

[R] **1** **Read the text below. What is 'the Canadian'? Where does it travel from and to? How long does the journey take?**

In 1885, Canadian engineers completed the Canadian Pacific Railway. It connected Montreal in the east to Vancouver in the west, and was the longest railway in the world. Today, you can make the amazing journey across Canada from Toronto to Vancouver on a special tourist train called the Canadian. The journey takes three full days and nights, and is over four and a half thousand kilometres long. Let's make an imaginary journey on the Canadian …

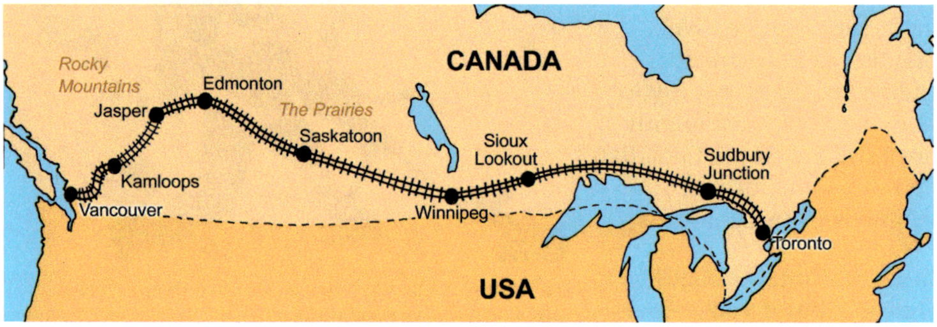

[R] **2** **Look at the map above and the pictures below, then listen and choose the correct answers on the next page.**

The train leaves Toronto

Forest and lakes near Sudbury Junction

Across the prairies

The Rocky Mountains

1 The Canadian would leave Toronto station at exactly … in the morning.
a 8 o'clock b 9 o'clock

2 At around 11 o'clock, you would see …
a the first trees of the forests. b the first mountains.

3 As you went to sleep at the end of your first day, you would maybe think …
a how comfortable your sleeping car is. b how big Canada is.

4 On day two, soon after Sioux Lookout, you would begin to see …
a lots of trees. b the prairies.

5 Canada is one of the world's largest producers of …
a wheat. b cattle.

6 As you went to sleep at the end of day two, you would perhaps think of …
a life on a Canadian farm. b a big steak.

7 On day three in Edmonton, you would be near the … part of your journey.
a most exciting b slowest

8 During the afternoon and evening, you would travel through two of … towns in the Rocky Mountains.
a the highest b the most beautiful

9 Unfortunately, your journey would end on day four at … in Vancouver.
a 8 o'clock in the morning b 8 o'clock in the evening

[R] **3 Do you remember these words and phrases? Match the English and German expressions.**

A	B
empty (land) • restaurant car • flat • to disappear • to grow • endless • from time to time • nearest neighbour • to reach	flach • von Zeit zu Zeit • endlos • nächste(r) Nachbar/in • (menschen)leer • erreichen • anbauen • Speisewagen • verschwinden

[M] **4 A German friend wants to know about the Canadian. Write her an email to describe the journey from Toronto to Vancouver. Write in German in your own words. Listen again and make more notes if necessary.**

[P/I] **5 Choose one of the projects.**

1 There are lots of interesting things which you can find out about Canada on the Internet: Canadian pop music, ice hockey, the Canadian Pacific Railway, famous cities like Montreal or Vancouver, the CN Tower, northern Canada ('Nunavut') . . . Choose one, and give a short talk to the class.

2 Imagine that you want to go on holiday to Canada. Look on the Internet for hotels. Choose one hotel and give the details (prices etc.) in English and German. (Tip: you'll also need to find out about Canadian dollars.)

ICH KANN JETZT …
- über ‚Bedingungen' reden und schreiben (Wenn …, dann …),
- manches über Kanada erzählen,
- einen längeren Hörtext verstehen und auf Deutsch zusammenfassen.

[R] **1 Read about Christian, and listen to the conversation.**

Christian Schulte works for an import-export company in Hamburg in Germany, but this year he is working for twelve months in the company's London office. At the weekends, Christian loves travelling around Britain and he often travels by train. In the UK, you can usually buy 'day return' tickets which are much cheaper than a normal return ticket. Christian is buying a ticket at a station in London at the moment.

Christian	Hello. I'd like a day return to Oxford, please.
Assistant	That's eighteen pounds. Thank you. Here's your ticket.
Christian	Could you tell me the time of the next train, please?
Assistant	Just a minute. The next train to Oxford leaves at nine fifteen. That's in about ten minutes.
Christian	And when does it arrive in Oxford?
Assistant	At ten ten.
Christian	What platform does the train leave from?
Assistant	Platform twelve.
Christian	Great. Thanks very much. Goodbye.

[R] **2 Answer the questions.**

1 Where does Christian normally work?
2 Where is he working this year?
3 What does he love doing at the weekends?
4 What is a day return ticket? Explain.
5 Where does Christian want to travel to today?
6 What time does the next train leave?
7 What time does it arrive?
8 What platform does it leave from?

[I] **3 Practise the dialogue with a partner.**

GRAMMAR SPOT: Das simple present für Fahrpläne

Wir benutzen das simple present, um über Flug-, Eisenbahn- und andere Fahrpläne zu sprechen:

What time **does** the train to Oxford **leave**, please?
– It **leaves** at 10.15 and it **arrives** in Oxford at 11.10.

[I] **4 Work with a partner to find the missing information.**

Partner B: Look at page 210.

Partner A: Below, you can see information about more trains from the station in London. But some times, platform numbers and ticket prices are missing. First, copy the table and ask your partner for the missing information. Then answer your partner's questions. (Numbers, dates and times: Klappumschlag A.)

DESTINATION	OXFORD	BRISTOL	CARDIFF	BIRMINGHAM
DEPARTURE	9.25	■	10.00	■
PLATFORM	■	3	■	6
ARRIVAL	■	11.15	■	12.04
SINGLE	£16	■	£47	■
RETURN	■	£70	■	£67
DAY RETURN	£18	■	£51	■

When does the train to … leave/arrive (please)?

What platform does it leave from?

How much is a single/return/day return ticket?

It leaves/arrives at …

(It leaves from) platform …

It's …

[I] **5 Now with your partner, use the information from the table in exercise 4 to buy a railway ticket like Christian. Decide where you want to travel to, and what sort of ticket you need. Take it in turns to be the assistant.**

→ Hello. I'd like …

ICH KANN JETZT …

- Auskunft für eine Bahnreise einholen,
- ein Bahn-Ticket in Großbritannien kaufen.

[R] **1** **This is a fabulous 1932 Ford Roadster – a classic American car!**
Can you find the parts of the car 1–15?

bumper • boot/trunk • headlight • gear stick • door • mirror • rear light • seat • wheel • steering wheel • windscreen • engine • exhaust • speedometer • tyre

[P] **2** **Complete the sentences with words from exercise 1.**

1 This Ford Roadster has the engine at the front and the … at the back. But in some cars (like the VW Beetle), the engine is at the back and the … is at the front.
2 You need these at night. The … at the back are red, and the … at the front are white.
3 The car has four wheels and four …
4 You turn the car left and right with the …
5 This Roadster has three gears. You change gear with the…
6 You can see how fast you are travelling with the…
7 The … is made of glass. You look through it when you are driving.

[R] **3 Read what Bob says and answer the questions.
True or not true? Correct the false sentences.**

"Hi. I'm Bob and I'm a mechanic at a garage in London. Lots of customers bring their cars to us regularly for a service. When we service a car, we change the oil and the oil filter. The old oil is always dirty. We also change the spark plugs so that the engine runs better. We check lots of other things, too – the exhaust, the tyres, the battery, the headlights, the brakes and so on. If there's a problem, we repair or replace things. After a car is two years old, it must have an MOT test every year. We do MOT tests at my garage. Our customers are always a bit nervous when they come to get their car after an MOT! They always ask: 'Is everything OK? Did it pass the MOT?'"

1 Bob works at a garage in the USA.
2 Lots of customers bring their car to Bob's garage every week for a service.
3 When Bob services a car, he changes the oil, the oil filter and the spark plugs.
4 He also checks the customers.
5 In Britain, cars must have an MOT test every two years.
6 Bob's customers are always happy when they come to get their car after an MOT.

[M] **4 You work at a garage in Germany. One of your customers is an English businessman. He is at your garage now to get his car after a service. Read your checklist. Can you help the customer and explain it to him in English?**

We changed the oil.

We checked …

There was a problem with … so we replaced …

The total cost is …

Ölwechsel	✓
Ölfilter wechseln	✓
Zündkerzen wechseln	✓
Bremse überprüfen	✓
Reifen überprüfen	Schlechter Zustand. Zwei neue Reifen vorne
Auspuff überprüfen	✓
Scheinwerfer überprüfen	✓
Batterie überprüfen	Batterie ersetzt
Gesamtbetrag	€885.00

ICH KANN JETZT …
- wichtige Teile eines Autos in English benennen,
- einer/em englischen Kundin/en einfache Informationen über eine Inspektion geben.

Unit 14 Unbelievable!

[P/I] **1** **Has a strange or unusual thing ever happened to you? When? What happened exactly? Tell the class.**

[R] **2** **Read this true story and answer the questions.**

Rainer Schuster was falling towards the earth at 200 kph …

Seconds earlier, three kilometres up, he had jumped from a plane with the other members of his German parachute team. Unfortunately, one of the other members of the team had hit Rainer when they jumped, and Rainer was now unconscious.

Below him, there were just miles and miles of the Lüneberger Heide. Flat. Empty. Well, almost empty – there was one pine tree. At the last minute, Rainer's emergency parachute opened automatically. It didn't stop him – it was too late – but Rainer crashed into the tree and the parachute caught in the branches. When he woke up, he was hanging from the tree. He had a broken arm. But he had survived! He was alive!

1 What kind of team was Rainer a member of?
2 What had happened seconds before the picture above?
3 What happened at the last minute? Did that stop Rainer? Why (not)?
4 Did Rainer hit the earth at 200 kph? Did he die or did he survive? Why?

[P] **3** **Can you translate these sentences into German?**

1 If Rainer had hit the earth at 200 kph, he would have died.
2 If he hadn't crashed into the tree, he wouldn't have survived.

R/P] **4** **Life is full of amazing coincidences. Here are two more true stories. Read them, then complete the sentences below.**

England, 1967. When the telephone number of his police station changed, an English policeman, Mr Mosardi, wanted to give a friend the new number (40116). But he made a mistake and gave the friend the number 40166. A couple of weeks later, Mr Mosardi was on patrol near a factory when he saw a light in a window. He went into the factory. Everything was OK, but suddenly a telephone rang in an office. Mr Mosardi went into the office and picked up the phone. It was his friend. The number of the phone in his hand was 40166!

Berkeley, California, 1974. Mrs Willard Lovell had a big problem! She had got up early, and had gone downtown to do some shopping. Now she was back at her apartment, but she couldn't open the door – she had forgotten her key. At that moment, the mailman arrived with a letter for her. It was from her brother. Two weeks earlier, he had stayed with Mrs Willard, and during his stay, he had borrowed a key for the apartment. In the letter was the key which he had just sent back!

1 Mr Mosardi made a mistake. He gave his friend the wrong number for the police station.
   a If he hadn't made (**not/make**) a mistake, he would have given (**give**) his friend the correct number.
   b But if he had … (**give**) his friend the correct number, his friend wouldn't … (**not/phone**) the factory.
   c And, of course, Mr Mosardi … (**not/hear**) the phone if he … (**not/go**) into the factory.
2 Mrs Willard's brother stayed with her and borrowed a key for her apartment during his stay.
   a If he … (**not/stay**) with her, he … (**not/borrow**) the key.
   b If he … (**not/borrow**) the key, he … (**not/send**) it back in a letter.
   c And the mailman … (**not/bring**) Mrs Willard the key that morning if her brother … (**not/send**) it back in a letter.

GRAMMAR SPOT: If-Sätze Typ 3

If + past perfect	would have/wouldn't have
If I had seen you, …	I would have said 'hello'.
If Mr Mosardi hadn't made a mistake, …	his friend wouldn't have phoned the factory.

→ Grammar summary, page 204

[R/P] **1** 'Urban myths' are stories which people tell about strange (and often grizzly) things. Sometimes these stories are true – usually they aren't! But we love hearing and telling them. Here are two famous stories.

The hook-hand

A young American couple on a date drove to a lonely wood to 'park'. While they were sitting in the car, they heard on the radio that a psychopath with a hook-hand had escaped from a hospital. After a while, there was a soft noise – like metal on the car. The girl was frightened. Her boyfriend said: "It's OK. Don't worry!" But the girl said: "Please! I really want to go NOW!" So the boyfriend drove home. He got out of the car and went to open the door for his girlfriend. On the door handle there was a hook!

What would you have done if you had been one of the teenagers and you had heard the noise?

Would you have …

a stayed in the wood?
b driven home quickly?
c opened the car door?

If I had heard the noise,
I would have …
I wouldn't have …

The bath full of ice

A businessman from Ohio in the USA was in Las Vegas. In the bar of his hotel, he met an attractive woman and they had a few drinks together. After a while, the businessman became unconscious. When he woke up, he was sitting in the bath in his hotel room. The bath was full of ice, and next to the bath was a telephone and a note which said: "Call 911 (the emergency number in the USA) or you will die!" He called an ambulance. At the hospital, the doctor looked at him and said: "Someone has taken one of your kidneys!"

What would you have done if you had woken up in the bath full of ice?

Would you have …

a called 911?
b thought: "This is a joke"?
c been very frightened?

If I …,
I would …
I wouldn't …

[P] **2** **Two American high school friends are looking at a website about amazing coincidences and urban myths. Complete their conversation with the correct forms of the verbs.**

Jesse I think all these urban myths are unbelievable! I don't think they happened at all.

Tyler I'm not sure. This guy in the bath full of ice, for example. The doctor found someone had taken his kidney. I think that if he **(1)** hadn't called **(not/call)** 911, he **(2) … (die)**.

Jesse How do you know someone had really taken his kidney?

Tyler Well, the police believed it. They warned tourists in Las Vegas about it!

Jesse What about the hook-hand story? Do you believe that? Do you think that the guy **(3) … (kill)** them if they **(4) … (stay)** in the wood?

Tyler No, that's like lots of stories. It just means: 'Don't park in the woods!' and 'Be good!' What about you? Do you believe the amazing coincidences?

Jesse Yes, I know they sound almost impossible, but I'm sure most of them are true. Like that guy in Germany who fell from the plane. He **(5) … (die)** if he **(6) … (not/crash)** into that tree.

Tyler Yeah, I think you can say that if he **(7) … (hit)** the earth at 200 kph, he **(8) … (not/survive)**!

[P] **3** **Complete the sentences with words from the table.**

Making words negative			
un-	**im-**	**in-**	**ir-**
believable conscious happy lucky usual	possible probable polite	credible correct complete	regular relevant

1 Something which you can't believe is unbelievable or …
2 An answer which is wrong is …
3 Rainer Schuster fell three kilometres and survived because he landed in a tree. He was very …
4 When you use verbs in English, you have to be careful that they aren't …
5 I think you can do this. It isn't …
6 OK, but this isn't usual. In fact, it's very …
7 He never says 'please' or 'thank you'. He's very …

[M] **4** * **A German friend wants to know about the stories which you have read so far in this unit. Choose one and give the main facts and ideas in German in your own words.**

▶ **TIPS AND TRICKS**

to be happy = sich freuen, fröhlich sein

to be lucky = Glück haben

[R] **1** **Read the magazine article.**

Accidental inventions

The world of science and technology also has its amazing coincidences. Here are three famous products which their inventors invented by accident.

Microwave ovens

One day in 1946, an American scientist called Percy Spencer with the Raytheon Company was testing a 'magnetron' – a piece of equipment which produces the strong waves which we use in RADAR. Suddenly, he noticed that the bar of chocolate in his pocket had melted. At a special frequency, the waves from a magnetron could cook food! Percy did some more experiments with popcorn, eggs and other things, and a few months later, he built the first microwave oven. The first commercial microwave oven came onto the market in 1947. It was as big as a refrigerator and cost $5,000!

Percy Spencer

Velcro®

One afternoon in 1941, the Swiss scientist Georges de Mestral came home after a walk with his dog. His trousers were covered with burrs which had stuck to the cloth. Under a microscope, Georges noticed that the burrs had thousands of tiny hooks. Ten years later, after a lot of work and a lot of experiments, he had invented Velcro – a fabric which has thousands of tiny nylon hooks and which sticks to cloth like the burrs.

Post-it® notes

Two men were behind our third famous product. Both worked for the 3M company in the USA. The first, Dr Spencer Silver, did some experiments to find a strong 'superglue' in 1959. Unfortunately (or perhaps fortunately), he wasn't successful. The glue which he invented wasn't 'super strong', but 'super weak'. "Interesting," he thought, "but not very useful." Then one evening 21 years later, Art Fry was singing in his church choir. His hymn book was full of bookmarks for the different hymns, but they fell out all the time and it was very annoying. Suddenly, he remembered Dr Silver's glue. That was it! Little notes which you could stick to a book but then pull off again easily. Post-it notes were born.

Art Fry

[R/P] **2 Copy and complete the table. Try to use your own words to answer the question.**

	Microwave ovens	Velcro	Post-it notes
Inventor(s)	■	■	■
Date	■	■	■
How did he/they invent the product?	■	■	■

[R/P] **3 True or not true? Correct the sentences which are false.**

1 The first commercial microwave ovens in 1947 were much smaller and cheaper than they are today.
2 Originally, Georges de Mestral got his idea for Velcro from nature.
3 Burrs stick to your clothes because they have thousands of tiny nylon hooks.
4 Art Fry got his idea for Post-it notes from another scientist's work two years earlier.

[R] **4 Find the words in the text.**

1 You keep food cold in this in your kitchen.
2 You stick things to other things with this.
3 You do this to test your ideas (in a laboratory, for example).
4 You use these so that you can quickly find a page in a book.
5 Very small.

[P] **5 Translate the missing parts of the sentences.**

1 Wenn die Tafel Schokolade in seiner Tasche nicht geschmolzen wäre, hätte Percy Spencer den Mikrowellenherd nicht erfunden.
If the chocolate bar in his pocket ..., Percy Spencer ... the microwave oven.
2 Art Fry sang gerade im Kirchenchor, als er die Idee für Post-it notes hatte.
Art Fry ... in the church choir when he suddenly ... the idea for Post-it notes.
3 Er erfand Post-it notes, 21 Jahre nachdem Dr Silver seinen Klebstoff erfunden hatte.
He invented Post-it notes 21 years after Dr Silver ... his glue.

[I] **6 Talk in class. What do you think we can learn from these stories about successful scientists, and how they think and work? Try to find words to describe the people in the stories.**

[P/I] **7 Choose one of the projects.**

1 There are some good sites on the Internet where you can find out about 'unbelievable' things – urban legends, amazing coincidences, UFOs, ghosts etc. Find a good story and tell the class.
2 Produce a class magazine in which you collect all your favourite 'unbelievable' stories.

ICH KANN JETZT ...

- über Bedingungen in der Vergangenheit sprechen und schreiben (‚Wenn dies oder das passiert wäre, ...'),
- kleine Erzählungen und interessante Fakten über Firmengeschichten usw. lesen und genießen.

[R/P] **1** **Read about Craig, then listen.**
What information is missing on the message form below?

Craig Davis is one of the reporters at a local newspaper in Dover in the south-east of England. It is called the Dover Express. Life in his office is always hectic. The newspaper has seven reporters and they are always busy. They write their stories in the office, but they are also often out of the office for interviews, to take photos and so on. Craig is on the phone at the moment …

Craig Dover Express. Craig Davis speaking.
Man Good morning. Could I speak to one of your reporters, please? Her name's Jeri Stone.
Craig I'm afraid Jeri is out of the office at the moment. Can I take a message for her?
Man Yes, OK. Thanks.
Craig Can I take your name?
Man It's Novis, Robert Novis.
Craig Could you spell that for me, please?
Man N-O-V-I-S.
Craig Thanks, Mr Novis. And what's your message?
Man I have an interview with Jeri tomorrow morning at 10 o'clock, but I'm afraid I can't make it. Can she please call me to arrange another time?
Craig Has she got your phone number, Mr Novis?
Man Yes, I think so, but I'll give it to you again. It's Dover 877139.
Craig OK. I've got all that. I'll give Jeri your message as soon as she gets in.
Man Thanks very much.
Craig You're welcome. Bye now.
Man Goodbye.

CULTURE TIPS:
THE PHONIC ALPHABET

People on the phone sometimes use words to make clear what letters they are saying A – Alpha, B – Bravo etc.). Look on the Internet and find out more – it's very helpful for spelling names, giving addresses etc.

TELEPHONE MESSAGE

TIME	10.20
FROM	Robert … (1)
TELEPHONE NUMBER	Dover … (2)

Jeri

He has an interview with you tomorrow morning at … (3) but he can't make it. Can you please call him to … (4)?

Craig

[R/P] **2** **Craig is taking more messages for Jeri.**
Copy and complete the three message forms.

Message 1

TELEPHONE MESSAGE

TIME	10.30
FROM	... (1)
TELEPHONE NUMBER	Dover ... (2)

Jeri

She's a photographer in Dover and ... (3) some great photos for you of ... (4).
Can you ... (5) to arrange a time for a meeting?

Craig

Message 2

TELEPHONE MESSAGE

TIME	11.00
FROM	... (6)
TELEPHONE NUMBER	Dover ... (7)

Jeri

He thinks that ... (8). The man has a ... (9) and Mr. X... (10).

Craig ☺

Message 3

TELEPHONE MESSAGE

TIME	11.35
FROM	... (11)
TELEPHONE NUMBER	(Mobile number) ... (12)

Jeri

She ... (13) Can you ... (14)

Craig

[R/P] **3** **Take it in turns with a partner to be Craig at the Dover Express and a caller who also wants to speak to Jeri. Jeri is still out of the office, of course.**

Partner A: You are the caller. First, think of what you want to say to Jeri. Then phone Craig and leave a message.

Partner B: You are Craig. Speak to the caller and write a message for Jeri. Then show your message to your partner. Are all the details correct?

ICH KANN JETZT ...

- eine kurze telefonische Nachricht aufgeben,
- eine telefonische Nachricht zusammenfassen und ausrichten.

[R] **1 Read the business letter and answer the questions below.**

Modebaum GmbH

Felixstraße 18, 60318 Frankfurt am Main
Tel. +49 (69) 28 33 47
E-Mail: info@modebaum.de
Web: www.modebaum.de

15 September 20..

Elegant Fashions Ltd
2 Bradstone Road
MANCHESTER
GB-M8 8WA

Dear Sir or Madam,

Request for sales catalogue and price lists

We were interested in your clothes which were on display at the recent trade fair in Frankfurt am Main.

We are a German retailer which sells fashion clothes and we have 29 stores around Germany.

Could you please send us your current sales catalogue and price lists? We would also be grateful for information about your delivery times and trade discounts which you offer.

We look forward to hearing from you soon.

Yours faithfully,

Olga Scharapova

Olga Scharapova
PURCHASING MANAGER

CULTURE TIPS: BEGINNING AND ENDING A LETTER

All letters begin with **Dear** … When we know the person's name, we write **Dear Mr/Ms** … When we don't know the person, we write **Dear Sir or Madam**. Letters which begin **Dear (name)**, end with **Yours sincerely**. Letters which begin **Dear Sir or Madam**, end **Yours faithfully**.

Careful!

- The subject ('Request for sales catalogue') comes **after** Dear …
- The first sentence of the letter begins with a CAPITAL letter.

1 Who wrote this letter? When (on what date)? To what company in England?
2 What company does the writer work for? What is the writer's job in her company?
3 The writer of this letter doesn't know the name of the person he or she is writing to. How can you see this from the letter?
4 The writer asks about a 'sales catalogue', 'price lists', 'delivery times' and 'trade discounts'. What do we call these in German?

[P] **2** **Read these notes and the useful phrases, then write one of the letters below.**

Enquiry letters (Anfragen)

One very important type of business letter is an enquiry letter. The letter on page 148 is an example. Enquiry letters are the first contact between two companies, and they ask for information. Often the writer would like a current sales catalogue, price lists, and information about delivery times and trade discounts. Sometimes we also ask for samples (Muster) of products. At the beginning of an enquiry letter we normally say how we first found out about the company – for example at a trade fair (Messe) or in a trade journal (Fachzeitschrift). And we give some short information about our company.

Useful phrases

We were interested in		your products on display at the recent trade fair in …	
		your advertisement in this month's (trade journal).	
We are a German		retailer.	
		company which makes …	
Could you please send us		your current sales catalogue and price lists?	
		samples of your products?	
We would also	be grateful for	information about	delivery times.
	like	details of	trade discounts.
Thank you in advance for your help.			
We look forward to hearing from you soon/shortly.			

Letter 1

You work for a company in Germany which makes toys. (Think of the name and address yourself.) You were at a trade fair recently in Dusseldorf and you saw some products of an English company which makes packaging. The company's name and address is Pack-It-All, 47 Old Road, Rossendale, Lancashire OL3 2WW, England. Write to the company to ask for a sales catalogue and price lists. You would also like information about delivery times and trade discounts which they offer.

Letter 2

You work for a retailer in Germany which sells food and which has 15 stores around Germany. (Think of the name and address yourself.) You saw an advertisement in this month's European Business Magazine from a Scottish company which makes jam. Its name and address are: MacGregor Ltd, 21 Highland Road, Dundee DD7 7PR, Scotland. Write a letter to the company to ask for a current sales catalogue and samples of the products. You would also be grateful for details of trade discounts which the company offers.

ICH KANN JETZT …

- einen einfachen Geschäftsbrief auf Englisch verstehen,
- eine einfache Anfrage auf Englisch schreiben.

Unit 15 What on earth are we doing?

[P/I] **1** **Work in a small group. How many trees, plants, birds and insects can you name in English in two minutes? Write a list.**

[R] **2** **Claire Bishop is a British scientist. Where is she at the moment? What is she doing?**

"This is the Amazon rainforest in South America. I'm here at the moment with an international team of scientists. We're studying the forest, and the plants, animals, birds and insects which live here. This forest, and the other rainforests are very important for the environment. First, they produce around 20 per cent of all the earth's oxygen. Second, around three-quarters of all the species of plants and animals in the world live in the rainforests. In fact, there are so many here that we know only 10 per cent of them. And third, the rainforests are 'the world's pharmacy'. Half the drugs and medicines which we use today came first from plants in the rainforests. Maybe there are plants here which can cure cancer or AIDS. We just don't know. And there is one terrible problem. Last year, we destroyed 300,000 square kilometres of forest, that's an area almost as big as Germany. In fact, every year we destroy about the same area. Since the 1950s, we have destroyed 50 per cent of the earth's rainforests. If we don't stop, in the next 50 years, we will destroy the other 50 per cent."

[R] **3** **Complete the sentences with information from the text.**

1 The Amazon and the other rainforests are important for the …
2 They produce around 20 per cent …
3 There are so many species of plants and animals that scientists …
4 Also, the ideas for half the drugs and medicines we use today …
5 Every year we destroy around …
6 Since the 1950s, we … and if we don't stop, in the next 50 years …

[R] **4** **Here is a leaflet about rainforests. Find sentences in the text in exercise 2 which give the same information as the sentences 1–6 in the leaflet.**
Example: (1) Last year, we destroyed 300,000 square kilometres of forest.

Save the rainforests!

What is happening with the earth's rainforests?

(1) Last year, 300,000 square kilometres of rainforest around the world were destroyed. (2) In fact, every year about 300,000 square kilometres are destroyed.
That's an area almost as big as Germany every year!
(3) Since the 1950s, 50 per cent of all the rainforests on earth have been destroyed. (4) If we don't stop, in the next 50 years, the other 50 per cent will be destroyed!

Why is this so bad?

- (5) 20 per cent of all the earth's oxygen is produced by the rainforests.
- Three-quarters of all the species of plants and animals in the world live in the rainforests – and at the moment, we know only 10 per cent of them.
- (6) Half the drugs and medicines which are used today came first from plants in the rainforests.
It is possible that there are plants in the forests which could cure cancer or AIDS.

What can I do?

- Become a member of one of the organisations which fight the destruction of the rainforests.
- It is mostly big, international companies which cut down the trees. Find out which and don't use their products.

[P] **5** **Give the missing passive forms of the verbs.**
Example: The trees in the forests produce lots of oxygen. ACTIVE
Lots of oxygen is produced by the trees in the forests. PASSIVE

1. We find new drugs in plants in the forests all the time.
New drugs … in plants in the forests all the time.
2. In fact, we found half our drugs first in plants in the forests.
In fact, half our drugs … first in plants in the forests.
3. In the last 50 years, we have destroyed half the world's rainforests.
Half the world's rainforests … in the last 50 years.
4. If we cut down the rainforests, we will kill millions of birds and animals.
If the rainforests … down, millions of birds and animals …

GRAMMAR SPOT: Das Passiv

- Die Passivform von Verben wird mit einer Form von to be und dem Partizip Perfekt (3. Form) gebildet. 'Von' in Passivsätzen wird durch das Wort by ausgedrückt.
- Passivsätze werden vor allem beim Schreiben benutzt, um Fakten auf eher unpersönliche Weise zu vermitteln.

	to be	3. Form	
Lots of trees	are	destroyed	by big companies.
	were		
	have been		
	will be		

 → Grammar summary, page 204

[R/P] **1** **Look at the diagram and complete the sentences below with the passive forms of the verbs.**

Global warming

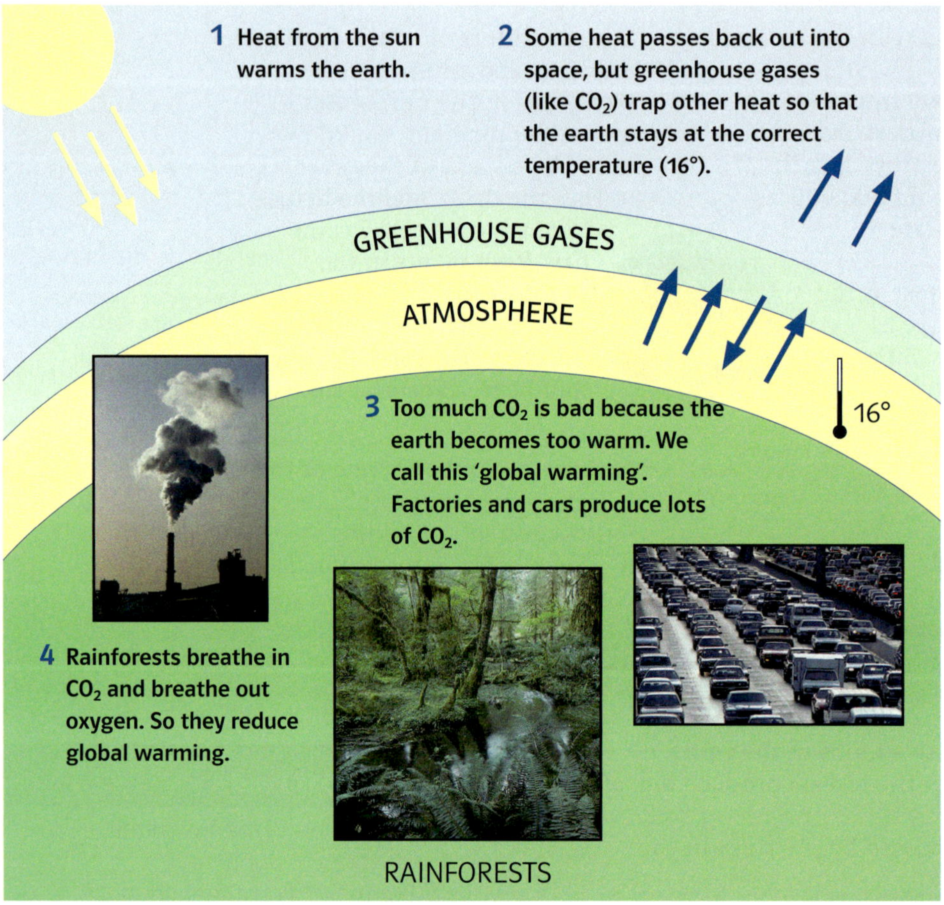

Example: The earth is warmed **(warm)** by heat from the sun.

1 Some heat passes back out into space, but other heat … **(trap)** by greenhouse gases (like CO_2) so that the earth stays at the correct temperature (16°).
2 Too much CO_2 is bad because the earth becomes too warm. This … **(call)** 'global warming'. Lots of CO_2 … **(produce)** by factories and cars.
3 CO_2 … **(breathe)** in by rainforests and oxygen … **(breathe)** out. Global warming … **(reduce)** by rainforests.

[P] **2** **Make passive sentences. Use the simple present.**

Example: cars/use/by/millions of people/every day
→ Cars are used by millions of people every day.

1 a lot of energy/use/the USA
2 millions of tonnes of CO_2/produce/factories around the world
3 thousands of kilometres of rainforest/destroy/every year
4 global warming/cause/people

[R] **3** **Choose the correct verbs in the list to complete the article below.**

were killed • was flooded • was made • were transported • was melted • was frozen

The next ice age?

Scientists don't always agree about global warming. Some believe that the earth will become warmer, others that it will, in fact, become colder. They say that ice at the north pole will melt and our weather will change. Then we will have another ice age. This was the story of the 2004 film, The Day After Tomorrow.

In the film, the ice at the north pole **(1)** … by global warming. There was a terrible storm and New York **(2)** … by a giant wave. Then suddenly, it became very, very cold and the city **(3)** … A scientist in the film survived, but millions of people across the USA **(4)** … At the end of the film, the survivors of the disaster **(5)** … to Africa and South America where they began a new life. Unbelievable? Well, yes and no. The theory is possible. But remember that the film **(6)** … in Hollywood, so everything was perhaps a bit more dramatic than real life!

[P] **4** **We can make many nouns in English if we add -ion to the verb. Use a dictionary or the wordlist at the end of the book to make nouns from these verbs. Then complete the sentences.**

produce → production • destroy • inform • invent • imagine • educate • decide

Example: Cars and factories produce CO_2. Our production of CO_2 is the main reason for global warming.

1 Another reason for global warming is the … of the rainforests. We destroy an area almost as big as Germany every year.
2 Governments around the world must educate people about global warming. … about the problem is very important.
3 You need a very good … to see what could happen in the future.
4 In the past, scientists often invented things which helped us with big problems. Hopefully, there will be … in the future which will help us with global warming.
5 If we want to stop global warming, we will have to make some difficult … We must decide what to do – and do it!

▶ TIPS AND TRICKS

Another ice age would be a disaster.

~~de~~saster

[M] **5** **A German friend is interested in the environment and asks you about the pages** * **so far in this unit. Make a list for her/him of ten important facts which you have learned. Write in German and use your own words.**

[R] **1** **Read the text.**

Energy from the wind

We produce a lot of CO_2 when we burn coal and oil (called 'fossil fuels'). These are often used in power stations, so one very good way to help with the problem of global warming is to use energy which does not come from fossil fuels. Two good examples are solar energy (energy from the sun) and hydroelectric energy (from water). A third, and one of the most important in Europe, is wind energy.

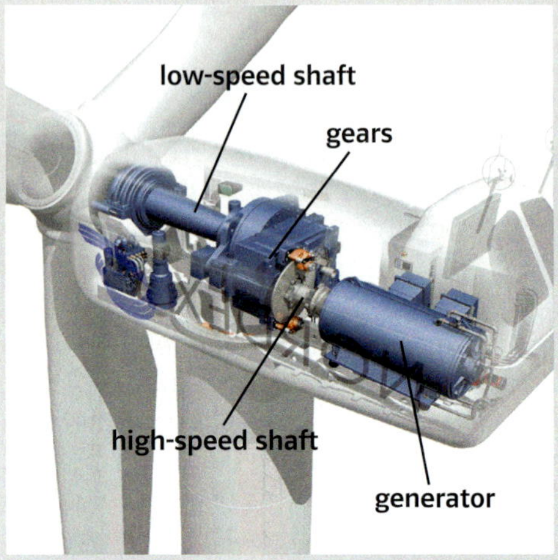

Wind energy is produced by the tall wind turbines which you sometimes see on top of hills when you travel on the motorway. Often, there are a number of these turbines together in 'wind farms'. Here's how a typical wind turbine works.

The turbine consists of a tower, rotor blades (normally there are three), and a nacelle, which sits on top of the tower and which contains all the important electrical and other equipment. As the wind blows, the rotor blades are turned at thirty to sixty times a minute. Inside the nacelle, the low-speed shaft is turned by the rotor blades. Thirty to sixty times a minute is not fast enough to produce electricity, so gears are used to increase the speed. With the gears, a second (high-speed) shaft is turned at 1,200–1,500 times a minute. The most important part of the turbine is the generator. It is connected to the high-speed shaft and it is used to produce the electricity itself.

[R] **2** **Complete the sentences with information from the text.**

1 Three important kinds of energy which do not come from fossil fuels are …
2 Of these, one of the most important in Europe is …
3 A group of wind turbines is a called a …
4 Wind turbines consist of three main parts: a tower, …
5 In a typical wind, the rotor blades are turned at between … and … times a …
6 The low-speed shaft is turned by the …
7 Gears are used to …
8 The high-speed shaft is turned at a speed of …
9 The electricity itself is produced by the …

[R] **3 Paul Richardson is a technician on a wind farm in the UK. He's talking about it and about wind energy in the UK. Listen and choose the correct answer.**

1 Paul works on a wind farm in the … of England.
a north b south
2 There are … wind turbines on the farm.
a five b fifteen
3 Each turbine is … metres tall.
a 70 b 17
4 The towers are made of …
a steel. b concrete.
5 People often say that wind farms are …
a noisy. b quiet.
6 The turbines are easy to look after and they last for about … years.
a twelve b twenty
7 Enough energy is produced by Paul's wind farm for … homes.
a 400 b 4,000
8 At the moment, the UK produces a lot … wind energy than Germany.
a more b less
9 But the government plans to increase the number of wind farms until … per cent of all energy comes from the wind.
a 10 b 20

[P] **4 Listen again to what Paul says. Then write a short summary in your own words. Begin like this:**

→ Paul works on a wind farm in the north of England …

[I] **5 Talk in class.**

From the different things which you have read in this unit, how important do you think the problem of global warming is? Why? What do you think we should do?

[P/I] **6 Choose one of the projects.**

1 Find out more about one aspect of global warming which interests you and give a short talk to the class.

2 The website young-europe.com is interested in the opinions of European teenagers about the environment. Write an email to the website with your ideas.

ICH KANN JETZT …

- komplexe Informationen verstehen und erläutern,
- über Umweltprobleme sprechen,
- Passivsätze benutzen, um Fakten zu vermitteln und Prozesse zu beschreiben.

[R] **1** **Here are some important departments in a typical manufacturing company. Can you match the English and German names for the departments?**

Marketing • Customer Service • Quality Control • Research and Development • Accounts • Sales • Distribution • Production • Purchasing	Verkauf • Forschung- und Entwicklung • Rechnungswesen • Qualitätssicherung • Marketing • Produktion • Kundendienst • Vertrieb • Einkauf

[R] **2** **What department do these people work in?**

1 We invent new products.

2 We buy the raw materials for the products.

3 We advertise the products.

4 We deal with customers' problems.

5 We manufacture the products.

6 We transport the products.

7 We look after the company's money.

8 We sell the products.

9 We check the products before they leave the factory.

CULTURE TIPS: ENGLISH FOR BUSINESS

Lots of English words are used in business in Germany, too – 'marketing' for example. Can you think of more?

[R] **3 The people on page 156 are all employees of a company called Suntech. It makes solar panels. How does a typical company like this work? Complete the text below with the names of the departments.**

How Suntech works

Solar panels on the roof of an office

The process begins with new products. These new products are invented by the **(1)** Research and Development Department. Next, the company must make the products, but first it needs raw materials – metals, plastics, glass and so on. The raw materials are bought by the **(2)** … Then the products are manufactured in the company's factory by the **(3)** … Department. Before the products can leave the factory, they must be perfect, and so they are checked by the **(4)** … Department. Now the company has its products, but how do customers know about them? Well, the company advertises them – in newspapers, on the Internet, on TV maybe. Products are advertised by the **(5)** … Department. The products are sold to customers by the **(6)** … Department. When a customer buys a product from Suntech, the solar panels are transported to their homes or offices. This is called 'distribution' and products are transported by the **(7)** … Normally, everything is fine, but if a customer has a problem, it is dealt with by the **(8)** … And finally, the company earns money. The company's finances are looked after by the **(9)** …

[I] **4 Interview a partner.**

You work in a department at Suntech. Make notes about your job. (Invent details yourself.) Take it in turns to interview your partner and write a short profile.

Name:
Department:
What my department does in the company: → In my department we …
Things I do in a typical day: → In a typical day I …
I like my job because:

What department do you work in?

What does your department do?

Can you describe a typical day?

Why do you like your job?

ICH KANN JETZT …

- wichtige Abteilungen in einem typischen Unternehmen nennen und über ihre Arbeit sprechen,
- ein kurzes Interview führen und die Informationen zusammenfassen.

[R] **1** **The pictures and texts below are from a leaflet called 'Save Energy!'
Match the pictures and the suggestions.**

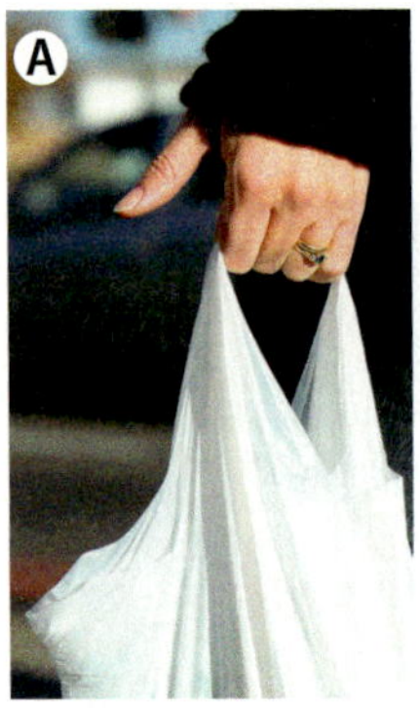

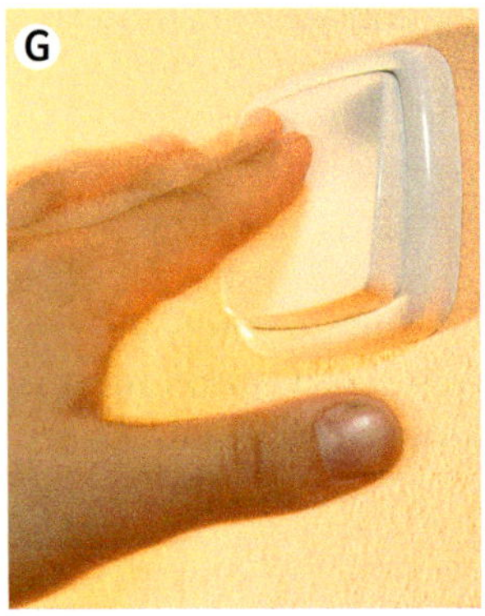

Save Energy!

1 30% of all energy is used in the home. One thing which you can do to save energy at home is to switch off lights when you don't need them.
2 When your computer is 'on standby', it still uses 50% of its normal energy. Switch off your computer when you are not using it.
3 Houses lose almost 50% of their energy if they are not insulated. Always make sure that your house or flat has good insulation.
4 Each litre of petrol which we use produces about 2 kg of carbon dioxide. Don't use your car if it isn't necessary. For longer journeys, always try to travel by bus or train.
5 And for shorter journeys, walk or go by bike. (You'll also be fitter if you do this, too!)
6 We use energy to produce water for our homes, and saving water is a very good way to save energy. One idea is to put a brick in your cistern. That way, you'll use less water.
7 We use energy when we manufacture things: metals and plastics, for example. Recycle, recycle, recycle! Take your cans and bottles to recycling centres.
8 And keep the plastic bags which you get at the supermarket. You can use them again!

[R] **2 The missing words in these sentences were all on page 158. What are they?**

1 When you use things again and again you … them.
2 It is a good idea to … off lights and computers when you don't need them.
3 If you put … in the roof of your house, it will stay warmer and you will lose less energy.
4 In a toilet, water comes from the …
5 If you use less energy, you … energy.

R/P] **3 Pauline Smith works for Friends of the Earth. Today she is doing a survey about energy. Look at Pauline's questions below and listen to the two interviews. Make notes of the people's answers, then choose one person and write a text about her or him.**

[1] **4 Now YOU. Do Pauline's survey in your class and then talk about the results. How green is your class?**

1 How many journeys do you make in a typical week? How many of the journeys do you make by car?

2 How often do you leave lights or computers on when you don't need them?

a often	b sometimes	c never

3 How often do you recycle rubbish (for example, bottles, cans, paper and plastic)?

a often	b sometimes	c never

4 How well do you think your house or flat is insulated?

a well	b it's OK	c badly

5 When you shop at a supermarket, do you:

a take your own shopping bag?
b get a plastic shopping bag from the store?
c use the plastic shopping bags again?

ICH KANN JETZT …

- über Energiesparen sprechen und schreiben,
- an einer Umfrage teilnehmen und über die Ergebnisse sprechen.

Unit 16 Talking about sport

[P/I] **1** **What's your favourite sport? Do you support a team? Do you have a favourite sportsman or woman?**

[R] **2** **Read about the football match.**
Yesterday afternoon, there was a dramatic football match in England between Manpool United and Liverchester. Liverchester scored three goals in the first half, and at half time the score was 3-nil. But then in the second half, Manpool scored four magnificent goals! The final score was 4–3 to Manpool.

[R] **3** **After the match, the two team managers talked to reporters. Which manager said what?**

I'm very happy with the result.

I'm a bit disappointed with the result.

We played badly in the first half, but the lads were magnificent in the second.

We played well in the first half, but the second half was a disaster.

We'll win next time!

[P] **4** **Mark Mason was one of the reporters at the match. Look at the Grammar Spot below and give the missing verbs in his article.**

Manpool beat Liverchester

By Mark Mason

In a dramatic match at Northfield Park yesterday, Manpool beat Liverchester 4–3. Manpool now go to the top of the league.

Liverchester scored three goals in the first half, but then after half-time, Manpool scored four, including two by the team's youngest player, Andy Frazer.

After the match, Manpool's manager Clive Townsend said that he (1) was very happy with the result. He said that Manpool (2) … badly in the first half, but that in the second his lads (3) … magnificent.

Liverchester's manager Marcel Arnaud said that he (4) … a bit disappointed with the result. He said that Liverchester (5) … really well until half time, but that the second half (6) … a disaster. Arnaud was still very confident about his team, however. He told reporters that Liverchester (7) … next time!

[P] **5** **Here are some comments by fans after the match yesterday. Report what they said.**

1 William: "Manpool are the best team in Europe!"
→ William said that Manpool …
2 Charlotte: "Andy Frazer was totally amazing. He was the best player on the field."
3 Pete: "Marcel Arnaud is rubbish! We need a new manager."
4 Daisy: "Liverchester are still the best. We'll beat Manpool next time!"

GRAMMAR SPOT: Reported speech (die indirekte Rede)

Wir benutzen die indirekte Rede, um zu berichten, was jemand in der Vergangenheit gesagt hat:

"I'm happy." (direkte Rede)	He said that he was happy. (indirekte Rede)

In der indirekten Rede verschieben wir die Zeitformen der Verben:

Direkte Rede	Indirekte Rede
Simple present: "I am happy."	Simple past: He said that he was happy.
Simple past: "We played well."	Past perfect: He said that they had played well.
Will: "We will win next time!"	Would: He said that they would win next time.

→ Grammar summary, page 205

[P] **1 Last week, Mark Mason interviewed Penny Hopper, a British international swimmer. Read what Penny said and complete the sentences below.**

I train five hours every day from Monday to Saturday.

I swim in the pool, I run, and I do exercises at a gym.

My training is different every week. One week I train for stamina, and another week for power or speed.

I love all sports but I don't have much time for them. I'm always busy with my swimming.

Penny told Mark that …

1 she trained five hours every day from Monday to Saturday.
2 she … in the pool, she …, and she … exercises at a gym.
3 her training … different every week. One week …
4 she … all sports, but …

[R/P] **2 Greg Heuberger is a disabled athlete in the States. Read below what Greg said in an interview about his life, then look at the sentences. Correct the sentences which are not true.**

"At high school my favourite sport was athletics, and after school I joined an athletics club in my hometown, Boise, Idaho. In 2002, I won the 100 and 200 metres in a national amateur athletics competition and in January 2003, I decided to become a professional. Two months later, I was in a car accident. I was in hospital for nearly six months. My friends were fantastic, however. One day, they gave me a sports wheelchair! I learned that there were lots of people like me, and in 2005 I took part in my first wheelchair athletics competition. One day, hopefully, I'll take part in the Paralympics – the Olympic Games for disabled athletes."

Greg said that …

1 after school, he had joined an athletics club in Chicago.
   → Not true. He said that after school, he …
2 at high school, his favourite sport had been athletics.
3 in 2002, he had won the 100 metres in a national competition.
4 in about March 2003, he had been in a motor-cycle accident.
5 his friends had given him a sports wheelchair.
6 one day, hopefully, he would take part in his first wheelchair athletics competition.

[P] **3 Said or told?**

Example: Marcel *said* that his team would win next time.

1 Clive … reporters that he was happy with the result.
2 Greg … in the interview that his favourite sport at high school had been athletics.
3 My friend … me that he supported Liverchester.
4 But he … that he didn't like Marcel Arnaud as a manager.

[P] **4 These English college students talked in a lesson yesterday about sport. What did they say?**

→ Sue said (that) her …
Paul told the class (that) his …

Sue

Paul

Chloe

Malik

Becky

Jason

[P] **5 Write 80–100 words with your ideas about sport – your favourite team, favourite sport, favourite sportsperson, or just sport in general.** *

[R] **1** **Read the magazine article.**

Around the world in 71 days, 14 hours, 18 minutes and 33 seconds

On 8 February 2005, at a quarter past midday, Ellen MacArthur sailed her trimaran into a harbour on the south coast of England. She had just broken the world record for the fastest solo journey around the world by boat.

At first sight, Ellen doesn't seem to be a 'typical' sailor. She is only 1m 57 tall and is a very quiet person. Her parents weren't sailors, and Ellen was born in 1978 in a part of England which isn't near the sea. As a young girl, however, she loved boats and sailing. At school, she saved all her pocket money and bought a small yacht. At the age of 18, she sailed solo around Britain.

Ellen's round-the-world journey in 2004 and 2005 began on the north coast of France and ended in England. On the way, she sailed past Africa, Australia and South America. The total distance was 43,000 kilometres. It is hard to imagine Ellen's amazing journey alone around the world. There were storms and icebergs, and on day 63 she almost hit a whale. One night, she had

to climb the 30-metre mast, in the dark and in a storm, to repair a sail. And during the 71 days of her journey she slept only five hours a day, in short 'catnaps' of 15 minutes.

There is no doubt that Ellen MacArthur is an extremely brave and incredibly determined person.

She is also a very modest person. Although she was alone on her boat, she would tell you very quickly that she had been part of a team – from the British company B&Q which gave the money for the boat, to the technicians and doctors who she could call on her radio 24 hours a day. And what did she say about her journey? "It's much more dangerous to drive your car!"

[R/P] **2** **Finish the sentences using information from the text. Use your own words when you can.**

1 Ellen's journey around the world began on 28 November 2004 and ended …
2 During her journey she sailed 43,000 kilometres from …
3 Ellen broke …
4 Ellen doesn't seem to be a 'typical' sailor because …
5 Some of the very dangerous things on her journey were …
6 Something which shows that Ellen is a very brave and determined person is …
7 Ellen was alone on her boat but we must remember that …
8 At the end of her journey, Ellen said that …

[R/P] **3 True or not true? Correct the false sentences.**

1 When Ellen sailed into the harbour on 8 February 2005, she had just broken the world record for the fastest journey around the world by a woman.
2 Most sailors look like Ellen, have her personality, and have parents and a birthplace like her.
3 Ellen paid for the yacht she bought at school herself.
4 Ellen's journey was 43,000 kilometres long and lasted a year.
5 There were lots of dangers for Ellen during her journey, and from the moment she began until the moment she finished, she couldn't sleep for longer than 15 minutes each time.
6 Ellen loves telling people very loudly about her journey and how brave she was.
7 During Ellen's journey, there were people she could call day or night if she needed help.
8 After her journey, Ellen said that it was much more dangerous to drive your car than to sail around the world.

[P] **4 Give words which mean the same as these words in the text.**

1 fastest (line 7)
2 began (line 25)
3 hard (line 3)

[P] **5 Give words which mean the opposite of these words in the text.**

1 quiet (line 12)
2 tall (line 11)
3 dangerous (line 17)

[P] **6 Give the corresponding ...**

1 verb: sailing → to sail
2 noun: to see
3 adjective: danger
4 adverb: easy

[I] **7 Talk in class. What do you think of Ellen MacArthur and what she did?**

[P/I] **8 Choose one of the projects.**

1 A press conference.
Find out about a famous sportsman or woman that you like. Then have a press conference in your class. Imagine that you are the famous person. The class must ask you questions about your life, then write a short article.

2 Do a survey in your class about sport. Here are some ideas, but you can think of others.
What's your favourite sport (1) to play (2) to watch?
Famous sports stars, like some footballers, earn too much money. True or false?
Sport is important in the world because it can bring countries together. True or false?
...

ICH KANN JETZT ...

- berichten, was Leute in der Vergangenheit gesagt haben,
- über das Thema Sport reden und schreiben,
- einen längeren und komplizierteren Text verstehen und besprechen.

[R] **1** **Read about CVs, then find the English expressions in Richard's CV below for:**

Lebenslauf • Schulbildung und Qualifikationen • Interessen • Lieblingsfächer • weiterführende Schule • Grundschule • Berufserfahrung • Fertigkeiten • persönliche Angaben

What is a CV?
When you apply for a job or a traineeship, one of your most important documents is your CV (Curriculum Vitae), your 'Lebenslauf'. CVs are often different in different countries, and it isn't easy to talk about your qualifications – they are different in different countries, too. Here is a typical CV for a young English person, Richard. Richard studied at a college in England. He finished in June 2007 and he got an NVQ (National Vocational Qualification) in Sport and Sports Science. NVQs are the important job qualifications which British students get at the end of their college course.

CURRICULUM VITAE

Personal details

Name: Richard Long
Address: 15 Kings Road
Littletown
LT3 4RT
Date of birth: 14 April 1989

Education and qualifications

Primary School: 1994–2000 Hamilton Primary School, Littletown
Secondary School: 2000–2005 Littletown Comprehensive School
Favourite subjects: Sport, Mathematics, English
College: 2005–2007 Littletown College of Further Education
Qualification: NVQ in Sport and Sports Science

Work experience

Part-time work: 2005–2007 Assistant at Littletown swimming pool

Skills

Computers: Microsoft Word, Microsoft Excel
Languages: French (basic)
Other: Red Cross First Aid Certificate

Interests

All sports
Reading
Travel

CULTURE TIPS: EXPLAINING GERMAN WORDS

To explain a German qualification, type of school etc to an English or American person you can use the phrase 'That's like ... in the UK/USA':

"I go to a Berufsfachschule in Germany – that's like an FE college in England."

2 Answer the questions about Richard's CV.

1 What is Richard's address? Which part of the address is the 'post code'?
2 When was he born?
3 Where did he go to primary school?
4 When did he start and finish primary school?
5 Where did he go to secondary school?
6 When did he start and finish secondary school?
7 What were his favourite subjects at secondary school?
8 When did he start college?
9 What course was he on at college?
10 What qualification did he get at college?
11 Does Richard have any work experience – for example, did he have a part-time job while he was at college?
12 What computer skills does he have? Which computer programs can he use?
13 What do you think Richard's mother tongue is? What other language(s) can he speak? How good is his knowledge of the other language(s)?
14 Does he have any other useful skills or qualifications?
15 What are Richard's hobbies and interests?

3 Now YOU.

1 Imagine that you finished your course at college last month. Write a CV for yourself. Use Richard's CV as a model.
2 Now work with a partner. Ask your partner about her/his CV and write a short summary.

When were you born?

Where did you go to primary/secondary school?

When did you start and finish …?

What were your favourite subjects?

When did you start college? What course …?

What qualification …?

→ Bernd/Martina was born on …
(S)he went to … primary school …

4 Richard would like to work for a time in Germany and he has sent his CV to the manager of a swimming pool in your town. The manager doesn't speak English and asks for your help. Give the main facts about Richard in German in your own words.

ICH KANN JETZT …

- einen typischen englischen Lebenslauf verstehen und auf Deutsch erklären,
- einen einfachen Lebenslauf auf Englisch schreiben,
- Fragen zu einem Lebenslauf stellen und beantworten.

[R] **1** **Safety at work is very important. The people below (A, B and C) all have dangerous jobs, and they are all wearing protective clothes and equipment. Look at the pictures and say which of the three is wearing ...**

1 boots
2 a face shield
3 gloves
4 goggles
5 an ear muff
6 an overall
7 a hard hat

A

B

C

[P] **2** **Why do people wear the things above? Make sentences with these words.**

Example: head → You wear a hard hat to protect your head.

1 ears
2 hands
3 eyes
4 face
5 feet
6 normal clothes

[I] **3** **Talk about the people in the pictures. Can you name their jobs? Can you name more dangerous jobs?**

[R] **4** **Signs are important in dangerous workplaces. Look at the signs below. Which signs give you the following information?**

1 You mustn't go out here.
2 You mustn't go in here.
3 Careful! Lasers!
4 This liquid burns!
5 Maximum speed 25 kph!
6 No mobiles!
7 You can stop a machine with this button.
8 You mustn't eat or drink here.
9 You must wear a hard hat.
10 You must wear goggles, an ear muff and boots.

> ▶ **TIPS AND TRICKS**
>
> Remember:
>
> You **must** …
> = Man muss …
>
> You **mustn't** …
> = Man darf nicht …

[M] **5** **The manager of your workshop wants to have the signs below in English and German. He asks you for a list of the signs in German. Can you help?**

A

B

C

D

E

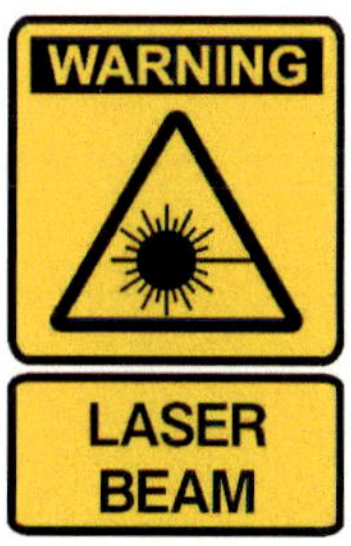

F

G

H

I

J

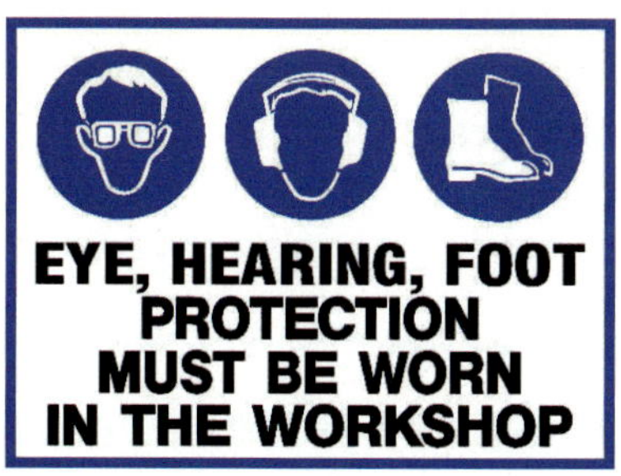

K

L

M

> **ICH KANN JETZT …**
>
> - über Sicherheit am Arbeitsplatz sprechen,
> - einige wichtige Schilder verstehen und auf Englisch erklären.

Unit 17 Working abroad

[P/I] **1 Would you like to work abroad in Britain or another country for six months?**

[R] **2 Read about Anna.**

The person using the computer is Anna from Germany. She's looking at a website called www.rausvonzuhaus.de. It's for young Germans wanting to work abroad. Anna finished her course at college a couple of months ago, and now she wants to work in Britain for a year before she starts a traineeship. On the website, she learns that there are lots of organisations helping young people like her. She even finds that young people working abroad for a short time can sometimes get money from the government.

[R] **3 Find sentences in the text which give the same information as these sentences.**

1 The person who is using the computer is Anna.
2 The website is for young Germans who want to work abroad.
3 There are lots of organisations which help young people like Anna.
4 Young people who work abroad can sometimes get government money.

GRAMMAR SPOT: Gekürzte Relativsätze (1)

Relativsätze werden manchmal gekürzt, indem ein Partizip statt who/which + ein Verb benutzt wird. Man kann eine -ing Form (Partizip Präsens) benutzen, um Relativsätze im present continuous oder im simple present zu kürzen.	The person who is using the computer is Anna. (present continuous)	The person using the computer is Anna.
	The website is for young Germans who want to work abroad. (simple present)	The website is for young Germans wanting to work abroad.

[P] **4 Here are two extracts from the website. Complete them with a shortened relative clause.**

AU PAIR
Au pairs live in a family and look after children. They also have to do some housework. People **(1) … (who work)** as au pairs get free accommodation and also some pocket money. Ninety per cent of au pairs are girls, but there are jobs for boys **(2) … (who want)** to be au pairs, too. Some families like having a 'big brother' for their kids.

VOLUNTEER WORK
Case study: Joachim Müller from Germany.
This is Joachim Müller. He's a typical volunteer. He's helping to build a youth club in Romania this year. The people **(3) … (who are standing)** next to Joachim in this photo are other volunteers from around the world. Young Germans **(4) … (who do)** volunteer work like Joachim get money from the government.

[R] **5 Read more about Anna and find the three sentences which give this information:**

1 There are lots of projects which are organised by environment agencies.
2 People who are employed on the project in Scotland live in a castle.
3 Anna finds the telephone number which is given on the website.

Anna thinks that a job as a volunteer would be great. She likes practical work and she finds that there are lots of projects organised by environment agencies in different countries, restoring old buildings for example. She finds that there's one project in Scotland to restore a castle. And people employed on the project even live in the castle. "Das wäre was für mich!" she thinks. She finds the telephone number given on the website and picks up the phone …

Grammar Spot: Gekürzte Relativsätze (2)

Relativsätze im Passiv werden mit einer 3. Form des Verbs (Partizip Perfekt) gekürzt.	There are lots of projects **which are organised** by environment agencies.	There are lots of projects **organised by** environment agencies.

→ Grammar summary, page 206

[P] **1** **Saskia is also from Germany. She's spending a year as an au pair in the States. Here she is with her American family, the Greenwalds. Who's who in the picture? Make sentences 1–3 below shorter, then make more sentences from the table.**

1 The woman who is wearing a blue top and white shorts is Mrs Greenwald.
→ The woman wearing …
2 The boy who is pouring lemonade is the Greenwalds' son, Wayne.
3 The girl who is sitting nearest to the camera is the Greenwalds' daughter, Marcie.

The man The woman The boy The girl	wearing holding taking	a yellow T-shirt some food from Saskia a dish of salad a blue dress sunglasses a pink top	is Mrs Greenwald. is Mr Greenwald. is Wayne. is Marcie. is Mrs Kowalski, a neighbour. is Saskia.

[P] **2** **Some American and British words are different. Make sentences like the example with words from the boxes.**
Example: People living in Britain say 'garden', but people living in the States say 'yard'.

In Britain they say …
garden • biscuit • holiday • lift • motorway • petrol • shop • town centre • trousers • underground

In the States they say …
cookie • gas • subway • vacation • yard • highway • elevator • downtown • store • pants

[P] **3** **Saskia sees notices, newspaper headlines and advertisements like those below every day in the States. Say them again as full sentences with who or which and a passive verb.**
Example: Do not park. Cars which are parked here will be towed away! → (A)

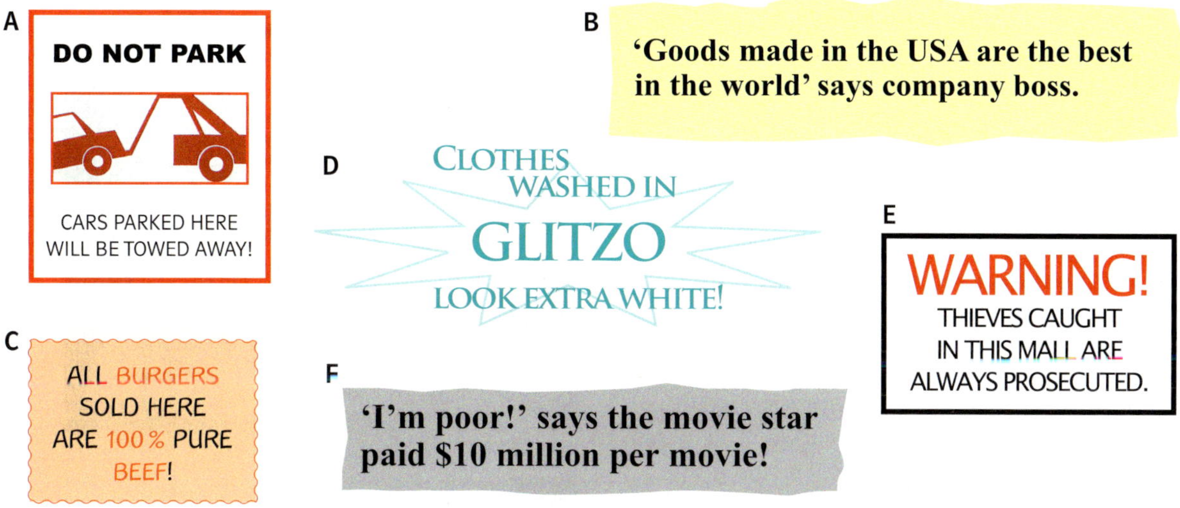

[P] **4** **Make shorter sentences with an -ing form (Partizip Präsens) or an -ed form (Partizip Perfekt).**

1 People who look after a family's children are called au pairs.
2 People who do voluntary work are called volunteers.
3 The person who is standing at the front of the classroom is my teacher.
4 The telephone number which is given on the website is 0207 755410.
5 She's working on a project which lasts six months.
6 The car which is parked in the street is Sam's.
7 People who are employed here always like their job.
8 Food which is cooked at home always tastes better.
9 The person who is using the mobile over there is Tom.

[P] **5** **Copy and complete the table, then write sentences with four of the words. (You need not complete the grey boxes.)**
Example: The website helped me very much – in fact, it was extremely helpful.

noun	verb	adjective	adverb
possibility		possible	possibly
help	**(1)**	helpful	helpfully
organisation	**(2)**		
(3)	to employ		
difference	to differ	**(4)**	differently
interest	to interest	**(5)**	interestingly
(6)	to govern		
improvement	**(7)**		
volunteer	**(8)**	voluntary	voluntarily

17 Working abroad

[R] 1 **Read the web page.**

Case studies > New Zealand > Dieter Veith (Germany)

A YEAR IN NEW ZEALAND

When Dieter Veith finished his apprenticeship as a carpenter in Germany two years ago, he decided to spend a year as a volunteer before he started working full time. Germany has a number of excellent organisations helping young people to find volunteer work, and it was through one of these organisations that Dieter found a project in New Zealand. Together with three other volunteers from around the world – one from Japan, one from Poland, and one from the United States – Dieter worked in a children's home near the New Zealand capital, Wellington. The home – run by the New Zealand government – provides accommodation for around 200 children. Many of the children living in the home are from disaster areas in the South Pacific and have lost their parents in floods or earthquakes. Dieter's main job in the home was to help the full-time staff, but as a qualified carpenter, he quickly found that he could also help with lots of day-to-day repairs and small construction projects. "I was busy from morning to night", says Dieter "but the year I spent in New Zealand was the best in my life. I learned so much about the world – and about myself – in those 12 months. And when I started looking for jobs back here in Germany afterwards, I found that employers were extremely interested in my experiences as a volunteer abroad. The boss of the company where I work now had been a volunteer, too, when he was younger, so we got on well together straight away."

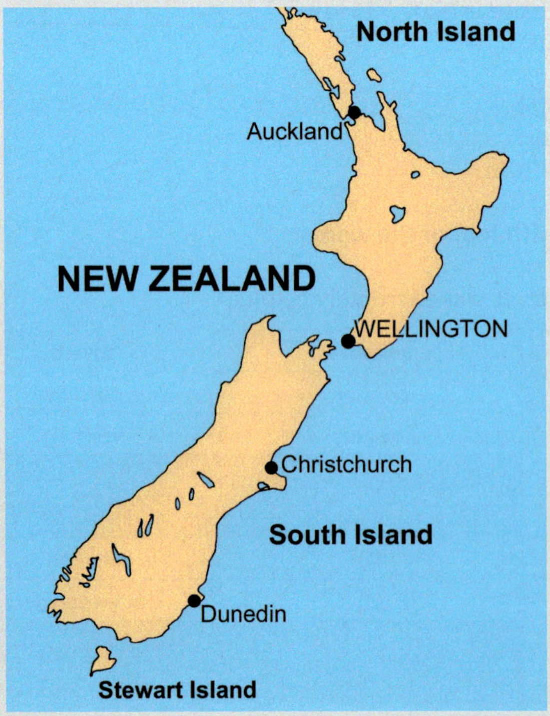

Click to hear Dieter

R/P] **2 True or not true? Correct the false sentences.**

1 Before he went to New Zealand, Dieter had been an apprentice in Germany.
2 There are only one or two organisations helping young people to find work as volunteers abroad.
3 Dieter worked in a children's home near the capital city of New Zealand.
4 He worked in the home with three other volunteers from Germany.
5 There are around 200 children living in the home.
6 Many of the children don't have parents because they died in disasters.
7 Dieter's main job in the home was to repair things.
8 Dieter said that the year he had spent in New Zealand had been the best in his life.
9 Dieter found that it was an advantage that he had spent a year abroad as a volunteer.

[P] **3 Give the corresponding ...**

to decide	→ noun: decision
to work	→ noun: ...
repair(s)	→ verb: ...
organisation	→ verb: ...
qualification	→ adjective: ...
extreme	→ adverb: ...

[P] **4 There are two mistakes in each sentence. Find and correct them.**

1 I decided to spent a jear as a volunteer before I started working.
2 I worked in a home in New Zeeland which was run by the goverment.
3 Employers were extremely intrested in my expreinces as a volunteer.

R/P] **5 Dieter is talking about his year in New Zealand.**
Listen and make notes under the headings below, then give a short report.

- Dieter's first week in New Zealand
- New Zealand the country
- The kids in the home
- The other volunteers
- Speaking English every day
- Feeling homesick

[I] **6 Talk in class. What do you think of Dieter's experiences in New Zealand? Would you like to work as a volunteer? Why (not)?**

P/I] **7 Choose one of the projects.**

1 Look online for information about au pair and volunteer work abroad and make a summary of the most important points in English.

2 New Zealand is a great country! Did you know, for example, that the film The Lord of the Rings was filmed there? Find out more and tell the class.

ICH KANN JETZT ...

- komplexere Sätze (z. B. mit Partizipien) verstehen,
- detaillierte Informationen verstehen, zusammenfassen und besprechen,
- über eine Arbeitsstelle im Ausland schreiben und diskutieren.

[P] **1 Read about Gabi and answer the questions about the job advert.**

Gabi Giesen is a student at a college in Stuttgart. She's on a business course, and at the moment, she's looking for a traineeship. This morning, Gabi saw this advertisement in the newspaper. It's by a big German retail company, but like a lot of big German companies nowadays, Jupiter's company language is English.

Hilfe! Ich muss mich auf Englisch bewerben!

TRAINEESHIPS

The German electronics retailer Jupiter is looking for young people interested in **Traineeships** in its branches around Germany. Candidates must currently be students on business or information technology courses in Germany. They must be keen to learn, be ready to work hard in a dynamic, modern company, and have a good knowledge of English. For further information, send your CV together with a covering letter in English to

1 Jupiter is a retail company. What kind of products do you think it sells in its shops?
2 The company is offering traineeships – where?
3 What kinds of students can apply?
4 How does the advert describe the personal qualities and the skills of the people who it is looking for?
5 What two things must you send to the company for further information?

[R] **2 With help from her friends and her teachers at college, Gabi writes her CV and a covering letter. You can see the letter on the next page. How does Gabi say these things:**

Meinen aktuellen Lebenslauf lege ich bei.

In den letzten zwei Jahren war ich als … tätig.

Ich würde mich sehr über die Möglichkeit freuen für Ihre Firma zu arbeiten.

Mit diesem Schreiben bewerbe ich mich …

Ich werde die Schule … beenden.

Für ein Vorstellungsgespräch stehe ich jederzeit zur Verfügung.

Mr Heinz Ockler
Personnel Department
Jupiter AG
Postfach 22186
70174 Stuttgart

Rosenstraße 20
70175 Stuttgart

19 April 20..

Dear Mr Ockler,

Traineeship

I am writing to apply for one of the traineeships which you advertised in the Stuttgarter Nachrichten of 19 April 20..

I am currently a student on a business course at a vocational college in Stuttgart. I will complete my course in June this year. I enclose my current CV.

For the last two years, I have worked part-time as a sales assistant in a large department store here in Stuttgart. I am extremely keen to learn, enjoy working hard, and I am one of the top students in my class in English. I would very much welcome the opportunity to work for your company.

I would be available for an interview at any time.

I look forward to hearing from you.

Yours sincerely,

Gabi Giesen

Gabi Giesen

[P] **3 Now YOU. Think of a traineeship which would interest you and write a letter.**

A letter of application

- I am writing about/I would like to apply for the traineeship which you advertised in … of (date).
- I am writing in response to your advertisement in … of (date).
- I am currently …
- I enclose/Please find enclosed my current CV.
- For the last … years, I have worked …
- I have work experience as …
- I would (very much) welcome the opportunity to work for/to start my career with your company.
- I would be available for an interview at any time.
- I look forward to hearing from you.

CULTURE TIPS: BEGINNING AND ENDING LETTERS

Do you remember the rules in English? Check back on page 148 if you're not sure.

ICH KANN JETZT …

- eine kurze Bewerbung auf Englisch schreiben.

[R] **1** **Christoph is a student at a vocational college in Germany. Last week, his English class practised some interview questions. Read the questions.**

1 Where were you born?
2 How long have you lived in the town where you live now?
3 Do you have any brothers and sisters?
4 What are your hobbies?
5 What's your favourite food?
6 What are your favourite subjects at college?
7 What time do your lessons normally begin and end each day?
8 How long have you learned English?
9 Tell me a bit about the town where you live.
10 Have you ever been to Britain or the USA?
11 What do you like doing in the evening?
12 What do you like doing at the weekend?
13 Do you have a favourite sport?
14 What sort of music do you like best?
15 Do you have a favourite movie? What is it? Can you tell me a bit about it?
16 How often do you use a computer?
17 How often do you use the Internet? What sorts of things do you do online?
18 Can you name a famous businessperson? What do you know about her or him?
19 Can you name a famous company? What can you say about it?
20 What job do you think you will have five years from now?

[R/P] **2** **Listen.**

Today, Christoph is having an interview. The interview is in German, but the interviewer asks him some questions in English. What answers does he give? Listen and make notes, then give a short report about Christoph.

→ Christoph was born in …

[I] **3** **Now YOU.**

Work with a partner. Take it in turns to be an interviewer who is asking some questions in English. Use Christoph's questions. You can think of some more questions too.

[R/I] **4** **What do you think is important in an interview? How can you make a good impression? Read the tips below, then talk in class.**

FIVE TIPS FOR A PERFECT INTERVIEW

- **Be a good listener.**
  Listen carefully when the interviewer is speaking and look interested. Never interrupt the interviewer.

- **Be honest.**
  Never say things which are not true in an interview. The interviewer will probably know! If you don't understand a question, ask. If you don't know an answer, say so.

- **Don't talk too much.**
  Answer the question, but then stop talking. Let the interviewer ask the next question.

- **Think about your body language.**
  When you sit still, you look confident. If you fidget, you look nervous. Sit up straight. If you slump, you look bored.

- **Always be positive.**
  Don't criticise your college, your teachers or your friends. If you are negative about them, then perhaps you will be negative about your new company!

[M] **5** **A German-speaking friend has an interview next week and wants to know about the interview tips above. Give the main ideas in German.**

ICH KANN JETZT …

- typische persönliche Fragen in einem Interview beantworten,
- einem Interview zuhören und den Inhalt weitergeben,
- über Interviews diskutieren.

Revision (2)

1 Read about Ben on his Internet blog and answer the questions below.

Ben's Blog

Hello! I'm Ben and this is my blog. I hope you'll enjoy reading a bit about my everyday life here in England and my ideas about the world.

1 September My first job

I finished my course at an FE college here in England three months ago at the end of June and got my NVQ in Sport and Sports Science. Then I went on holiday. I spent July in Canada. I came back here in August. I got a part-time job in a big sports shop in town. I really enjoyed it. One day, I was working in the shop when Greg, the manager, said: "Would you like a permanent job here, Ben?" I said "Yes". He said: "OK!". And that was it, the shortest job interview in history! Today was my first day full time. My first, real job.

1 When did Ben finish his college course?
2 What did he do after he had finished his course?
3 What did he do after he had come back to England?
4 What happened one day while Ben was working in the shop?

The past perfect and the past continuous

After Ben had finished his course he went on holiday. (Past perfect)
Ben was working in the shop one day when the manager said: "Would you like a job?" (Past continuous)

When do we use these two tenses?

2 Here's more of Ben's blog. Complete it with who or which.

18 September Good and bad things about my job

The job here is great. The people (1) … work here are all young and we are good friends. Greg, the guy (2) … is the manager, is fine. The big company (3) … owns all 42 shops in the UK is famous, and the goods (4) … we sell are high quality. Bad things about the job? Some of the customers (5) … we get in the shop are a bit difficult. Of course, 'the customer is always right', so we must always be polite. My biggest problem is that I have to work Monday to Saturday. (Fortunately, I don't have to work on Sundays). And Saturday I normally play football for my team. I think I'll talk to Greg about this soon.

3 In two sentences in exercise 2, you can leave out who and which. Which two?

Relative pronouns

When do we use who and which in relative sentences?
When can we leave out who and which?

4 Say if these sentences in Ben's blog in exercise 2 are true or not true. Correct the false sentences.

1 Greg has to work on Mondays.
2 He mustn't work on Sundays.
3 He needn't be polite with his customers.

Must, have to ...

List the English verbs for:
muss – muss nicht – darf nicht.

5 Infinitive or -ing form? Choose the correct form.

20 October
Say hello to the new Benmobile

OK, it isn't a Rolls Royce, but it's mine! I couldn't afford **(1) to buy/buying** a car when I was a student, but I saw this great old Mini in the paper last weekend and decided **(2) to buy/buying** it straight away. Fantastic! I love **(3) to drive/driving** around town in it and next month I hope **(4) to go/going** on holiday to Wales with a couple of guys from the shop. I like the black colour, but a friend suggested **(5) to paint/painting** it red. Now I'm not sure ...

Verbs + infinitive; verbs + -ing form

After some verbs we use the infinitive, after others the -ing form. Find examples in Ben's blog above.

6 Find one conditional sentence type 1 and two conditional sentences type 2 in Ben's blog below. Choose one of his questions and write him an email.

1 November
Thanks for all the emails ... and some more questions

A big 'thanks' to everyone who emailed me with suggestions for colours for the Benmobile. I think I'll keep it black!
OK. Yesterday, some friends and I played the game 'What if...?' Here are two of the questions for you...
1 If you were an animal, which animal would you like to be?
2 If you had a time machine, which time (past or future) would you visit?
If you send me your answers, I'll put them on the blog next week.

Conditional sentences (If-Sätze)

- **Types 1 and 2:** what tenses do we use in types 1 and 2? When do we use use type 1 or type 2? (tip: 'concrete' or imaginary situations?)
- **Type 3:** complete this type 3 sentence. What tenses do we use? Translate it into German.
  If I ... (see) you, I ... (say) 'hello'! (But I didn't see you, so I didn't say 'hello'.)

7 Here's Ben's blog for 15 December. Answer the questions below.

15 December I sometimes get angry

Here are some facts about the goods in our shop. We sell trainers. They are sold in our shop for £50-£80. The trainers aren't made here in Europe. They are made (often by children) in poor countries and they earn perhaps £2 a day for their work. Footballs are sold in the shop for £20-£40. They are also made by people in poor countries. The workers are paid 10p per football. Question: Who gets all the money?

1 How much are trainers sold for in Ben's shop?
2 Where are the trainers made?
3 How much do the people who make the trainers earn?
4 Is the situation the same for footballs?

The passive

Active: We sell trainers in our shop.
Passive: Trainers are sold in our shop.

Find the **passive** verbs in Ben's blog. How do we make the **passive** form?
How do we say 'von' in passive sentences in English?

8 Finish the sentences below this part of Ben's blog. Use reported speech.

30 January Goodbye Michael Warner?

So will Manpool's best player Michael Warner leave Manpool and go to play for a Spanish team? Michael said:

MONDAY:	"I'm very happy at Manpool."
TUESDAY:	"No, a Spanish team didn't offer me £80m last week."
WEDNESDAY:	"Yes, a Spanish team offered me a lot of money last week."
THURSDAY:	"The weather in Spain is fantastic."
FRIDAY:	"I'll visit Madrid next week for a holiday."

Example: On Monday, Michael said that he was very happy at Manpool.
1 On Tuesday, he told reporters that a Spanish team … offered him £80m.
2 On Wednesday, he said that…
3 On Thursday, Michael told…
4 On Friday, …

Reported speech (indirekte Rede)

- How do verb tenses change when we use reported speech?
- What is the difference between 'he said' and 'he told'?

9 Make the sentences below shorter with an -ing form or -ed form.

1 The person who writes this blog is Ben.
→ The person writing …
2 The car which is standing in the street is mine.
3 Footballs which are made in poor countries are expensive in Europe.

Shortened relative sentences

When do we use an -ing form and when do we use an -ed form to shorten sentences with who and which?

Anhang

Extra reading texts

1 American high schools (after unit 9)

1 Read the text once and find out:

- How old are American teenagers when they start high school?
- When does the day in a typical high school start and finish?
- What happens for most pupils in high school in the afternoons?

You have probably seen American high schools in movies or TV programmes, so you know that they are a very 'typical' part of American life. All young Americans go to high school – or at least start high school; about 5 per cent 'drop out' and don't finish.

Let's look quickly at the American education system in general. In the USA, education begins at the age of six and lasts for everyone until they are 18. Most children also spend a year in 'kindergarten' before school at the age of five. Americans call the 12 years of school from 6–18 'grades'. The first school which children go to is elementary school, and is for the first to fifth grades, that is for ages six to 11. Next comes middle school or 'junior high school': sixth to eighth grades, ages 12–14. And then, finally, there is high school (sometimes called 'senior high school') for the four years of ninth to twelfth grades. A typical high school student is between 15 and 18 years old.

High schools can be different in different parts of America because all the states in the USA have their own laws about education. But here is a fairly typical day. It begins early at 7.30. Students arrive on foot or by one of the famous 'school buses' and for the first 15 minutes from 7.30–7.45 they go to their 'homeroom' – the classroom where they meet their 'homeroom teacher'. She or he talks to them about general things, or problems, and makes announcements. The first lesson of the day begins at 7.45. Lessons normally last 45 minutes, with five minutes between each lesson. Students have around an hour for lunch at midday and most eat at school. The last lesson of the day finishes at 2.30.

The last classroom lesson finishes at 2.30, but for most students this is not the end of the school day. Activities, and in particular sports activities, are an extremely important part of high school life. Football (American football, that is) is probably the most important activity of all. High school teams play in their own leagues and hundreds of students from the school come to the matches and watch their teams enthusiastically. There are always 'cheerleaders' with the teams, groups of girls who dance and march.

Americans always remember the years which they spend at their high school. For many, they are the best years of their life.

(409 words)

to drop out die Schule abbrechen • **education system** Bildungswesen, Schulsystem • **grade** Jahrgangsstufe • **their own laws** ihre eigenen Gesetze • **to make an announcement** eine Ansage machen

2 Read again and answer these questions.

1 What percentage of young Americans start high school? How many finish?
2 What are the three main kinds of schools in America, and what do Americans call the 12 years of school?
3 Why are high schools in different states not always exactly the same?
4 Give one of the things that a homeroom teacher does with her or his class in the mornings.
5 How long are lessons in a high school?

6 The players in high school football teams are boys. What can girls do to take part actively in the football matches?
7 How do Americans often remember their years at high school?

3 Find these useful words and expressions in the text in English.

1 wahrscheinlich (line 1)
2 zumindest (line 3)
3 im Alter von (line 6)
4 schließlich (line 9)
5 allgemeine Dinge (line 16)
6 insbesondere (line 21)

2 London (after unit 10)

1 Before you read the text, try to answer the questions below. Then read and check your answers.

- How many (millions of) people live in London?
- Can you name two famous places in London?
- What important event will take place in London in 2012? (Tip: sport)

London is Britain's capital and by far its biggest city. Around 7.2m people live here permanently – about one in seven of the population of England. Hundreds of thousands of commuters also arrive in London every day to work, and at 9 o'clock in the morning and again at 5 o'clock in the afternoon the London underground (Londoners call it 'the tube') is full of people. These are the 'rush hours', and they are not good times to travel if you are a visitor! You also notice immediately when you visit London that it is a very multicultural city. About half of all Britain's ethnic minority people live here in the capital. Altogether, the people of London speak over 250 different languages.

London has many different faces. For the people who live in London every day, it is just 'home'. Londoners often say that the city is like a lot of small villages. The part of London where they live has its own shops, markets, cinemas and restaurants and they usually visit the city centre only to shop for clothes or for a special meal.

For businesspeople, London is a world business centre. The most famous part for business is the 'City' (with a capital 'c'). It is here that you find the Bank of England, the London Stock Exchange (with New York and Tokyo one of the three most important in the world) and the offices of big companies. All of the UK's media companies are in London, too, including all the national newspapers and the BBC.

For tourists, London is simply one of the most popular cities in the world. Around 13m people visit the city every year to go to its theatres and museums; to take photos of Buckingham Palace, the Houses of Parliament, and Trafalgar Square; to shop in Oxford Street; or just to sit in one of London's parks. Thirty per cent of London is parks and it is one of the 'greenest' cities in Europe. One of London's newest sights is the London Eye, near the Houses of Parliament next to the River Thames. It opened in 2000, and from the top of the 130 metre-high wheel, you can see all over London. In 2012, London will probably get even more visitors. The Olympic Games will take place in London that year.

London really has something for everyone. Go and visit it one day!

(403 words)

commuter Pendler/in • **underground** U-Bahn • **rush hour** Hauptverkehrszeit • **to notice** merken • **altogether** insgesamt • **face** Gesicht • **stock exchange** Börse • **sight** Sehenswürdigkeit • **from the top of** vom höchsten Punkt • **wheel** Rad

2 Answer the questions.

1 Why are 9 am and 5 pm not good times to travel in London?
2 How do Londoners themselves often describe London?
3 What is 'the City' in London?
4 Why is London one of the greenest cities in Europe?
5 Why do you think visitors to London like the London Eye so much?

3 Give these useful words and expressions from the text in German.

1 by far (line 1)
2 immediately (line 6)
3 Houses of Parliament (line 20)
4 River Thames (line 23)
5 even more (line 25)

4 Complete the definitions.

1 Someone who travels into a city each day to work is a …
2 Someone who lives permanently in London is a …
3 A city where people from many different ethnic groups live is a … city.
4 A place where people buy and sell shares (Aktien) is a …

3 Shopping on the Internet (after unit 11)

1 Before you read the text, write down one reason why you think many people like shopping online, and one reason why some people don't like it.

In Europe and the USA, over 60 per cent of people who use the Internet at home have now bought at least one thing online, and with broadband in more and more homes, and with many TVs which now connect to the Internet, this number is growing very quickly every year. So why do – or don't – people like shopping online?

Lots of surveys show that there are three main reasons why people often prefer the Internet to a normal shop. The first is convenience. It is quick, you don't have to travel to town, and the companies which sell goods online deliver them directly to your door. For some people – old people, for example – the Internet can be the only way to shop at all. The second reason is cost. You can 'shop around', compare prices, and find the best deals. Online retailers often have 'special offers' – free delivery, for example – and so goods can be cheaper than in the shops. The third reason is that online shopping is not as stressful as normal shopping. It is private, you have time to think, and you are not in a crowded shop or busy town centre. Of all three reasons, convenience is the most important for over 75 per cent of people.

If over 60 per cent of people now shop online, there are also almost 40 per cent who don't like Internet shopping, and the same surveys show why this happens. Again, there are three main reasons. The first, and most important, is security. People are simply not sure that it is safe to shop online. Newspapers often have stories about criminals who steal credit card details or websites which aren't real websites but just a 'scam'. People are particularly worried when they buy goods from another country, and don't know the laws which those countries have about e-commerce. The second and also very important reason is that online, you can't see and touch goods as you can in a shop. You can't get help from a shop assistant. And if you are buying clothes, you can't try them on. Perhaps for this reason, the most popular goods on the Internet are not things like clothes, but music downloads and airline tickets.

And finally, the third reason is that some people like shopping. Convenience and price are fine, but they just like going to town, meeting people and looking round shops.

(407 words)

to connect (to) angeschlossen werden (an) • **to grow** wachsen, zunehmen • **main reason** Hauptgrund • **convenience** Komfort, Bequemlichkeit • **to shop around** Preise vergleichen • **deal** Angebot • **retailer** Einzel-händler/in • **special offer** Sonderangebot • **crowded** überfüllt, voll • **security** Sicherheit • **to steal** stehlen • **scam** Betrug • **to touch** anfassen, berühren • **to try on** anprobieren

2 Answer the questions.

1 What are two reasons why the number of people who shop online is growing quickly?
2 Why is shopping online so convenient?
3 Give two reasons why goods which you buy online can be cheaper.
4 Why isn't shopping on the Internet as stressful as shopping in town?
5 How does reading newspapers sometimes make people nervous about shopping online?
6 Security is one reason why people sometimes don't like shopping online. What other two reasons does the text give us?

3 Match the verbs on the left and the phrases on the right. Then use three complete expressions to write three sentences yourself about shopping on the Internet.

1 to shop	a quickly
2 to grow	b credit card details
3 to deliver	c online
4 to compare	d things (e.g. clothes) with your hand
5 to steal	e goods directly to your door
6 to touch	f prices
7 to look	g round (e.g. shops)

4 Route 66 (after unit 12)

1 Read the text once and find out:

- Where does the road begin and end?
- How long is it?
- Can you still travel along Route 66 today?

Route 66 is a part of American history. Today, it isn't a real road which you can travel on from end to end. Only about 80% of the old road still exists, and in some places it has become a normal, modern US highway. But if you have a map, and if you really want to find the road, it is possible. The American Highway Department (which looks after roads in the USA) has put up signs for 'Historic Route 66' and travelling along the road is a popular holiday for people from all over the world.

Route 66 begins in America's biggest industrial city, Chicago, in the north-east, and ends in Los Angeles in the south-west. Between the two, it runs through eight American states. After Chicago, Illinois, it crosses the wide, flat prairies of Missouri, Kansas and Oklahoma; past the oil-wells of Texas, then crosses the deserts of New Mexico and Arizona (it is very close here to the Grand Canyon), and finally arrives at the coast in LA, California. 2,448 miles, 3,940 kilometres.

People began building Route 66 in 1926. In those days, there were no American highways as we know them today, and Route 66 was the first, long-distance road across America. Because the road was mostly flat, and it was very quick, it soon became popular with truck drivers. Soon, little restaurants, cafés, and motels started appearing beside the road, then, as other people began using the route, little museums, zoos, and other attractions appeared – all with owners who wanted to attract visitors. The signs and advertisements became more and more amazing, some bigger than houses. Some of America's famous restaurants started here: McDonald's in San Bernardino, for example, and the 'Big Texan' Steak House where, if you could eat all of your enormous 2.5 kilo steak, your meal was free!

Route 66 began disappearing in the 60s and 70s, but in every state today there are Route 66 societies which try to preserve the road and its history. Many of the old restaurants and other places along the route are now museums.

One great way to see Route 66 is on a Harley-Davidson motor bike. From its offices in Chicago and LA, you can rent a bike for a holiday on the historic road and travel alone or in a group. If you love the 'old America', then travelling along Route 66 on a Harley is definitely for you!

(407 words)

to be part of something zu etwas gehören • **department** Amt • **(road) sign** (Straßen)schild • **to run through** führen durch • **to cross** durchqueren • **prairie** Prärie • **oil-well** Ölquelle • **long-distance (road)** Fern(straße) • **attraction** Attraktion • **owner** Besitzer/in • **to attract** anziehen • **to disappear** verschwinden • **society** Verein • **to preserve** bewahren, erhalten • **definitely** ganz bestimmt, sicherlich

2 True or not true? Correct the false sentences.

1 People from all over the world like travelling along Route 66.
2 Route 66 runs through six American states.
3 It is easy to visit the Grand Canyon from Route 66.
4 Route 66 was the first long road across America.
5 Truck drivers began using the road because there were lots of good restaurants.
6 In one restaurant on Route 66, your meal was free if you could eat the 2.5 kilo steak.
7 You can still see some of the old restaurants on Route 66 because they are museums.
8 The text says that one great way to see the road is to buy a Harley-Davidson.

3 Find the words or phrases in the text which complete these sentences.

1 People often need a … to find roads and towns. (line 3)
2 A town where there are a lot of factories etc. is an … town. (line 7)
3 In 1926, there were no highways in America … today. (line 14)
4 A person who owns a restaurant is the restaurant's … (line 18)
5 Some people travel along Route 66 on a Harley together with other people … (line 28)

5 English around the world (after unit 13)

1 Before you read the text, can you write down:

- four countries where English is the language of the country?
- one reason why so many people around the world today also speak English?

When we read about Canada or Australia or the USA, we accept naturally that people there speak English. Of course – it is the language of the country. But why? These places are very far from England! Why do so many people around the world speak English?

For Canada, Australia and the USA – and in fact for lots of other countries such as New Zealand, South Africa, India and several countries in Africa (altogether around 1.5 billion people), the reason is that they were once part of a worldwide British Empire. From 1620, when the first English settlers arrived in America on the ship called the Mayflower, and for the next 300 years, the British travelled all over the world and established colonies. The small colony in New England in the north-east of the modern USA was the first. Then came Canada in 1763; in 1770, Australia (where the British sent all the criminals they didn't want!); in 1840, New Zealand; and from around 1850, India and many countries in Africa. In 1921, the British Empire covered 37 million square kilometres (about a third of the earth), and one person in four worldwide spoke or heard English every day.

The British Empire began disappearing after World War II, but English as a world language didn't disappear. In fact, in the 20th century it became even more important. Canadians, Australians and so on continued speaking English, of course. But now English started becoming popular in other places. The reason this time wasn't the British Empire. It was the importance of the USA, now the most powerful nation on earth. English became worldwide the language of American culture – the language of Coca-Cola, of chewing gum, of McDonald's, of jeans, and, of course, of movies.

Today, English is the world language. It is the international language of business, of sport, of science, of the media, of technology, of computers, – and, of course, of the Internet. This new global English isn't 'British' or 'American'. People speak it with many different accents, and if they use some slightly different words or phrases in their country, it isn't 'wrong'. Nobody knows exactly how many people in the world will soon speak English, but right now, about 1 billion people – including you! – are learning it. One thing is certain, however: there will be many more English speakers in the world than 'English' people in Britain.

(404 words)

such as wie (zum Beispiel) • **empire** Reich • **settler** Siedler/in • **to establish** gründen • **square kilometre** Quadratkilometer • **importance** Wichtigkeit, Bedeutung • **powerful** mächtig • **chewing gum** Kaugummi • **science** Wissenschaft • **slightly** etwas, leicht • **including** einschließlich

2 True or not true? Correct the false sentences.

1 The first British colony was in New England in America.
2 Australia became a British colony in 1840, and India in 1921.
3 In 1921, everyone in the world spoke English.
4 The reason why English became even more important in the 20th century was that America became the most powerful nation on earth.
5 The Internet is one of the reasons why English is a world language today.
6 The text says that only people who live in England speak English correctly.

3 Find these words and phrases in the text in English.

1 eigentlich (line 4)
2 namens (line 7)
3 jede vierte Person (line 13)
4 diesmal (line 17)
5 eins ist aber sicher (line 26)

6 Manchester old and new (after unit 14)

1 Read the text once and find out:

- Why was the city important between 1750 and 1950? What happened in the 1980s and 90s?
- What typical 'old Manchester' product does Jack Botham make and sell?

Manchester is one of England's biggest cities after London. It is in the north-west of England, not far from other famous northern cities like Liverpool. And, of course, it has a very famous football team. Manchester is not just 'another typical English city', however. The city in the past and the modern city now show us exactly how Britain was, and how it is today.

The story of Manchester begins with the Industrial Revolution. From around 1750, engineers in Britain started inventing machines like the steam engine and machines to spin cotton. The first factories appeared in northern England (where there is coal, iron, water and all the other things necessary for industry). With its factories and the cotton from its colonies, Britain quickly became the richest country in the world, and Manchester was the centre of the British cotton industry. In the 19th century, around four-fifths of all the cotton clothes in the world came from Manchester. Although the city itself was extremely rich, however, life for the people who worked in the factories – many of them only small children – was extremely hard. They worked long hours for very little money and lived in small houses in narrow, dirty streets. The sky was permanently black with smoke from the factories.

Manchester remained a big, industrial town and the centre of the world textile industry until about 1950. Then other countries began producing cheaper goods. The factories in northern England closed, there was mass unemployment, and cities like Manchester and Liverpool 'died'. But this isn't the end of the story. In the 1980s and 90s, hundreds of new companies in the media, financial, IT and other industries began moving into the city. It got a new city centre with modern, attractive buildings and developed the best public transport system in Britain. The narrow, dirty streets disappeared, and the old factories became modern flats. Many big, international companies opened new offices in the city. Restaurants, cafés, theatres and bars opened, and only London now has more night clubs. Manchester is again one of Britain's most successful cities.

A few things of the 'old' Manchester remain, however. In a street near the city centre you can find 'Jack Botham's Pie Shop'. Jack makes Manchester's best meat pies. He and his family have been selling the pies, and the people of Manchester have been buying and eating them for over 100 years. The only difference today is that Jack also sells his pies on the Internet!

(417 words)

steam engine Dampfmaschine • **to spin (cotton)** (Baumwolle) spinnen • **coal** Kohle • **iron** Eisen • **necessary** nötig • **narrow** eng • **smoke** Rauch • **to remain** bleiben • **mass unemployment** Massenarbeitslosigkeit • **night club** Nachtlokal • **(meat) pie** Fleischpastete

2 Answer the questions.

1 In what region of England is Manchester? Why was this region important during the Industrial Revolution?
2 Why exactly was Manchester so rich in the 19th century?
3 Were factory workers in Manchester also rich?
4 Why did factories in northern England start closing in around 1950?
5 Give two examples of how Manchester today is a successful, modern city.
6 Where can people who don't live in Manchester (or even in England) buy Jack Botham's pies?

3 Look at the Grammar Spot, then answer the questions with the present perfect continuous.

1 How long have Jack Botham and his family been selling meat pies in Manchester?
→ He has been …
2 How long have the people of Manchester been eating Jack's pies?
3 How long have you been living in the town where you live now?
4 How long have you been sitting in the room where you're sitting now?
5 How long have you been learning English?
6 How long have you and your friends been using mobile phones?

GRAMMAR SPOT: Das present perfect continuous

- **Das present perfect mit since und for**
  Das present perfect wird oft mit since und for benutzt, um die Frage: How long … ? zu beantworten (Unit 5):
  How long has Nick lived in Australia? He's lived there for 16 years.
- **Die Verlaufform des present perfect: das present perfect continuous**
  Wollen wir die Länge und Stetigkeit der Handlung betonen, können wir in solchen Sätzen auch eine Verlaufsform des present perfect (das present perfect continuous) benutzen.
  Diese Zeitform wird gebildet aus has/have + been + -ing-Form.

How long has Mrs Jackson been living in her house? She has been living there for over 60 years! How long have you been learning English? I have been learning English since I was about 10 years old.	I have he has she has we have you have they have	I've he's she's we've you've they've	been	learning

TIPP: Wenn Sie selber schreiben oder sprechen, bleiben Sie beim present perfect: In diesen Sätzen wird es immer richtig sein. Seien Sie nur bereit, dem present perfect continuous in Texten zu begegnen.

7 Life in the future (after unit 15)

1 Read the text once. Which one of the following things does the text NOT talk about?
clothes • jewellery • food in the future • talking computers • computers which can understand human feelings • virtual reality in schools • how people can be wrong about the future

What can we expect from the world of the future? Three things are certain: life will be very different; the changes will be exciting; and you will see them! Here are a few ideas about life in the future from various experts.

Why have just a picture on your T-shirt when you can have a moving video picture? Many experts say that clothes in the future will be very different. New textiles and new computer technology will come together so that clothes can show video pictures, change colour (for example, become bright and colourful when we meet a friend!), and become warmer or cooler as the weather changes. Clothes can also become 'computers'. They will be able to store music (like your MP3 player now), connect to the Internet when you want information, and store personal information about you. If you don't want your T-shirt to do this, you can use your watch or jewellery. These new 'intelligent' clothes won't need batteries. The warmth from your body or solar energy will be enough.

Computers will be, of course, at the heart of many changes in our life in the future, and the next big step will be how we communicate with them. In the next few years, computers will begin understanding our voices and we will simply talk to them – and they will talk to us. Many experts also say that computers will become more 'human'. They will know from our voice and our face if we are happy or sad, relaxed or stressed, and will react to our feelings. Already in some call centres, computers analyse the voices of callers and warn the call centre workers if a person is angry.

You have probably seen 'virtual reality' in movies – where someone wears a helmet and gloves which are connected to a computer, and can then see, hear and feel imaginary situations. Virtual reality will become much more important in the future, sometimes just for fun (imagine a computer game in which you really meet aliens!), or for more serious things. Virtual reality computers are already used by pilots and surgeons for training, but in the future, schools could have virtual reality classrooms where you can see the past in your history lesson.

Before we become too confident about these ideas, however, we should remember some things which people have said in the past. In 1903, a professor of mathematics at a university in America wrote: "Heavier-than-air flight is impossible. People will never fly". Six months later, the Wright Brothers flew the world's first plane.

(430 words)

change (noun) Veränderung • **various** verschiedene(r, s) • **moving (adjective)** (sich) bewegend • **bright and colourful** hell und bunt • **jewellery** Schmuck • **step** Schritt • **voice** Stimme • **human** menschlich • **call centre** telefonischer Kundendienst • **helmet** Helm • **gloves** Handschuhe • **alien** Außerirdische/r • **surgeon** Chirurg/in • **confident** zuversichtlich • **heavier-than-air flight** Fliegen mit Luftfahrzeugen, die schwerer als Luft sind

2 True or not true? Correct the false sentences.

1 Many experts say that in the future we will be able to store music and personal information in our clothes.
2 We won't be able to have conversations with computers in the next few years.
3 Computers will become more 'human', that's to say, they'll begin walking and eating.
4 There will be virtual reality computer games in the future where you will be able to see, hear and feel imaginary situations – like meeting aliens.
5 Virtual reality is already used now by some people for training.
6 In the future, school pupils will be able to travel in time.
7 Six months before the Wright Brothers flew the first plane, an American professor had said that people would never fly.

3 Match parts A and B of these expressions from the text, then use three of the complete expressions to write sentences yourself about life in the future.

A	B
1 moving video	a energy
2 to change	b a person's feelings
3 to store	c colour
4 solar	d flight
5 to react to	e reality
6 virtual	f picture
7 heavier-than-air	g information

8 Drugs and sport (after unit 16)

1 Before you read the text, write down:

- one reason why perhaps people use drugs in sport
- one example of how people use drugs in sport
- one reason why people should not use drugs in sport.

Imagine. You're a professional, international sportsman or woman. Six months from now, you're going to run in the Olympics, or take part in the world basketball championship, or try to break a world record in skiing. If you're successful, you (and your team) will be famous, perhaps even rich. Thousands, maybe even millions of people in your country will be proud and happy. You'll have a medal which you can show to people for the rest of your life. And then you know that there is a drug, maybe a drug which no-one will ever be able to detect. If you take it, you'll run faster, play better, be stronger. Will you take the drug, or will you say 'no'?

Drugs in sport are nothing new. In fact, the problem is very old. There are stories about athletes in the Olympic Games in Greece 2,000 years ago who ate a special kind of mushroom to become stronger and who were banned from the competition. But it was in the 20th century that drugs became a serious problem in sport, as more and more sportspeople competed in more and more competitions. Some of the first serious cases were in the Tour de France cycle race in the 1940s and 50s, when two cyclists died from drugs. Later, there were many famous examples of athletes from Eastern Europe, especially the old East Germany, who used drugs to break a whole series of world records. One female athlete took so many drugs that she became a man. Ben Johnson was another very famous Canadian sprinter who took drugs at the Olympics and who has never taken part in them again since then.

Many different kinds of drugs are used in sport, not just drugs which help you to run faster. Strong painkillers, for example, can help sportspeople in hard contact sports like boxing and ice hockey. Sedative drugs can keep snooker players calm so that their hands are steady. And there are drugs which can keep you awake so that you can train longer.

Why is it so important, then, that drugs aren't used by sportspeople? The answer is very simple. In all sports, people must win fairly, that's to say, they must all have the same chance. Also, although world records get better all the time, they must be real records. If someone does something which is only possible because of chemicals, the record has no meaning. And finally, drugs are dangerous and sportspeople who take them can damage their health (and their minds). There's no point in being the world champion if you die as a result.

(438 words)

proud stolz • **medal** Medaille • **to detect** aufspüren, nachweisen • **to ban** verbieten • **a (whole) series of** eine (ganze) Reihe von • **sprinter** Kurzstreckenläufer/in • **painkiller** Schmerzmittel • **sedative** Beruhigungsmittel • **steady** ruhig • **to keep awake** wach halten • **fairly** fair, gerecht • **real** echt • **chemicals** Chemikalien • **(to have no) meaning** bedeutungslos, wertlos sein • **mind** Psyche • **there's no point (in)** es hat keinen Sinn (zu) • **as a result** als Folge

2 Answer the questions.

1 In the first paragraph, the text asks readers to answer a question. What is the question?
2 What 'drug' did Greek athletes use in the Olympic Games 2,000 years ago?
3 Why did drugs become a serious problem in the 20th century?
4 The text gives three examples of some people who took drugs. In which three countries were these people athletes?
5 Give an example from the text of how people in different sports use different types of drugs.
6 What three reasons does the text give why people in sport should not take drugs?

3 Give the missing English words in these expressions from the text.

1 to … a record	einen Rekord brechen
2 … new	nichts Neues
3 … … more sportspeople	immer mehr Sportsleute
4 to die … drugs	an Drogen sterben
5 to keep someone …	jmdn. wach halten
6 to have the … …	die gleiche Chance haben
7 drugs can … your …	Drogen können Ihrer Gesundheit schaden

9 How different are the British and the Germans? (after unit 17)

1 Read the text once and say which statement below you think describes best the main idea.

- There are a few important differences between British and German people.
- British and German people are totally different.
- There aren't any important differences between British and German people.

We all know that the modern world of work is global. We also know that there are cultural differences between people from different nations. 'Other countries, other customs'. But we usually think that these differences exist only between us Europeans and, say, the Japanese or perhaps the Americans. There aren't any problems, we say, when Europeans meet Europeans.

In fact, there are very important differences between Europeans, and if we have to work with people from other European countries, we have to know what they are. Let's take the British and the Germans as an example. On the whole, people from Germany and Britain are very similar. We're all northern Europeans (so, for example, we have perhaps more in common than with the Spanish or the Italians). But here are a couple of examples of things which can go wrong.

Situation one. Some British and German people are in an important meeting. Everyone is very serious. Suddenly, one of the British people tells a joke. The British laugh, the Germans are amazed. A joke in a meeting? And right now when we're talking about a problem? For British people, humour is extremely important. The joke means: "Stop! Let's think about this for a moment. Perhaps that problem isn't so bad. Let's take a break and relax." Humour for the British is like oil in a machine – the machine functions better with it than without it.

Situation two. A German and a British colleague are talking. The German colleague makes a suggestion. The British colleague says: "Yes, that's interesting." The German thinks: "Great. He (or she) agrees!" In fact, the British colleague is saying that he (or she) doesn't find the suggestion very good! 'Interesting' means "OK, but it's just one idea and I think there are better ones." British people are famous for their 'yes' which means 'no'. They don't like disagreeing directly. In fact, they find Germans who do this very rude!

So what can you do when you have to work with British (or Spanish, or French, or Japanese…) people so that you don't have problems? Well, the first thing is to know that there will be differences. Your colleagues from another country are not 'crazy' or 'lazy' or 'silly'. They just have different ideas. Try to understand how they think, and be ready to learn! The second thing, is that the more often you meet and work with colleagues from another country, the easier you will find it. Who knows, perhaps you will even begin telling jokes in meetings and saying 'yes' when you mean 'no'!

(433 words)

other countries, other customs andere Länder, andere Sitten • **on the whole** im Großen und Ganzen • **similar** ähnlich • **(to have) in common** gemeinsam (haben) • **to make a suggestion** einen Vorschlag machen • **rude** unhöflich • **silly** albern • **the more often … the easier** je öfter … desto leichter

2 Continue these statements with ideas and information from the text. Try to use your own words. You can write more than one sentence if necessary.

1 People often think that there are only differences between Europeans and, say, Japanese people, but …
2 Germans are amazed if a British person tells a joke in a meeting, but …
3 In Britain, 'yes' doesn't always mean …
4 What can you do so that you don't have problems if you work with people from other countries? Well, …

3 Copy and complete this table. Use your dictionary if necessary. (You needn't complete the empty boxes.)

VERB	NOUN	ADJECTIVE
to differ	(1)	different
	(2)	important
	seriousness	(3)
to suggest	(4)	
to interest	(5)	interesting
to disagree	(6)	
	rudeness	(7)
	(8)	lazy
to know	(9)	

So geht's …
10 Tipps zum Englischlernen

TIPP 1

GRAMMATIK

Kaum jemand paukt gerne Grammatik, doch führt kein Weg daran vorbei. Die unregelmäßigen Verben sind dabei die halbe Miete. Wenn Sie die „draufhaben", fallen Ihnen die Zeiten sowie indirekte Rede, Aktiv/Passiv und if-Sätze viel leichter. Nehmen Sie sich jeden Tag ein Verb vor. Überlegen Sie auch, wie sich Verben in Gruppen zusammenfassen lassen (zum Beispiel drink-drank-drunk und sing-sang-sung).

Und wie wäre es, wenn Sie sich einmal die Woche hinsetzen und vier (beliebige) Sätze aus der aktuellen Unit abschreiben? Auch so prägt sich Grammatik ein!

TIPP 2

PROJEKTARBEIT: GEZIELTE GRUPPENARBEIT

Jede Unit in Gateway macht Projektvorschläge, aus denen Sie Ihren Interessen folgend auswählen können. Erfolgreiche Projekt- und Gruppenarbeit braucht Regeln:

- Legen Sie exakt fest, was Sie erarbeiten möchten. Fassen Sie das Thema nicht zu weit, sonst verlieren Sie leicht den Überblick.
- Als Nächstes: Planen Sie die einzelnen Arbeitsschritte. Das ist besonders wichtig, wenn Sie in einer Gruppe arbeiten. Wo finden Sie die notwendigen Informationen? Wer macht was bis wann?
- In welcher Form präsentieren Sie Ihre Ergebnisse? Referat? Plakat? Website? Klären Sie solche Fragen frühzeitig, um dann gezielt und effektiv arbeiten zu können.

TIPP 3

UMGANG MIT LESE- UND HÖRTEXTEN

Lassen Sie sich von längeren Lese- und Hörtexten nicht verrückt machen. Und greifen Sie nicht gleich zum Wörterbuch. Beachten Sie stattdessen folgende Tipps:

- Vor dem ersten Lesen/Hören: Was verraten Überschriften und Bilder über den Inhalt des Textes? Mutmaßen Sie, worum es geht, das hilft beim anschließenden Verstehen.
- Lesen oder hören Sie den Text als Nächstes ein- oder zweimal, ohne an einzelnen Wörtern hängen zu bleiben. Völlig normal, wenn Sie nicht gleich alles verstehen.
- Danach erst ist Detailverständnis gefragt. Bevor Sie das Wörterbuch zücken, überlegen Sie, ob Sie einzelne Wörter, Ausdrücke, ganze Sätze, nicht doch aus dem Zusammenhang verstehen können. Dies ist eine ganz eigene Fähigkeit, aber wie alle anderen auch kann sie trainiert werden!

TIPP 4

VOKABELLERNEN

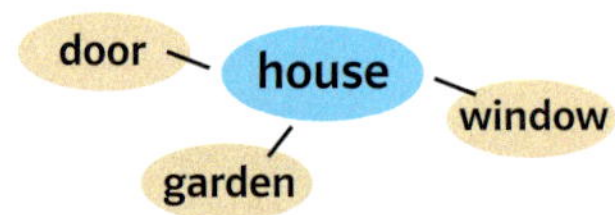

Lernen Sie regelmäßig Vokabeln, nicht erst am Ende der Unit oder kurz vor der Arbeit. Fünf Vokabeln jeden Tag bringen mehr als eine lange Liste auf einmal.

Und noch etwas: Stellen Sie Wörter zu Wortfeldern zusammen, z.B. alle Wörter zum Thema house oder alle zum Wortfeld college. Unser Gehirn lernt und erinnert sich leichter, wenn das Gelernte in Gruppen abgespeichert wird.

Lernen Sie Vokabeln im Zusammenhang, d.h. in einem kurzen Satz oder einer Wendung. Dann müssen Sie später nicht erst überlegen, wie es verwendet wird. Beispiel: home – at home – to go home. Weitere Beispiele finden Sie im Vokabelanhang.

TIPP 5
SPRECHEN UND SCHREIBEN

K
I
S
S

Wetten, Sie finden Lesen und Hören auf Englisch einfacher als Sprechen und Schreiben? Das geht den meisten Leuten so. Der Schlüssel zum Erfolg:
KISS = **K**eep **I**t **S**hort and **S**imple.
Vermeiden Sie lange und komplizierte Sätze, die Sie Wort für Wort ins Englische übersetzen. Konzentrieren Sie sich stattdessen auf einfache, knappe Sätze, bei denen Sie sich sicher fühlen. Lieber einfach und richtig als kompliziert und falsch.

TIPP 6
WÖRTERBUCHARBEIT

Ein zweisprachiges Wörterbuch ist wichtig, hat aber seine Tücken! Denn meistens bietet es mehrere Übersetzungen, und woran erkennt man die richtige? Am besten: Schlagen Sie die Übersetzung, für die Sie sich entschieden haben, als Gegenbeweis in der anderen Hälfte des Wörterbuchs nach.

TIPP 7
KLASSENARBEITEN UND PRÜFUNGEN

- Fangen Sie rechtzeitig mit dem Lernen an, aber hören Sie auch rechtzeitig wieder auf. Nicht bis unmittelbar vor der Arbeit lernen!
- Während der Arbeit: Lesen Sie die Aufgabenstellung genau durch. Sie verschenken unnötig Punkte, wenn Sie nicht auf das antworten, was gefragt ist.
- Auch wenn's nervt: Lesen Sie die Arbeit mindestens einmal durch, bevor Sie sie abgeben. Irgendwas findet man immer!

TIPP 8
WIE HÄLT MAN EIN REFERAT?

Das A und O eines guten Referats: Sagen Sie Ihrem Publikum, worüber Sie sprechen werden (Today I'd like to talk about …), sprechen Sie dann darüber und fassen Sie anschließend zusammen, was Sie gerade gesagt haben!

Setzen Sie visuelle Hilfen ein. Denn: Wir lernen zu 80 % über das Sehen, nur zu 20 % über das Hören. Schreiben Sie Stichwörter an die Tafel, bereiten Sie eine Folie mit Bildern/Grafiken vor. Davon profitieren nicht nur Ihre Zuhörer, sondern auch Sie – denn so prägt sich der Ablauf Ihres Referats besser bei Ihnen ein.

TIPP 9
MEIN HOBBY? ENGLISCH.

chips **pop song** **computer** **hamburger** **jeans**

Englisch begegnet man heute überall – auf Kinoplakaten, in Zeitschriften, im Internet, in der Werbung, im Fernsehen, in Popsongs. Sperren Sie Augen und Ohren auf. Versuchen Sie z.B. Ihr aktuelles Lieblingslied zu verstehen oder schalten Sie, wenn Sie einen Film auf DVD schauen, auf die englische Spur um.

TIPP 10
UND ZUM SCHLUSS …

Ein kluger Kopf hat einmal gesagt, mit dem Sprachenlernen sei es wie mit dem Autofahren: Übung macht den Meister! Wir können die Theorie noch so gut beherrschen, es ist erst die Praxis, die uns zu guten Autofahrern macht. Auch eine Sprache müssen Sie üben und üben, bis es irgendwann wie von selbst geht und Sie kaum noch Fehler machen. Und denken Sie daran: So schwer ist das alles nicht, das haben schon andere vor Ihnen geschafft!

Unit 1 A day in my life

TO WORK	TO WATCH
I work he/she/it works we work you work they work	I watch he/she/it watches we watch you watch they watch
TO GO	**TO STUDY**
I go he/she/it goes we go you go they go	I study he/she/it studies we study you study they study

Das simple present: -s, -es oder -ies?
- Im simple present wird an die meisten Verben (wie to work) nach he/she/it ein -s angehängt.
- Die Endung -es wird bei Verben benutzt, die z. B. auf s, ss, x, ch oder sh enden – hier wäre es schwer, ein -s auszusprechen.
- To go und to do bekommen die Endung -es.
- Verben, die auf einen Konsonanten + -y enden, bekommen die Endung -ies.

I always get up at 6 o'clock. (Vollverb)
I'm never late for lessons. (to be)

Häufigkeitsadverbien (always, often, never usw.)
Häufigkeitsadverbien stehen vor einem Vollverb, aber nach to be.

I have a brother = I've got a brother.

I have a shower every morning at 7.30.
~~I've got a shower every morning at 7.30.~~

Do you have a sister? Have you got a sister?
I don't have a car. I haven't got a car.

TO HAVE GOT
I have got he/she/it has got we/you/they have got

Verneinung	Frageform
I haven't got he/she/it hasn't got we haven't got you haven't got they haven't got	have I got? has he/she/it got? have we got? have you got? have they got?

To have und to have got
- To have und to have got sind meistens austauschbar im Sinne von 'besitzen'.
- In einigen feststehenden Ausdrücken, z. B. to have a shower, ist nur to have möglich.
- **Vorsicht!** To have bildet Fragen und Verneinungen mit do/does/don't/doesn't. To have got folgt anderen Regeln.

Unit 2 Stay in touch!

I'm he's/she's/it's we're you're they're	working	I'm not working She isn't working Are you working? Are they working?

Das present continuous: Bildung
- Das present continuous wird mit to be + -ing Form gebildet.
- Fragen und Verneinungen werden mit den Frage- und Verneinungsformen von to be gebildet.

(Schreibweise → S. 206)

Present continuous
What is Marco doing at the moment?
He's sitting in his room. He's looking at a message from his friend.

What is Matt doing this week?
He's spending five days in the mountains. He's snowboarding and he's having a great time with his friends.

Present continuous oder simple present?
Das present continuous wird für Aktivitäten verwendet, die:
- gerade jetzt im Augenblick des Sprechens stattfinden,
- auf einen gegenwärtigen Zeitraum begrenzt sind.

Es wird häufig mit Zeitangaben wie at the moment, right now, this week verwendet.

Simple present
I live in Germany.
I am a student at a vocational college.
People in England speak English.

I often send text messages to my friends.
Jenna always chats to her friends in the evenings.

Das simple present wird verwendet:
- für Tatsachen, die für eine längere Zeit gültig sind,
- mit Häufigkeitsadverbien, um auszudrücken, was jemand **oft**, **regelmäßig** usw. tut.

Unit 3 What's your favourite food?

Adjektiv	Komparativ	Superlativ
small healthy	smaller healthier	smallest healthiest
delicious	more delicious	most delicious
good bad	better worse	best worst

Salad is nicer than burgers. ~~... nicer as ...~~

Die Steigerung des Adjektivs
- Kurze (einsilbige) Adjektive und Adjektive auf -y bilden Komparativ und Superlativ mit -er/-est.
- Für längere Adjektive wird more und most verwendet.
- Good und bad sind unregelmäßig.
- 'Als' in Sätzen mit einem Komparativ heißt than.

big	bigger	biggest
nice	nicer	nicest
happy	happier	happiest

Adjektive + -er/-est: Schreibweise
- Adjektive, die auf einen Vokal plus einen Konsonanten enden, verdoppeln den Konsonanten.
- Bei Adjektiven mit -e am Ende entfällt das e.
- Bei Adjektiven mit -y am Ende wird das y zu i.

Unit 4 Famous people

Ein regelmäßiges Verb: TO WORK

I worked he/she/it worked we/you/they worked	Did you work? Did he/they/we work?	she didn't work we didn't work

Ein unregelmäßiges Verb: TO GO

I went he/she/it went we/you/they went	Did you go? Did he/they/we go?	she didn't go we didn't go

TO BE

I/he/she/it was we/you/they were	Was he? Was I? Were you? Were they?	I wasn't she wasn't we weren't you weren't

Das simple past: Bildung

- Regelmäßige Verben bilden das simple past mit -ed.
  (Schreibweise → S. 206)
- Unregelmäßige Verben bilden das simple past mit Sonderformen, die gelernt werden müssen. (Unregelmäßige Verben → Klappumschlag D)

- Fragen im simple past werden bei allen Verben mit did, Verneinungen mit didn't gebildet.
- Vorsicht bei Fragen und Verneinungen:
  ~~Did you worked …~~ ~~We didn't went …~~

- To be benutzt im simple past die Formen was/were. Fragen und Verneinungen werden nicht mit did/didn't gebildet.

Julia Roberts was born in 1967.
I saw the movie Erin Brockovich on TV last week.
My family came to Germany five years ago.
When I was very young, I loved trains.

Die Verwendung des simple past

Das simple past wird verwendet, um Ereignisse in der Vergangenheit zu schildern, die jetzt abgeschlossen sind. Es wird häufig mit Zeitangaben wie in 1993, last year (week/month usw.), three years ago, when I was very young benutzt.

Unit 5 Where I live

I have he has she has it has we have they have	I've he's she's it's we've they've	worked gone

Have you worked?
Has she gone?
I haven't worked.
He hasn't gone.

Das present perfect (1): Bildung

- Das present perfect wird aus to have und dem Partizip Perfekt (3. Form) gebildet.
- Das Partizip Perfekt von regelmäßigen Verben hat die gleiche Form wie das simple past und endet auf -ed. (Schreibweise → S. 206) Unregelmäßige Verben haben Sonderformen. (Unregelmäßige Verben → Klappumschlag D)
- Fragen im present perfect werden gebildet, indem has/have und das Subjekt die Stellung im Satz tauschen. Verneinungen werden mit hasn't/haven't gebildet.

Simple past
We came to Australia in 1975.
We bought our house in Sydney 10 years ago.

Present perfect
How long have you lived in Australia?
We have lived in Australia since 1975.
(**since** + **Zeitpunkt**: 1975)
How long have you lived in your house?
We have lived in our house for 10 years.
(**for** + **Zeitraum**: 10 years)
~~We live in our house for 10 years/since 1997.~~

Present perfect oder simple past? (1)

- Das simple past wird verwendet, um Ereignisse in der Vergangenheit zu schildern, die jetzt abgeschlossen sind.
- Das present perfect drückt einen Zustand aus, der in der Vergangenheit begann und bis in die Gegenwart andauert. Häufig wird es mit since und for benutzt, um die Frage How long ...? zu beantworten. Dabei wird since für einen Zeitpunkt, for für einen Zeitraum verwendet.

Unit 6 Have you ever ...?

Have you ever played hockey?
Yes, I have./No, I haven't.
I haven't played hockey but I've played football.

Have you ever been to England?
= Have you ever gone to England?

Das present perfect (2)

- Das present perfect wird außerdem verwendet, um auszudrücken, ob bzw. dass man etwas schon einmal gemacht hat. Es beantwortet häufig die Frage: Have you ever ...?
- To be wird in solchen Sätzen im Sinne von to go benutzt.

Present perfect ohne Zeitangabe.
I've been to New York.
I've seen all the Harry Potter movies.
I've eaten Japanese food.

Simple past mit Zeitangabe.
I went to New York with my family in 2004.
I saw a Harry Potter movie on TV yesterday.
I ate Japanese food last week in Dusseldorf.

Present perfect oder simple past? (2)

- Das present perfect drückt aus, ob/dass man etwas schon einmal (irgendwann bis jetzt) gemacht hat. Dabei ist unwichtig wann, wo usw. Es wird also ohne Zeitangabe benutzt.
- Das simple past wird mit Zeitangaben wie in 1993, last year/week/month usw. benutzt, um konkret über Ereignisse in der Vergangenheit zu erzählen.

Unit 7 The Internet

I got a quick answer to my email.
(= Adjektiv + Substantiv)
Emails are quick and easy.
(= to be + Adjektiv)
Some people speak very quickly.
(= Adverb: beschreibt wie einige Leute reden)

Adjektive und Adverbien
- Adjektive beschreiben Personen und Sachen. Sie stehen meist vor einem Substantiv oder nach to be.
- Adverbien beschreiben, wie etwas passiert. Sie beziehen sich auf ein Verb.

Adjektiv	Adverb
quick safe wonderful	quickly safely wonderfully
easy	easily
simple	simply
automatic	automatically
good	well
fast	fast

Adverbien: Bildung
- Adverbien werden gebildet, indem an das Adjektiv (auch an Adjektive die auf -e und -ful enden) -ly angehängt wird.
- Bei Adjektiven mit der Endung -y wird das -y zu -ily.
- Die Endung -le wird zu -ly.
- -ic wird zu -ically.
- Die Adverbform zu good ist well.
- Einige Adverbien haben die gleiche Form wie das Adjektiv.

I he/she/it we/you/ they	can can't	could couldn't	use a computer

Can/can't/could/couldn't
- Das Verb can/can't (simple past: could/couldn't) bleibt in allen Personen unverändert.
- Es wird mit dem Infinitiv ohne to benutzt.

Unit 8 Career plans

In five years from now, I will be 22.
I think the world of work will be very different in the future.
What are you going to do when you finish college? – I'm going to travel around Europe.

Die Zukunft: going to und will
- Um Tatsachen, Vorhersagen und Vermutungen auszudrücken, wird will verwendet.
- Um über Pläne und Vorhaben zu reden, wird going to verwendet.

I will he will we will you will they will	I'll he'll we'll you'll they'll	I won't he won't we won't you won't they won't	work

Where will you work in your new job?

Will
Will bleibt in allen Personen unverändert. Die Kurzform 'll wird fast immer beim Sprechen und häufig auch beim Schreiben benutzt. Die Verneinung wird mit won't gebildet. Bei Fragen tauschen will und das Subjekt die Stellung im Satz.

What are you doing next Wednesday?
I'm visiting a client at 10 o'clock. Then I'm meeting Mr Jones at lunchtime.

Das present continuous für Termine
Das present continuous wird oft für Handlungen benutzt, die fest geplant sind.

Unit 9 Love at first sight

I was watching TV yesterday ...
(= past continuous, Handlung 1)
... when my mobile rang.
(= simple past, Handlung 2)
Zoe was eating popcorn when she met Dylan.
Zoe met Dylan while she was eating popcorn.

Das past continuous: Verwendung
- Das past continuous drückt aus, dass etwas gerade im Gang war, als sich etwas Neues ereignete. Für diese neue, zweite Handlung wird das simple past benutzt.
- When wird mit dem simple past, while mit dem past continuous verwendet.

I was he/she/it was we were you were they were	working.	I wasn't working He wasn't working Were you working? Were they working?

Das past continuous: Bildung
- Das past continuous wird aus was/were und einer -ing-Form gebildet. Fragen und Verneinungen werden mit den Fragen- und Verneinungsformen von was/were gebildet.

(Schreibweise → S. 206)

Unit 10 Living together

He's the pop star. – Welcher Popstar?
He's the pop star who was at the festival last week.
It's a festival. – Welches Fest?
It's a festival which takes place every summer.

He's the pop star who was at the festival.

Relativsätze
- Um Personen und Sachen genauer zu beschreiben, wird ein Satzteil hinzugefügt, der mit who oder which beginnt.
- Who für Personen, which für Sachen.
- Vor who und which steht kein Komma.

He's the pop star who was at the festival.
(who = Subjekt)
He's the man who I met last week.
(who = Objekt)
It's a festival which takes place every year.
(which = Subjekt)
It's a festival which Asha likes very much.
(which = Objekt)
He's the man (who) I met last week.
It's a festival (which) Asha likes very much.

Who/which als Subjekt und Objekt
- Im Relativsatz können who und which Subjekt oder Objekt sein.
- TIPP! Wenn who und which Subjekt des Satzes sind, stehen sie direkt vor einem Verb. Sind sie Objekt des Satzes dann steht zwischen ihnen und dem Verb ein anderes Wort.
- Wenn who und which Objekt des Satzes sind, kann man sie weglassen.

There are more people in Germany than in Britain but China has the most people.
Pete eats fewer biscuits every day than Jim, but Sarah eats the fewest biscuits every day.

Americans spend more money on ice cream than Europeans, but New Zealenders spend the most money on it.
Pete drinks less water every day than Jim, but Sarah drinks the least water.

More, the most/fewer, the fewest/ less, the least
- Um zählbare Substantive miteinander zu vergleichen, werden more, the most, fewer, the fewest gebraucht.
- Für Vergleiche von nicht zählbaren Substantiven (Zeit, Geld, Wasser usw.) werden more, the most, less, the least verwendet.

Unit 11 Teenage life

In England you must/have to drive on the left.

He's so rich that he doesn't have to/needn't work.

You mustn't drive on the left in Germany!

Modale Hilfsverben (must/have to usw.)
- Must/have to drücken aus, dass etwas notwendig ist: Man muss …
- Don't have to/needn't drücken aus, dass etwas nicht notwendig ist: Man muss nicht/ braucht nicht …
- Mustn't drückt aus, dass etwas nicht erlaubt ist: Man darf nicht …

I he/she/it we/you/they	must mustn't needn't	do that

I he/she/it we/you/they	have has have	don't have to doesn't have to don't have to	do that

Modale Hilfsverben: Schreibweise
- Must/mustn't bleiben in allen Personen unverändert. Sie werden mit dem Infinitiv ohne to benutzt.
- Needn't bleibt ebenfalls in allen Personen gleich und wird mit dem Infinitiv ohne to verwendet.
- Have to und don't have to werden mit einer Form von to have + Infinitiv mit to gebildet.

Unit 12 Famous companies

I he/she/it we/you/they	had	hadn't	worked gone

Had you seen/Had she seen the film before?

Das past perfect
Das past perfect wird aus had/hadn't + Partizip Perfekt (3. Form) gebildet. (Schreibweise → S. 206)
Bei Fragen tauschen had und Subjekt ihre Stellung im Satz.

1. Ereignis	2. Ereignis
We studied unit 12.	We did a class test.

After we had studied (past perfect) unit 12, we did (simple past) a class test.
She became a film star, but before that she had been a pop singer.
My teacher was angry because I hadn't done my homework.

Das past perfect: Verwendung
- Das past perfect wird verwendet, um ein Ereignis zu schildern, das vor einem zweiten Ereignis in der Vergangenheit stattfand. Für das zweite Ereignis benutzt man das simple past.
- Sätze mit past perfect sind häufig an den Schlüsselwörtern after, before (that) und because zu erkennen.

+ -ing Form

(1) enjoy, hate, like, love, not mind (nichts dagegen haben), prefer
(2) begin, continue (etw. weiterhin tun), start, stop
(3) imagine, miss (vermissen, etwas zu tun), practise, suggest (vorschlagen)

Verben + -ing Form oder Infinitiv
- Nach bestimmten Verben folgt eine -ing Form, nach anderen ein Infinitiv.
- Verben + -ing Form sind:
  (1) Verben des Mögens und Nicht-Mögens (like, hate, love …)
  (2) Verben des Beginnens, Fortsetzens und Beendens (begin, continue, stop …)
  (3) andere Verben wie imagine, practise und suggest.

+ Infinitiv	
agree, (can) afford (es leisten), decide, hope, learn, manage (es schaffen), offer, plan, promise, try, want, would like	• Verben + Infinitiv sind z. B. want, decide, learn, plan. • Vorsicht! Nach like folgt die -ing Form, aber nach would like der Infinitiv.

Unit 13 Destination Canada

if-Teil	**Hauptteil**
If I went to Canada,	I would visit Toronto.

Hauptteil	**if-Teil**
I would visit Toronto	if I went to Canada.

If-Sätze: Satzbau

If-Sätze bestehen aus if-Teil und Hauptteil und können sowohl mit dem Hauptteil als auch mit dem if-Teil anfangen. Beginnt der Satz mit dem if-Teil, steht ein Komma zwischen if- und Hauptteil. Beginnt er mit dem Hauptteil, ist kein Komma nötig.

Typ 1

if + simple present	will
If you run,	you'll catch your plane.

Typ 2

if + simple past	would
If you lived in Canada,	you would speak English every day.

If you would live in Canada, ~~you would speak English every~~ day.

If-Sätze Typ 1 und 2

- If-Sätze (Typ 1) benutzen das simple present im if-Teil und will im Hauptteil. Sie drücken aus, was unter bestimmten Bedingungen ganz konkret in der Zukunft geschehen kann.
- If-Sätze (Typ 2) haben das simple past im if-Teil und would im Hauptteil. Sie werden benutzt, um über eventuelle Situationen zu sprechen.
- Vorsicht! Would wird nie zweimal in einem if-Satz (Typ 2) benutzt.

I he/she/it we/you/they	would	wouldn't	go

I'd go, he'd go, she'd go, it'd go, we'd go, you'd go, they'd go
Where would you go if you visited Canada?

Would

- Would/wouldn't bleibt in allen Personen unverändert.
- 'd wird häufig beim Sprechen und oft auch beim Schreiben benutzt.
- Fragen bildet man, indem man die Stellung im Satz von would und Subjekt vertauscht.

The train leaves London at 10.00.
What time does it arrive in Manchester?
It arrives in Manchester at 13.00.

Das simple present für Fahrpläne

Das simple present plus Zeitangaben wird gebraucht, um Angaben zu Flug-, Zug- und anderen Fahrplänen zu machen.

Unit 14 Unbelievable!

If I had seen you in town yesterday, I would have said 'hello'!
(But I didn't see you, so I didn't say 'hello'.)

Typ 3

if + past perfect	would have
If I had seen you,	I would have said 'hello'.

If-Sätze Typ 3
- If-Sätze (Typ 3) schildern Ereignisse in der Vergangenheit, die unter gewissen Bedingungen hätten passieren können – die aber nicht zustande gekommen sind.
- Sie werden mit dem past perfect und would have gebildet.

I he/she/it we/you/they	would wouldn't	have	said gone worked

I'd he'd/she'd/it'd we'd/you'd/they'd	have	said gone worked

What would you have said?

If I'd (I had) been there, I'd (I would) have been very frightened!

Would have
- Nach would have/wouldn't have folgt das Partizip Perfekt (3. Form). (Schreibweise → S. 206)
- Die Kurzform 'd have wird beim Sprechen und Schreiben benutzt. Fragen bildet man, indem man would und Subjekt vertauscht.
- Vorsicht! Die Kurzform 'd kann sowohl had als auch would ersetzen. Nicht verwechseln!

Unit 15 What on earth are we doing?

Lots of people drink Coca-Cola. **(Aktiv)**
Coca-Cola is drunk by lots of people. **(Passiv)**

(1) Scientists discover many important new drugs every year.
➔ Many important new drugs are discovered by scientists every year.

(2) We/People destroy thousands of square kilometres of rainforest every year.
➔ Thousands of square kilometres of rainforest are destroyed every year.

Das Passiv
- Man kann passive Sätze als ‚umgedrehte' aktive Sätze ansehen, wobei das Objekt des aktiven Satzes zum Subjekt des passiven Satzes wird.
- Passive Sätze werden verwendet:
  (1) wenn das Objekt eines aktiven Satzes hervorgehoben werden soll. In diesen Sätzen wird das deutsche ‚von' durch by wiedergegeben;
  (2) wenn das Subjekt des aktiven Satzes eigentlich unwichtig ist und völlig weggelassen werden kann.

Simple present	
is/are (isn't/aren't)	destroyed
Simple past	
was/were (wasn't/weren't)	destroyed
Present perfect	
has been/have been (hasn't been/haven't been)	destroyed
Will	
will be (won't be)	destroyed

Das Passiv: Bildung
- Das Passiv wird aus to be und dem Partizip Perfekt (3. Form) gebildet. (Schreibweise → S. 206)
- Die verschiedenen Zeiten werden mit den entsprechenden Zeiten von to be gebildet.
- Verneinungen werden mit den Verneinungsformen von to be gebildet.

Unit 16 Talking about sport

"I like sport." **(direkte Rede)**
Tom said that he liked sport. **(indirekte Rede)**

"I swim every day."
He said that he swam every day.
He told me/his friend that he swam every day.
~~He said me that … He told that …~~

The manager told the reporter (that) she was very happy about the match.

"I love all sports but my favourite is hockey."
➔ She said that she loved all sports but that her favourite was hockey.

Die indirekte Rede
- Mit der indirekten Rede wird berichtet, was jemand in der Vergangenheit gesagt hat.
- Das Berichtete wird oft mit said oder told + that eingeführt. Vorsicht! Nach said folgt direkt das Gesagte, nach told muss ein Objekt benutzt werden.
- That kann weggelassen werden.

- Pronomen wie I und we werden in der indirekten Rede zu he/she und they, Possessivpronomen wie my zu his/her usw.

direkte Rede	indirekte Rede
simple present	simple past
I play	she played
simple past	past perfect
I played	she had played
will	would
I will play	she would play

Die Verschiebung der Zeiten in der indirekten Rede
In der indirekten Rede werden die Zeitformen der Verben verschoben.

Unit 17 Working abroad

The person who lives next door is called John.
→ The person living next door is called John.
The girl who is sitting by the window is Ann.
→ The girl sitting by the window is Ann.

Things which are bought on the Internet are sometimes cheaper.
→ Things bought on the Internet are sometimes cheaper.

Gekürzte Relativsätze

- Relativsätze können gekürzt werden, indem ein Partizip anstelle von who/which + Verb verwendet wird.
- Relativsätze mit who/which + simple present oder present continuous werden durch eine -ing Form (Partizip Präsenz) gekürzt.
- Relativsätze im Passiv können durch eine -ed Form (Partizip Perfekt) gekürzt werden.
- (Schreibweise -ing und -ed Formen → siehe unten)

VERBEN: ÜBERSICHT

-ing und -ed Formen: Schreibweise

work – working, speak – speaking want – wanted, start – started	An die meisten Verben wird einfach -ing oder -ed angehängt.
have – having, phone – phoning love – loved, change – changed	Verben, die auf -e enden, verlieren das -e vor -ing und bekommen nur die Endung -d statt -ed.
sit – sitting, win – winning shop – shopped, jog – jogged Aber: say – saying, show – showing, fix – fixed	Kurze einsilbige Verben, die auf einen Vokal und einen Konsonanten enden, verdoppeln den Konsonanten vor -ing und -ed. Ausnahmen sind Verben, die auf -y, -x oder -w enden.
visit – visiting, listen – listening happen – happened, develop – developed Aber: begin – beginning, travel – travelling/travelled, quarrel – quarrelling/quarrelled	Die meisten längeren Verben, die auf einen Vokal und einen Konsonanten enden, verdoppeln den Konsonanten vor -ing und -ed nicht. Ausnahmen: begin, travel, quarrel.
die – dying, lie – lying	Bei Verben, die auf -ie enden, wird das -ie zu -y vor -ing.
marry – married, study – studied	Bei Verben, die auf -y enden, wird das -y zu -i vor -ed.

DIE ZEITEN

	Zeit	Bildung
I live in Germany. I often go to the cinema.	**Simple present** I work	Infinitiv ohne to
I'm reading this at the moment. My friend is spending a week in London right now.	**Present continuous** I am working	am/is/are + Verb + -ing
We watched a good movie on TV yesterday.	**Simple past** I worked	Infinitiv ohne to + -ed
I was watching TV yesterday when my mobile rang.	**Past continuous** I was working	was/were + Verb + -ing
I have lived here for five years. Have you ever been to Australia?	**Present perfect** I have worked	has/have + Partizip Perfekt (3. Form)
(I think that) life in the year 2050 will be very different from life today.	**Will** I will work	will + Infinitiv ohne to
I'm going to look for a job in the States when I finish college.	**Going to** I'm going to work	am/is/are + going + Infinitiv mit to
After she had finished her work, she went home and relaxed.	**Past perfect** I had worked	had + Partizip Perfekt (3. Form)
If I had a lot of money, I would travel round the world.	**Would** I would work	would + Infinitiv ohne to
If you had studied more, you would have got a better mark in your test.	**Would have** I would have worked	would have + Partizip Perfekt (3. Form)
Das Passiv		
German cars are sold all over the world.	**Simple present** Coke is drunk	am/is/are + Partizip Perfekt (3. Form)
The telephone was invented by Alexander Graham Bell in 1876.	**Simple past** Coke was drunk	was/were + Partizip Perfekt (3. Form)
Rice has been eaten in China for thousands of years.	**Present perfect** Coke has been drunk	has/have been + Partizip Perfekt (3. Form)
Your order will be delivered tomorrow.	**Will** Coke will be drunk	will be + Partizip Perfekt (3. Form)

Partner files

Vorkurs

C5

Partner B:

DEPARTURES			
Flight	To	Time	Check in
?	ROME	09:15	A27
LH 853	MUNICH	?	A4
?	ANTALYA	09:25	A19
LH 438	CHICAGO	09:30	?
LX 1215	ZURICH	?	C18
?	MADRID	09:50	A12
KL 1845	AMSTERDAM	10:00	?
BA 935	?	10:05	A25

What's the flight number of the flight to …?
– It's …
What time's the flight to …?
– It's at …
What's the check-in desk for …?
– It's …
What's the destination of flight number …/the flight at …?
– It's …

Unit 10

At work 4

Partner B:
Answer your partner's questions about the helium bed (B). Then ask questions to get details of invention A below.

What's it called?
How do you use it?
What does it consist of?

A

DIMENSIONS
Part A
Height: …
Width: …
Length: …
Weight: …

Part B
Diameter: …

B The helium bed

The bed consists of two parts: Part A, a bed and Part B, a handle. The bed is filled with helium – so it's weightless! During the day it floats to the ceiling. Then when you want to sleep, you pull the bed down with the handle.

DIMENSIONS
Part A
Height: 30 cm
Width: 190 cm
Length: 90 cm
Weight: Nothing
Part B
Length: 1 m

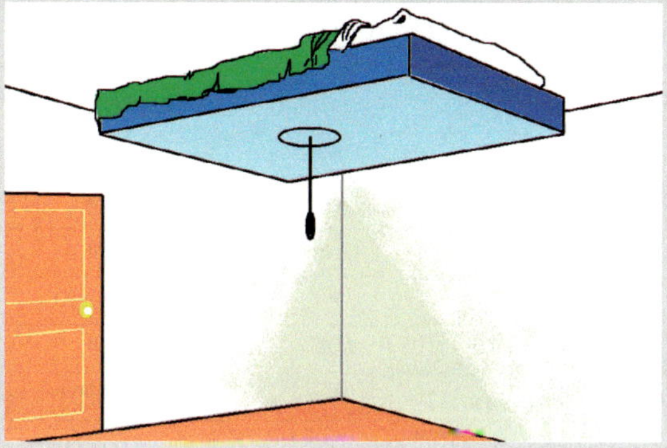

Unit 11

Gateway to work 4

Partner B:
You are a sales assistant at the computer shop. Use the information below to answer your partner's questions on the telephone.

ComputerWorld. (Your name) speaking. How can I help you? …

Your shop
The name of your shop is ComputerWorld

Sale dates
Your sale is on all this week and next week. It ends on Friday next week.

Sale details
All the computers in your shop are in the sale. You have (desktop) PCs, laptops and handhelds.

Makes
You have all the top makes. (Think of some names yourself.)

Prices
All the computers in the sale are half-price (that's 50% off!). You have PCs from around £200, laptops from £250 and handhelds from only £100.

Special offer
With all the PCs you get a free printer!

Opening hours
You are open seven days a week from 8 am to 8 pm.

UNIT 13
Gateway to work 4

Partner B:
Below you can see more information about trains from the station in London – but some times, platform numbers and ticket prices are missing. First, copy the table. Answer your partner's questions then ask your partner for the missing information in your table. (Numbers, dates and times: Klappumschlag A.)

DESTINATION	OXFORD	BRISTOL	CARDIFF	BIRMINGHAM
DEPARTURE	■	09.30	■	10.03
PLATFORM	12	■	11	■
ARRIVAL	10.20	■	12.40	■
SINGLE	■	£35	■	£33.50
RETURN	£32	■	£94	■
DAY RETURN	■	£40	■	£35

When does the train to … leave/arrive (please)?

What platform does it leave from?

How much is a single/return/day return ticket?

It leaves/arrives at …

(It leaves from) platform …

It's …

Unit 7
Focus 5

Answers:

1953 first successful colour TV programmes
1967 first pocket calculator
1969 ________
1971 first email
1973 first commercial mobile phones
1991 World Wide Web

Unit 11
Listening and reading 1

Answers (in order):

Boys	Girls
Car mechanic	Office clerk
Electronic technician	Doctor's assistant
Plumber	Shop assistant
Painter and decorator	Dentist's assistant

Hörtexte

Vorkurs

1 A

This is Dusseldorf International Airport. Every day, there are 500 flights to and from the airport and there are people here from all over the world. At a big international airport like Dusseldorf, one language is the world language ... English.

6 D

Remember Jason, Laura and Rachel from page 8? They live in England and they go to college in London. They're students on a media studies course. This week, their class is at Dusseldorf airport. They've got a project. It's to interview people at the airport and to take photos. They're with the man below at the moment.

Jason	Hi. I'm Jason and this is Laura and Rachel.
Dirk	Hi. Nice to meet you. I'm Dirk.
Jason	Thanks very much for this interview.
Dirk	You're welcome. How can I help?
Laura	We've got some questions about your job. Is that OK?
Dirk	Sure.
Laura	OK. Where do you work?
Dirk	At Airport City. It's a big business park near Dusseldorf airport with a conference centre and a hotel.
Laura	Do you work at the conference centre?
Dirk	No, I work at the hotel. I'm a receptionist.
Rachel	When do you work? What's a typical day?
Dirk	Well, it depends. The hotel is open 24 hours. Sometimes I work in the morning, sometimes in the afternoon and evening, and sometimes at night.
Jason	What do you do when you're at work?
Dirk	I welcome guests, I answer the phone, I help people when they've got a problem – lots of things.
Laura	Do you speak English in your job?
Dirk	Oh yes, every day. Our guests are from all over the world.
Jason	Do you like your job?
Dirk	Of course! It's great.

Unit 1

5 Gateway to work

Hi there. I'm Martin. This is me at home in the morning. OK. I work six days a week, from Monday to Saturday. I sometimes work from 9 o'clock in the morning to 3 o'clock in the afternoon, and I sometimes work from 3 o'clock in the afternoon to 9 o'clock in the evening. So I'm not a secretary or a bank employee or a car mechanic, for example. What do I do when I'm at work? Well, I have about 20 clients and I work with each client for an hour. My clients are men and women, young and old. One of my clients at the moment is a dancer, another is a footballer, and another is a man who is, well, a bit too fat. I help my clients with exercises, training, and tips about food and a healthy lifestyle. So. Where do I work and what's my job? What do you think?

Unit 2

1 Listening and reading

Mary	Excuse me. I'm doing a survey about cell phones. Do you have a couple of minutes for some questions?
Man	Yeah, sure.
Mary	Great. Thanks. First, do you have a cell phone?
Man	Yeah.
Mary	Which of these do you do with your phone? Do you phone friends, family, work colleagues?
Man	Yeah, of course.
Mary	Do you send text messages?
Man	Yeah.
Mary	Do you send picture or video messages?
Man	No.
Mary	Play games?
Man	No, never!
Mary	Take photos?
Man	Hmm, yeah, sometimes.
Mary	OK. In a typical week, how many minutes do you normally talk on your phone?
Man	In a typical week? Er, about forty, fifty minutes maybe.
Mary	So between thirty and sixty?
Man	Yeah.
Mary	How many text messages do you send?
Man	Ten, fifteen maybe.
Mary	You don't send picture or video messages, you said. So zero for that. OK. Great. When you choose a new phone, which one of these things is the most important for you? It's a good size. It looks good. It's efficient and easy to use. You can play good games on it. The camera is good.
Man	It's efficient and easy to use.
Mary	Great. Just two more quick questions. Can I ask your age?
Man	Sure. I'm thirty-four.
Mary	And what's your occupation?
Man	I'm a high school teacher.
Mary	That's it. Thanks very much.
Man	You're welcome.

3 Listening and reading

Mary	Excuse me. I'm doing a survey about cell phones. Do you have a couple of minutes for some questions?
Girl	Yeah, cool.
Mary	Great. Thanks. First, do you have a cell phone?
Girl	Yeah, of course.

Mary Which of these do you do with your phone? Do you phone friends, family, work colleagues?
Girl Yeah. Well, friends.
Mary OK. Do you send text messages?
Girl Yeah.
Mary Do you send picture or video messages?
Girl I send picture messages. So, yeah.
Mary Play games?
Girl Yeah, I do that, too.
Mary Take photos?
Girl Yeah.
Mary OK. In a typical week, how many minutes do you normally talk on your phone?
Girl Minutes in a week? OK. I talk about twenty, thirty minutes every day, so in a week, that's … ?
Mary Between a hundred and twenty and two hundred and forty?
Girl Yeah, that's cool.
Mary Great. And how many text messages do you send?
Girl Oh, er, sixty, seventy maybe.
Mary Between fifty and a hundred?
Girl Yeah. Between fifty and a hundred.
Mary And picture messages?
Girl Maybe one a day, so in a week, six or seven.
Mary Great. OK, now, when you choose a new phone, which one of these things is the most important for you? It's a good size. It looks good. It's efficient and easy to use. You can play good games on it. The camera is good.
Girl That's easy. It looks good.
Mary Just two more questions. Can I ask your age?
Girl I'm seventeen.
Mary And what's your occupation?
Girl I'm a high school student.
Mary That's it. Thanks very much.
Girl You're welcome.

2 Gateway to work

Christa Hotel zur Post. Sie sprechen mit Christa Merten. Wie kann ich behilflich sein?
Man Do you speak English, please?
Christa Of course. Christa Merten speaking. How can I help you?
Man Oh great, thanks very much. I'd like to book a room, please.
Christa Certainly. Can I take your name, please?
Man Yes, it's Ogilvie. John Ogilvie.
Christa How do you spell that, please?
Man O-G-I-L-V-I-E.
Christa Thank you, Mr Ogilvie. When would you like the room?
Man For two nights, from 15 to 17 November.
Christa Is that a single or a double room?
Man A single room, please.
Christa Yes, that's fine. May I take a credit card number? That just confirms the booking.
Man Yes. It's an American Express Card, number 7166 8883 2190 0557.
Christa And the expiry date?
Man Er, 6/2009.
Christa OK. I've got all that. Thank you for calling the Hotel zur Post, Mr Ogilvie. We look forward to seeing you soon.
Man Thanks very much. Bye.
Christa Goodbye.

Unit 3

3 Gateway to work

Schwein	pork	Erbsen	peas
Rind	beef	Zwiebeln	onions
Lamm	lamb	Kartoffeln	potatoes
Hähnchen	chicken	Pommes frites	chips
Pute	turkey	Reis	rice
Wurst	sausage	Nudeln	noodles
Schinken	ham	Käse	cheese
Fisch	fish	Ei	egg
Suppe	soup	Schlagsahne	whipped cream
Salat	salad	Obsttorte	fruit tart
Tomate	tomato	Eis	ice cream
Spargel	asparagus	Soße, Sauce	sauce
Champignons	mushrooms		
Karotten	carrots		

Unit 4

3 Gateway to work

Jane Well, welcome to the club Susan. Can I just ask you some questions and put your details on to our computer?
Susan Sure.
Jane Great, thanks. OK, today's date is the seventeenth of February. What's your full name, please?
Susan Susan Elizabeth James.
Jane And what's your date of birth?
Susan The fifteenth of July 1987.
Jane So that's fifteen, oh seven, eighty-seven. And your address, Susan.
Susan Thirty-four, Vine Street, Banbury.
Jane That's Vine, V-I-N-E, yeah?
Susan That's right.
Jane Thirty-four, Vine Street, Banbury and that's Oxfordshire. Do you know your post code?
Susan Yes, it's OX5 2WW.
Jane OX5 2WW. Great. Now some phone numbers and things. What's your home phone number?
Susan Oh one two nine five for Banbury, of course, then six double one, seven three nine.
Jane Oh one two nine five, six double one, seven three nine. Have you got a mobile?
Susan Yes. The number is oh double seven eight six, seven three nine, three nine two.
Jane Sorry, I didn't get all that. Could you say it again?

Susan	Sure. Oh double seven eight six.
Jane	Oh double seven eight six.
Susan	Seven three nine, three nine two.
Jane	Seven three nine, three nine two.
Susan	That's it.
Jane	And what about an email address?
Susan	S dot James at hotmail dot com.
Jane	Hotmail dot com. Right, nearly finished, Susan. Just a couple of questions now for our records. Your height. How tall are you?
Susan	In feet and inches or metres and centimetres?
Jane	Metres and centimetres if you can.
Susan	One metre seventy.
Jane	Great. And your weight at the moment? In kilos?
Susan	Oh dear! Sixty-five kilos.
Jane	Thanks very much. OK, here's your membership number, Susan. Do you want to write this down?
Susan	Yes, let me get a pen. OK.
Jane	It's one one five six.
Susan	One one five six.
Jane	Nine zero zero nine zero.
Susan	Nine zero zero ...?
Jane	Nine zero.
Susan	Yes, I've got that.
Jane	Fine. That's all. Now, let's get a cup of coffee!
Susan	Great idea!

Unit 5

1 Listening and reading

Interviewer	Hi, Jack, and thanks for the interview.
Jack	G'day! No problem!
Interviewer	How long have you been a road train driver?
Jack	A truckie? For about 20 years.
Interviewer	And where in Australia do you drive?
Jack	I drive all over the country, but I work for a company in Perth, and I drive mostly in western Australia.
Interviewer	How are the roads where you drive?
Jack	Well, most big Australian towns are on the coast. We call central Australia the 'outback', and it's pretty empty. In the desert, the roads aren't really roads at all, just tracks.
Interviewer	How big is a road train, Jack?
Jack	Big! My road train is 50 metres long and it weighs about 140 tonnes. It's got 62 wheels! And it's fast. When you drive a road train, you start and you don't stop. I normally travel at about 100, maybe 110 kilometres an hour. When I want to stop, it takes two kilometres!
Interviewer	How long are your journeys?
Jack	Normally, about a week.
Interviewer	Where do you eat and sleep?
Jack	Well there are little restaurants and motels on the road, but my truck has got a bed, a fridge, a cooker and a TV. I usually sleep in the truck.
Interviewer	Jack, thanks very much.
Jack	You're welcome!

3 Gateway to work

1 Go straight up here, under the railway bridge, until you come to a roundabout. It's in front of you.
2 Go straight up here and take the first left. That's Sheep Street. Go straight on at the traffic lights and at the roundabout, turn right. That's North Road. Go under the motorway bridge and it's on the left.
3 Go straight up here. Take the first left and then the first right. Go past the railway station and it's on the left.

Unit 6

2 Listening and reading

Lots of different people hire helicopters from us at Northern Air Services, but one day last month, it was exciting, because a film company hired a helicopter for the day. The star of the film was Brad Pitt and he was there, too.

The day – it was a Wednesday – started at 8 o'clock. Lots of people from the film company arrived with cameras and lights and microphones and other things. Then at 9 o'clock the film director arrived with Brad. They drank some coffee, then at about 10 o'clock they started filming. In the first scene, Brad was in a car, and he drove very fast across the airport.

Everything was OK until about midday. Then there was a big problem. The next scene was the scene with the helicopter. A man with a machine gun in the helicopter wanted to kill Brad – but the actor who was the man in the helicopter wasn't there!

The director talked a lot on his mobile, then he talked to my boss. And then, the director and my boss looked at me! After a minute or two, they came over. My boss said: "Tim, this is Mr Steinberg, the film director." I said "hello" and then Mr Steinberg said: "Tim, have you ever been in a movie?" I laughed and said: "No, never." Then he said: "Would you like to be in a movie?" and I said "Yes, of course!" "Great!" said Mr Steinberg, "Then you're the guy in the helicopter!"

They gave me the machine gun – it was just a dummy, of course, but it was very loud – and I put on my baseball cap and an old jacket and climbed into the helicopter. In the helicopter with me was a guy from the film company.

The pilot took off, and we flew into the air. Below me, I saw the car again with Brad. The pilot flew down near to the car. I sat in the door of the helicopter and waited. Then the guy from the film company looked at me and shouted: "Now!" I fired the machine gun. It was absolutely great!

Five minutes later we landed again. My boss and the film director smiled and said: "Congratulations, Tim. Excellent!" And then Brad Pitt came over and he said: "Good work, Tim!" and he shook my hand. It was fantastic.

So that's my story. Now, if people ask me: "Have you ever been in a movie?" I say: "Yeah, sure. Brad Pitt and I are best friends!"

1 Gateway to work

Conversation 1

Leo	Schuhmann Architects, guten Tag.
Woman	Oh, hi. Could I speak to Mr Waldmann, please?
Leo	Who's calling, please?
Woman	It's Diane Smith. I'm the English project engineer on the new museum project in London.
Leo	One moment, please, Ms Smith. I'm putting you through now.

Conversation 2

Leo	Schuhmann Architects, guten Tag.
Man	Do you speak English, please?
Leo	Certainly. My name's Leo Besold. How may I help you?
Man	Thanks. Could I speak to Ms Henneke, please?
Leo	I'm sorry but she isn't in the office at the moment. Can she call you back this afternoon?
Man	Yes, OK.
Leo	Who's calling please?
Man	It's Fredrik Olsson. I'm the Swedish project manager on your project in Stockholm.
Leo	Thanks, Mr Olsson. Does Ms Henneke have your number?
Man	Yes, she does.
Leo	I'll tell her as soon as she comes into the office.
Man	Thanks. Bye.
Leo	You're welcome. Goodbye.

Unit 7

1 Listening and reading

Michael wants to buy a new computer game, so he goes to his favourite online games store, Games World. There, he can browse easily through an e-catalogue and search for products. He finds his game (Robot Wars II). Great! It's on special offer at the moment and there's 20% off! He puts the game quickly in his shopping trolley.

When you shop online, it's important that you can buy things safely – that no one can steal your credit card number, for example. Like all good e-commerce companies, Games World uses a 'secure socket layer' (SSL). That means that all the customer's information is encrypted. Michael logs on, then goes to the checkout with his game. He types in his credit card number, and Games World takes the money immediately from his account.

So that Michael knows that everything is OK, Games World now sends him a quick email. It confirms that he has bought Robot Wars II.

Three days later, the postperson delivers a small package to Michael's house. Fantastic! It's his game! Now he can play Robot Wars II happily on his Playstation!

3 Gateway to work

"There are hundreds of thousands of websites on the Internet, so it's really important that your website is not just good, but extremely good! What's an extremely good website? Well, I have four golden rules. One, it's easy to find on the web. You need a good name for your company, a name that people can find easily with a search engine. The best names often say already what you can buy – Montana Bread, for example. Rule number two is: the website is easy to read. Good websites are simple. Don't use too many colours, and don't put too much information on a page. People read very quickly on the Internet. Rule number three: the website is easy to navigate. What does that mean? It means that you can go from one part of the website to another part quickly and easily. Organise your web pages clearly, and use good, clear buttons. And my final rule is: a good website downloads quickly. Flash animation and lots of pictures are nice, but often the home page then downloads very slowly. On the Internet, people don't like to wait! After four or five seconds they exit your website and look at the next one! Those are my four golden rules!"

Unit 8

2 Listening and reading

I'll never forget my first day at work! It was Monday the first of September last year. I got up, had my breakfast and put on my smart new clothes. I wanted to take the bus to work. When I left the house, I looked at my watch – I was a bit late, so I ran to the bus stop. I was in the middle of the street when suddenly a big BMW came round the corner very fast. It stopped, but it almost hit me. I was already nervous and I shouted at the driver: "You stupid idiot!" Then I caught the bus and went to work. I arrived at work at about five to nine. Perfect. A very nice woman gave me a cup of coffee, then she said: "OK, would you like to come with me? I'll take you to your boss's office." She opened the door – and my new boss was the man in the BMW! It was terrible and I think my face became very red. Things at work are fine now, and my boss is really very nice, but the first week was a bit difficult!

4 At work

Jeffrey	Jeffrey Taylor speaking.
Inge	Good morning, Mr Taylor. This is Inge Wegener from Aqua Showers.
Jeffrey	Oh, hello, Ms Wegener. How can I help you?

Inge I'd like to visit you the week after next, that's the week of the first to the sixth of May. Is that possible?
Jeffrey Just a minute, I'll look at my diary. OK. I'm afraid I'm busy all day on Monday and Tuesday. How about Wednesday?
Inge I'm visiting a customer in London in the morning, but I'm free in the afternoon.
Jeffrey Hmm. I'm afraid I can't make Wednesday afternoon.
Inge How about Thursday morning?
Jeffrey Yes, that looks fine. Is 10 o'clock OK for you?
Inge Yes, 10 o'clock is fine.
Jeffrey Great. I look forward to seeing you then.
Inge Thanks very much. Yes, I look forward to seeing you, too. Bye now.

Unit 9

5 At work

I've been a teacher at Long Park Primary School in Cardiff for ten years. I teach the pupils in the second year. There are twenty-five children in my class, boys and girls. In England and Wales, children start primary school at the age of five, so my pupils are about six years old. The pupils will spend six years at my school, then they'll go to a secondary school when they're eleven.

I'm with my class all day and we have all our lessons together. The school day begins at 9 o'clock and finishes at a quarter past three. The children get an hour at lunchtime and they usually stay at school. In some big schools there's a kitchen and the children can eat a hot meal. But we haven't got a kitchen at Long Park School, and the children bring sandwiches and a drink. In all schools in England and Wales we give the children fruit, too – an apple, an orange or a banana, for example.
In most primary schools in the UK the children wear a uniform, and we have a uniform here in my school – a white shirt or blouse, a tie (for the boys and for the girls), grey trousers for the boys and grey skirts for the girls. When it's cold, the children also wear a grey pullover.
We're always busy at the school. There are our normal lessons, but we also have clubs every day, sometimes at lunchtime and sometimes after school. For example, we have a swimming club every week, and a dance class. It's hard work, but I love my job and I don't want to change!

Unit 10

5 Listening and reading

My grandma lives with me and my mum and dad. She's great, and she often tells me stories about the early days, when she first moved to England.

My grandad came to England in 1961 and Grandma came two years later in 1963. She came on a boat and the journey lasted 15 days. When she arrived, the first thing she noticed was the weather. It was terribly cold! Another problem was shopping. There were some Pakistani people in England then, but not many, and it was difficult to buy the things which Grandma wanted when she cooked food for Grandad. She was very happy when the first Pakistani food shop opened.

People in the town were very nice, very friendly. Grandma couldn't speak English at first and one day she got lost in town. A man and woman helped her. Grandma could say her address, and the man and woman brought her back to the house.

My favourite story is about Grandma's job. She worked in a factory for about six months, and all the other women in the factory were British. On her first day at work, Grandma had some food with her for her lunch. In Pakistan, people always share food, so when all the women were together at lunchtime, Grandma offered them some food. They were all very surprised! And Grandma was surprised that the British women didn't offer her their food!

3 At work

Steve IT department. Steve Johnson speaking.
Erica Hi, Steve, it's Erica here from the sales department.
Steve Oh, hi Erica. How are you this morning?
Erica Fine, thanks. And you?
Steve Yeah, great thanks. How can I help?
Erica I think you've got a new laser printer for us, Steve. Is that right?
Steve Yes, that's right.
Erica I want to plan the office a bit here. Could you give me the dimensions of the printer?
Steve Sure. Just a minute. OK. Are you ready?
Erica Go ahead.
Steve Right, well, the printer is forty-one centimetres high.
Erica Forty-one.
Steve Fifty-one centimetres wide.
Erica Fifty-one wide.
Steve And forty-seven centimetres deep.
Erica Forty-seven deep. OK. And what about the cable? What's the length of the cable?
Steve Two point five metres. And the diameter is five millimetres if you want to know that, too.
Erica Great. So the printer is forty-one centimetres high by fifty-one centimetres wide by forty-seven centimetres deep, and the cable is two point five metres long and five millimetres across. Oh – and I nearly forgot the weight! How much does the printer weigh?
Steve Thirty-six point three kilos.
Erica Thirty-six point three kilogrammes. Steve, that's great. Thanks a lot.
Steve You're welcome, Erica. See you.
Erica Yeah, bye Steve. And thanks again.

Unit 11

4 Listening and reading

TAB Hi Marlies. You're from Amsterdam in the Netherlands.
Marlies Hi. Yes, that's right.
TAB What career are you training for?
Marlies I'm training to be a painter and decorator.
TAB Why did you choose that job?
Marlies At school, my favourite subject was always art, and when I was a kid I always loved painting things. Then in my last year at school, my class visited some firms in our town. I spent a day with some painters and decorators, and I thought it was great.
TAB How did your parents and your friends react to your career choice?
Marlies At first, they were all a bit sceptical, but then they saw that it was the right job for me, and now everyone supports me a hundred per cent.
TAB Are you the only girl apprentice in your firm?
Marlies No, there's another girl. Together, there are two girls and two boys.
TAB How do the other people in your firm react to you?
Marlies Sometimes the men in the firm want to help me, for example, when I have to carry heavy things. I have to explain that it isn't necessary. I'm pretty tall and strong, so I can do all the work easily.
TAB What do you think? Why aren't there more girls in jobs like painter and decorator?
Marlies Girls often just think: 'I can't do that.' But they're wrong. Girls can do everything that guys do.

1 Gateway to work

Man The Bikeshop. Jeff speaking.
Mike Oh, hi. I'm ringing about your advertisement in the paper this morning. Is the sale still on?
Man Yes, it's on all week. It ends on Sunday.
Mike Great! Could you tell me a bit about the bikes you have in the sale?
Man Sure. We've got all sorts of bikes – BMX, mountain bikes, road bikes ... Are you interested in anything in particular?
Mike Yes, mountain bikes.
Man Oh right, OK. We've got about 30 at the moment in the sale.
Mike What makes do you have?
Man Trax, Bergen and Sunrider.
Mike What sort of offers do you have on the Sunrider bikes?
Man Just a minute. We have the new Sunrider 20X at 30 per cent off.
Mike That sounds great. And the sale is on until Sunday, you said?
Man That's right. But hurry. We're selling the bikes fast!
Mike OK. Thanks a lot for your help.
Man You're welcome.
Mike Great. Bye.

3 At work

Woman Planet Office. Kelly speaking. How can I help you?
Nikki I'd like to order some items from your catalogue, please.
Woman Certainly. Can I take your name, please?
Nikki Yes, It's Moss, M-O-double S.
Woman And your address, Ms Moss?
Nikki 123 Bridge Road, Bristol BS5 3XK.
Woman Thank you. So, what would you like to order?
Nikki The desk, please. The catalogue number is ED 1478.
Woman That's on special offer at the moment, so it's only £150. Anything else?
Nikki Yes, the office chair, catalogue number AX 5153.
Woman The chair is available in blue, grey or red. Which colour would you prefer?
Nikki Blue, please.
Woman OK. One chair, in blue. Anything else, Ms Moss?
Nikki No, that's all.
Woman That comes to £249, then. How would you like to pay?
Nikki By credit card.
Woman Could you give me your credit card number, please?
Nikki It's a Visa card, 4142 6517 7178 9923.
Woman Fine. Thank you very much. We'll deliver your order in about seven days.
Nikki Thanks. Bye now.
Woman Goodbye, Ms Moss. And thank you again for your order.

Unit 13

2 Listening and reading

Let's imagine a journey across Canada from Toronto to Vancouver on the Canadian.

Day one of your journey. At exactly 9 o'clock in the morning, the Canadian would leave Toronto station. At first, you would travel through the city, past the CN Tower. Then you would leave Toronto behind you, and at around 11 o'clock, you would see the first trees of Canada's forests. In front of you now, there would be hundreds of kilometres of wonderful, empty land with only lakes and tall trees. At about 4 o'clock in the afternoon, the train would halt for a short while at the small town of Sudbury Junction. In the evening, you would have a delicious meal in the restaurant car, then perhaps go to the comfortable sleeping car. As you went to sleep at the end of your first day, you would maybe think how big and empty Canada is!

Day two. Your first, short stop today would be in the small town of Sioux Lookout. Around the town, there would still be forest and lakes, but very soon, this would begin to change. The land would become flat, the trees would disappear, and soon you would see the prairies. Canada is one of the world's biggest producers of wheat, and this is where Canadians grow it. If you looked out of the window now, you would see only endless fields with just a large farm from time to time. In the afternoon, you would halt at the first big city since Toronto – Winnipeg. Then it would be 'all aboard!' again. As you went to sleep later, you would perhaps think of life on a Canadian farm, where your nearest neighbour is 100 kilometres away!

Day three. While you were asleep, the train would travel through Saskatoon at about 2 o'clock in the morning. The first halt for you would be in Edmonton, another large and important town, at around 8 o'clock. The train would stop here for about forty minutes and it would take on water, food and diesel fuel. The air here in Edmonton would already feel cold. You would be near the most exciting part of your holiday – the amazing journey through the Rocky Mountains. Soon you would see the mountains and lakes, and at 2 o'clock in the afternoon, you would reach Jasper, one of the most beautiful and famous towns in the Rockies. Then it would be on to another beautiful, small town in the mountains, Kamloops, at around 6 o'clock. When you went to sleep today, you would perhaps think of the amazing engineers who built the first railway through these mountains.

Day four. You would reach your destination, Vancouver, at 8 o'clock in the morning. You would say goodbye to the other passengers on the train, and then perhaps go into the city for a good breakfast. Unfortunately, your journey across Canada on the Canadian would be over.

Unit 14

2 Gateway to work

1

Craig Dover Express. Craig Davis speaking.
Woman Good morning. Could I speak to Jeri Stone, please?
Craig I'm afraid she's out of the office at the moment. Can I take a message for her?
Woman Yes, great, thanks.
Craig Can I take your name, please?
Woman Yes, it's Theresa Lewis. That's T-H-E-R-E-S-A, L-E-W-I-S.
Craig Thanks, Ms Lewis. And what's your message?
Woman I'm a photographer here in Dover and I have some great photos for Jeri of the football match yesterday. Can she ring me to arrange a time for a meeting?
Craig Does Jeri have your number, Ms Lewis?
Woman No. I'll give it to you. It's Dover 155133.
Craig 155133. OK. I've got all that. I'll give Jeri your message as soon as she gets in.
Woman Thanks very much.
Craig You're welcome. Bye now.
Woman Bye.

2

Craig Dover Express. Craig Davis speaking.
Man Could I speak to your reporter Jeri Stone, please?
Craig I'm sorry. Jeri isn't here at the moment. Can I take a message?
Man Yes, OK.
Craig Can I take your name, please?
Man No, that isn't important. Just say my name is X.
Craig Mr X?
Man That's right. Mr X.
Craig OK, Mr X. What's your message?
Man I think my neighbour is a psychopath. The man has a hook-hand and I hear strange noises at night.
Craig He has a hook-hand and you hear strange noises at night?
Man That's correct.
Craig OK. I've got that. Can I take your telephone number, Mr X?
Man No! Goodbye!
Craig Er, goodbye!

3

Craig Dover Express. Craig Davis speaking.
Woman Oh, hi. Could I speak to Jeri, please?
Craig I'm afraid she's out of the office at the moment. Can I take a message?
Woman Oh, yes please. Thanks very much. This is her sister Kate.
Craig Oh, hello! Jeri often talks about you. What's your message, Kate?
Woman I'll be in Dover tomorrow. Can Jeri phone me so that we can meet? I'll give you my mobile number. It's 07786 915427.
Craig Sorry. 07786 …
Woman 915427.
Craig Thanks. I've got all that. I'll give Jeri your message as soon as she gets in.
Woman Thanks a lot. Bye.
Craig Bye.

Unit 15

3 Listening and reading

Hi. I'm Paul and I'm a technician on a wind farm in the UK. A lot of the wind farms in the UK are in the north of England, and the one where I work is there, too. It's relatively small - we've got five turbines on the farm. I think myself that they look great. Each turbine is white, 70 metres tall, and made of steel. People often say that wind farms are noisy. In fact, this isn't true. They're incredibly quiet. They're also easy to look after and they last for around 20 years. So they aren't as expensive as, say, normal power stations. At the farm, we produce energy for the town nearby. We produce enough energy for 4,000 homes. Right now, the UK produces a lot less wind energy than some other countries – Germany or

Denmark, for example. But the government here is very interested in new forms of energy, and over the next ten years, it plans to increase the total number of wind farms until 10 per cent of all the nation's energy comes from the wind.

3 At work

Interview 1

Pauline Excuse, me. I'm doing a survey about how people use energy. Have you got a couple of minutes?
Woman Sure.
Pauline Thanks. First, a question about transport. How many journeys do you make in a typical week?
Woman Well, I travel to and from work every day, and at the weekend I go shopping. So, say, twelve journeys.
Pauline How many of the journeys do you make by car?
Woman All of them. I always travel by car.
Pauline Now a question about energy in the home. How often do you leave lights or computers on when you don't need them? Often, sometimes or never?
Woman Often, I'm afraid. I leave my computer on all the time.
Pauline This is a question about recycling. Again, it's sometimes, often or never. How often do you recycle rubbish – for example bottles, cans, paper and plastic?
Woman Oh, I think recycling is very important. Often.
Pauline OK. Next, a question about insulation. How well do you think your house or flat is insulated? Would you say: well, it's OK, or badly?
Woman I'm afraid I don't know exactly, but I think it's OK.
Pauline Just one more question. About bags in supermarkets. When you shop at a supermarket, do you (a) take your own shopping bag? (b) get a plastic shopping bag from the store? (c) use the plastic shopping bags again?
Woman I always get a plastic shopping bag from the store.
Pauline That's it. Thank you very much for your time.
Woman You're welcome.

Interview 2

Pauline Excuse, me. I'm doing a survey about how people use energy. Have you got a couple of minutes?
Man Yes, OK.
Pauline Thanks. First, a question about transport. How many journeys do you make in a typical week?
Man I go to work, I visit friends, I go shopping ... about 20, I'd say.
Pauline How many of the journeys do you make by car?
Man Not many. Some weeks I don't use my car at all. I normally travel by bike or by bus.
Pauline Now a question about energy in the home. How often do you leave lights or computers on when you don't need them? Often, sometimes or never?
Man I try to switch off lights, but I'm afraid I sometimes forget! And I'm afraid I often leave my computer on. So, the answer is often.
Pauline This is a question about recycling. Again, it's sometimes, often or never. How often do you recycle rubbish – for example bottles, cans, paper and plastic?
Man That's easy. Always.
Pauline OK. Next, a question about insulation. How well do you think your house or flat is insulated? Would you say: well, it's OK, or badly?
Man That's important, too. I live in a house and it's well insulated.
Pauline Just one more question. About bags in supermarkets. When you shop at a supermarket, do you (a) take your own shopping bag? (b) get a plastic shopping bag from the store? (c) use the plastic shopping bags again.
Man I have my own shopping bag.
Pauline That's it. Thank you very much for your time.
Man OK. Bye.
Pauline Goodbye.

Unit 17

5 Listening and reading

My first week in New Zealand was hard. Everything was new – the people, the job, the country, and, of course the language. But after a short time, it became much better. As a volunteer, I had a flat with the other volunteers on the project and we did lots of things together. We were quickly best friends, and so I didn't feel at all lonely. New Zealand is a great country. At the weekends, and in my short holiday, I travelled around the two islands. They are both very beautiful and the people are really friendly. I spoke English all year! Because the other volunteers were from different countries, we spoke English together, and in the home I spoke English with the kids. I think my English became really good after about three months. Now, I can speak the language easily – some people say I have a New Zealand accent! I liked being with the kids in the home. Lots of the kids had problems, and it was good that I could help. They respected me, and that was a good feeling. Of course, while I was in New Zealand I didn't forget Germany, and I was sometimes homesick. But I learned in my year abroad that I can do things alone, without help, and that was a good lesson, too. Now I know I can travel and meet new people and that I will be OK.

2 At work

Interviewer I have some questions for you now in English, Christoph.
Christoph Fine.
Interviewer Where were you born?

Christoph	I was born in Vienna in Austria.
Interviewer	But you live in Karlsruhe now, is that right?
Christoph	Yes, my parents moved here when I was very young.
Interviewer	So how long have you lived in Karlsruhe?
Christoph	I've lived here for 15 years.
Interviewer	Do you have any brothers and sisters?
Christoph	I have one brother.
Interviewer	And you are a student at the moment at a college in Karlsruhe?
Christoph	Yes, that's right.
Interviewer	What time do your lessons normally begin and end each day?
Christoph	I usually begin at 8 o'clock in the morning, and I have lessons until about 1 o'clock or half past one.
Interviewer	What do you like doing at the weekend?
Christoph	I like meeting my friends. I often play football on Saturday – I like sport very much. I sometimes go to the cinema, too.
Interviewer	What about computers? How often do you use the Internet?
Christoph	Every day. I often use the Internet for my homework at college, and I often chat online to my friends. We play games online sometimes, too.
Interview	Just one more question, Christoph. What job do you think you'll have in, say, five years from now?
Christoph	I don't know. I like my course at college very much, and I'm sure that I want to be an electrician. I think I'll also be an electrician in five years from now, but perhaps I'll have my own small company.
Interviewer	Thank you, Christoph. Those are all my questions in English.

Grundwortschatz

Als bekannt vorausgesetzt, hier aber nicht gelistet werden:
Wochentage, Monate, Zahlen, konjugierte Formen von be, Subjektpronomen

A

a/an ein(e)
about über, ungefähr
address Adresse
after nach
afternoon Nachmittag
again wieder
age Alter
airport Flughafen
all alle(s)
all over (the world) überall (auf der Welt)
almost fast
already schon, bereits
also auch
always immer
am vormittags (nur nach Uhrzeiten)
and und
animal Tier
another noch eine(r, s), ein(e) andere(r, s)
answer; to answer Antwort; beantworten
any irgendein(e)
apple Apfel
arm Arm
arrival Ankunft
to arrive ankommen
aunt Tante
to ask (questions) fragen, (Fragen) stellen
at an, auf, in, bei
away weg

B

back zurück
bad schlecht, schlimm
bag Tasche
ball Ball
bank Bank
bathroom Bad(ezimmer)
to be sein
beautiful schön
because weil
bed Bett
bedroom Schlafzimmer
before bevor, vor
to begin anfangen
behind hinter, hinten
below unter, unten
best beste(r, s)
better besser
bicycle Fahrrad
big groß
bike Fahrrad
bird Vogel
birthday Geburtstag
bit (a ~) (ein) bisschen
black schwarz
blond blond
blue blau
book Buch
boss Chef(in)
both beide
bottle Flasche
box Schachtel, Kiste
boy Junge
bread Brot
breakfast Frühstück
to bring bringen
Britain Großbritannien
brother Bruder
brown braun
bus(-es) Bus(se)
business Geschäft
but aber
butter Butter
to buy kaufen
by (car/bus) mit (dem Auto/dem Bus)

C

café Café
cake Kuchen
can Dose; können
camera Kamera, Fotoapparat
car Auto
card (credit~) (Kredit)karte
careful vorsichtig, sorgfältig
cash Bargeld
cash machine Bankautomat
cat Katze
centre Zentrum
chair Stuhl
cheap billig
to check (über)prüfen
cheese Käse
child(-ren) Kind(er)
chocolate Schokolade
Christmas Weihnachten
church Kirche
cinema Kino
city (Groß)stadt
class (Schul)klasse
classroom Klassenzimmer
clean sauber
clever klug, schlau
clock (Wand)uhr
to close schließen
closed geschlossen
clothes Kleidung
coffee Kaffee
coke Cola
cold kalt
college Hochschule
colour Farbe
to come kommen
to complete fertig stellen
to cook kochen
copy; to copy Kopie; kopieren, abschreiben
correct; to correct korrekt, richtig; korrigieren
to cost kosten
to count zahlen
country(-ies) Land (Länder)
cow Kuh
cup Tasse

D

dad Papa
date Datum, Verabredung
daughter Tochter
day Tag
desk Schreibtisch
dialogue Dialog
dictionary Wörterbuch
different verschieden, unterschiedlich
difficult schwierig, schwer
dinner Abendessen
dirty dreckig, schmutzig
to discuss besprechen, diskutieren
to do machen, tun
doctor Arzt, Ärztin
dog Hund
door Tür
drink; to drink Getränk; trinken

E

ear Ohr
early früh
easy leicht
to eat essen
egg Ei
to email eine E-Mail schreiben
empty leer
end Ende, Schluss
England England
Europe Europa
European europäisch
evening Abend
every jede(r, s)
example Beispiel
exercise Übung
expensive teuer
Excuse me! Entschuldigung!
eye Auge

F

face Gesicht
fact Tatsache
to fall fallen
false falsch
family Familie
far weit, fern
fast schnell
father Vater
to feel fühlen
film Film
to find finden
fine fein, schön
to finish beenden, abschließen
first erste(r, s)
fish Fisch
flat Wohnung
flower Blume
to fly fliegen
food Essen, Nahrung
foot (on ~) (zu) Fuß
football Fußball

for für
to forget vergessen
free frei, kostenlos
friend Freund(in)
from von, aus
in front of vor
fruit (~ juice) (Obst)saft
full voll
fun Spaß

G

garage Garage
garden Garten
gate Tor
Germany Deutschland
to get bekommen, erhalten
girl Mädchen
to give geben
glass Glas
to go gehen
good gut
good morning guten Morgen
goodbye auf Wiedersehen
grandfather Großvater
grandmother Großmutter
great großartig
green grün
grey grau
guest Gast

H

hair Haar
half halb
hand Hand
to happen geschehen, passieren
happy glücklich
hard schwer
hat Hut
to hate hassen
to have (got) haben
head Kopf
to hear hören
hello hallo
to help helfen
her ihr(e)
here hier
him ihm, ihn
his sein(e)
holiday Urlaub, Ferien
home Zuhause
at home zu Hause
homework Hausaufgabe
hot heiß, scharf
house Haus
how wie
how many wie viele
how much wie viel
how old wie alt
hungry hungrig
husband Ehemann

I

ice cream Eiskrem
idea Idee, Vorstellung
if wenn, falls, ob
ill krank
important wichtig
in in
interesting interessant
international international
interview Interview, Vorstellungsgespräch
to interview befragen
into in (... hinein)
to introduce vorstellen
its sein(e), ihr(e)

J

jacket Jacke
job Arbeit, Beruf
juice (fruit ~) (Obst)saft
just einfach, nur, gerade

K

to keep (be)halten, aufbewahren
kilometre Kilometer
kitchen Küche
knee Knie
knife (knives) Messer
to know wissen, kennen

L

language Sprache
large weit, groß
last letzte(r, s)
late (zu) spät
to laugh lachen
to learn lernen
to leave (ver)lassen, abfahren
left links
leg Bein
lesson Unterrichtsstunde
letter Brief, Buchstabe
life (lives) Leben
to like mögen
litre Liter
like this so
list Liste
to listen (zu)hören
little klein, wenig
to live leben
living room Wohnzimmer
long lang
to look at betrachten, ansehen
lots of viel(e)
loud laut
love; to love Liebe; lieben
lunch Mittagessen

M

machine Maschine, Gerät, Automat
magazine Zeitschrift
to make machen
man (men) Mann (Männer)
many viele
map (Land)karte
to marry heiraten
to match passen, zuordnen
maybe vielleicht
me mir, mich
to mean bedeuten
meat Fleisch
to meet treffen
media Medien
media studies Kommunikationswissenschaft
metre Meter
middle Mitte; mittlere(r, s)
mile Meile
milk Milch
minute Minute
mistake Fehler
mobile (phone) Mobiltelefon
moment (at the ~) (im) Moment
money Geld
month Monat
moped Mofa, Moped
more mehr
morning Morgen
mother Mutter
motorbike Motorrad
mouth Mund
Mr Herr (Anrede)
Mrs Frau (Anrede für eine verheiratete Frau)
Ms Frau (Anrede)
much viel
mum Mama
music Musik
must müssen
my mein(e)

N

name Name
near nahe
to need brauchen
never nie(mals)
new neu
news Nachrichten
newspaper Zeitung
next nächste(r, s)
nice nett, schön, hübsch
nice to meet you angenehm, sehr erfreut
night Nacht
noise Lärm, Geräusch
noisy laut
normal normal
normally normalerweise
not nicht
nothing nichts
notepad Notizblock, Merkzettel
now jetzt
number Zahl, Nummer

O

o'clock Uhr
of von, aus
of course natürlich
off aus, weg, von
office Büro
often oft, häufig
old alt
on an, auf, bei, in
once einmal, einst
only nur, erst
open offen
to open öffnen
or oder
other andere(r, s)
our unser(e)
over mehr als

P

page Seite
paper Papier
parents Eltern
park Park
to park parken

partner Partner(in)
passenger Passagier(in)
to pay (be)zahlen
pen Stift, Füller
pencil Bleistift
people Leute, Volk
perhaps vielleicht
person Person
phone Telefon
photo(graph) Foto(graf)
picture Bild
place Platz, Ort, Stelle
plane Flugzeug
plate Teller, Platte, Schild
to play spielen
please bitte
plural Plural
pm nachmittags (nur nach Uhrzeiten)
police(-man/-woman) Polizist(in)
poor arm
possible möglich
price Preis
problem Problem
project Projekt
pupil Schüler(in)
to put setzen, legen, stellen

Q

question Frage
quick(ly) schnell

R

rain; to rain Regen; regnen
to read lesen
really wirklich
red rot
to relax entspannen, sich erholen
to remember sich erinnern, daran denken
rich reich
right richtig, rechts
river Fluss
road Straße
room Zimmer, Raum
rule Regel
to run laufen, rennen

S

sad traurig
same der-/die-/dasselbe
to say sagen
school Schule
schoolbag Schultasche
sea Meer
seat Sitz
second zweite(r, s)
secretary Sekretär(in)
to see sehen, verstehen
to seem (er)scheinen
to sell verkaufen
to send schicken, senden
sentence Satz
shoe Schuh
shop Geschäft, Laden
shop assistant Verkäufer(in)
short kurz
shopping Einkauf
to show zeigen
to shut schließen
sister Schwester
to sit sitzen
sky Himmel
to sleep schlafen
slow langsam
small klein
so so
some einige
son Sohn
soon bald
(I'm) sorry tut mir Leid
to speak sprechen
sport Sport
to stand stehen
to start anfangen, beginnen
station Bahnhof
to stop beenden, anhalten
story Geschichte
street Straße
student Schüler(in), Student(in)
to study studieren, untersuchen
suddenly plötzlich
summer Sommer
sun Sonne
sure sicher
sweets Süßigkeiten
to swim schwimmen

T

table Tabelle, Tisch
to take nehmen, brauchen, dauern
to take off ausziehen, abheben
to talk reden, sprechen
tall groß
tea Tee
teacher Lehrer(in)
(tele)phone Telefon
television Fernsehen
to tell erzählen, sagen
terrible schrecklich, furchtbar
thanks, thank you danke
that der/die/das
the der/die/das
their ihr(e)
then dann
there dort
there is/are es gibt
thing Ding, Sache
to think denken, glauben, meinen
these diese
this diese(r, s)
those diese
time Zeit
tired müde
to an, auf, nach, zu
today heute
toilet Toilette, WC
tomorrow morgen
tonight heute Abend, heute Nacht
too auch
town Stadt
train Zug
trainers Turnschuhe
tram (Straßen)bahn
to travel reisen
tree Baum
trousers Hose(n)
true wahr, echt
to try versuchen
typical typisch
TV Fernsehen, Fernsehapparat

U

uncle Onkel
under unter
underground U-Bahn
to understand verstehen
until bis
to use benutzen, verwenden
usually gewöhnlich

V

very sehr
village Dorf
to visit besuchen

W

to wait warten
waiter Kellner(in)
to walk gehen, laufen, spazieren
to want wollen
warm warm
to wash waschen
to watch beobachten, zuschauen
water Wasser
to wear tragen
weather Wetter
week Woche
weekend Wochenende
welcome willkommen
to welcome willkommen heißen, begrüßen
well gut; gesund; also
what was
what time um wie viel Uhr
when wann
where wo
which welche(r, s)
white weiß
who wer, wem, wen
why warum
wife (wives) Ehefrau(en)
winter Winter
with mit
without ohne
woman(-men) Frau(en)
wonderful herrlich, traumhaft, wundervoll
word Wort
work; to work Arbeit; arbeiten
world Welt
to write schreiben
wrong falsch

Y

year Jahr
yellow gelb
yesterday gestern
young jung
your dein(e), euer/eure

Vocabulary – Unitbegleitendes Wörterverzeichnis

Abkürzungen und Zeichen

pl	= Plural, Mehrzahl	=	entspricht	1	Vor den Vokabeln finden Sie immer die jeweiligen Übungsnummern der Unit
sb	= somebody	≠	heißt nicht		
sth	= something	↔	ist das Gegenteil von		
AE	= Amerikanisches Englisch	→	ist verwandt mit		
BE	= Britisches Englisch	!	Achtung!	blue	Tapescript-Vokabel

---

orkurs A

	English ['ɪŋglɪʃ]	englisch	! Nationalitäten schreibt man immer groß: Sam is from London. He's English.
1	**question** ['kwestʃən]	Frage	Question: How old are you?
	flight [flaɪt]	Flug	to fly → a flight
	like [laɪk]	wie	The London Eye looks like a big wheel.
2	**sign** [saɪn]	Zeichen, (Verkehrs)schild	
	German ['dʒɜ:mən]	deutsch	I can speak German. I can say: "Guten Tag!"
	phrase [freɪz]	Ausdruck, (Rede)wendung	'Good' is a word, 'be good at' is a phrase.
	departure [dɪ'pɑ:θse]	Abflug	The departure was at 10 o'clock.
	baby change ['beɪbɪ ˌtʃeɪndʒ]	Wickelraum	
	meeting point ['mi:tɪŋ ˌpɔɪnt]	Treffpunkt	
	passport control [ˌpɑ:spɔ:t kən'trəʊl]	Passkontrolle	
5	**to take it in turns** [ˌteɪk‿ɪt‿ɪn 'tɜ:nz]	sich abwechseln	
7	**Athens** ['æθənz]	Athen	
	Vienna [vɪ'enə]	Wien	
	France [frɑ:nts]	Frankreich	
	Sweden ['swi:dən]	Schweden	
	Austria ['ɒstrɪə]	Österreich	
	Italy ['ɪtəlɪ]	Italien	! Die erste Silbe wird betont.
	Greece [grɪ:s]	Griechenland	
	Turkey ['tɜ:kɪ]	Türkei	Tarik's grandma lives in Turkey.
	Rome [rəʊm]	Rom	
9	**to ask around** [ˌɑ:sk‿ə'raʊnd]	herumfragen	
10	**over there** [ˌəʊvə 'ðeə]	dort drüben	Your things are over there.
11	**form** [fɔ:m]	Form, Formular	Type in your name and address in this form.
	North Rhine Westphalia [ˌnɔ:θ raɪn west'feɪlɪə]	Nordrhein-Westfalen	
12	**to fill in** [fɪl‿'ɪn]	ausfüllen	These days you can fill in forms on a computer.
	hometown [ˌhəʊm 'taʊn]	Heimatort, Heimatstadt	
	grammar spot ['græmə ˌspɒt]	etwa: Grammatikecke	

orkurs B

1	**to be on one's way to ...** [ˌbi:‿ɒn wʌnz 'weɪ tə]	auf dem Weg nach ... sein	
	handluggage ['hænd ˌlʌgɪdʒ]	Handgepäck	
	tissue ['tɪʃu:]	Papiertaschentuch	
2	**countable** ['kaʊntəbl]	zählbar	
	uncountable [ʌn'kaʊntəbl]	unzählbar	
5	**ruler** ['ru:lə]	Lineal	

	calculator ['kælkjʊ,leɪtə]	Rechner	
6	**in English** [ɪn‿'ɪŋglɪʃ]	auf Englisch	
	tip [tɪp]	Rat(schlag), Tipp	! Schreibweise
	bar [bɑ:]	Riegel	Mrs Dixon is buying two bars of chocolate.
	loaf [ləʊf]	Laib	
	tin [tɪn]	Büchse, Dose	Our dog eats a tin of dog food every day.
	tomato [tə'mɑ:təʊ]	Tomate	
	carton ['kɑ:tn]	hier: Tüte	! Betonung
7	**to choose (chose, chosen)** [tʃu:z, tʃəʊz, tʃəʊzn]	auswählen	Which colour pen do you want? You can choose.
11	**gram** [græm]	Gramm	
12	**of one's own** [,əv wʌnz‿əʊn]	eigen	

Vorkurs C

1	**order** ['ɔ:də]	Ordnung, Reihenfolge	ABDCE...: the letters are in the wrong order.
	call [kɔ:l]	hier: Aufruf	
	monitor ['mɒnɪtə]	Bildschirm, Monitor	
	screen [skrɪ:n]	Leinwand, Bildschirm	TVs and computers have a screen.
	check-in agent ['tʃek‿ɪn‿,eɪdʒənt]	etwa: Schalter-angestellte(r)	
	luggage ['lʌgɪdʒ]	Gepäck	! keine Mehrzahl
	boarding pass ['bɔ:dɪŋ ,pɑ:s]	Bordkarte	You need a boarding pass to get on the plane.
	to depart [dɪ'pɑ:t]	abfliegen	
	hour ['aʊə]	Stunde	! Das h wird nicht gesprochen.
	security check [sɪ'kjʊərətɪ ,tʃek]	Sicherheitskontrolle	
	staff [stɑ:f]	Mitarbeiter, Personal	Airport staff work on the ground.
	to board [bɔ:d]	einsteigen (in)	We can board the plane now.
	destination [,destɪ'neɪʃn]	Ziel(ort)	
	Asia ['eɪʃə]	Asien	
	Africa ['æfrɪkə]	Afrika	
	America [ə'merɪkə]	Amerika	
2	**to go with** ['gəʊ wɪð]	gehören zu	
	each [ɪ:tʃ]	jede(r, s)	These bags are only a pound each.
3	**a lot (of)** [ə 'lɒt‿əv]	sehr; viele	I've got a lot of friends.
	in German [ɪn 'dʒɜ:mən]	auf Deutsch	
	to check in [tʃek‿'ɪn]	einchecken	
	to find out [faɪnd‿'aʊt]	herausfinden	Sorry, I don't know, but I can find out for you.
	present ['preznt]	Geschenk	These are Jenny's birthday presents.
	someone ['sʌmwʌn]	jemand	someone = somebody
5	**missing** ['mɪsɪŋ]	fehlend	MISSIN_: there is a letter missing!
	Munich ['mju:nɪk]	München	
6	**abbreviation** [ə,bri:vɪ'eɪʃn]	Abkürzung	

Vorkurs D

3	**simple present** [,sɪmpl 'preznt]	einfache Gegenwart	
4	**trainee** [,treɪ'ni:]	Praktikant(in)	
	hangar ['hæŋə]	Hangar, Flugzeughalle	
	engineer [,endʒɪ'nɪə]	Ingenieur(in)	
	Russia ['rʌʃə]	Russland	
	Russian ['rʌʃn]	Russe, Russin; russisch	
5	**reporter** [rɪ'pɔ:tə]	Reporter(in)	! Aussprache
	e-zine ['i: ,zi:n]	etwa: Internet-Magazin	
	Thanks very much. [,θæŋks verɪ 'mʌtʃ]	Vielen Dank.	
	You're welcome. [jɔ: 'welkəm]	Gern geschehen.	Thank you for a lovely meal. – You're welcome.

6	**conference centre** ['kɒnfərəns‿sentə]	Konferenzzentrum	AE: center
	to depend [dɪ'pend]	darauf ankommen	
	receptionist [rɪ'sepʃnɪst]	Empfangsmitarbeiter(in)	
	course [kɔ:s]	Kurs	
7	**conversation** [ˌkɒnvə'seɪʃn]	Gespräch, Unterhaltung	Their conversation was so loud that I couldn't sleep.
	group [gru:p]	Gruppe	
11	**lemonade** [ˌlemə'neɪd]	Limonade	
	Chinese [tʃaɪ'nɪ:z]	Chinese, Chinesin; chinesisch	! Die zweite Silbe reimt sich mit please.
12	**modern** ['mɒdn]	modern	
13	**to test** [test]	prüfen, testen	
	yourself [jɔ:'self]	dich; dir	You shouldn't talk about yourself all the time.
	introduction [ˌɪntrə'dʌkʃn]	Einführung	This book has a long introduction.
	Cologne [kə'ləʊn]	Köln	

Unit 1 A day in my life

Focus

1	**activity** [æk'tɪvətɪ]	Aktivität	
	to get up [get‿'ʌp]	aufstehen	= to get out of bed
2	**above** [ə'bʌv]	oben	
	sometimes ['sʌmtaɪmz]	manchmal	
	to tidy ['taɪdɪ]	aufräumen	Laura tidies her room every day.
3	**adverb** ['ædvɜ:b]	Adverb	'Quick' is an adjective, 'quickly' is an adverb.
	main verb ['meɪn ˌvɜ:b]	Vollverb	
5	**health and social care** [ˌhelθ‿ənd ˌsəʊʃl 'keə]	Gesundheits- und Sozialwesen	
	aloud [ə'laʊd]	laut	She reads stories aloud to her children.
	half past (seven) [ˌhɑ:f pɑ:st 'sevn]	halb(acht)	
	to have a shower [ˌhæv‿ə 'ʃaʊə]	duschen	
	quarter (past/to) ['kwɔ:tə pɑ:st/tə]	Viertel (nach/vor)	2.45: quarter to three; 3.15: quarter past three
	for a while [ˌfər‿ə 'waɪl]	eine Zeit lang	
	supper ['sʌpə]	Abendessen	
6	**midday** [ˌmɪd'die]	Mittag	
7	**expression** [ɪk'spreʃən]	Ausdruck	
	to end [end]	enden, aufhören	How does the film end?
8	**adverb of frequency** [ˌædvɜ:b‿əv 'fri:kwənsɪ]	Häufigkeitsadverb	

Practice

1	**American** [ə'merɪkən]	Amerikaner(in); amerikanisch	American football is different to British football.
	high school ['haɪ ˌsku:l]	etwa: Mittelschule, Oberschule	A school in the USA for people between the ages of 15 and 18.
	spellings ['spelɪŋz]	Schreibweise	
	to bike [baɪk]	(mit dem) Rad fahren	He bikes to work.
	though [ðəʊ]	aber, dennoch	You can ask her, though she will say no.
	busy ['bɪzɪ]	beschäftigt	I must do a lot of things today. I'm busy.
	part-time job [ˌpɑ:t‿taɪm 'dʒɒb]	Teilzeitstelle	
2	**bracket** ['brækɪt]	Klammer	
3	**statement** ['steɪtmənt]	Aussage(satz)	
	negative ['negətɪv]	hier: Verneinung	Isn't is a negative form of to be.
6	**something** ['sʌmθɪŋ]	etwas	I'm hungry. I need something to eat.
	cereal ['sɪərɪəl]	Frühstückszerealien	She eats cereal for breakfast.
7	**maths** [mæθs]	Mathe	
8	**to collect** [kə'lekt]	sammeln	Jenny collects posters.
	heading ['hedɪŋ]	Überschrift	

	to add [æd]	hinzufügen	
	meal [mi:l]	Mahlzeit, Essen	Breakfast and lunch are meals.
9	**to underline** [ˌʌndəˈlaɪn]	unterstreichen	

Listening and reading

1	**career** [kəˈrɪə]	Laufbahn, Karriere	
	company [ˈkʌmpənɪ]	Firma, Unternehmen	My mum works for an American company.
	release [rɪˈli:s]	hier: Veröffentlichung	
	studio [ˈstju:ðieu]	Studio	
	to prepare [prɪˈpeə]	vorbereiten	Dad is preparing lunch. = Dad is getting lunch ready.
	canteen [kænˈti:n]	Kantine	
	footballer [ˈfʊtbɔ:lə]	Fußballspieler(in)	
	national league [ˌnæʃnl͜ ˈli:g]	etwa: Bundesliga	
	certainly [ˈsɜ:tnlɪ]	sicher(lich), bestimmt	I certainly want to come to your birthday party.
	postman [ˈpəʊstmən]	Briefträger, Postbote	
	a couple of [ə ˈkʌpl͜ əv]	ein paar	
3	**factory** [ˈfæktrɪ]	Fabrik, Werk	They make cars in factories.
	famous [ˈfeɪməs]	berühmt	I know David Beckham. He is very famous.
	singer [ˈsɪŋə]	Sänger(in)	to sing → singer
	special [ˈspeʃl]	besondere(r,s)	! Aussprache: Das c wird sh ausgesprochen.
	to call [kɔ:l]	hier: nennen	My name is Michael, but you can call me Mike.
4	**opposite** [ˈɒpəzɪt]	entgegengesetzt	'Yes' is the opposite of 'no'.
	meaning [ˈmi:ŋin]	Bedeutung	What's the meaning of to describe? – It means: to say what a thing or a person looks like.
	exactly [ɪgˈzæktlɪ]	genau	It's my birthday today. I'm now exactly 18.
6	**favourite** [ˈfeɪvrɪt]	Lieblings-	My favourite sport is football.
	musician [mjʊˈzɪʃn]	Musiker(in)	

Gateway to work

1	**description** [dɪˈskrɪpʃn]	Beschreibung	description → to describe
	architect [ˈɑ:kɪˌtekt]	Architekt(in)	
	worker [ˈwɜ:kə]	Arbeiter(in)	worker → to work
	hundred [ˈhʌndrəd]	Hundert	
	employee [ɪmˈplɔɪi:]	Angestellte(r)	The company has 500 employees.
	bricklayer [ˈbrɪkˌleɪə]	Maurer	
	chef [ʃef]	Koch, Köchin	
	driver [ˈdraɪvə]	Fahrer(in)	A driver can drive a car, a bus or a taxi.
	fashion designer [ˈfæʃn dɪˌzaɪnə]	Modeschöpfer(in)	
	hairdresser [ˈheəˌdresə]	Frisör(in)	
	IT technician [aɪˈti: tekˌnɪʃn]	Informatiker(in)	
	journalist [ˈdʒɜ:nəlɪst]	Journalist(in)	'Jour-' wird gesprochen wie 'Ger-' in German.
	mechanic [mɪˈkænɪk]	Mechaniker(in)	
	nurse [nɜ:s]	Krankenschwester	Nurses work in hospitals.
	plumber [ˈplʌmə]	Klempner(in)	
	police officer [pəˈli:s͜ ˌɒfisə]	Polizeibeamte(r)	
	sales representative [ˈseɪlz reprɪˌzentətɪv]	Handelsvertreter(in)	
	social worker [ˈsəʊʃl ˌwɜ:kə]	Sozialarbeiter(in)	
	technician [tekˈnɪʃn]	Techniker(in)	
	to design [dɪˈzaɪn]	entwerfen	Cool T-shirt, Tom. – Yes, I designed it.
	to cut (cut, cut) [kʌt, kʌt, kʌt]	schneiden	
	hospital [ˈhɒspɪtl]	Krankenhaus	He's in hospital with a broken leg.
	to repair [rɪˈpeə]	reparieren	My computer is broken. Can you repair it?
	building [ˈbɪldɪŋ]	Gebäude, Bau	Skyscrapers and houses are buildings.
	product [ˈprɒdʌkt]	Produkt	! Betonung

	to protect [prə'tekt]	(be)schützen	The police protect you from criminals.
	to catch (caught, caught) [kætʃ, kɔ:t, kɔ:t]	fangen	Throw me the ball and I will catch it.
	criminal ['krɪmɪnl]	Verbrecher(in)	There are more criminals in big cities.
	to install [ɪn'stɔ:l]	installieren, montieren	
	water pipe ['wɔ:tə ˌpaɪp]	Wasserleitung	
	to build (built, built) [bɪld, bɪlt, bɪlt]	bauen	building → to build
	cable ['keɪbl]	Kabel	
	to look after [lʊk‿'ɑ:ftə]	sich kümmern um	David looks after the baby when his mum isn't there.
	telephone ['telɪfəʊn]	Telefon	My telephone number is two – seven – oh – five.
	cable ['keɪbl]	Kabel	
	to drive (drove, driven) [draɪv, drəʊv, 'drɪvn]	fahren	People drive a car or a bus – but they ride a bike.
	lorry ['lɒrɪ]	Lastwagen	Jack drives a lorry from London to Manchester.
	to program ['prəʊgrəm]	programmieren	
5	**healthy** ['helθɪ]	gesund	health → healthy
	client ['klaɪənt]	Kunde, Kundin	
	dancer ['dɑ:nsə]	Tänzer(in)	
	This is me. [ˌðɪs‿ɪz 'mi:]	Das bin ich.	
	at work [ət 'wɜ:k]	bei der Arbeit	
	too [tu:]	hier: zu	My old shoes are too small.
	fat [fæt]	dick	Fast food makes you fat.
6	**summary** ['sʌmərɪ]	Zusammenfassung	A summary is a short version of a text.

Unit 2 Stay in touch!

Focus

1	**to stay in touch** [ˌsteɪ‿ɪn 'tʌtʃ]	in Kontakt bleiben	They met a year ago but they stay in touch.
	mobile (phone) [ˌməʊbaɪl 'fəʊn]	Mobiltelefon, Handy	**!** Im Englischen heißt es nie 'handy'.
	to chat [tʃæt]	plaudern, chatten	
	postcard ['pəʊstˌkɑ:d]	Postkarte	Jenny is writing a postcard to her boyfriend.
2	**vocational college** [vəʊˌkeɪʃnl 'kɒlɪdʒ]	etwa: Berufsschule	
	even ['i:vn]	selbst, sogar	We'll never win, even if we play really well.
	right now [ˌraɪt 'naʊ]	im Augenblick	I'll do it later. Right now I'm having lunch.
	floor [flɔ:]	Boden	The book is on the floor.
	message ['mesɪdʒ]	Nachricht	Hello, can I leave a message for Robert?
	the States [ðə 'steɪts]	die (Vereinigten) Staaten	I'd love to go to the States.
	cell (phone) (AE) ['sel ˌfəʊn]	Mobiltelefon, Handy	
	UK (= United Kingdom) [ˌju:'keɪ, ju:ˌnaɪtɪd 'kɪŋdəm]	Vereinigtes Königreich	He lives in the UK.
4	**present continuous** [ˌpreznt kən'tɪnjʊəs]	Verlaufsform der Gegenwart	
5	**spring** [sprɪŋ]	Frühling	= the months of March, April and May
	autumn ['ɔ:təm]	Herbst	
	sunny ['sʌni]	sonnig	sun → sunny
	mountain ['maʊntɪn]	Berg	
	snowy ['snəʊɪ]	verschneit	
	to ski [ski:]	Ski laufen/fahren	**!** 'sk' wird wie der Anfang von school ausgesprochen.
	to snowboard ['snəʊˌbɔ:d]	snowboarden	
	to spend (spent, spent) [spend, spent, spent]	verbringen, ausgeben	**!** to spend ≠ spenden
	to stay [steɪ]	bleiben, übernachten	We can go to the cinema, or we can stay at home.
	youth hostel ['ju:θ ˌhɒstl]	Jugendherberge	On our class trip we stayed at a youth hostel.
6	**to quarrel** ['kwɒrəl]	streiten, zanken	

	Practice		
1	**to come over** [kʌm͜ˈəʊvə]	herüberkommen, vorbeikommen	Can you come over this afternoon?
	to jog [dʒɒg]	joggen, dauerlaufen	Lisa is jogging with her dog.
2	**to write out sth in full**	etw. ausformulieren	
	capital letter [ˌkæpɪtl͜ˈletə]	Großbuchstabe	
3	**to dance** [dɑ:ns]	tanzen	The music is great – let's dance.
	to smile [smaɪl]	lächeln	To laugh at somebody is nasty, to smile at somebody is nice.
5	**instant message** [ˌɪnstənt ˈmesɪdʒ]	Onlinenachricht	
	screen name [ˈskri:n͜ˌneɪm]	Codename	
	guy [gaɪ]	Typ, Kerl	The guy invited me for coffee.
8	**trip** [trɪp]	Ausflug, Reise, Fahrt	Ben and Adam are going on a trip to New York today.
9	**to imagine** [ɪˈmædʒɪn]	sich vorstellen	Can you imagine what it is like to work in the States?
	Dear, [dɪə]	Liebe(r),	
	to camp [kæmp]	campen, zelten	They camped in the woods for a week.
	to give sb one's love	jdm. Grüße bestellen	When you see her, give her my love.
	See you soon. [ˌsi: jə ˈsu:n]	Bis bald.	
	best wishes [ˌbest ˈwɪʃɪz]	viele/beste Grüße	
	kiss [kɪs]	Kuss	
	Listening and reading		
	market research [ˈmɑ:kɪt rɪˌsɜ:tʃ]	Marktforschung	
	survey [ˈsɜ:veɪ]	Untersuchung, Umfrage	With a survey you can find out about people's opinions.
	colleague [ˈkɒli:g]	Kollege, Kollegin	
	text message [ˈtekst ˌmesɪdʒ]	SMS	You can send a text message on your mobile phone.
	game [geɪm]	Spiel	
	to take photos [teɪk ˈfəʊtəʊz]	Fotos machen	
	size [saɪz]	Größe	Have you got this T-shirt in a different size, please?
	to look [ˈlʊk]	hier: aussehen	Your new mobile really looks cool!
	efficient [ɪˈfɪʃnt]	effizient	He has a very efficient secretary.
	occupation [ˌɒkjʊˈpeɪʃn]	Beruf	
	between [bɪˈtwi:n]	zwischen	We always have a break between lessons.
	That's it. [ðæts͜ˈɪt]	Das war's.	
4	**parents (pl)** [ˈpeərənts]	Eltern	
	to agree [əˈgri:]	zustimmen, übereinstimmen	I agree with you. = I think what you say is right.
5	**to think of** [ˈθɪŋk͜əv]	hier: sich überlegen	Think of your favourite TV programme. What is it?
	Gateway to work		
	to spell [spel, spelt, spelt]	buchstabieren	Spell Tom. – T-O-M.
	single room [ˈsɪŋgl ˌru:m]	Einzelzimmer	
	double room [ˈdʌbl ˌru:m]	Doppelzimmer	
	fully booked [ˌfʊlɪ ˈbʊkt]	ausgebucht	We can't stay. It's fully booked.
	may (might) [meɪ, maɪt]	dürfen, können	May I sit here?
	credit card [ˈkredɪt ˌkɑ:d]	Kreditkarte	
	expiry date [ɪkˈspaɪərɪ ˌdeɪt]	Ablaufdatum, Verfallstermin	
	to look forward to [ˌlʊk ˈfɔ:wəd tə]	sich freuen auf	! + -ing-form
2	**to confirm** [kənˈfɜ:m]	bestätigen	Can you confirm that you will come?
	booking [ˈbʊkɪŋ]	Buchung	The hotel has no bookings today.
3	**to practise** [ˈpræktɪs]	üben	I play football. I practise on Monday and Wednesday.
	caller [ˈkɔ:lə]	Anrufer(in)	to call → caller

4	**businessman** ['bɪznəsmæn]	Geschäftsmann	
	to decide [dɪ'saɪd]	sich entscheiden, beschließen	Coffee or tea? – I don't know. I can't decide.
	to repeat [rɪ'pi:t]	wiederholen	To say (or do) sth again.
5	**phone call** ['fəʊn ˌkɔ:l]	Telefonanruf	When you phone somebody, you make a phone call.
	note [nəʊt]	Notiz	Listen to the teacher and make notes.

Unit 3 What's your favourite food?

Focus

2	**banana** [bə'nɑ:nə]	Banane	Apples, oranges and bananas are all fruit.
	biscuit ['bɪskɪt]	Keks	**!** Biscuit ≠ Biskuit
	fries (AE) [fraɪz]	Pommes	
	carrot ['kærət]	Möhre, Karotte, Mohrrübe	
	kiwi ['ki:wi:]	Kiwi	
	mixed [mɪkst]	gemischt	Sugar and salt mixed is not nice!
	salad ['sæləd]	Salat	**!** Die erste Silbe wird betont.
	orange ['ɒrɪndʒ]	Orange	Oranges are usually orange!
	pea [pi:]	Erbse	
	sausage ['sɒsɪdʒ]	Wurst, Würstchen	
	curry sauce ['kʌrɪ ˌsɔ:s]	Currysauce	
	spaghetti [spə'getɪ]	Spaghetti	
	strawberry ['strɔ:brɪ]	Erdbeere	
3	**kind** [kaɪnd]	Art, Sorte	What kind of music do you like, David?
	vegetable ['vedʒtəbl]	Gemüse	Amy's family eats lots of vegetables from their garden.
	main meal [ˌmeɪn 'mi:l]	Hauptmahlzeit	He eats his main meal in the evening.
	part [pɑ:t]	Teil, Rolle	Let's play a game. Which part do you want?
	popular ['pɒpjʊlə]	beliebt	Everyone likes her. She is very popular.
4	**British** ['brɪtɪʃ]	britisch	The Leinerts are German, and the Crofts are British.
	chips (pl) [tʃɪps]	Pommes frites (BE), Chips (AE)	
	crisps (pl) [krɪsps]	Chips	
	together [tə'geðə]	zusammen, gemeinsam	They go everywhere together.
	grandma ['grænˌmɑ:]	Oma, Omi	Your mother's or your father's mother.
	grandad ['grænˌdæd]	Opa, Opi	grandad = grandfather
	originally [ə'rɪdʒnəlɪ]	ursprünglich	
	India ['ɪndɪə]	Indien	
	delicious [dɪ'lɪʃəs]	lecker, köstlich	Yummy! This cake is delicious.
	curry ['kʌrɪ]	Curry(gericht)	
	to prefer [prɪ'fɜ:]	vorziehen, lieber mögen	I prefer rice to spaghetti.
5	**vanilla** [və'nɪlə]	Vanille	

Practice

1	**chain** [tʃeɪn]	Kette	There is a chain of shops across the country.
	menu ['menju:]	Speisekarte	Waiter, what's on the menu today?
	chicken ['tʃɪkɪn]	Huhn	They get fresh eggs from their chicken.
	medium ['mi:dɪəm]	mittel	
	onion ['ʌnjən]	Zwiebel	**!** Aussprache
	ring [rɪŋ]	Ring	
	regular ['regjʊlə]	regelmäßig, normal	A large not a regular portion, please.
	portion ['pɔ:ʃn]	Teil, Portion	Two portions of chips, please.
2	**adjective** ['ædʒɪktɪv]	Adjektiv	
	comparative [kəm'pærətɪv]	Komparativ	
	superlative [sʊ'pɜ:lətɪv]	Superlativ	

4	**consumer** [kən'sju:mə]	Konsument(in)	
	in fact [ɪn 'fækt]	tatsächlich, vielmehr	I don't like fish, in fact I hate it!
	New Zealander [nju: 'zi:ləndə]	Neuseeländer(in)	
	per [pɜ:]	pro	He drove a 100 miles per day.
	Swiss [swɪs]	Schweizer(in); schweizerisch	
	flavour ['fleɪvə]	Geschmack(srichtung)	I don't like that ice cream flavour.
	per cent [pə 'sent]	Prozent	
	nut [nʌt]	Nuss	I like chocolate with fruit and nuts.
	cookie (AE) ['kʊkɪ]	Keks	
	caramel ['kærəˌmel]	Karamell	
	finally ['faɪnlɪ]	schließlich, letztendlich	We waited an hour and finally he came.
	sweet [swi:t]	süß	Children like sweet food.
	chilli ['tʃɪlɪ]	Chili	
	Japanese [ˌdʒæpn'i:s]	Japaner(in); japanisch	
	exotic [ɪg'zɒtɪk]	exotisch, fremdartig	
	garlic ['gɑ:lɪk]	Knoblauch	
	potato (pl -es) [pə'teɪtəʊ, pə'teɪtəʊz]	Kartoffel	
	strange [streɪndʒ]	sonderbar	What's that strange noise? I'm frightened!
	Japan [dʒə'pæn]	Japan	! Aussprache.
5	**customer** ['kʌstəmə]	Kunde, Kundin	A customer buys things in a shop.
	assistant [ə'sɪstnt]	Hier: Kellner(in)	
	dessert [dɪ'zɜ:t]	Nachtisch, Dessert	Children often like this more than the main course.
	to come to ['kʌm tə]	sich belaufen auf	How much does that come to? – £410.
	Here you are. [ˌhɪə jə‿'ɑ:]	Bitte schön.	Where's my pen? – Here you are.
	Enjoy your meal. [ɪnˌdʒɔɪ jə 'mi:l]	Guten Appetit.	
7	**to translate** [træns'leɪt]	übersetzen	

Listening and reading

1	**article** ['ɑ:tɪkl]	Artikel	! Schreibung und Aussprache
	generally ['dʒenrəlɪ]	generell, im Allgemeinen	Generally, I go to bed at 11:00.
	unhealthy [ʌn'helθɪ]	ungesund	It's unhealthy to watch five hours of TV every day.
	truth [tru:θ]	Wahrheit	true → the truth
	soda (drink) (AE) ['səʊdə ˌdrɪŋk]	Limonade	
	to contain [kən'teɪn]	enthalten, beinhalten	A glass of water contains no calories.
	calory ['kælrɪ]	Kalorie	
	fresh [freʃ]	neu, frisch	The milk from the farm is really fresh.
	sugar ['ʃʊgə]	Zucker	! Das s wird wie sh ausgesprochen.
	tooth (pl teeth) [tu:θ, ti:θ]	Zahn	
	body ['bɒdɪ]	Körper	
	overweight [ˌəʊvə'weɪt]	übergewichtig	These days too many people are overweight.
	to enjoy [ɪn'dʒɔɪ]	genießen	The concert was great. I really enjoyed it.
	around [ə'raʊnd]	hier: ungefähr	The car can go around 200 kph.
	instead of [ɪn'sted‿əv]	anstatt, anstelle	They have a holiday in winter instead of in summer.
3	**approximately** [ə'prɒksɪmətlɪ]	etwa, ungefähr	The plane lands at approximately 17:50.
6	**pie chart** ['paɪ ˌtʃɑ:t]	Kuchendiagramm	
	recipe ['resɪpɪ]	(Koch)Rezept	! Aussprache. Recipe is for food, not medicine!
	dish [dɪʃ]	Gericht	Spaghetti carbonara is an Italian dish.

Gateway to work

	furniture (no pl) ['fɜ:nɪtʃə]	Möbel	! Singular: Their furniture is very old.
	lunchtime ['lʌntʃˌtaɪm]	Mittagspause	
	works [wɜ:ks]	Werkanlage	
	soup [su:p]	Suppe	A bowl of hot soup is good on a cold day.

	pork [pɔ:k]	Schwein(efleisch)	
	apple strudel ['æpl ˌstru:dl]	Apfelstrudel	
	sauce [sɔ:s]	Soße	I love ice cream with chocolate sauce.
	What about ...? [ˌwɒt‿ə'baʊt]	Was ist mit ...?, Wie wäre es mit ...?	What about going to the football game this Saturday?
	beef [bi:f]	Rind(fleisch)	
	lamb [læm]	Lamm	! Aussprache: Das b wird nicht ausgesprochen.
	turkey ['tɜ:kɪ]	Pute	We always eat turkey at Christmas.
	ham [hæm]	Schinken	I'd like some sandwiches. – Cheese and tomato? Or ham?
	asparagus [ə'spærəgəs]	Spargel	
	mushroom ['mʌʃru:m]	Pilz	
	rice [raɪs]	Reis	Risotto is a rice dish.
	noodle [nu:dl]	Nudel	
	whipped cream [ˌwɪpt 'kri:m]	Schlagsahne	
	fruit tart ['fru:t‿ˌtɑ:t]	Obsttorte	
5	**visitor** ['vɪzɪtə]	Besucher(in)	to visit → visitor
	to explain [ɪk'spleɪn]	erklären	Can you explain what this word means?

Unit 4 Famous people

Focus

	to name [neɪm]	(be)nennen	Name the first man on the moon.
	businessperson ['bɪznəsˌpɜ:sn]	Geschäftsmann, -frau	
	author ['ɔ:θə]	Autor(in)	
	scientist ['saɪəntɪst]	Wissenschaftler(in)	Scientists have to be good at maths.
2	**biography** [baɪ'ɒgrəfɪ]	Biografie	The story of a person's life.
	details ['di:teɪlz]	Angaben	
	date of birth [ˌdeɪt‿əv 'bɜ:θ, ˌdeɪts‿əv 'bɜ:θ]	Geburtsdatum	
	birthplace ['bɜ:θˌpleɪs]	Geburtsort	
	real [rɪəl]	echt, wirklich	Do you know how to make a real English breakfast?
	actor, actress ['æktə, 'æktrəs]	Schauspieler(in)	
	star sign ['stɑ: ˌsaɪn]	Sternzeichen	What's your star sign? – Taurus.
	Scorpio ['skɔ:pɪəʊ]	Skorpion (Sternzeichen)	
	dark [dɑ:k]	dunkel	In the night you can't see because it's dark.
	blonde [blɒnd]	blond	Her mother is blonde.
	height [haɪt]	Höhe, Größe	high → height
	foot (pl feet) [fʊt, fi:t]	Fuß (= 30,48 cm)	
	inch [ɪntʃ]	Zoll (= 2,54 cm)	
	cameraman ['kæmrəˌmæn]	Kameramann	
	twin [twɪn]	Zwilling	She's got twins, a boy and a girl.
	born [bɔ:n]	geboren	He was born in Germany.
	residence ['rezɪdns]	Wohnsitz, Wohnung	But his main residence is in Switzerland.
3	**vacuum cleaner** ['vækjʊəm ˌkli:nə]	Staubsauger	
	salesman ['seɪlzmən]	Händler, Verkäufer	
	vet [vet]	Tierarzt	
	movie (AE) ['mu:vɪ]	(Kino)Film	
	to change [tʃeɪndʒ]	(ver)ändern	She changes her car every year.
	successful [sək'sesfl]	erfolgreich	He's very successful at his job.
	to fall in love with [ˌfɔ:l‿ɪn 'lʌv wɪð]	sich verlieben in	She lives in Italy. She fell in love with the country.
	smile [smaɪl]	Lächeln	a smile → to smile
	breakthrough ['breɪkθru:]	Durchbruch	My English was bad. The breakthrough was a trip to the USA. Now I can speak well.
	to appear [ə'pɪə]	erscheinen, auftreten	She appeared in more than 50 films.

	to become (became, become) [bɪ'kʌm, bɪ'keɪm, bɪ'kʌm]	werden	! to become ≠ bekommen
	overnight [ˌəʊvə'naɪt]	über Nacht	
	to star [stɑː]	eine Hauptrolle spielen	
	brilliant ['brɪljənt]	großartig, hervorragend	I like this song. It's brilliant.
	to win (won, won) [wɪn, wʌn, wʌn]	gewinnen	She came first and won the race.
	to earn [ɜːn]	verdienen	Lisa has got a good job and earns a lot of money.
	fantastic [fæn'tæstɪk]	fantastisch	Surfing is fantastic.
	highest-paid ['haɪəstˌpeɪd]	bestbezahlt	
4	**(not) at all** [ˌnɒt‿ət‿'ɔːl]	überhaupt (nicht)	I didn't like that movie at all.
	I see. [aɪ 'siː]	Ich verstehe.	That's why I'm late. – I see. OK.
	simple past [ˌsɪmpl 'pɑːst]	einfache Vergangenheit	

Practice

1	**irregular** [ɪ'regjʊlə]	unregelmäßig	irregular → regular
	on the set [ˌɒn ðə 'set]	am Drehort	
	director [də'rektə]	Direktor(in), Regisseur(in)	
	midnight ['mɪdˌnaɪt]	Mitternacht	The clocks change at midnight in October.
2	**on the left** [ˌɒn ðə 'left]	links	In Britain they drive on the left.
3	**usual** ['juːʒʊəl]	gewöhnlich, üblich	9 o'clock is the usual time to start work.
	beach [biːtʃ]	Strand	Mark is playing on the beach. He's making a castle.
	neighbour ['neɪbə]	Nachbar(in)	Your neighbour lives in the house next to your house.
5	**north** [nɔːθ]	Norden	
	to separate ['seprət]	(sich) trennen	It's bad for children when parents separate.
	to grow up [grəʊ‿'ʌp]	aufwachsen	= to become an adult
	to join [dʒɔɪn]	(sich) anschließen (an), beitreten	I'm a member of the karate club. I joined it last year.
	solo ['səʊləʊ]	solo; Solo-	
	wild [waɪld]	wild	Lions don't live on farms. They're wild.
	drug [drʌg]	Droge	It is dangerous to take drugs.
	song [sɒŋ]	Lied	Let's sing a song.
	to release [rɪ'liːs]	veröffentlichen	They released this film in London last week.
	enormous [ɪ'nɔːməs]	enorm, riesig	My girlfriend wears enormous earrings.
	songwriter ['sɒŋˌraɪtə]	Komponist(in)	
	alive [ə'laɪv]	am Leben, lebendig	My grandpa's father is still alive. He's 96.
6	**whole** [həʊl]	ganz	David spent a whole week in New York.

Listening and reading

1	**surprise** [sə'praɪz]	Überraschung	Good to see you! What a surprise!
	founder ['faʊndə]	Gründer	
	north-west [ˌnɔːθ'west]	Nordwesten	
	university [ˌjuːnɪ'vɜːsətɪ]	Universität	
	lawyer ['lɔːjə]	Rechtsanwalt, -anwältin	
	programming language	Programmiersprache	
	to found [faʊnd]	gründen	Last year Bill founded his own company.
	to produce [prə'djuːs]	produzieren, herstellen	to produce → product
	revolution [ˌrevə'luːʃn]	Revolution	
	alone [ə'ləʊn]	allein	She lives alone in the middle of town.
	version ['vɜːʃn]	Version, Ausgabe	I enjoyed the book better than the film.
	head office [ˌhed‿'ɒfɪs]	Zentrale, Hauptsitz	
	library ['laɪbrərɪ]	Bibliothek, Bücherei	There are thousands of books in a library.
	underground garage [ˌʌndəgraʊnd 'gærɑːʒ]	Tiefgarage	Park your car in the underground garage.
	shy [ʃaɪ]	schüchtern, scheu	She never speaks, she's very shy.

	generous ['dʒenərəs]	großzügig, freigebig	He buys everybody drinks. He's generous.
	to give away [ˌgɪv‿ə'weɪ]	weggeben, verschenken	He gave away everything to his children.
2	**to describe** [dɪ'skraɪb]	beschreiben	Can you describe the man who stole your bag?
6	**talk** [tɔ:k]	Gespräch, Vortrag	**!** Das l wird nicht ausgesprochen.
8	**to find out about** [faɪnd‿'aʊt‿əˌbaʊt]	sich informieren über	Before I go on holiday, I find out about the country.

Gateway to work

1	**keyboard** ['ki:ˌbɔ:d]	Keyboard, hier: Tastatur	
	printer ['prɪntə]	Drucker(in), Drucker	How many copies a minute does your printer print?
	plant [plɑ:nt]	Pflanze	
	mouse (pl mice) [maʊs, maɪs]	Maus	
	filing cabinet ['faɪlɪŋ ˌkæbɪnət]	Aktenschrank	He closes his filing cabinet before he leaves the office.
	calendar ['kælɪndə]	Kalender	Calendars are usually for 12 months.
	radiator ['reɪdɪˌeɪtə]	Heizkörper	It is cold. Turn the radiator on.
	window ['wɪndəʊ]	Fenster	Can we open the window?
	notice board ['nəʊtɪs ˌbɔ:d]	schwarzes Brett	
	cuddly toy [ˌkʌdlɪ 'tɔɪ]	Kuscheltier	
2	**finances (pl)** ['faɪnænsɪz]	Finanzen	
	to keep (kept, kept) [ki:p, kept, kept]	(be)halten, führen	You keep milk in the fridge.
	record ['rekɔ:d]	Aufzeichnung	
	member ['membə]	Mitglied	Are you a member of a football club?
	personal ['pɜ:snəl]	persönlich	
	post code ['pəʊst ˌkəʊd]	Postleitzahl	
	area code ['eərɪə ˌkəʊd]	Vorwahl	
3	**to note down** [ˌnəʊt 'daʊn]	notieren	Can you note down this information?
	separate ['seprət]	einzeln, gesondert	The children sleep in separate bedrooms.
	sheet of paper [ˌʃi:t‿əv 'peɪpə]	Blatt Papier	I must write a list. Have you got a sheet of paper?
	start date ['stɑ:t ˌdeɪt]	Starttermin	
	weight [weɪt]	Gewicht	I lost weight last year – 5 kilos.
	membership number ['membəʃɪp]	Mitgliedsnummer	
	to save [seɪv]	hier: speichern	Always save documents on your computer.
	to edit ['edɪt]	bearbeiten	
	to delete [dɪ'li:t]	löschen	If you don't like something you wrote, delete it.
	nearly ['nɪəlɪ]	fast, beinahe	Are you OK? You nearly fell over.
	centimetre ['sentɪˌmi:tə]	Zentimeter	
	Oh dear! [ˌəʊ 'dɪə]	Du meine Güte!	
	to write down [raɪt 'daʊn]	aufschreiben	Homework is on the board. Write it down, please.
	to let (let, let) [let, let, let]	lassen	I was late last night: my friend didn't let me go home!

Unit 5 Where I live

Focus

2	**Australia** [ɒs'treɪlɪə]	Australien	
	south-east [ˌsaʊθ'i:st]	Südosten	
	(the) most [ðə 'məʊst]	(die) meisten	Most people live in cities.
	coast [kəʊst]	Küste	The coast is where the land ends and the sea starts.
	capital ['kæpɪtl]	Hauptstadt	London is the capital of England.
	to immigrate ['ɪmɪˌgreɪt]	einwandern	Millions of people have immigrated to Australia.
	to cook a barbecue [ˌkʊk‿ə 'bɑ:bɪkju:]	grillen	
	since [sɪns]	seit	I've waited since 5 o'clock!
	outside [ˌaʊt'saɪd]	außen, außerhalb, im Freien, draußen	outside ↔ inside
	break [breɪk]	Pause	After the first two lessons we always have a break.

	secondary school ['sekəndrɪ ˌsku:l]	etwa: weiterführende Schule	
	final year [ˌfaɪnl 'jɪə]	Abschlussklasse	
	vocational school [vəʊˌkeɪʃnl 'sku:l]	etwa: Berufsschule	
	electrician [ɪˌlek'trɪʃn]	Elektriker(in)	
3	**population** [ˌpɒpjʊ'leɪʃn]	Bevölkerung	London has a large population.
	average ['ævrɪdʒ]	durchschnittlich	The average family has two children.
	temperature ['temprətʃə]	Temperatur	! Die erste Silbe wird betont.
4	**diagram** ['daɪəˌgræm]	Diagramm	A diagram can make things clearer.
5	**present perfect** [ˌpreznt 'pɜ:fɪkt]	Perfekt	

Practice

2	**history** ['hɪstrɪ]	Geschichte	In history lessons you learn about life in the past.
	Aborigine [ˌæbə'rɪdʒənɪ]	Ureinwohner(in) Australiens	
	inhabitant [ɪn'hæbɪtənt]	Einwohner(in)	
	Native American [ˌneɪtɪv‿ə'merɪkən]	amerikanische(r) Ureinwohner(in)	Another word for (American) Indian.
	BC (= before Christ) [ˌbi:'si:, bɪˌfɔ: 'kraɪst]	vor Christus	
	Englishman ['ɪnglɪʃmən]	Engländer	
	to land [lænd]	landen	The plane landed five minutes ago.
	Australian [ɒs'treɪlɪən]	Australier(in); australisch	Australian wine is world famous.
	prison ['prɪzn]	Gefängnis	Criminals go to prison.
	multicultural [ˌmʌltɪ'kʌltʃərəl]	multikulturell	London and New York are multicultural cities.
	on the right [ˌɒn ðə 'raɪt]	rechts	There's a big supermarket on the right.
	Asian ['eɪʃn]	Asiat(in); asiatisch	Chinese people and people from India are Asians.
3	**tense** [tens]	Tempus, Zeitform	The simple present is a tense.
4	**rainforest** ['reɪnˌfɒrɪst]	Regenwald	
	desert ['dezət]	Wüste	There's no water in the desert.
	rock [rɒk]	Fels, Stein	A rock is a hard thing to sit on.
	south-eastern [saʊθ‿'i:stən]	südöstlich	
	south [saʊθ]	Süden	
	east [i:st]	Osten	
	west [west]	Westen	
	northern ['nɔ:ðən]	nördlich	
	southern ['sʌðən]	südlich	
	eastern ['i:stən]	östlich	
	western ['westən]	westlich	
	north-western [ˌnɔ:θ 'westən]	nordwestlich	
	central ['sentrəl]	zentral, in der Mitte gelegen	Central London has a lot of traffic.
5	**to compare** [kəm'peə]	vergleichen	Compare the two pictures. Are they the same?

Listening and reading

1	**across** [ə'krɒs]	über	We went across the river in a boat.
	outback ['aʊtˌbæk]	Busch, Hinterland	Life in the outback is very quiet.
	road train ['rəʊd ˌtreɪn]	Lastzug	
	truck [trʌk]	Lastwagen	truck = lorry
	to carry ['kærɪ]	tragen, transportieren	Can you carry this box for me, please?
	cattle (pl) ['kætl]	Vieh	Cattle eat grass.
	oil [ɔɪl]	Öl	
	means [mi:nz]	Mittel	Cars, buses and taxis are different means of transport.
	freight [freɪt]	Fracht	
	transport ['trænspɔ:t]	Transport	! Betonung

	G'day (informal, AUS) [gəˈdeɪ]	Tag, hi, hallo	
	mostly [ˈməʊstlɪ]	hauptsächlich, meistens	We're mostly out at the weekend.
	pretty [ˈprɪtɪ]	ziemlich	The nights are pretty cold, and the days pretty hot.
	track [træk]	Spur, Feldweg	He left the road and walked down the track.
	to weigh [weɪ]	wiegen	These shopping bags weigh too much.
	tonne [tʌn]	metrische Tonne	
	wheel [wiːl]	Rad	A bike has got two wheels.
	journey [ˈdʒɜːnɪ]	Reise	It's a long journey from here to Berlin by car.
	fridge [frɪdʒ]	Kühlschrank	It stays cold in the fridge.
	cooker [ˈkʊkə]	Herd, Kocher	
4	**everywhere** [ˈevrɪweə]	überall	= in all places
5	**sand** [sænd]	Sand	You can make castles with sand on the beach.
	round [raʊnd]	rund	The earth is round.
6	**boring** [ˈbɔːrɪŋ]	langweilig	Driving through the desert is boring.
	exciting [ɪkˈsaɪtɪŋ]	aufregend, spannend	Surfing is exciting.
	lonely [ˈləʊnlɪ]	einsam	Life in the outback can be lonely.
7	**to draw (drew, drawn)** [drɔː, druː, drɔːn]	zeichnen	Let's draw a picture with our pencils.
	kangaroo [ˌkæŋgəˈruː]	Känguru	

Gateway to work

1	**to deliver** [dɪˈlɪvə]	(aus)liefern	They deliver the newspaper every day.
	horse [hɔːs]	Pferd	You can ride a bike or you can ride a horse.
	supermarket [ˈsuːpəˌmɑːkɪt]	Supermarkt	
	multi-storey car park [ˌmʌltɪ stɔːrɪ]	Parkhaus	
	industrial estate [ɪnˌdʌstrɪəl‿ɪˈsteɪt]	Gewerbegebiet	
	motorway [ˈməʊtəˌweɪ]	Autobahn	
	railway station [ˈreɪlweɪ ˌsteɪʃn]	Bahnhof	
	bus station [ˈbʌs‿ˌsteɪʃn]	Bushaltestelle	
2	**(for) help** [fə ˈhelp]	(um) Hilfe	I don't speak the language. I'll ask this lady for help.
	to follow [ˈfɒləʊ]	folgen	Follow me, please!
	directions (pl) [dɪˈrekʃny]	Wegbeschreibung	I'm lost. I need directions.
	to look for [ˈlʊk fɔː]	suchen nach	I'm looking for my mobile. Do you know where it is?
	straight [streɪt]	gerade	Walk straight along this road.
	up [ʌp]	hinauf	
	traffic light [ˈtræfɪk ˌlaɪt]	Ampel	If there is a roundabout, you don't need traffic lights.
	to turn [tɜːn]	sich drehen, abbiegen	Turn left!
	along [əˈlɒŋ]	entlang	The track goes along the river.
	past [pɑːst]	vorbei/vorüber an	Go past the cinema and look for the sign.
	bridge [brɪdʒ]	Brücke	A bridge goes over a river.
	roundabout [ˈraʊndəˌbaʊt]	Kreisel, Kreisverkehr	
3	**railway** [ˈreɪlweɪ]	Bahn(hof)	
4	**tourist** [ˈtʊərɪst]	Tourist(in)	There are too many tourists on this island.
	to go on [gəʊ‿ˈɒn]	weitergehen	Don't stop at the bridge. Go on.

Unit 6 Have you ever ...?

Focus

	ever [ˈevə]	je(mals)	Have you ever been to Berlin? – Yes, once.
1	**unusual** [ʌnˈjuːʒʊəl]	unüblich, ungewöhnlich	He's got red hair – that's unusual.
	funny [ˈfʌnɪ]	lustig, witzig, komisch	Comics can be funny.
2	**jump** [dʒʌmp]	Sprung	
	terrifying [ˈterəˌfaɪɪŋ]	erschreckend, Furcht einflößend	
3	**crazy** [ˈkreɪzɪ]	verrückt	What a crazy idea!

4	**competition** [ˌkɒmpəˈtɪʃn]	Wettbewerb	
	feeling [ˈfiːlɪŋ]	Gefühl	to feel → feeling
	amazing [əˈmeɪzɪŋ]	erstaunlich, toll	
	concert [ˈkɒnsət]	Konzert	Let's go to the rock concert next Saturday.
5	**stage** [steɪdʒ]	Bühne	There is a stage in every theatre.
	marathon [ˈmærəθn]	Marathon	
6	**piece of paper** [ˌpiːs‿əv ˈpeɪpə]	Blatt Papier	
	to guess [ges]	(er)raten	Guess how old my grandmother is! – 95? 100?

Practice

1	**to save** [seɪv]	hier: sparen	You can save money or time.
	somewhere [ˈsʌmweə]	irgendwo	somebody – something – somewhere
	Egypt [ˈiːdʒɪpt]	Ägypten	
	pyramid [ˈpɪrəmɪd]	Pyramide	
	fascinating [ˈfæsɪneɪtɪŋ]	faszinierend	
	chaotic [keɪˈɒtɪk]	chaotisch	
	Kenya [ˈkenjə]	Kenia	
	Moscow [ˈmɒskəʊ]	Moskau	
2	**extreme sport** [ɪkˈstriːm ˌspɔːt]	Extremsportart	
	dangerous [ˈdeɪndʒərəs]	gefährlich	Don't go so fast – it's dangerous!
	rock climbing [ˈrɒk‿klaɪmɪŋ]	Klettern, Klettersport	! Aussprache: climbing
	rock climber [ˈrɒk‿klaɪmə]	Kletterer(in)	
	to climb [klaɪm]	(er)klettern, besteigen	
	high [haɪ]	hoch	Mt Everest is the highest mountain in the world.
	California [ˌkælɪˈfɔːnɪə]	Kalifornien	
	to reach [riːtʃ]	erreichen	When we reached the hotel, we were tired.
	top [tɒp]	Spitze, Gipfel	We reached the top in the evening.
	probably [ˈprɒbəblɪ]	wahrscheinlich	It's so hot! It's probably 40°.
3	**excited** [ɪkˈsaɪtɪd]	aufgeregt	Today is my birthday party. I'm very excited!
	absolutely [ˈæbsəluːtlɪ]	absolut, wirklich	
	amazed [əˈmeɪzd]	erstaunt	Very surprised.
	bored [bɔːd]	gelangweilt	! boring = langweilig; bored = gelangweilt
	fascinated [ˈfæsɪneɪtɪd]	fasziniert	
	interested (in) [ˈɪntrəstɪd‿ɪn]	interessiert (an)	I'm interested in music. = I think music is interesting.
	terrified [ˈterəfaɪd]	erschreckt	= very, very frightened
4	**title** [ˈtaɪtl]	Titel	! Schreibweise

Listening and reading

1	**engineering** [ˌendʒɪˈnɪərɪŋ]	Technik, Maschinenbau	
	helicopter [ˈhelɪˌkɒptə]	Hubschrauber	You can't fly far in a helicopter.
	to charter [ˈtʃɑːtə]	chartern	
	to hire [ˈhaɪə]	mieten, leihen	You can hire a car at the airport.
	whatever [wɒtˈevə]	was (auch immer)	Take whatever you want!
	to service [ˈsɜːvɪs]	pflegen, warten	You should service your car once a year.
	extra [ˈekstrə]	besonders, Extra-	Can I have extra chips, please?
	firm [fɜːm]	Firma, Unternehmen	
	to be based (in ...) [bɪ ˈbeɪst‿ɪn]	seinen Sitz (in ...) haben	The company is based in London.
2	**advertising company** [ˈædvətaɪzɪŋ]	Werbeagentur	
	scene [siːn]	Szene	This is a very boring scene in the film.
	machine gun [məˈʃiːn ˌgʌn]	Maschinengewehr	
	to kill [kɪl]	töten	I don't like that film. They kill too many people.
	pilot [ˈpaɪlət]	Pilot(in)	A pilot flies a plane or a helicopter.
	down [daʊn]	hinunter	to go down ↔ to go up

	to fire ['faɪə]	abdrücken, feuern	
	congratulations [kənˌgrætʃʊ'leɪʃnz]	Glückwunsch, Glückwünsche	You won the race. Congratulations!
	light [laɪt]	Licht	The room is dark. I'll get a light.
	microphone ['maɪkrəfəʊn]	Mikrofon	! Betonung
	to put on [pʊt‿'ɒn]	anziehen, aufsetzen	It's cold. Put this hat on.
	to shout [ʃaʊt]	schreien	I can't hear you. You will have to shout.
	excellent ['eksələnt]	ausgezeichnet	
	to shake (shook, shaken) [ʃeɪk, ʃʊk, 'ʃeɪkən]	schütteln	When you meet somebody, you often shake hands.
3	**to direct** [dɪ'rekt]	Regie führen	
	player ['pleɪə]	Spieler	player → to play
	gun [gʌn]	Gewehr, Pistole	In the USA more people have guns.
5	**above** [ə'bʌv]	über	There's a nice picture above the table.
8	**skateboarding** ['skeɪtˌbɔ:dɪŋ]	Skateboardfahren	
	surfing ['sɜ:fɪŋ]	Surfen	You can go surfing in Australia.
	skydiving ['skaɪˌdaɪvɪŋ]	Fallschirmspringen	
	result [rɪ'zʌlt]	Ergebnis	The results is: Liverpool 2 – Arsenal 0

Gateway to work

1	**worldwide** [ˌwɜ:ld'waɪd]	weltweit, global	
	museum [mju:'zi:əm]	Museum	
	to call [kɔ:l]	(an)rufen	He called at 2 o'clock in the morning!
	Swedish ['swi:dɪʃ]	schwedisch	
	Bye! [baɪ]	Tschüs!	
	to put through [pʊt 'θru:]	durchstellen, verbinden	Can you put me through to Mr Williams, please?
3	**speaker** ['spi:kə]	Sprecher(in)	speaker → to speak
4	**to invent** [ɪn'vent]	erfinden	Who invented paper? – The Chinese.

nit 7 The Internet

Focus

2	**president** ['prezɪdənt]	Präsident(in)	
	in Spanish [ɪn 'spænɪʃ]	auf Spanisch	He spoke to me in Spanish.
	Spain [speɪn]	Spanien	
	global ['gləʊbl]	global, weltweit	
3	**instant messenger** [ˌɪnstənt 'mesɪdʒə]	Onlinenachrichtendienst	
5	**technology** [tek'nɒlədʒɪ]	Technik	! Aussprache: Das ch wird wie k gesprochen.
	moon [mu:n]	Mond	
	to surf [sɜ:f]	surfen	
	pocket calculator [ˌpɒkɪt 'kælkjʊleɪtə]	Taschenrechner	

Practice

1	**site** [saɪt]	hier: Seite	
	to search ['sɜ:tʃ]	suchen	I can't find it. I've searched everywhere!
	antivirus [ˌæntɪ'vaɪrəs]	Antivirus-	
	ringtone ['rɪŋtəʊn]	Klingelton	
	everything ['evrɪθɪŋ]	alles	Everything is OK.
2	**to ride (rode, ridden)** [raɪd, rəʊd, 'rɪdn]	fahren; reiten	He rides his bike to work.
3	**quiet** ['kwaɪət]	leise, ruhig	Be quiet! Don't say a word.
4	**inventor** [ɪn'ventə]	Erfinder(in)	
	military ['mɪlɪtrɪ]	Militär	
	everyone ['evrɪwʌn]	jede(r); alle	= everybody
	atomic research centre [əˌtɒmɪk rɪ'sɜ:tʃ]	Atomforschungszentrum	
	Switzerland ['swɪtsələnd]	die Schweiz	

	document ['dɒkjʊmənt]	Dokument	
	system ['sɪstəm]	System	
	simple ['sɪmpl]	einfach	= easy
	method ['meθəd]	Methode	
	horrible ['hɒrəbl]	fürchterlich, schrecklich	
	safe [seɪf]	sicher	This product is very safe.
	over ['əʊvə]	(her)über	I bought my car over a friend, not a newspaper.
	invention [ɪn'venʃn]	Erfindung	The invention of emails has changed the world.
	technical ['teknɪkl]	technisch, technologisch	He doesn't understand technical things.
5	**singular** ['sɪŋgjʊlə]	Singular, Einzahl	
	knowledge (no pl) ['nɒlɪdʒ]	Wissen, Kenntnis(se)	
	glasses (pl) ['glɑːsɪz]	Brille	! My glasses ARE on the table.
	spectacles (pl) ['spektəklz]	Brille	
	scissors (pl) ['sɪzəz]	Schere	! The scissors ARE on my desk.
6	**track** [ˌtræk]	hier: Titel	

Listening and reading

1	**e-commerce** [ˌiː'kɒmɜːs]	elektronischer Handel	
	stage [steɪdʒ]	hier: Arbeitsgang, Phase	
	robot ['rəʊˌbɒt]	Roboter	Robots can make cars.
	catalogue ['kætəˌlɒg]	Katalog	
	war [wɔː]	Krieg	
	trolley ['trɒlɪ]	Einkaufswagen	
	payment ['peɪmənt]	(Be)zahlung	
	secure socket layer [sɪˌkjʊə 'sɒkɪt ˌleɪə]	SSL-Verbindung	
	checkout ['tʃekaʊt]	Kasse	That supermarket has ten checkouts.
	confirmation [ˌkɒnfə'meɪʃn]	Bestätigung	The confirmation comes as an email.
	delivery [dɪ'lɪvrɪ]	(Aus)lieferung	Delivery is in five days.
	to steal (stole, stolen) [stiːl, stəʊl, 'stəʊlən]	stehlen	Some people try to steal money on the Internet.
	to encrypt [ɪn'krɪpt]	chiffrieren, verschlüsseln	
	to log on [lɒg‿'ɒn]	sich anmelden, sich einwählen	
	to type in [taɪp‿'ɪn]	eintippen	Type in your name and address.
	immediately [ɪ'miːdɪətlɪ]	sofort	Can you come now? – OK, I'm leaving immediately.
	account [ə'kaʊnt]	Konto	Where do you have your bank account?
	to browse [braʊz]	blättern, schmökern	
	special offer [ˌspeʃl‿'ɒfə]	Sonderangebot	Special offer today: Jeans only £15.
	postperson ['pəʊstˌpɜːsn]	Postbote (-botin)	
	package ['pækɪdʒ]	Paket	A package came for you today.
2	**store** [stɔː]	Laden, Geschäft	Another word for a shop.

Gateway to work

1	**state** [steɪt]	Staat	There are over 50 states in the USA.
	advantage [əd'vɑːntɪdʒ]	Vorteil	In basketball, it's an advantage to be tall.
	to log in [lɒg‿'ɪn]	einloggen	
	to contact ['kɒntækt]	Kontakt aufnehmen mit	You can contact me by phone or email.
	stuff (informal) [stʌf]	Zeug	
	to believe (in) [bɪ'liːv‿ɪn]	glauben (an)	
	squishy ['skwɪʃɪ]	matschig	
2	**itself** [ɪt'self]	sich (selbst)	
	button ['bʌtn]	Knopf, Taste	
	to click [klɪk]	klicken	
	directly [dɪ'rektlɪ]	direkt	She came here directly from the station.

	basic ['beɪsɪk]	grundlegend, grundsätzlich	In the first year of English you learn a lot of basic language.
	login ['lɒgɪn]	Anmeldung	
3	**designer** [dɪ'zaɪnə]	Layouter(in), Gestalter(in)	
	extremely [ɪk'stri:mlɪ]	extrem, äußerst	
	to navigate ['nævɪˌgeɪt]	lenken, navigieren	
	to exit ['eksɪt]	verlassen, beenden	
	search engine ['sɜ:tʃ‿endʒɪn]	Suchmaschine	
	to organise ['ɔ:gəˌnaɪz]	einrichten, ordnen	
	clear [klɪə]	klar, eindeutig	Do you understand? – Yes, that's very clear.
	final ['faɪnl]	letzte(r, s)	! Die ersten Buchstaben reimen sich mit 'nine'.
	animation [ˌænɪ'meɪʃn]	Animation	
5	**toy** [tɔɪ]	Spielzeug	Children play with toys.
	hot rod (informal) [hɒt 'rɒd]	frisiertes Auto	
	tyre ['taɪə]	Reifen	
	paint [peɪnt]	Farbe, Lack	
	low [ləʊ]	niedrig, tief	high ↔ low

Unit 8 Career plans

Focus

2	**farm** [fɑ:m]	Bauernhof	Food comes from farms in the country.
	plan [plæn]	Plan	
	future ['fju:tʃə]	Zukunft	past → present → future
	Poland ['pəʊlənd]	Polen	
	nursing ['nɜ:sɪŋ]	Krankenpflege	
	apprenticeship [ə'prentɪsʃɪp]	Ausbildung, Lehre	You do an apprenticeship for three years.
	construction [kən'strʌkʃn]	Bau(gewerbe)	
	Me too. [mi: 'tu:]	Ich auch.	
	Denmark ['denmɑ:k]	Dänemark	
	seriously ['sɪərɪəslɪ]	im Ernst	The story is really true. Seriously!
	agricultural [ˌægrɪ'kʌltʃrəl]	landwirtschaftlich	
	Ireland ['aɪələnd]	Irland	
4	**positive** ['pɒzətɪv]	positiv	
	negative ['negətɪv]	negativ	
	frightening ['fraɪtnɪŋ]	beängstigend, erschreckend	That was a frightening film.
	strict [strɪkt]	streng	My boss is very strict. She often says "Don't ...!"
	to be able to [bi:‿'eɪbl tə]	können	My job is near home. So I am able to walk there.

Practice

1	**electronics** [ˌelek'trɒnɪks]	Elektronik	
	travel ['trævl]	Reise	
	tourism ['tʊərɪzm]	Tourismus	
	catering ['keɪtərɪŋ]	Gastronomie, Hotel- und Gaststättengewerbe	
	hairdressing ['heədresɪŋ]	Frisieren; Friseurberuf	
	motor ['məʊtə]	Motor, Auto	
	mechanics [mɪ'kænɪks]	Mechanik	
	art [ɑ:t]	Kunst	She likes art because she's good at drawing.
	travel agent ['trævl‿eɪdʒnt]	Reisebürokaufmann/-frau	You can book holidays at the travel agent's.
	nursery ['nɜ:srɪ]	Kindergarten, Hort	
	hairdressing salon [ˌheədresɪŋ sə'lu:n]	Friseursalon	
3	**working hours** ['wɜ:kɪŋ‿aʊəz]	Geschäftszeiten	She works hard. Her working hours are long.

	duty ['dju:tɪ]	Aufgabe	
	to serve [sɜ:v]	servieren, bedienen	They serve steak with chips.
	stock [stɒk]	Lager(bestand)	Does that shop have a good stock of things?
	to water ['wɔ:tə]	gießen	In summer you have to water the garden every day.
	wages (pl) ['weɪdʒɪz]	Arbeitslohn	They pay good wages.
	uniform ['ju:nɪfɔ:m]	Uniform	Pupils in England wear school uniforms.
	apron ['eɪprən]	Schürze	Cooks wear aprons.
4	**preposition** [ˌprepə'zɪʃn]	Präposition	
	to look up [lʊk‿'ʌp]	nachschlagen	You can look up words in a dictionary.
5	**spelling mistake** [ˌspelɪŋ mɪ'steɪk]	Rechtschreibfehler	

Listening and reading

1	**headline** ['hedlaɪn]	Schlagzeile	Read this headline.
	to read through [ri:d 'θru:]	durchlesen	Before you write, read through the exam carefully.
	experience [ɪk'spɪərɪənts]	Erfahrung	He worked in the USA. It was a wonderful experience.
	the do's and don'ts [ðə ˌdu:z‿ən 'dəʊnts]	was man tun und nicht tun sollte	
	nervous ['nɜ:vəs]	nervös	! Die erste Silbe wird betont.
	to worry ['wʌrɪ]	sich Sorgen machen	You worry too much. Relax!
	traffic ['træfɪk]	Verkehr	I'm late. The traffic was terrible.
	smart [smɑ:t]	elegant	She always wears smart clothes.
	workshop ['wɜ:kˌʃɒp]	Werkstatt	
	hard hat ['hɑ:d ˌhæt]	Schutzhelm	
	way [weɪ]	Art und Weise	I'm found a new way to learn vocabulary.
	stupid ['stju:pɪd]	dumm, blöd	= silly
	suggestion [sə'dʒestʃn]	Vorschlag	Can I make a suggestion? Let's go on a short holiday.
	friendly ['frendlɪ]	freundlich	
	impression [ɪm'preʃn]	Eindruck	What was your impression of the new teacher?
2	**own** [əʊn]	eigene(r, s)	! Verwende 'own' nie ohne my/your/his/her etc.
	watch [wɒtʃ]	Armbanduhr	
	bus stop ['bʌs‿stɒp]	Bushaltestelle	
	round [raʊnd]	um … herum	
	corner ['kɔ:nə]	Ecke	Most rooms have four corners.
	to hit (hit, hit) [hɪt, hɪt, hɪt]	hier: anfahren	
	idiot ['ɪdɪət]	Idiot, Trottel	It's very rude to call sb an idiot.
	to catch (caught, caught) [kætʃ, kɔ:t, kɔ:t]	hier: erreichen, erwischen	I catch the 8 o'clock bus every day.
4	**reason** ['ri:zn]	Grund	Why did you do it? What was the reason?
6	**frightened** ['fraɪtnd]	erschreckt, erschrocken	Some people are frightened of big dogs.
	attractive [ə'træktɪv]	attraktiv, gut aussehend	
8	**further education** [ˌfɜ:ðər‿edjʊ'keɪʃn]	Aus- und Weiterbildung	
	report [rɪ'pɔ:t]	Bericht	There's the report you asked for.

Gateway to work

1	**training course** ['treɪnɪŋ ˌkɔ:s]	Kurs, Lehrgang, Schulung	
	How do you do [ˌhaʊ djʊ 'du:]	Guten Tag	
	organiser ['ɔ:gəˌnaɪzə]	Organisator(in), Veranstalter(in)	
	Pleased to meet you. [ˌpli:zd tə 'mi:t jə]	Es freut mich, dich/Sie kennen zu lernen.	
	during ['djʊərɪŋ]	während	He works hard during the day.
	myself [maɪ'self]	mich/mir (selbst)	I made it myself.
	north-east [ˌnɔ:θ'i:st]	Nordosten	
	visit ['vɪzɪt]	Besuch	It's his third visit to Germany.
	not quite [nɒt 'kwaɪt]	nicht ganz	Is lunch ready? – Not quite.

4	**culture** ['kʌltʃə]	Kultur	
	first name ['fɜ:st ˌneɪm]	Vorname	My first name is Jack.
	straight away [ˌstreɪt‿ə'weɪ]	sofort	They became friends straight away.
	formal ['fɔ:ml]	förmlich	His boss is very formal.
	situation [ˌsɪtʃu'eɪʃn]	Situation	
	everyday ['evrɪdeɪ]	alltäglich	Traffic is an everyday problem in this city.
	serious ['sɪərɪəs]	ernst(haft)	He doesn't laugh, he's very serious.
	unmarried [ʌn'mærɪd]	ledig, unverheiratet	He's forty, but he's still unmarried.

At work

1	**shower** ['ʃaʊə]	Dusche	
	department store [dɪ'pɑ:tmənt ˌstɔ:]	Kaufhaus	They sell everything in a department store.
	to attend [ə'tend]	besuchen, teilnehmen an	He has to attend a meeting morning and afternoon.
	trade fair ['treɪd ˌfeə]	Messe	
	sales [seɪlz]	Verkauf, Vertrieb	
2	**diary** ['daɪərɪ]	Terminkalender	Her diary is very full this week.
4	**to phone** [fəʊn]	anrufen	
	I'm free. [aɪm 'fri:]	hier: Ich habe Zeit.	I'm free on Monday and Tuesday.
	This is ... ['ðɪs‿ɪz]	hier: Hier spricht ...	
	just a minute [ˌdʒʌst‿ə 'mɪnɪt]	einen Augenblick/ Moment bitte	
	I'm afraid ... [ˌaɪm‿ə'freɪd]	Tut mir Leid, aber ...	I'm afraid I can't come.
	How about ...? [ˌhaʊ‿ə'baʊt]	Wie wäre es mit ...?	How about going for a long walk?
5	**Is that convenient?** [ˌɪz ðæt kən'vi:nɪənt]	Passt Ihnen das?	

Unit 9 Love at first sight

Focus

	love at first sight [ˌlʌv‿ət fɜ:st 'saɪt]	Liebe auf den ersten Blick	
2	**dream** [dri:m]	Traum	
	(shopping) mall (AE) ['ʃɒpɪŋ 'mɔ:l]	Einkaufszentrum	
	boyfriend ['bɔɪˌfrend]	Freund (eines Mädchens)	Robert is Becky's boyfriend.
	locker ['lɒkə]	Schließfach, Spind	Sam is putting his clothes in his locker.
	girlfriend ['gɜ:lˌfrend]	Freundin (eines Jungen)	Ben is happy. He's got a new girlfriend.
	to sit down [sɪt 'daʊn]	sich (hin)setzen	I'm tired. I must sit down for a minute.
4	**while** [waɪl]	während, als	He called me while I was doing my homework.
6	**past continuous** [ˌpɑ:st kən'tɪnjʊəs]	Verlaufsform der Vergangenheit	

Practice

2	**everybody** ['evrɪˌbɒdɪ]	jede(r); alle	everybody ↔ nobody
	to hold (held, held) [həʊld, held, held]	halten	Hold this for a moment, please.
	to hold hands [həʊld 'hændz]	Händchen halten	
	joke [dʒəʊk]	Witz	Jokes make people laugh.
	buffet ['bʊfeɪ]	Büfett	
3	**to ring (rang, rung)** [rɪŋ, ræŋ, rʌŋ]	klingeln	Is your mobile ringing?
	to text [tekst]	eine SMS-Nachricht senden, simsen	
4	**to go wrong** [gəʊ 'rɒŋ]	schief gehen	Yesterday, I lost my money – everything went wrong!
	to arrange [ə'reɪndʒ]	hier: ausmachen	We arranged to go this weekend.
	unfortunately [ʌn'fɔ:tʃnətlɪ]	leider	Unfortunately I don't speak Spanish.
	to bet (bet, bet) [bet, bet, bet]	wetten	The sun is shining now, but I bet it will rain later.
	to turn round [ˌtɜ:n 'raʊnd]	(sich) umdrehen	
5	**object pronoun** ['ɒbdʒɪkt ˌprəʊnaʊn]	Pronomen im Akkusativ	
7	**necessary** ['nesəsrɪ]	nötig, notwendig	It won't be necessary to book tickets before.
	the Rhine [ðə 'rain]	der Rhein	

Listening and reading

2	**lawn** [lɔ:n]	Rasen	
	main building [ˌmeɪn ˈbɪldɪŋ]	Hauptgebäude	
	advice [ədˈvaɪs]	Rat(schlag)	! some advice: Let me give you some advice.
	grass [grɑ:s]	Gras	
	towards [təˈwɔ:dz]	in Richtung (auf)	I saw her. She was coming towards me.
	hair style [ˈheəˌstaɪl]	Frisur	
	dress [dres]	Kleid	What a nice dress!
	to flirt [flɜ:t]	flirten	
	jealous [ˈdʒeləs]	eifersüchtig	Tim likes Susan. I'm so jealous.
	to cry [kraɪ]	weinen	She was so sad that she cried.
	raindrop [ˈreɪnˌdrɒp]	Regentropfen	
	to stamp [stæmp]	stampfen	
	wet [wet]	nass	It's rainy today. My hair is wet.
	speaker [ˈspi:kə]	hier: Lautsprecher	
	amplifier [ˈæmplɪˌfaɪə]	Verstärker	
	equipment (no pl) [ɪˈkwɪpmənt]	Ausrüstung, Gerät(e)	A rock band needs a lot of equipment.
	heavy [ˈhevɪ]	hier: heftig	
	pretty [ˈprɪtɪ]	hübsch	She's a pretty girl. She's got a very pretty face.
	kind [kaɪnd]	nett, freundlich	A kind person is good to others.
	helpful [ˈhelpfl]	hilfsbereit	Nico is going to come and help. He's really helpful.
3	**happy ending** [ˌhæpɪ‿ˈendɪŋ]	Happyend	
4	**to kiss** [kɪs]	küssen	
5	**lipstick** [ˈlɪpˌstɪk]	Lippenstift	
	personality [ˌpɜ:səˈnælətɪ]	Persönlichkeit	He's kind and friendly – a nice personality.
	opposite [ˈɒpəzɪt]	Gegenteil	'Yes' is the opposite of 'no'.
6	**romantic** [rəʊˈmæntɪk]	romantisch	
	silly [ˈsɪlɪ]	albern, dumm	That's a silly game.
	sexist [ˈseksɪst]	sexistisch	
	good-looking [ˌgʊdˈlʊkɪŋ]	gut aussehend	What is Nico like? – He's very good-looking.
	slim [slɪm]	schlank, schmal, dünn	
	sporty [ˈspɔ:tɪ]	sportlich	
	figure [ˈfɪgə]	hier: Figur	
	intelligent [ɪnˈtelɪdʒənt]	intelligent	
	honest [ˈɒnɪst]	ehrlich	An honest person always tells the truth.
7	**discussion** [dɪˈskʌʃn]	Diskussion, Gespräch	

Gateway to work

1	**to offer** [ˈɒfə]	(an)bieten	Can I offer you a drink?
	nursery school [ˈnɜ:srɪ ˌsku:l]	Kindergarten	
	head teacher [ˌhed ˈti:tʃə]	Rektor(in), Schulleiter(in)	
	bed and breakfast [ˌbed‿ən ˈbrekfəst]	(Frühstücks)pension	A bed and breakfast is cheaper than a hotel.
	floor [flɔ:]	hier: Etage, Stockwerk	The department store has six floors.
	corridor [ˈkɒrɪˌdɔ:]	Flur, Gang, Korridor	
3	**to role-play** [ˈrəʊlˌpleɪ]	Rollenspiel spielen	
	conference room [ˈkɒnfrəns ˌru:m]	Besprechungsraum	
	to take a seat [ˌteɪk‿ə ˈsi:t]	Platz nehmen	Why are you standing? Take a seat.
	polite [pəˈlaɪt]	höflich	rude ↔ polite
	offer [ˈɒfə]	Angebot	
	request [rɪˈkwest]	Bitte, Wunsch	

At work

1	**ankle** [æŋkl]	(Fuß)knöchel	
	chest [tʃest]	Brust(korb)	

	elbow ['elbəʊ]	Ellbogen	
	nose [nəʊz]	Nase	
	shoulder ['ʃəʊldə]	Schulter	I can't use my left arm. My shoulder hurts.
	stomach ['stʌmək]	Magen, Bauch	
	tummy ['tʌmɪ]	Bauch	
	toe [təʊ]	Zeh(e)	
2	**to bite (bit, bitten)** [baɪt, bɪt, 'bɪtn]	beißen	My cat bit me today.
	to smell [smel, smelt, smelt]	riechen	That smells good! I'm hungry.
	to move [muːv]	(sich) bewegen, umziehen	Mr Jackson's back hurts, he can't move.
	to bend (bent, bent) [bend, bent, bent]	beugen, biegen	Can you bend that long piece of wood?
4	**headache** ['hedeɪk]	Kopfschmerzen, Kopfweh	**!** Singular: I've got a bad headache.
	to twist one's ankle [ˌtwɪst wʌnz‿'æŋkl]	mit dem Fuß umknicken	
	I feel sick. [ˌaɪ fiːl 'sɪk]	Mir ist schlecht/übel.	
	to hurt (hurt, hurt) [hɜːt, hɜːt, hɜːt]	(sich) verletzen	
	cold [kəʊld]	Erkältung, Schnupfen	She's got a cold. She is staying in bed.
5	**tablet** ['tæblɪt]	Tablette	
	aspirin ['æsprɪn]	Aspirin	
	paracetamol [ˌpærə'siːtəmɒl]	Paracetamol	
	plaster ['plɑːstə]	Pflaster	
	wound [wuːnd]	Wunde	
	to rest [rest]	(sich) ausruhen	They rested after the long trip.
	to lie down (lay, lain) [laɪ 'daʊn, leɪ 'daʊn, leɪn 'daʊn]	sich hinlegen	You are tired. Why don't you lie down?
	ice [aɪs]	Eis	
	to bandage ['bændɪdʒ]	bandagieren, verbinden	
6	**primary school** ['praɪmərɪ ˌskuːl]	Grundschule	
	to teach (taught, taught) [tiːtʃ, tɔːt, tɔːt]	lehren, unterrichten	
	club [klʌb]	Klub, Verein	health club
	shirt [ʃɜːt]	Hemd	
	blouse [blaʊs]	Bluse	
	tie [taɪ]	Krawatte	He always wears a shirt and tie.
	skirt [skɜːt]	Rock	Sarah's new skirt is very nice.
	pullover ['pʊləʊvə]	Pullover	
	swimming ['swɪmɪŋ]	Schwimmen	I like swimming.
	dance [dɑːns]	Tanz(en)	The music is great – let's dance!
	hard [hɑːd]	hier: hart	Teaching can be a hard job.

Unit 10 Living together

Focus

1	**nationality** [ˌnæʃə'nælətɪ]	Nationalität, Staatsangehörigkeit	What's your nationality? – I'm German.
2	**cousin** ['kʌzn]	Cousin(e)	My aunt and uncle are my cousin's parents.
	to take place [teɪk 'pleɪs]	stattfinden	The market takes place three times a week.
	grandparents ['græn,peərənts]	Großeltern	
	Bangladesh [ˌbæŋglə'deʃ]	Bangladesch	
	stall [stɔːl]	(Verkaufs)stand	There are lots of different stalls at the market.
	jewellerey (no pl) ['dʒuːəlrɪ]	Schmuck	She never wears jewellerey.
	to sing (sang, sung) [sɪŋ, sæŋ, sʌŋ]	singen	She always sings when she drives her car.
7	**programme** ['prəʊgræm]	Programm	There's an interesting programme on TV tonight.
	subject ['sʌbdʒɪkt]	(Schul)fach	The first lesson today is maths – my favourite subject.

Practice

1	**society** [sə'saɪətɪ]	Gesellschaft	Britain and India are very different societies.
	ethnic ['eθnɪk]	ethnisch	
	minority [maɪ'nɒrətɪ]	Minderheit	
	area ['eərɪə]	Gebiet, Gegend	In many areas of the world they speak English.
	Caribbean [ˌkærɪ'bi:ən]	karibisch	
	island ['aɪlənd]	Insel	Britain is an island.
	China ['tʃaɪnə]	China	
	Jamaica [dʒə'meɪkə]	Jamaika	
	Bangladeshi [ˌbæŋglə'deʃɪ]	Bangladescher(in); bangladeschisch	
	Indian ['ɪndɪən]	Inder(in); indianisch	She comes from India, so she cooks Indian food.
	Jamaican [dʒə'meɪkən]	Jamaikaner(in); jamaikanisch	
	Pakistani [ˌpɑ:kɪ'stɑ:nɪ]	Pakistaner(in), pakistanisch	
3	**continent** ['kɒntɪnənt]	Kontinent	
	Antarctica [æn'tɑ:ktɪkə]	die Antarktis	
	North America [ˌnɔ:θ‿ə'merɪkə]	Nordamerika	
	South America [ˌsaʊθ‿ə'merɪkə]	Südamerika	
4	**immigrant** ['ɪmɪgrənt]	Einwanderer(in)	Immigrants come from many countries to work.
	carnival ['kɑ:nɪvl]	Jahrmarkt	
	crowd [kraʊd]	(Menschen)menge	There was a big crowd at the scene of the accident.
	to last [lɑ:st]	dauern	Hot weather doesn't usually last very long.
	atmosphere ['ætməsˌfɪə]	Atmosphäre	The atmosphere at the party was great!
	race [reɪs]	Rasse	
	energy ['enədʒɪ]	Energie	He's got a lot of energy – he can dance all night.

Listening and reading

1	**generation** [ˌdʒenə'reɪʃn]	Generation	
	a few [ə 'fju:]	ein paar	Can you wait a few minutes?
	qualified ['kwɒlɪˌfaɪd]	qualifiziert, kompetent	He is a qualified mechanic.
	professional [prə'feʃnl]	Berufstätige(r) mit qualifizierter Ausbildung	
	cleaner ['kli:nə]	Reinigungskraft	to clean → a cleaner
	to vary ['veərɪ]	sich ändern, sich unterscheiden	
	to integrate ['ɪntɪˌgreɪt]	(sich) integrieren	Immigrants in societies have to integrate.
	contrast ['kɒntrɑ:st]	Kontrast, Gegensatz	
	sadly ['sædlɪ]	traurigerweise, leider	Sadly, I never saw him again.
	prejudice ['predʒʊˌdɪs]	Vorurteil	
	against [ə'genst]	gegen	We will play against seven different teams.
	despite [dɪ'spaɪt]	trotz	She works in a restaurant, despite the bad wages.
	difficulty ['dɪfɪkltɪ]	Schwierigkeit	He had a lot of difficulties with his parents.
	however [haʊ'evə]	aber, jedoch	He was rich. However, he wasn't happy.
4	**noun** [naʊn]	Hauptwort, Substantiv	
	to succeed [sək'si:d]	Erfolg haben	
5	**boat** [bəʊt]	Boot	
	to notice ['nəʊtɪs]	bemerken, wahrnehmen	Sarah looked a bit annoyed. – Really? I didn't notice.
	to get lost [get 'lɒst]	sich verirren	I didn't know the town. I got lost.
	to share [ʃeə]	teilen	I forgot my lunch. Can I share yours?
	surprised [sə'praɪzd]	überrascht	He came very late. We were surprised to see him.

7	**industry** ['ɪndəstrɪ]	Industrie	There isn't much industry in Africa.
	around [ə'raʊnd]	rund um, um … herum	

Gateway to work

1	**bar chart** ['bɑː ˌtʃɑːt]	Balkendiagramm	
	percentage [pə'sentɪdʒ]	Prozentsatz	
	African ['æfrɪkən]	Afrikaner(in); afrikanisch	Mali is an African country.
	point [pɔɪnt]	hier: Komma	! 1.5 = 1 POINT 5
3	**few** [fjuː]	wenig	
5	**aged** [eɪdʒd]	im Alter von	
	leisure (time) ['leʒə ˌtaɪm]	Freizeit	Fifty years ago people had less leisure.
7	**topic** ['tɒpɪk]	Thema	Another word for 'subject'.
	opinion [ə'pɪnjən]	Meinung, Ansicht	In my opinion, we should use cars less.
	to smoke [sməʊk]	rauchen	

At work

1	**dimension** [daɪ'menʃn]	Ausmaß, Raumangabe	
	scooter ['skuːtə]	Roller	
	plastic ['plæstɪk]	Plastik, Kunststoff	
	pipe [paɪp]	Rohr	
	wide [waɪd]	breit, weit	It's too wide, we can't get it through the door.
	deep [diːp]	tief	
	by [baɪ]	hier: mal	
	heavy ['hevɪ]	schwer	I can't carry this box – it's too heavy.
	across [ə'krɒs]	hier: quer (durch)	It's 1 metre across.
	diameter [daɪ'æmɪtə]	Durchmesser	
	width [wɪdθ]	Breite, Weite	
	depth [depθ]	Tiefe	The pool has a depth of 2 metres.
	length [leŋθ]	Länge	It has a length of 50 metres.
3	**department** [dɪ'pɑːtmənt]	Abteilung	Big companies have many departments.
	How are you? [ˌhaʊ‿'ɑː jə]	Wie geht es Ihnen?	
	to plan [plæn]	planen, anlegen	
	ready ['redɪ]	fertig, bereit	Are you ready? – Yes, let's go!
	to go ahead [ˌgəʊ‿ə'hed]	fortfahren, weitermachen	Go ahead. I'm listening.
	millimetre ['mɪlɪˌmiːtə]	Millimeter	
4	**ski** [skiː]	Ski	! 'sk' wird wie 'sch' in 'school' ausgesprochen.
	fan [fæn]	Ventilator, Gebläse	
	to consist of [kən'sɪst‿əv]	bestehen aus	

Unit 11 Teenage life

Focus

	to take a break [ˌteɪk‿ə 'breɪk]	eine Pause einlegen	Why don't you stop and take a break?
	competition [ˌkɒmpə'tɪʃn]	hier: Preisausschreiben	
	sun cream ['sʌn ˌkriːm]	Sonnenkrem	
	plus [plʌs]	plus	There are twenty-three in our class plus our teacher.
	fashion ['fæʃn]	Mode	If you like fashion, you want to know about clothes.
2	**prize** [praɪz]	Preis, Gewinn	You can win a prize for the best school project.
3	**driving licence** ['draɪvɪŋ ˌlaɪsns]	Führerschein	
	L-plate ['elˌpleɪt]	Anfänger-Warnschild	
	to take off [teɪk‿'ɒf]	entfernen, abnehmen	Sit down. Take off your coat.
	driving test ['draɪvɪŋ ˌtest]	Fahrprüfung	Can you take the driving test after 50 lessons?
	to pass [pɑːs]	hier: bestehen	If you work, you will pass the test.
	theory ['θɪərɪ]	Theorie	
	examiner [ɪg'zæmɪnə]	Prüfer(in)	

	driving school ['draɪvɪŋ ˌsku:l]	Fahrschule	
	licence ['laɪsns]	Führerschein	Have you got a driving licence?
	lift [lɪft]	Mitfahrgelegenheit	Can I give you a lift to school?
	petrol ['petrəl]	Benzin	Petrol is very expensive these days.
	Practice		
1	**private** ['praɪvət]	privat	! Das englische Wort hat ein e.
	file [faɪl]	Datei	
	to insult [ɪn'sʌlt]	beleidigen, beschimpfen	He said he was fat – he insulted him!
2	**photographer** [fə'tɒgrəfə]	Fotograf(in)	
	No way! [ˌnəʊ 'weɪ]	Auf keinen Fall!	! Umgangssprache
	ordinary ['ɔ:dnərɪ]	normal, gewöhnlich	
3	**beauty** ['bju:tɪ]	Schönheit	
	care [keə]	Sorgfalt	He washes his car with great care.
	success [sək'ses]	Erfolg	If you work hard, you may have success.
	stressful ['stresfl]	stressig	
	careless ['keələs]	achtlos	He broke a plate because he was careless.
	helpless ['helpləs]	hilflos	If you can't walk, you are helpless.
	useless ['ju:sləs]	nutzlos	I can't do it – I'm useless!
	to break down [breɪk 'daʊn]	eine Panne haben	The car broke down in the mountains.
	no one ['nəʊ wʌn]	niemand	I shouted, but no one answered.
	Listening and reading		
1	**traditional** [trə'dɪʃnl]	traditionell, herkömmlich	In that country they wear traditional clothes.
	doctor's assistant ['dɒktəz‿əˌsɪstənt]	Arzthelfer(in)	
	electronic technician [elek'trɒnɪk tekˌnɪʃn]	Elektroniker(in)	
	office clerk ['ɒfɪs ˌklɑ:k]	Bürokaufmann, -frau	
	painter and decorator [ˌpeɪntər‿ən 'dekəreɪtə]	Maler und Tapezierer	
	dentist's assistant ['dentɪsts‿əˌsɪstənt]	Zahnarzthelfer(in)	
2	**industrial** [ɪn'dʌstrɪəl]	industriell	
	natural ['nætʃərəl]	natürlich	! Betonung
	choice [tʃɔɪs]	Wahl	You have a choice – this one or that one?
	to support [sə'pɔ:t]	unterstützen	Their parents support them in everything they do.
	to react (to) [rɪ'ækt‿tə]	reagieren (auf)	
	bond [bɒnd]	Verbindung	
	comment ['kɒment]	Kommentar, Äußerung	! Betonung
	to expect [ɪk'spekt]	erwarten	Your present was a big surprise, I didn't expect it.
4	**Netherlands** ['neðələndz]	Holland, Niederlande	
	artist ['ɑ:tɪst]	Künstler(in)	
	geography [dʒi:'ɒgrəfɪ]	Erdkunde, Geographie	In geography we learn about different countries.
	sceptical ['skeptɪkl]	skeptisch	I don't think it is a good idea – I'm sceptical.
	critical ['krɪtɪkl]	kritisch	Some people are always critical of things.
	strong [strɒŋ]	stark	
	enough [ɪ'nʌf]	genug	Have we got enough milk for breakfast?
	to paint [peɪnt]	malen, anstreichen	The walls are dirty, so we must paint them.
6	**profile** ['prəʊfaɪl]	Profil	
8	**to include** [ɪn'klu:d]	berücksichtigen, beinhalten	
	Gateway to work		
1	**advertisement** [əd'vɜ:tɪsmənt]	Anzeige, Reklame	The newspaper is full of advertisements.
	sale [seɪl]	hier: Schlussverkauf	There are always sales after Christmas.

	up to ['ʌp tə]	bis (zu)	They live up to 100 years.
	to be on [bɪ‿'ɒn]	hier: laufen	The race is on.
	sort [sɔ:t]	Typ, Art, Sorte	
	in particular [ɪn pə'tɪkjʊlə]	besonders, speziell	
	reduction [rɪ'dʌkʃn]	Preisnachlass, Rabatt	
	to sound [saʊnd]	klingen	I like your music – it sounds good.
	to hurry ['hʌrɪ]	sich beeilen	Hurry up, we're late!
4	**ad (= advertisement)** [æd]	Anzeige, Reklame	
	sales assistant ['seɪlz‿əˌsɪstənt]	Verkäufer(in)	
	handheld ['hændˌheld]	tragbares Gerät	
	make [meɪk]	Marke	What make of mobile do you have?
	opening hours ['əʊpənɪŋ‿ˌaʊəz]	Öffnungszeiten	The shop has long opening hours.
	enquiry [ɪn'kwaɪrɪ]	Erkundigung, Anfrage	I can answer all your enquiries.
	deal [di:l]	hier: Angebot	I got a good deal, it was very cheap.

At work

1	**telecoms** ['telɪkɒmz]	Fernmeldewesen	
	item ['aɪtəm]	Posten, Objekt, Artikel	That's an expensive item!
	available [ə'veɪləbl]	verfügbar, erhältlich	Sorry, there are no more available.
	lamp [læmp]	Lampe	
	bookcase ['bʊkˌkeɪs]	Bücherregal	
	waste bin ['weɪst ˌbɪn]	Abfalleimer	
2	**to order** ['ɔ:də]	bestellen	People who don't want to prepare their own food often order a pizza.
3	**order** ['ɔ:də]	hier: Bestellung	They waited one hour for their order.
	else [els]	sonst (noch)	I've done the shopping. Do we need anything else?
	quantity ['kwɒntətɪ]	Anzahl, Menge	
	total ['təʊtl]	Summe	That's a total of £20.

nit 12 Famous companies

Focus

2	**border** ['bɔ:də]	Grenze	
	particularly [pə'tɪkjʊləlɪ]	besonders	particularly good = especially good
	creamy ['kri:mɪ]	sahnig	
	to borrow ['bɒrəʊ]	leihen	Can I borrow this book? – OK, but give it back.
	gas station (AE) ['gæs‿ˌsteɪʃn]	Tankstelle	= garage (BE)
	instant ['ɪnstənt]	sofortig	
	to grow (grew, grown) [grəʊ, gru:, grəʊn]	wachsen	The town has grown a lot in ten years.
	Belgium ['beldʒəm]	Belgien	
	Luxembourg ['lʌksəmbɜ:g]	Luxemburg	
	although [ɔ:l'ðəʊ]	obwohl, obgleich	He speaks German although he's English.
	still [stɪl]	(immer) noch, noch immer	Is Lisa 18? – No, she's still 17.
3	**infinitive** [ɪn'fɪnətɪv]	Infinitiv	'To win' is an infinitive.
5	**past perfect** [ˌpɑ:st 'pɜ:fɪkt]	Plusquamperfekt, Vorvergangenheit	

Practice

1	**(a month) ago** [ə ˌmʌnθ‿ə'gəʊ]	vor (einem Monat)	I saw him a month ago.
	to manage ['mænɪdʒ]	(es) schaffen	It wasn't an easy job – but I've managed it!
	hire car ['haɪə ˌkɑ:]	Mietwagen	They had a hire car on holiday.
	to manufacture [ˌmænjʊ'fæktʃə]	herstellen, produzieren	
	cop (slang) [kɒp]	Bulle	
	gear [gɪə]	Gang	Cars have four or five gears.

	speed [spi:d]	Geschwindigkeit	
	motor cycle ['məʊtə,saɪkl]	Motorrad	
	shed [ʃed]	Schuppen	There is a shed in the garden.
	headquarters [,hed'kwɔ:təz]	Stammsitz, Zentrale	
	to afford [ə'fɔ:d]	sich leisten	That's too expensive. I can't afford it.
	to promise ['prɒmɪs]	versprechen	I'll be back at 7 o'clock, I promise.
	to hope [həʊp]	hoffen	I hope I will get a good job.
2	**wood** [wʊd]	Holz	Tables and chairs are made of wood.
	electric [ɪ'lektrɪk]	elektrisch, Elektro-	He's using an electric drill to put the shelves up.
	wizard ['wɪzəd]	hier: Genie	
	businesswoman ['bɪznəs,wʊmən]	Geschäftsfrau	
	environmentally friendly [ɪn,vaɪrənmentlɪ 'frendlɪ]	umweltfreundlich	Wind energy is environmentally friendly.
	soap [səʊp]	Seife	Wash your hands with soap and water.

Listening and reading

1	**to suggest** [sə'dʒest]	vorschlagen	I suggest we stay at home.
	paragraph ['pærə,grɑ:f]	Absatz, Abschnitt	
	nobody ['nəʊbɒdɪ]	niemand	Is there anybody outside? – No, nobody.
	to be a leader [,bɪ‿ə 'li:də]	führend sein	
	to lie (lay, lain) [laɪ, leɪ, leɪn]	liegen	
	in ruins [ɪn 'ru:ɪnz]	in Trümmern	After the bombs the city was in ruins.
	electricity [ɪ,lek'trɪsətɪ]	Strom, Elektrizität	
	proper ['prɒpə]	richtig, echt, ordentlich	Not fast food, I need proper food!
	physicist ['fɪzɪsɪst]	Physiker(in)	
	electrical [ɪ'lektrɪkl]	elektrisch	
	broken ['brəʊkən]	kaputt, gebrochen	
	to employ [ɪm'plɔɪ]	beschäftigen	They employ people in ten countries.
	black market [,blæk 'mɑ:kɪt]	Schwarzmarkt	
	laboratory [lə'bɒrətərɪ]	Labor	
	transistor [træn'zɪstə]	Transistor	
	portable ['pɔ:təbl]	tragbar	Have you seen my new portable TV?
	pot [pɒt]	Topf	
	to burn [bɜ:n]	(ver)brennen	Be careful – don't burn the toast!
	including [ɪn'klu:dɪŋ]	einschließlich	We were ten, including my friend.
	to die [daɪ]	sterben	Robert's grandpa died four years ago.
4	**fortunately** ['fɔ:tʃənətlɪ]	glücklicherweise	Fortunately we found a bank.

Gateway to work

1	**manager** ['mænɪdʒə]	hier: Geschäftsführer(in)	
	to correspond [,kɒrɪ'spɒnd]	korrespondieren	
	personnel [,pɜ:sə'nel]	Personal	
	reply [rɪ'plaɪ]	Antwort	Another word for 'answer'.
	inbox ['ɪn,bɒks]	Eingang	
	to attach [ə'tætʃ]	anhängen	He attached a document to the email.
	further ['fɜ:ðə]	weitere(r, s)	Do you have any further ideas?
	Kind regards [,kaɪnd rɪ'gɑ:dz]	Herzliche Grüße	
2	**figure** ['fɪgə]	hier: Zahl	Do you have the latest figures?
	How are things? [,haʊ‿ə 'θɪŋz]	Wie geht's?	
	security camera [sɪ'kjʊərətɪ ,kæmərə]	Überwachungskamera	
	asap (= as soon as possible)	so bald wie möglich	
	in advance [ɪn‿əd'vɑ:ns]	im Voraus	If you want to be sure, get a ticket in advance.
	All the best [,ɔ:l ðə 'best]	Alles Gute	
	hectic ['hektɪk]	hektisch	

3	**informal** [ɪnˈfɔːml]	formlos, locker	formal ↔ informal
	to reply [rɪˈplaɪ]	antworten	Do you reply to every email?

At work

1	**cookbook** [ˈkʊkˌbʊk]	Kochbuch	
	pub [pʌb]	Kneipe, Lokal	A place to go and have drinks and talk to friends.
	tasty [ˈteɪstɪ]	schmackhaft, lecker	This sandwich is tasty.
	stereotype [ˈsterɪəˌtaɪp]	Stereotyp, Klischee	
3	**to fry** [fraɪ]	braten	fry an egg – bake a cake – boil potatoes
	soft [sɒft]	weich	Butter is soft.
	to simmer [ˈsɪmə]	köcheln lassen	simmer the water
	balsamic vinegar [bɔːlˌsæmɪk ˈvɪnɪgə]	Balsamicoessig	
	pepper [ˈpepə]	Pfeffer	
	salt [sɔːlt]	Salz	
	to serve [sɜːv]	hier: reichen für	The recipe serves six.
	ingredient [ɪnˈgriːdɪənt]	Zutat	I have to buy lots of ingredients for this recipe.
	to peel [piːl]	schälen	peel an orange
	to chop [tʃɒp]	hacken	
	clove of garlic [ˌkləʊv‿əv ˈgɑːlɪk]	Knoblauchzehe	
	olive oil [ˈɒlɪv‿ɔɪl]	Olivenöl	
	teaspoon [ˈtiːˌspuːn]	Teelöffel	A teaspoon is smaller than a tablespoon.
	dried [draɪd]	getrocknet	I love dried tomatoes!
	oregano [ˌɒrɪˈgɑːnəʊ]	Oregano	
	quality [ˈkwɒlətɪ]	Qualität, Eigenschaft	
	tinned [tɪnd]	konserviert, in Dosen	I like fresh fruit, not tinned fruit.
	tablespoon [ˈteɪblˌspuːn]	Esslöffel	
	handful [ˈhændfʊl]	Handvoll	
	basil [ˈbæzl]	Basilikum	
	method [ˈmeθəd]	hier: Zubereitung	There are many methods to cook rice.
	to stir [stɜː]	rühren	stir the pot
	meanwhile [ˈmiːnˌwaɪl]	zwischenzeitlich, unterdessen	
	to boil [bɔɪl]	kochen	If you boil eggs or potatoes, you cook them in water.
	salted [ˈsɔːltɪd]	gesalzen	
	to mix [mɪks]	(ver)mischen	
	beer [bɪə]	Bier	
	baking powder [ˈbeɪkɪŋ ˌpaʊdə]	Backpulver	
	to heat [hiːt]	erhitzen	heat the oven
	to beat (beat, beaten) [biːt, biːt, ˈbiːtn]	hier: verrühren	Beat eggs to make an omelette.
	mixture [ˈmɪkstʃə]	Mischung	
	thick [θɪk]	dick	thin ↔ thick
	to dust [dʌst]	bestäuben	
	to dip [dɪp]	tauchen	
	oven [ˈʌvn]	Backofen	She bakes bread in the oven.
	to dry [draɪ]	trocknen	Dry the meat well before you put it in the oven.

nit 13 Destination Canada

Focus

2	**in time** [ɪn ˈtaɪm fə]	rechtzeitig	We'll be just in time for the beginning of the film.
	to miss [mɪs]	fehlen, verpassen	I miss you. = Du fehlst mir.
4	**surprising** [səˈpraɪzɪŋ]	überraschend	It's surprising what a big country Canada is.
5	**polar bear** [ˈpəʊlə ˌbeə]	Eisbär	

Practice

1	**port** [pɔ:t]	Hafen	Hamburg and Bremen are ports.
	facility [fə'sɪlətɪ]	Einrichtung	All the hotels have great facilities.
	bath [bɑ:θ]	Bad	
	car park ['kɑ: ˌpɑ:k]	Parkplatz	There's a big car park for 100 cars in town.
	public ['pʌblɪk]	öffentlich	The garden is private, but the park is public.
	nearby [ˌnɪə'baɪ]	in der Nähe	There are taxis nearby.
	Canadian [kə'neɪdɪən]	Kanadier(in); kanadisch	
2	**province** ['prɒvɪns]	Gebiet, Provinz	In most provinces they speak English.
	French [frentʃ]	Franzose/Französin; französisch	Many people speak French in Canada.
	mainly ['meɪnlɪ]	hauptsächlich	They mainly speak French in Quebec.
	community college [kə'mju:nətɪ ˌkɒlɪdʒ]	etwa: berufsbildende Schule	
	national ['næʃnəl]	national, National-	
	beginning [bɪ'gɪnɪŋ]	Anfang	beginning ↔ ending
	term [tɜ:m]	Schuljahresabschnitt	There are three terms in a school year.

Listening and reading

1	**to connect** [kə'nekt]	verbinden	
	imaginary [ɪ'mædʒɪnərɪ]	imaginär, in der Vorstellung	
2	**forest** ['fɒrɪst]	Wald	
	lake [leɪk]	See	You can swim in the lake.
	prairie ['preərɪ]	Prärie	
	comfortable ['kʌmftəbl]	bequem	You need comfortable shoes for walking.
	producer [prə'dju:sə]	Erzeuger, Hersteller	France is a producer of wine.
	wheat [wi:t]	Weizen	Canada is a big producer of wheat.
	land [lænd]	Land	All the land there is forest.
	to halt [hɔ:lt]	anhalten	
	restaurant car ['restərɒnt ˌkɑ:]	Speisewagen	
	flat [flæt]	flach	Country where there are no hills is flat.
	to disappear [ˌdɪsə'pɪə]	verschwinden	He stayed for an hour, then he disappeared.
	to grow (grew, grown)	hier: anbauen	They grow a lot of vegetables and fruit.
	endless ['endləs]	endlos, unendlich	
	All aboard! [ˌɔ:l‿ə'bɔ:d]	Alles einsteigen!	
	to be asleep [ˌbɪ‿ə'sli:p]	schlafen	
	halt [hɔ:lt]	Halt	
	to take on [teɪk‿'ɒn]	hier: aufnehmen, laden	
	fuel ['fju:əl]	Treibstoff	The cost of fuel is high.
	air [eə]	Luft	The air in the mountains is clear.

Gateway to work

1	**day return ticket** [ˌdeɪ rɪ'tɜ:n ˌtɪkɪt]	Tagesrückfahrkarte	
	return ticket [rɪ'tɜ:n ˌtɪkɪt]	Rückfahrkarte	A return ticket, please. I'm coming back tonight.
	platform ['plætˌfɔ:m]	Gleis	

At work

fabulous ['fæbjʊləs]	fabelhaft, sagenhaft	
classic ['klæsɪk]	klassisch	
engine ['endʒɪn]	Motor	Almost all cars have the engine in front of the driver.
boot [bu:t]	hier: Kofferraum	Suitcases go in the boot of the car.
trunk (AE) [trʌŋk]	hier: Kofferraum	
steering wheel ['stɪərɪŋ ˌwi:l]	Lenkrad	
headlight ['hedˌlaɪt]	Scheinwerfer, Vorderlicht	

	rear light ['rɪə ˌlaɪt]	Rücklicht	
	exhaust [ɪg'zɔ:st]	Auspuff	
	bumper ['bʌmpə]	Stoßstange	
	windscreen ['wɪnd͵skri:n]	Windschutzscheibe	Always keep the windscreen clean.
	mirror ['mɪrə]	Spiegel	There's always a mirror in the bathroom.
	gear stick ['gɪə ˌstɪk]	Schaltknüppel	
	speedometer [spɪ'dɒmɪtə]	Tachometer	
3	**service** ['sɜ:vɪs]	hier: Inspektion	The car needs a service every 15,000 kms.
	to change [tʃeɪndʒ]	hier: austauschen, wechseln	We should change the tyres in the winter.
	filter ['fɪltə]	Filter	
	spark plug ['spɑ:k ˌplʌg]	Zündkerze	
	battery ['bætərɪ]	Batterie	Your mobile won't work without a battery.
	brake [breɪk]	Bremse	
	MOT test [ˌeməʊ'ti: ˌtest]	etwa: TÜV-Prüfung	
4	**to replace** [rɪ'pleɪs]	ersetzen	If the spark plugs are old, replace them.
	total cost ['təʊtl ˌkɒst]	Gesamtkosten	The total cost of a car is high.

nit 14 Unbelievable!

Focus

	unbelievable [ˌʌnbɪ'li:vəbl]	unglaublich	
2	**earth** [ɜ:θ]	Erde	The earth is round.
	kph (= kilometres per hour)	kmh	Stundenkilometer
	up [ʌp]	hier: weiter oben	
	to jump [dʒʌmp]	springen	
	parachute ['pærə͵ʃu:t]	Fallschirm	
	to hit (hit, hit) [hɪt, hɪt, hɪt]	treffen, schlagen	I hit my head on the door.
	unconscious [ʌn'kɒnʃəs]	bewusstlos	After I hit my head, I was unconscious.
	pine tree ['paɪn ˌtri:]	Kiefer, Pinie	
	emergency [ɪ'mɜ:dʒənsɪ]	Notfall; Not-	It's an emergency, call the police!
	automatic [ˌɔ:tə'mætɪk]	automatisch	
	to crash [kræʃ]	stürzen	The car crashed into the lorry.
	to catch (caught, caught)	hier: sich verfangen	I caught my coat in the door.
	branch [brɑ:ntʃ]	Ast	A tree has branches.
	to wake up (woke, woken) [weɪk‿'ʌp, wəʊk‿'ʌp, ˌwəʊkən‿'ʌp]	aufwecken, aufwachen	I wake up later on Sunday.
	to hang (hung, hung) [hæŋ, hʌŋ, hʌŋ]	hängen	
	to survive [sə'vaɪv]	überleben	He crashed into the lorry but he survived.
4	**coincidence** [kəʊ'ɪnsɪdəns]	Zufall	We were both in the same café – what a coincidence!
	police station [pə'li:s‿ˌsteɪʃn]	Polizeiwache	
	patrol [pə'trəʊl]	Patrouille, Polizeistreife	
	to pick up [pɪk‿'ʌp]	abnehmen	
	downtown (AE) ['daʊn͵taʊn]	in der Innenstadt, im Stadtzentrum	= in the city centre (BE)
	apartment (AE) [ə'pɑ:tmənt]	Wohnung	= flat (BE)
	key [ki:]	Schlüssel	
	mailman (AE) ['meɪl͵mæn]	Briefträger, Postbote	
	stay [steɪ]	Aufenthalt	Our stay was not long.

Practice

1	**urban** ['ɜ:bən]	städtisch, urban	
	myth [mɪθ]	Mythos	
	grizzly ['grɪzlɪ]	etwa: grausig, schauderhaft	

	hook [hʊk]	Haken	You catch fish with hooks.
	couple ['kʌpl]	Paar	There were a lot of couples, no single people.
	wood [wʊd]	hier: Wald	A wood is smaller than a forest.
	psychopath ['saɪkəʊˌpæθ]	Psychopath	
	to escape [ɪ'skeɪp]	(ent)fliehen, entkommen	The prisoner escaped over the wall.
	soft [sɒft]	hier: leise	The music was so soft I couldn't hear it.
	metal ['metl]	Metall	
	to get out [get‿'aʊt]	aussteigen	
	handle ['hændl]	Griff	The handle of that pot is hot.
	ambulance ['æmbjʊləns]	Krankenwagen	She must go to hospital. Call an ambulance!
	kidney ['kɪdnɪ]	Niere	
2	**to warn** [wɔ:n]	warnen	The police warned us to drive slowly.
	impossible [ɪm'pɒsəbl]	unmöglich	I don't believe it. It's impossible!
3	**believable** [bɪ'li:vəbl]	glaubwürdig, glaubhaft	
	conscious ['kɒnʃəs]	bewusst	I'm awake, I'm conscious.
	unhappy [ʌn'hæpɪ]	unglücklich	She's unhappy with her new job.
	lucky ['lʌkɪ]	glücklich	Lucky you! You've won the first prize.
	unlucky [ʌn'lʌkɪ]	unglücklich	I'm unlucky – I crashed the car.
	probable ['prɒbəbl]	wahrscheinlich	I will probably work in a big city.
	improbable [ɪm'prɒbəbl]	unwahrscheinlich	It's improbable that I will earn £ 1,000,000.
	impolite [ˌɪmpə'laɪt]	unhöflich	He didn't say 'sorry'. That's impolite.
	credible ['kredəbl]	glaubwürdig	
	incredible [ɪn'kredəbl]	unglaublich	That's an incredible story.
	incorrect [ˌɪnkə'rekt]	falsch, unrichtig	That's not true, it's incorrect.
	complete [kəm'pli:t]	fertig, komplett	
	incomplete [ˌɪnkəm'pli:t]	unvollständig, unfertig	I can't send this letter, it's incomplete.
	relevant ['reləvənt]	relevant, entsprechend	
	irrelevant [ɪ'reləvənt]	belanglos, unerheblich	
4	**so far** ['səʊ fɑ:]	so weit, bisher	We have read 14 units so far.
	to be lucky ['lʌkɪ]	Glück haben	

Listening and reading

1	**accidental** [ˌæksɪ'dentl]	zufällig, versehentlich	
	science ['saɪəns]	(Natur)wissenschaft	! Aussprache
	by accident [baɪ‿'æksɪdənt]	zufällig	I met him in town by accident.
	microwave ['maɪkrəˌweɪv]	Mikrowelle	
	magnetron ['mægnətrɒn]	Magnetfeldröhre	
	piece of equipment [ˌpi:s‿əv‿ɪ'kwɪpmənt]	Ausrüstungsgegenstand	
	wave [weɪv]	Welle	In a storm at sea there are big waves.
	radar ['reɪdɑ:]	Radar, Funkmesstechnik	
	pocket ['pɒkɪt]	Tasche	Sarah has got 50p in her pocket.
	to melt [melt]	schmelzen	The sun melts chocolate or butter.
	frequency ['fri:kwənsɪ]	Frequenz	
	experiment [ɪk'sperɪmənt]	Experiment	! Betonung
	commercial [kə'mɜ:ʃl]	kommerziell	
	onto ['ɒntə]	auf	on + to = onto
	market ['mɑ:kɪt]	Markt	
	refrigerator [rɪ'frɪdʒəˌreɪtə]	Kühlschrank	
	Velcro ['velkrəʊ]	Klettverschluss	
	walk [wɔ:k]	Spaziergang	He has a walk every evening.
	to cover (with) ['kʌvə wɪð]	bedecken (mit)	In autumn the roads are covered with leaves.
	burr [bɜ:]	Klette	
	to stick (stuck, stuck) [stɪk, stʌk, stʌk]	kleben (bleiben)	Use glue to stick things together.
	cloth [klɒθ]	Stoff	This cloth is very warm. It's for winter clothes.

	microscope ['maɪkrəˌskəʊp]	Mikroskop	
	tiny ['taɪnɪ]	winzig	Some insects are so tiny we can't see them.
	fabric ['fæbrɪk]	Stoff	They sell many beautiful fabrics.
	glue [gluː]	Klebstoff	The glass is broken. Perhaps we can use glue.
	weak [wiːk]	schwach	weak ↔ strong
	choir ['kwaɪə]	Chor	A choir is a group of people who sing together.
	hymn book ['hɪm ˌbʊk]	Gesangbuch	
	bookmark ['bʊkˌmɑːk]	Lesezeichen	
	hymn [hɪm]	Kirchenlied, Hymne	
	to fall out [fɔːl‿'aʊt]	herausfallen	The boy fell out of the tree.
	annoying [ə'nɔɪɪŋ]	ärgerlich	It is annoying that I didn't see the film.
	to pull off [pʊl‿'ɒf]	abziehen, entfernen	
7	**legend** ['ledʒənd]	Legende	An old story that may be true in parts.
	ghost [gəʊst]	Geist	Sometimes there are stories of ghosts in old houses.

Gateway to work

1	**local** ['ləʊkl]	örtlich, hiesig	The schools in your area are your local schools.
	I can't make it. [ˌaɪ kɑːnt 'meɪk‿ɪt]	Ich kann es nicht schaffen.	
2	**to ring (rang, rung)** [rɪŋ, ræŋ, rʌŋ]	hier: anrufen	I rang her three times yesterday.
	to get in [get‿'ɪn]	zurückkehren	

At work

1	**Dear Sir or Madam** [dɪə ˌsɜːr‿ɔː 'mædəm]	Sehr geehrte Damen und Herren	
	to be on display [ˌbɪ‿ɒn dɪ'spleɪ]	ausgestellt sein	The new clothes were on display in the shop.
	recent ['riːsənt]	kürzlich, neulich	Have you seen a recent newspaper?
	retailer ['riːˌteɪlə]	Einzelhändler	
	current ['kʌrənt]	aktuell, gegenwärtig	The current situation is difficult.
	grateful ['greɪtfl]	dankbar	I'm grateful for your help.
	trade discount ['treɪd‿dɪskaʊnt]	Handelsrabatt	
	Yours faithfully/sincerely [jɔːz 'feɪθflɪ]	Mit freundlichen Grüßen	
	purchasing manager ['pɜːtʃəsɪŋ ˌmænɪdʒə]	Einkaufsleiter	
	subject ['sʌbdʒɪkt]	hier: Betreff	
	writer ['raɪtə]	Autor(in), Verfasser(in)	
2	**type** [taɪp]	Typ, Art, Sorte	She always wears the same type of jeans.
	contact ['kɒntækt]	Kontakt	
	sample ['sæmpl]	Muster	Sometimes they give you samples of perfume.
	trade journal ['treɪd‿dʒɜːnl]	Fachblatt, Fachzeitschrift	
	shortly ['ʃɔːtlɪ]	in Kürze, bald	He's coming soon, so we will see him shortly.
	packaging ['pækɪdʒɪŋ]	Verpackungsmaterial	
	Scottish ['skɒtɪʃ]	schottisch	Scottish weather is colder than English weather.
	Scotland ['skɒtlənd]	Schottland	

nit 15 What on earth are we doing?

Focus

1	**insect** ['ɪnsekt]	Insekt	
2	**environment** [ɪn'vaɪrənmənt]	Umwelt	We must look after our environment.
	oxygen ['ɒksɪdʒən]	Sauerstoff	
	species (pl species) ['spiːʃiːz, 'spiːʃiːz]	Spezies, Art	Many species of insects live in the forest.
	pharmacy (AE) ['fɑːməsɪ]	Apotheke	
	drug [drʌg]	hier: Medikament, Arznei	
	medicine ['medsn]	Medizin, Medikament	When you are ill you need medicine.

	to cure [kjʊə]	heilen	
	cancer ['kænsə]	Krebs	
	to destroy [dɪ'strɔɪ]	zerstören	The storm destroyed many houses.
	square kilometre ['skweə ˌkɪləmi:tə]	Quadratkilometer	
4	**leaflet** ['li:flət]	Prospekt, Broschüre	She gave me a leaflet about the Amazon forest.
	to save [seɪv]	hier: retten	The doctor saved my life.
	organisation [ˌɔ:gənaɪ'zeɪʃn]	Organisation	
	to fight (fought, fought) [faɪt, fɔ:t, fɔ:t]	(be)kämpfen	Medicines help us fight illnesses.
	destruction [dɪ'strʌkʃn]	Zerstörung	
	to cut down [kʌt 'daʊn]	fällen	Where can the animals live if we cut down the trees?
5	**passive** ['pæsɪv]	Passiv	
	active ['æktɪv]	Aktiv	

Practice

1	**warming** ['wɔ:mɪŋ]	Erwärmung	
	heat [hi:t]	Hitze	
	to warm [wɔ:m]	(er)wärmen	Is this milk warmed?
	to pass back [pɑ:s 'bæk]	hier: zurückstrahlen	
	out [aʊt]	hinaus	
	space [speɪs]	Weltraum	There are millions of planets in space.
	greenhouse ['gri:nˌhaʊs]	Treibhaus	In a greenhouse you can grow plants in winter.
	gas [gæs]	Gas	
	to trap [træp]	einschließen	
	to breathe [bri:ð]	atmen	I like to breathe the early morning air.
	to reduce [rɪ'dju:s]	reduzieren, vermindern	I must reduce weight.
2	**to cause** [kɔ:z]	verursachen, auslösen	
3	**to flood** [flʌd]	(über)fluten, überschwemmen	The town was flooded by the storm.
	to transport [træn'spɔ:t]	transportieren	Oil is transported by ship.
	to freeze (froze, frozen) [fri:z, frəʊz, ' frəʊzn]	(er)frieren, gefrieren	The lake was frozen by the cold wind.
	ice age ['aɪs‿eɪdʒ]	Eiszeit	
	north pole [ˌnɔ:θ 'pəʊl]	Nordpol	
	storm [stɔ:m]	Sturm	In a storm small boats stay in the harbour.
	giant ['dʒaɪənt]	riesig	
	survivor [sə'vaɪvə]	Überlebende(r)	The survivors were taken away by helicopter.
	disaster [dɪ'zɑ:stə]	Katastrophe, Unglück	Storms and hurricanes are disasters.
	dramatic [drə'mætɪk]	dramatisch	
4	**production** [prə'dʌkʃn]	Produktion, Herstellung	
	to inform [ɪn'fɔ:m]	informieren	You will be informed soon.
	to educate ['edjʊˌkeɪt]	unterrichten, ausbilden	He was educated in England.
	government ['gʌvnmənt]	Regierung	
	hopefully ['həʊpflɪ]	hoffnungsvoll, hoffentlich	Hopefully they will come to the party.

Listening and reading

1	**wind** [wɪnd]	Wind	In the north of England there is more wind and rain.
	coal [kəʊl]	Kohle	You can burn wood or coal in the fire.
	fossil fuel ['fɒsl ˌfju:əl]	fossiler Brennstoff	
	power station ['paʊə ˌsteɪʃn]	Kraftwerk	Power stations produce electricity.
	solar energy [ˌsəʊlər‿'enədʒɪ]	Solarenergie	Solar energy is better than fossil fuel.
	hydroelectric energy [haɪdrəʊɪˌlektrɪk‿'enədʒɪ]	Wasserkraft	
	turbine ['tɜ:baɪn]	Turbine	
	hill [hɪl]	Hügel	A hill is smaller than a mountain.

	tower ['taʊə]	Turm	
	rotor blade ['rəʊtə ˌbleɪd]	Rotorblatt	
	nacelle [nə'sel]	Motorengehäuse	
	as [æz]	hier: wenn	As I left, she arrived.
	to blow (blew, blown) [bləʊ, blu:, bləʊn]	blasen, wehen	
	inside ['ɪnˌsaɪd]	innen; hier: im Inneren	
	shaft [ʃɑ:ft]	hier: Welle	
	to increase [ɪn'kri:s]	erhöhen, steigern	The price of gas has been increased.
	generator ['dʒenəˌreɪtə]	Generator	
3	**steel** [sti:l]	Stahl	Steel is produced in Germany.
	concrete ['kɒŋkri:t]	Beton	
	relatively ['relətɪvlɪ]	relativ	
	total number [ˌtəʊtl 'nʌmbə]	Gesamtzahl	
6	**aspect** ['æspekt]	Aspekt, Gesichtspunkt	! Betonung
	to interest ['ɪntrəst]	interessieren	I am interested in what you said.

Gateway to work

1	**manufacturing company** [mænjʊˌfæktʃərɪŋ 'kʌmpənɪ]	Herstellungsbetrieb	
	customer service ['kʌstəmə ˌsɜ:vɪs]	Kundendienst	
	quality control ['kwɒlətɪ kənˌtrəʊl]	Qualitätssicherung	
	research [rɪ'sɜ:tʃ]	Forschung	
	development [dɪ'veləpmənt]	Entwicklung	
	accounts [ə'kaʊnts]	Rechnungswesen	
	distribution [ˌdɪstrɪ'bju:ʃn]	Vertrieb	
2	**raw material** [ˌrɔ: mə'tɪərɪəl]	Rohstoff	Germany must import a lot of raw materials.
	to advertise ['ædvəˌtaɪz]	(be)werben, Werbung machen für	The job was advertised in the newspaper.
	to deal with ['di:l wɪð]	sich befassen mit	If you don't deal with a problem, it won't go away.
3	**solar panel** [ˌsəʊlə 'pænl]	Sonnenkollektor	
	process ['prəʊses]	Verfahren, Vorgang	

At work

1	**to switch on/off** [swɪtʃ‿'ɒn, swɪtʃ‿'ɒf]	an-/ausschalten	Switch on the lights.
	to lose (lost, lost) [lu:s, lɒst, lɒst]	verlieren	Don't lose her telephone number.
	to insulate ['ɪnsjʊˌleɪt]	isolieren, dämmen	It is cold here. We need to insulate our houses well.
	to make sure [meɪk 'ʃɔ:]	sichergehen, dafür sorgen	
	insulation [ˌɪnsjʊ'leɪʃn]	Isolierung, Dämmung	It's very warm. You have good insulation!
	carbon dioxide [ˌkɑ:bən daɪ'ɒksaɪd]	Kohlendioxid	
	brick [brɪk]	Ziegelstein	Houses are made of bricks.
	cistern ['sɪstən]	Spülkasten, Wasserkasten	
	to recycle [ri:'saɪkl]	recyceln, wieder verwerten	Most things can be recycled.
	to keep (kept, kept) [ki:p, kept, kept]	hier: aufbewahren	Where do you keep the butter?
2	**roof** [ru:f]	Dach	He has insulated his roof.
3	**transport** ['trænspɔ:t]	hier: Verkehrsmittel	! Betonung
	rubbish ['rʌbɪʃ]	Müll	

nit 16 Talking about sport

Focus

1	**sportsman/-woman** ['spɔ:tsmən, 'spɔ:tsˌwʊmən]	Sportler(in)	
2	**to score** [skɔ:]	erzielen, schießen	Our team scored a goal and we won 1–0.

	goal [gəʊl]	Tor	
	score [skɔ:]	Spielstand	What's the score? = Wie steht es?
	nil [nɪl]	Null	We won 3 – nil.
	magnificent [mæg'nɪfɪsnt]	wunderbar, großartig	That old Rolls-Royce is magnificent.
3	**disappointed** [ˌdɪsə'pɔɪntɪd]	enttäuscht	The other team were very disappointed.
	the lads [ðə 'lædz]	die Jungs	
4	**to beat (beat, beaten)** [bi:t, bi:t, bi:tn]	schlagen	We beat the other team on Saturday.
	league [li:g]	Liga	
	confident ['kɒnfɪdənt]	zuversichtlich, selbstbewusst	I'm confident we will win.
5	**to report** [rɪ'pɔ:t]	berichten	You should report it to the police.
	field [fi:ld]	Wiese, Feld, Platz	Football is played on a field.
	reported speech [rɪˌpɔ:tɪd 'spi:tʃ]	indirekte Rede	

Practice

1	**swimmer** ['swɪmə]	Schwimmer(in)	Lisa often swims. She's a good swimmer.
	gym (= gymnasium) [dʒɪm, dʒɪm'neɪzɪəm]	Turnhalle	! keine Schule
	stamina ['stæmɪnə]	Ausdauer	He runs for hours. He has a lot of stamina.
	power ['paʊə]	Kraft	He's got a lot of power in his arms – he often trains.
2	**disabled** [dɪs'eɪbld]	behindert	Disabled people can use this door.
	athlete ['æθli:t]	Athlet(in), Sportler(in)	! Betonung
	athletics [æθ'letɪks]	Leichtathletik	
	amateur ['æmətə]	Amateur-, Hobby-	
	professional [prə'feʃnəl]	hier: Profi	
	accident ['æksɪdənt]	Unfall	A lot of people die every year in car accidents.
	wheelchair ['wi:lˌtʃeə]	Rollstuhl	
	to take part (in) [teɪk 'pɑ:t‿ɪn]	teilnehmen (an)	She took part in the 100 metre race.
	the Olympic Games [ˌðɪ‿əˌlɪmpɪk 'geɪmz]	die Olympischen Spiele	
4	**Formula One** [ˌfɔ:mjələ 'wʌn]	Formel Eins	
	motor racing ['məʊtə ˌreɪsɪŋ]	Autorennsport	
	totally ['təʊtlɪ]	völlig, total	I totally agree with what you say.
5	**in general** [ɪn 'dʒenərəl]	im Allgemeinen	In general I am interested in all sports.

Listening and reading

1	**to sail** [seɪl]	segeln	Ships sail in the sea.
	trimaran ['traɪməˌræn]	Trimaran	
	harbour ['hɑ:bə]	Hafen	The weather is bad, so the boats are in the harbour.
	to break (broke, broken) [breɪk, brəʊk, 'brəʊkən]	brechen	
	record ['rekɔ:d]	hier: Rekord	Around the world in seven days is a record.
	at first sight [ət ˌfɜ:st 'saɪt]	auf den ersten Blick	
	sailor ['seɪlə]	Segler(in)	
	sailing ['seɪlɪŋ]	Segeln	Sailing is not for me – I don't like water.
	yacht [jɒt]	Jacht	
	total distance [ˌtəʊtl 'dɪstəns]	Gesamtstrecke	
	iceberg ['aɪsˌbɜ:g]	Eisberg	
	whale [weɪl]	Wal	Whales are not fish, but they live in the sea.
	mast [mɑ:st]	Mast	
	dark [dɑ:k]	Dunkelheit	Are you afraid of the dark?
	sail [seɪl]	Segel	
	catnap (informal) ['kætˌnæp]	Nickerchen	
	doubt [daʊt]	Zweifel	She never had any doubts.
	brave [breɪv]	tapfer	Ellen was brave to sail round the world.
	determined [dɪ'tɜ:mɪnd]	entschlossen	She is determined to finish the race.

	modest ['mɒdɪst]	bescheiden	He doesn't say much – he's very modest.
3	**danger** ['deɪndʒə]	Gefahr	If you follow the rules, there is no danger.
6	**corresponding** [ˌkɒrɪ'spɒndɪŋ]	entsprechend, dazugehörig	
8	**press conference** ['pres ˌkɒnfərəns]	Pressekonferenz	

Gateway to work

1	**CV (= curriculum vitae)** [ˌsiː'viː, kəˌrɪkjʊləm 'viːtaɪ]	Lebenslauf	
	to apply [ə'plaɪ]	sich bewerben	He applied for only one job and was offered it.
	traineeship [ˌtreɪ'niːʃɪp]	Ausbildungsplatz	
	qualification [kwɒlɪfɪ'keɪʃn]	Qualifikation	
	National Vocational Qualification [ˌnæʃnəl vəʊˌkeɪʃnəl kwɒlɪfɪ'keɪʃn]	etwa: nationale berufsbezogene Qualifikation	
	education [ˌedjʊ'keɪʃn]	(Aus)bildung	You need a good education for your future life.
	comprehensive school [kɒmprɪ'hensɪv]	Gesamtschule	
	mathematics [ˌmæθə'mætɪks]	Mathematik	
	skill [skɪl]	Fähigkeit, Fertigkeit	Painting or sailing are skills.
	Red Cross [ˌred 'krɒs]	Rotes Kreuz	
	first aid [ˌfɜːst‿'eɪd]	erste Hilfe	
	certificate [sə'tɪfɪkət]	Bescheinigung, Zeugnis	
	interest ['ɪntrəst]	Interesse	
2	**program** ['prəʊgræm]	Programm	! program = computer; programme = TV
	mother tongue ['mʌðə ˌtʌŋ]	Muttersprache	My mother tongue is German.
3	**model** ['mɒdl]	Modell	

At work

1	**safety** ['seɪftɪ]	Sicherheit	safe → safety
	protective clothes [prəˌtektɪv 'kləʊðz]	Arbeitsschutzkleidung	For certain jobs protective clothes are important.
	boot [buːt]	Stiefel	You wear boots, not shoes, for walking in snow.
	face shield ['feɪs ˌʃiːld]	Gesichtsschutzschild	
	glove [glʌv]	Handschuh	Shoes for your feet and gloves for your hands.
	goggles (pl) ['gɒglz]	Schutzbrille	
	ear muff ['ɪə ˌmʌf]	Ohrenschützer	
	overall ['əʊvərˌɔːl]	Arbeitskittel, -mantel	
4	**workplace** ['wɜːkˌpleɪs]	Arbeitsplatz, Arbeitsstelle	
	liquid ['lɪkwɪd]	Flüssigkeit	Water is a liquid.
	maximum ['mæksɪməm]	Maximal-, maximal	
5	**no entry** [nəʊ‿'entrɪ]	Zutritt verboten	
	exit ['eksɪt]	Ausgang	There is always an EXIT sign in the cinema.
	to prohibit [prəʊ'hɪbɪt]	verbieten	Smoking is prohibited here.
	warning ['wɔːnɪŋ]	Warnung	Don't do it! That's a warning.
	beam [biːm]	Strahl	
	forklift truck ['fɔːklɪft‿ˌtrʌk]	Gabelstapler	
	fire extinguisher ['faɪər‿ɪkˌstɪŋgwɪʃə]	Feuerlöscher	
	protection [prə'tekʃn]	Schutz	Gloves, goggles, hard hats offer protection.
	emergency stop [ɪ'mɜːdʒənsɪ ˌstɒp]	Not-Aus-Einrichtung	

Unit 17 Working abroad

Focus

	abroad [ə'brɔːd]	im/ins Ausland	
4	**contract** ['kɒntrækt]	Vertrag	When you begin a new job you get a contract.
	shortened ['ʃɔːtnd]	gekürzt, verkürzt	

	relative clause [ˌrelətɪv ˈklɔːz]	Relativsatz	
	au pair [əʊ ˈpeə]	Au-pair-Mädchen/-Junge	
	housework [ˈhaʊsˌwɜːk]	Hausarbeit	I do my housework on Saturdays.
	accommodation [əˌkɒməˈdeɪʃn]	Unterkunft, Wohnung	What was your accommodation on holiday like?
	case study [ˈkeɪs‿stʌdɪ]	Fallbeispiel, Fallstudie	
	volunteer [ˌvɒlənˈtɪə]	Freiwillige(r), Ehrenamtliche(r)	Volunteers are not paid for their work.
	Romania [rʊˈmeɪnɪə]	Rumänien	
5	**agency** [ˈeɪdʒənsɪ]	Agentur	
	castle [ˈkɑːsl]	Schloss	! Das t in castle wird nicht gesprochen.
	practical [ˈpræktɪkl]	praktisch	I like to work with my hands. I like practical work.
	to restore [rɪˈstɔː]	restaurieren	That old table has been restored.

Practice

1	**to pour** [pɔː]	eingießen, einschenken	Can I pour you a drink?
	dish [dɪʃ]	hier: Schale, Schüssel	a dish of fruit
	sunglasses (pl) [ˈsʌnˌglɑːsɪz]	Sonnenbrille	Your sunglasses ARE here.
2	**yard (AE)** [jɑːd]	Garten	
	lift [lɪft]	Aufzug, Fahrstuhl	
	gas (AE) [gæs]	hier: Benzin	
	subway (AE) [ˈsʌbˌweɪ]	U-Bahn	
	vacation (AE) [vəˈkeɪʃn]	Urlaub, Ferien	How long is your vacation?
	highway (AE) [ˈhaɪˌweɪ]	Schnellstraße, Autobahn	
	elevator (AE) [ˈeləveɪtə]	Aufzug, Fahrstuhl	Taking the elevator is much quicker than walking.
	pants (pl) (AE) [pænts]	Hose	
3	**to tow away** [ˌtəʊ‿əˈweɪ]	abschleppen	The police towed my car away.
	goods (pl) [gʊdz]	Ware	The quality of his goods is bad.
	pure [pjʊə]	rein, pur	pure orange juice
	thief (pl thieves) [θiːf, θiːvz]	Dieb	A thief stole my money.
	to prosecute [ˈprɒsɪˌkjuːt]	strafrechtlich verfolgen	
4	**voluntary** [ˈvɒləntərɪ]	freiwillig	You don't have to give money – it's voluntary.
	to taste [teɪst]	schmecken	Mm! This cake tastes fantastic!
5	**possibility** [ˌpɒsəˈbɪlətɪ]	Möglichkeit	Is there a possibility that I can pay later?
	difference [ˈdɪfrəns]	Unterschied	Can you see the difference between these pictures?
	to differ [ˈdɪfə]	sich unterscheiden	
	to govern [ˈgʌvn]	regieren	The party governs the country very well.
	improvement [ɪmˈpruːvmənt]	Verbesserung	They have made many improvements to their house.

Listening and reading

1	**New Zealand** [njuː ˈziːlənd]	Neuseeland	
	carpenter [ˈkɑːpɪntə]	Tischler(in), Zimmerer(in)	A carpenter works with wood.
	to provide [prəˈvaɪd]	liefern, bereitstellen	Volunteers are provided with food.
	Pacific [pəˈsɪfɪk]	Pazifik	
	earthquake [ˈɜːθˌkweɪk]	Erdbeben	Did you hear about the terrible earthquake?
	day-to-day [ˌdeɪtəˈdeɪ]	alltäglich	There are some day-to-day problems.
	repair [rɪˈpeə]	Reparatur	
	afterwards [ˈɑːftəwədz]	hinterher, danach, später	I'm going to town. I'll come to you afterwards.
	to get on [get‿ˈɒn]	auskommen, sich verstehen	There is a new trainee at work. We get on very well.
3	**decision** [dɪˈsɪʒn]	Entscheidung	to decide → decision
5	**to feel homesick** [ˌfiːl ˈhəʊmsɪk]	Heimweh haben	After a month, he felt homesick.
	accent [ˈæksnt]	Akzent	I can't understand a Scottish accent.

	to respect [rɪ'spekt]	respektieren, achten	
7	**lord** [lɔ:d]	Herr	

Gateway to work

1	**retail** ['ri:teɪl]	Einzelhandel	
	nowadays ['naʊəˌdeɪz]	heutzutage	Nowadays you needn't wear a tie at work.
	branch [brɑ:ntʃ]	hier: Filiale	
	candidate ['kændɪˌdeɪt]	Bewerber(in)	How many candidates are there for the job?
	keen [ki:n]	eifrig, leidenschaftlich	I'm very keen to learn the job.
	dynamic [daɪ'næmɪk]	dynamisch	
	covering letter ['kʌvərɪŋ ˌletə]	Begleitschreiben, Bewerbung	
	advert ['ædvɜ:t]	Anzeige, Reklame	
2	**to advertise** ['ædvəˌtaɪz]	hier: ausschreiben	
	to enclose [ɪn'kləʊz]	beilegen	I enclose the photo that you asked for.
	opportunity [ˌɒpə'tju:nətɪ]	Gelegenheit, Chance	The job is in London. It is a great opportunity!
3	**in response** [ˌɪn rɪ'spɒns]	als Antwort	

At work

4	**listener** ['lɪsnə]	Zuhörer(in)	
	to interrupt [ˌɪntə'rʌpt]	unterbrechen	Don't interrupt the boss when she is speaking!
	still [stɪl]	still	Keep your arm still. Don't move it.
	to fidget ['fɪdʒɪt]	herumzappeln	Children often fidget.
	to sit up straight [ˌsɪt‿ʌp 'streɪt]	gerade sitzen	My grandmother was taught to always sit up straight.
	to slump [slʌmp]	zusammensacken	Don't slump in your chair – it's bad for your back.
	to criticise ['krɪtɪˌsaɪz]	kritisieren	

Vocabulary – Alphabetisches Wörterverzeichnis

In dieser alphabetischen Wortliste ist das gesamte Vokabular aus dem unitbegleitenden Wörterverzeichnis enthalten.
Die Angaben hinter den Einträgen geben die Fundstelle an, z. B. 22 = Seite 22.

A

a couple of 26 ein paar
a few 104 ein paar
a lot (of) 14 sehr; viele
abbreviation 15 Abkürzung
Aborigine 55 Ureinwohner(in) Australiens
above 22 oben
above 67 über
abroad 170 im/ins Ausland
absolutely 65 absolut, wirklich
accent 175 Akzent
accident 162 Unfall
accidental 144 zufällig, versehentlich
accommodation 171 Unterkunft, Wohnung
account 74 Konto
accounts 156 Rechnungswesen
across 57 über
across 108 hier: quer (durch)
active 151 Aktiv
activity 22 Aktivität
actor, actress 46 Schauspieler(in)
ad 117 Anzeige, Reklame
to add 25 hinzufügen
adjective 40 Adjektiv
advantage 76 Vorteil
adverb 22 Adverb
adverb of frequency 23 Häufigkeitsadverb
advert 176 Anzeige, Reklame
to advertise 156 (be)werben, Werbung machen für
to advertise 177 hier: ausschreiben
advertisement 116 Anzeige, Reklame
advertising company 66 Werbeagentur
advice 94 Rat(schlag)
to afford 122 sich leisten
African 106 Afrikaner(in); afrikanisch
afterwards 174 hinterher, danach, später
against 104 gegen
aged 107 im Alter von
agency 171 Agentur
(a month) ago 122 vor (einem Monat)
to agree 35 zustimmen, übereinstimmen
agricultural 78 landwirtschaftlich
air 135 Luft
alive 49 am Leben, lebendig
All aboard! 135 Alles einsteigen!
All the best 127 Alles Gute
alone 50 allein
along 60 entlang
aloud 23 laut
although 120 obwohl, obgleich
amateur 162 Amateur-, Hobby-
amazed 65 erstaunt
amazing 63 erstaunlich, toll
ambulance 142 Krankenwagen
American 24 Amerikaner(in); amerikanisch
amplifier 94 Verstärker
animation 77 Animation
ankle 98 (Fuß)knöchel
annoying 144 ärgerlich
Antarctica 102 die Antarktis
antivirus 72 Antivirus-
apartment (AE) 141 Wohnung
to appear 47 erscheinen, auftreten
apple strudel 44 Apfelstrudel
to apply 166 sich bewerben
apprenticeship 78 Ausbildung, Lehre
approximately 42 etwa, ungefähr
apron 81 Schürze
architect 28 Architekt(in)
area 102 Gebiet, Gegend
area code 52 Vorwahl
around 42 hier: ungefähr
around 105 rund um, um … herum
to arrange 93 hier: ausmachen
art 80 Kunst
article 41 Artikel
artist 115 Künstler(in)
as 154 hier: wenn
asap (= as soon as possible) 127 so bald wie möglich
Asia 14 Asien
Asian 56 Asiat(in); asiatisch
to ask around 9 herumfragen
asparagus 44 Spargel
aspect 155 Aspekt, Gesichtspunkt
aspirin 99 Aspirin
assistant 41 hier: Kellner(in)
(not) at all 47 überhaupt (nicht)
at first sight 164 auf den ersten Blick
at work 29 bei der Arbeit
Athens 8 Athen
athlete 162 Athlet(in), Sportler(in)
athletics 162 Leichtathletik
atmosphere 103 Atmosphäre
atomic research centre 73 Atomforschungszentrum
to attach 126 anhängen
to attend 86 besuchen, teilnehmen
attractive 83 attraktiv, gut aussehend
au pair 171 Au-pair-Mädchen/-Junge
Australia 53 Australien
Australian 56 Australier(in); australisch
Austria 8 Österreich
author 45 Autor(in)
automatic 140 automatisch
autumn 31 Herbst
available 118 verfügbar, erhältlich
average 54 durchschnittlich

B

baby change 6 Wickelraum
baking powder 129 Backpulver
balsamic vinegar 128 Balsamicoessig
to bandage 99 bandagieren, verbinden
bar 11 Riegel
bar chart 106 Balkendiagramm
basic 76 grundlegend, grundsätzlich
basil 129 Basilikum
bath 132 Bad
battery 139 Batterie
BC (= before Christ) 56 vor Christus
to be a leader 124 führend sein
to be able to 79 können
to be asleep 135 schlafen

to be based (in ...) 66 seinen Sitz (in ...) haben
to be lucky 143 Glück haben
to be on 116 hier: laufen
to be on display 148 ausgestellt sein
to be on one's way to ... 10 auf dem Weg nach ... sein
beach 48 Strand
beam 169 Strahl
to beat (beat, beaten) 129 hier: verrühren
to beat (beat, beaten) 161 schlagen
beauty 113 Schönheit
to become (became, become) 47 werden
bed and breakfast 96 (Frühstücks)pension
beef 44 Rind(fleisch)
beer 129 Bier
beginning 133 Anfang
Belgium 120 Belgien
believable 143 glaubwürdig, glaubhaft
to believe (in) 76 glauben (an)
to bend (bent, bent) 98 beugen, biegen
best wishes 33 viele/beste Grüße
to bet (bet, bet) 93 wetten
between 34 zwischen
to bike 24 (mit dem) Rad fahren
biography 46 Biografie
birthplace 46 Geburtsort
biscuit 37 Keks
to bite (bit, bitten) 98 beißen
black market 124 Schwarzmarkt
blonde 46 blond
blouse 99 Bluse
to blow (blew, blown) 154 blasen, wehen
to board 14 einsteigen (in)
boarding pass 14 Bordkarte
boat 105 Boot
body 42 Körper
to boil 129 kochen
bond 114 Verbindung
bookcase 118 Bücherregal
booking 36 Buchung
bookmark 144 Lesezeichen
boot 138 hier: Kofferraum
boot 168 Stiefel
border 120 Grenze
bored 65 gelangweilt
boring 58 langweilig
born 46 geboren
to borrow 120 leihen
boyfriend 90 Freund (eines Mädchens)
bracket 24 Klammer
brake 139 Bremse
branch 140 Ast
branch 176 hier: Filiale
brave 164 tapfer
break 54 Pause
to break (broke, broken) 164 brechen
to break down 113 eine Panne haben
breakthrough 47 Durchbruch
to breathe 152 atmen
brick 158 Ziegelstein
bricklayer 28 Maurer
bridge 60 Brücke
brilliant 47 großartig, hervorragend
British 38 britisch
broken 124 kaputt, gebrochen
to browse 74 blättern, schmökern
buffet 92 Büfett
to build (built, built) 28 bauen
building 28 Gebäude, Bau
bumper 138 Stoßstange
to burn 124 (ver)brennen
burr 144 Klette
bus station 60 Bushaltestelle
bus stop 83 Bushaltestelle
businessman 37 Geschäftsmann
businessperson 45 Geschäftsmann, -frau
businesswoman 123 Geschäftsfrau
busy 24 beschäftigt
button 76 Knopf, Taste
by 108 hier: mal
by accident 144 zufällig
Bye! 68 Tschüs!

C

cable 28 Kabel
cable 28 Kabel
calculator 11 Rechner
calendar 52 Kalender
California 65 Kalifornien
call 14 hier: Aufruf
to call 27 hier: nennen
to call 68 (an)rufen
caller 36 Anrufer(in)
calory 42 Kalorie
to camp 33 campen, zelten
Canadian 132 Kanadier(in); kanadisch
cancer 150 Krebs
candidate 176 Bewerber(in)
canteen 26 Kantine
capital 54 Hauptstadt
capital letter 32 Großbuchstabe
car park 132 Parkplatz
caramel 41 Karamell
carbon dioxide 158 Kohlendioxid
care 113 Sorgfalt
career 26 Laufbahn, Karriere
careless 113 achtlos
Caribbean 102 karibisch
carnival 103 Jahrmarkt
carpenter 174 Tischler(in), Zimmerer(in)
carrot 38 Möhre, Karotte, Mohrrübe
to carry 58 tragen, transportieren
carton 11 hier: Tüte
case study 171 Fallbeispiel, Fallstudie
castle 171 Schloss
catalogue 74 Katalog
to catch (caught, caught) 28 fangen
to catch (caught, caught) 83 hier: erreichen, erwischen
to catch (caught, caught) 140 hier: sich verfangen
catering 80 Gastronomie, Hotel- und Gaststättengewerbe
catnap (informal) 164 Nickerchen
cattle 58 Vieh
to cause 152 verursachen, auslösen
cell (phone) (AE) 30 Mobiltelefon, Handy
centimetre 53 Zentimeter
cereal 25 Frühstückszerealien
certainly 26 sicher(lich), bestimmt
certificate 166 Bescheinigung, Zeugnis
chain 39 Kette
to change 47 (ver)ändern
to change 139 hier: austauschen, wechseln
chaotic 64 chaotisch
to charter 66 chartern
to chat 30 plaudern, chatten
to check in 14 einchecken
check-in agent 14 etwa: Schalter-angestellte(r)
checkout 74 Kasse
chef 28 Koch, Köchin
chest 98 Brust(korb)
chicken 40 Huhn
chilli 41 Chili
Chinese 19 Chinese, Chinesin; chinesisch

chips (pl) 38 Pommes frites (BE), Chips (AE)
choice 114 Wahl
choir 144 Chor
to choose (chose, chosen) 12 auswählen
to chop 129 hacken
cistern 158 Spülkasten, Wasserkasten
classic 138 klassisch
cleaner 104 Reinigungskraft
clear 77 klar, eindeutig
to click 76 klicken
client 29 Kunde, Kundin
to climb 65 (er)klettern, besteigen
cloth 144 Stoff
clove of garlic 129 Knoblauchzehe
coal 154 Kohle
coast 53 Küste
coincidence 141 Zufall
cold 98 Erkältung, Schnupfen
colleague 34 Kollege, Kollegin
to collect 25 sammeln
Cologne 20 Köln
to come over 32 herüberkommen
to come to 41 sich belaufen auf
comfortable 135 bequem
comment 114 Kommentar, Äußerung
commercial 144 kommerziell
community college 133 etwa: berufsbildende Schule
company 26 Firma, Unternehmen
comparative 40 Komparativ
to compare 57 vergleichen
competition 63 Wettbewerb
competition 110 hier: Preisausschreiben
complete 143 fertig, komplett
comprehensive school 166 Gesamtschule
concert 63 Konzert
concrete 155 Beton
conference centre 18 Konferenzzentrum
conference room 97 Besprechungsraum
confident 161 zuversichtlich, selbstbewusst
to confirm 36 bestätigen
confirmation 74 Bestätigung
congratulations 66 Glückwunsch, Glückwünsche
to connect 134 verbinden
conscious 143 bewusst
to consist of 109 bestehen aus
construction 78 Bau(gewerbe)
consumer 40 Konsument(in)
to contact 76 Kontakt aufnehmen mit
to contain 42 enthalten, beinhalten
continent 102 Kontinent
contract 171 Vertrag
contrast 104 Kontrast, Gegensatz
conversation 18 Gespräch, Unterhaltung
to cook a barbecue 54 grillen
cookbook 128 Kochbuch
cooker 58 Herd, Kocher
cookie (AE) 41 Keks
cop (slang) 122 Bulle
corner 83 Ecke
to correspond 126 korrespondieren
corresponding 165 entsprechend, dazugehörig
corridor 96 Flur, Gang, Korridor
countable 11 zählbar
couple 142 Paar
course 18 Kurs
cousin 100 Cousin(e)
to cover (with) 144 bedecken (mit)
covering letter 176 Bewerbungsschreiben, Bewerbung
to crash 140 stürzen
crazy 62 verrückt
creamy 120 sahnig
credible 143 glaubwürdig
credit card 36 Kreditkarte
criminal 28 Verbrecher(in)
crisps (pl) 39 Chips
critical 115 kritisch
to criticise 179 kritisieren
crowd 103 (Menschen)menge
to cry 94 weinen
cuddly toy 52 Kuscheltier
culture 85 Kultur
to cure 150 heilen
current 148 aktuell, gegenwärtig
customer 41 Kunde, Kundin
customer service 156 Kundendienst
to cut (cut, cut) 28 schneiden
to cut down 151 fällen
CV 166 Lebenslauf

D

dance 99 Tanz(en)
to dance 32 tanzen
dancer 29 Tänzer(in)
danger 165 Gefahr
dangerous 65 gefährlich
dark 46 dunkel
dark 164 Dunkelheit
date of birth 46 Geburtsdatum
day return ticket 136 Tagesrückfahrkarte
day-to-day 174 alltäglich
deal 117 hier: Angebot
to deal with 156 sich befassen mit
Dear 33 Liebe(r)
Dear Sir or Madam 148 Sehr geehrte Damen und Herren
to decide 37 sich entscheiden, beschließen
decision 175 Entscheidung
deep 108 tief
to delete 53 löschen
delicious 39 lecker, köstlich
to deliver 59 (aus)liefern
delivery 74 (Aus)lieferung
Denmark 78 Dänemark
dentist's assistant 114 Zahnarzthelfer(in)
to depart 14 abfliegen
department 109 Abteilung
department store 86 Kaufhaus
departure 6 Abflug
to depend 18 darauf ankommen
depth 108 Tiefe
to describe 50 beschreiben
description 28 Beschreibung
desert 56 Wüste
to design 28 entwerfen
designer 77 Layouter(in), Gestalter(in)
despite 104 trotz
dessert 41 Nachtisch, Dessert
destination 14 Ziel(ort)
to destroy 150 zerstören
destruction 151 Zerstörung
details (pl) 46 Angaben
determined 164 entschlossen
development 156 Entwicklung
diagram 54 Diagramm
diameter 108 Durchmesser
diary 86 Terminkalender
to die 124 sterben
to differ 173 sich unterscheiden
difference 173 Unterschied
difficulty 104 Schwierigkeit
dimension 108 Ausmaß, Raumangabe
to dip 129 tauchen
to direct 67 Regie führen
directions (pl) 60 Wegbeschreibung
directly 76 direkt

director 47 Direktor(in), Regisseur(in)
disabled 162 behindert
to disappear 135 verschwinden
disappointed 160 enttäuscht
disaster 153 Katastrophe, Unglück
discussion 95 Diskussion, Gespräch
dish 43 Gericht
dish 172 hier: Schale, Schüssel
distribution 156 Vertrieb
the do's and don'ts 82 was man tun und nicht tun sollte
doctor's assistant 114 Arzthelfer(in)
double room 36 Doppelzimmer
doubt 164 Zweifel
down 66 hinunter
dramatic 153 dramatisch
to draw (drew, drawn) 59 zeichnen
dream 90 Traum
dress 94 Kleid
dried 129 getrocknet
to drive (drove, driven) 28 fahren
driver 28 Fahrer(in)
driving licence 111 Führerschein
driving school 111 Fahrschule
driving test 111 Fahrprüfung
drug 49 Droge
drug 150 hier: Medikament, Arznei
to dry 129 trocknen
during 84 während
to dust 129 bestäuben
duty 81 Aufgabe
dynamic 176 dynamisch

E

each 14 jede(r, s)
ear muff 168 Ohrenschützer
to earn 47 verdienen
earth 140 Erde
earthquake 174 Erdbeben
east 57 Osten
eastern 57 östlich
e-commerce 74 elektronischer Handel
to edit 53 bearbeiten
to educate 153 unterrichten, ausbilden
education 166 (Aus)bildung
efficient 34 effizient
Egypt 64 Ägypten
elbow 98 Ellbogen
electric 123 elektrisch, Elektro-
electrical 124 elektrisch
electrician 54 Elektriker(in)
electricity 124 Strom, Elektrizität
electronic technician 114 Elektroniker(in)
electronics 80 Elektronik
elevator (AE) 172 Aufzug, Fahrstuhl
else 119 sonst (noch)
emergency 140 Notfall; Not-
emergency stop 169 Not-Aus-Einrichtung
to employ 124 beschäftigen
employee 28 Angestellte(r)
to enclose 177 beilegen
to encrypt 74 chiffrieren, verschlüsseln
to end 23 enden, aufhören
endless 135 endlos, unendlich
energy 103 Energie
engine 138 Motor
engineer 17 Ingenieur(in)
engineering 66 Technik, Maschinenbau
Englishman 56 Engländer
to enjoy 42 genießen
Enjoy your meal. 41 Guten Appetit.
enormous 49 enorm, riesig
enough 115 genug
enquiry 117 Erkundigung, Anfrage
environment 150 Umwelt
environmentally friendly 123 umweltfreundlich
equipment (no pl) 94 Ausrüstung, Gerät(e)
to escape 142 (ent)fliehen, entkommen
ethnic 102 ethnisch
even 30 selbst, sogar
ever 62 je(mals)
everybody 92 jede(r); alle
everyday 85 alltäglich
everyone 73 jede(r); alle
everything 72 alles
everywhere 58 überall
exactly 27 genau
examiner 111 Prüfer(in)
excellent 66 ausgezeichnet
excited 65 aufgeregt
exciting 59 aufregend, spannend
exhaust 138 Auspuff
exit 169 Ausgang
to exit 77 verlassen, beenden
exotic 41 exotisch, fremdartig
to expect 114 erwarten
experience 82 Erfahrung
experiment 144 Experiment
expiry date 36 Ablaufdatum, Verfallstermin
to explain 44 erklären
expression 23 Ausdruck
extra 66 besonders, Extra-
extreme sport 65 Extremsportart
extremely 77 extrem, äußerst
e-zine 17 etwa: Internet-Magazin

F

fabric 144 Stoff
fabulous 138 fabelhaft, sagenhaft
face shield 168 Gesichtsschutzschild
facility 132 Einrichtung
factory 27 Fabrik, Werk
to fall in love with 47 sich verlieben in
to fall out 144 herausfallen
famous 27 berühmt
fan 109 Ventilator, Gebläse
fantastic 47 fantastisch
farm 78 Bauernhof
fascinated 65 fasziniert
fascinating 64 faszinierend
fashion 110 Mode
fashion designer 28 Modeschöpfer(in)
fat 29 dick
favourite 27 Lieblings-
to feel homesick 175 Heimweh haben
feeling 63 Gefühl
few 106 wenig
to fidget 179 herumzappeln
field 161 Wiese, Feld, Platz
to fight (fought, fought) 151 (be)kämpfen
figure 95 hier: Figur
figure 127 hier: Zahl
file 112 Datei
filing cabinet 52 Aktenschrank
to fill in 9 ausfüllen
final 77 letzte(r, s)
final year 54 Abschlussklasse
finally 41 schließlich, letztendlich
finances (pl) 52 Finanzen
to find out 14 herausfinden
to find out about 50 sich informieren über
to fire 66 abdrücken, feuern
fire extinguisher 169 Feuerlöscher
firm 66 Firma, Unternehmen
first aid 166 erste Hilfe

first name 85 Vorname
flat 135 flach
flavour 41 Geschmack(srichtung)
flight 6 Flug
to flirt 94 flirten
to flood 153 (über)fluten, überschwemmen
floor 30 Boden
floor 96 hier: Etage, Stockwerk
to follow 60 folgen
foot (pl feet) 46 Fuß (= 30,48 cm)
footballer 26 Fußballspieler(in)
for a while 23 eine Zeit lang
forest 134 Wald
forklift truck 169 Gabelstapler
form 9 Form, Formular
formal 85 förmlich
fortunately 125 glücklicherweise
fossil fuel 154 fossiler Brennstoff
to found 50 gründen
founder 49 Gründer
France 8 Frankreich
to freeze (froze, frozen) 153 (er)frieren, gefrieren
freight 58 Fracht
French 133 Franzose/Französin; französisch
frequency 144 Frequenz
fresh 42 neu, frisch
fridge 58 Kühlschrank
friendly 82 freundlich
fries (AE) 38 Pommes
frightened 83 erschreckt, erschrocken
frightening 79 beängstigend, erschreckend
fruit tart 44 Obsttorte
to fry 128 braten
fuel 135 Treibstoff
fully booked 36 ausgebucht
funny 62 lustig, witzig, komisch
furniture (no pl) 43 Möbel
further 126 weitere(r, s)
further education 83 Aus- und Weiterbildung
future 78 Zukunft

G

G'day (informal, AUS) 58 Tag, hi, hallo
game 34 Spiel
garlic 41 Knoblauch
gas 152 Gas
gas (AE) 172 hier: Benzin
gas station (AE) 120 Tankstelle
gear 122 Gang
gear stick 138 Schaltknüppel
generally 41 generell, im Allgemeinen
generous 50 großzügig, freigebig
geography 115 Erdkunde, Geographie
to get in 147 zurückkehren
to get lost 105 sich verirren
to get on 174 auskommen, sich verstehen
to get out 142 aussteigen
to get up 22 aufstehen
ghost 145 Geist
giant 153 riesig
girlfriend 90 Freundin (eines Jungen)
to give away 50 weggeben, verschenken
to give sb one's love 33 jdm. Grüße bestellen
glasses (pl) 73 Brille
global 70 global, weltweit
glove 168 Handschuh
glue 144 Klebstoff
to go ahead 109 fortfahren, weitermachen
to go on 60 weitergehen
to go with 14 gehören zu
to go wrong 93 schief gehen
goal 160 Tor
goggles (pl) 168 Schutzbrille
good-looking 95 gut aussehend
goods (pl) 173 Ware
to govern 173 regieren
government 153 Regierung
gram 13 Gramm
grandad 39 Opa, Opi
grandma 39 Oma, Omi
grandparents 100 Großeltern
grass 94 Gras
grateful 148 dankbar
Greece 8 Griechenland
greenhouse 152 Treibhaus
grizzly 142 etwa: grausig, schauderhaft
group 18 Gruppe
to grow (grew, grown) 120 wachsen
to grow (grew, grown) 135 hier: anbauen
to grow up 48 aufwachsen
to guess 63 (er)raten
gun 67 Gewehr, Pistole
guy 33 Typ, Kerl
gym (= gymnasium) 162 Turnhalle

H

hair style 94 Frisur
hairdresser 28 Frisör(in)
hairdressing 80 Frisieren; Friseurberuf
hairdressing salon 80 Friseursalon
half past (seven) 23 halb(acht)
halt 135 Halt
to halt 135 anhalten
ham 44 Schinken
handful 129 Handvoll
handheld 117 tragbares Gerät
handle 142 Griff
handluggage 10 Handgepäck
to hang (hung, hung) 140 hängen
happy ending 95 Happyend
harbour 164 Hafen
hard 99 hier: hart
hard hat 82 Schutzhelm
to have a shower 23 duschen
head office 50 Zentrale, Hauptsitz
head teacher 96 Rektor(in), Schulleiter(in)
headache 98 Kopfschmerzen, Kopfweh
heading 25 Überschrift
headlight 138 Scheinwerfer, Vorderlicht
headline 82 Schlagzeile
headquarters 122 Stammsitz, Zentrale
health and social care 23 Gesundheits- und Sozialwesen
healthy 29 gesund
heat 152 Hitze
to heat 129 erhitzen
heavy 94 hier: heftig
heavy 108 schwer
hectic 127 hektisch
height 46 Höhe, Größe
helicopter 66 Hubschrauber
(for) help 60 (um) Hilfe
helpful 94 hilfsbereit
helpless 113 hilflos
Here you are. 41 Bitte schön.
high 65 hoch
high school 24 etwa: Mittelschule, Oberschule
highest-paid 47 bestbezahlt
highway (AE) 172 Schnellstraße, Autobahn
hill 154 Hügel
to hire 66 mieten, leihen
hire car 122 Mietwagen
history 55 Geschichte

to hit (hit, hit) 83 hier: anfahren
to hit (hit, hit) 140 treffen, schlagen
to hold (held, held) 92 halten
to hold hands 92 Händchen halten
hometown 9 Heimatort, Heimatstadt
honest 95 ehrlich
hook 142 Haken
to hope 122 hoffen
hopefully 153 hoffnungsvoll, hoffentlich
horrible 73 fürchterlich, schrecklich
horse 59 Pferd
hospital 28 Krankenhaus
hour 14 Stunde
housework 171 Hausarbeit
How about ...? 87 Wie wäre es mit ...?
How are things? 127 Wie geht's?
How are you? 109 Wie geht es Ihnen?
How do you do 84 Guten Tag
however 104 aber, jedoch
hundred 28 Hundert
to hurry 116 sich beeilen
to hurt (hurt, hurt) 98 (sich) verletzen
hydroelectric energy 154 Wasserkraft
hymn 144 Kirchenlied, Hymne
hymn book 144 Gesangbuch

I

I can't make it. 146 Ich kann es nicht schaffen.
I feel sick. 98 Mir ist schlecht/übel.
I see. 47 Ich verstehe.
I'm afraid ... 87 Tut mir Leid, aber ...
I'm free. 87 hier: Ich habe Zeit.
ice 99 Eis
ice age 153 Eiszeit
iceberg 164 Eisberg
idiot 83 Idiot, Trottel
imaginary 134 imaginär, in der Vorstellung
to imagine 33 sich vorstellen
immediately 74 sofort
immigrant 103 Einwanderer(in)
to immigrate 54 einwandern
impolite 143 unhöflich
impossible 143 unmöglich
impression 82 Eindruck
improbable 143 unwahrscheinlich
improvement 173 Verbesserung
in advance 127 im Voraus
in English 11 auf Englisch
in fact 40 tatsächlich, vielmehr
in general 163 im Allgemeinen
in German 14 auf Deutsch
in particular 116 besonders, speziell
in response 177 als Antwort
in ruins 124 in Trümmern
in time 130 rechtzeitig
inbox 126 Eingang
inch 46 Zoll (= 2,54 cm)
to include 115 berücksichtigen, beinhalten
including 124 einschließlich
incomplete 143 unvollständig, unfertig
incorrect 143 falsch, unrichtig
to increase 154 erhöhen, steigern
incredible 143 unglaublich
India 39 Indien
Indian 102 Inder(in); indianisch
industrial 114 industriell
industrial estate 60 Gewerbegebiet
industry 105 Industrie
to inform 153 informieren
informal 127 formlos, locker
ingredient 129 Zutat
inhabitant 55 Einwohner(in)
insect 150 Insekt
inside 154 innen; hier: im Inneren
to install 28 installieren, montieren
instant 120 sofortig
instant message 33 Onlinenachricht
instant messenger 71 Onlinenachrichtendienst
instead of 42 anstatt, anstelle
to insulate 158 isolieren, dämmen
insulation 158 Isolierung, Dämmung
to insult 112 beleidigen, beschimpfen
to integrate 104 (sich) integrieren
interest 166 Interesse
to interest 155 interessieren
interested (in) 65 interessiert (an)
to interrupt 179 unterbrechen
introduction 20 Einführung
to invent 69 erfinden
invention 73 Erfindung
inventor 73 Erfinder(in)
Ireland 78 Irland
irregular 47 unregelmäßig
irrelevant 143 belanglos, unerheblich
Is that convenient? 87 Passt Ihnen das?
island 102 Insel
IT technician 28 Informatiker(in)
Italy 8 Italien
item 118 Posten, Objekt, Artikel
itself 76 sich (selbst)

J

Japanese 41 Japaner(in); japanisch
jealous 94 eifersüchtig
jewellerey (no pl) 100 Schmuck
to jog 32 joggen, dauerlaufen
to join 48 (sich) anschließen (an), beitreten
joke 92 Witz
journey 58 Reise
jump 62 Sprung
to jump 140 springen
just a minute 87 einen Augenblick/ Moment bitte

K

kangaroo 59 Känguru
keen 176 eifrig, leidenschaftlich
to keep (kept, kept) 52 (be)halten, führen
to keep (kept, kept) 158 hier: aufbewahren
key 141 Schlüssel
keyboard 50 Keyboard, hier: Tastatur
kidney 142 Niere
to kill 66 töten
kind 38 Art, Sorte
kind 94 nett, freundlich
Kind regards 126 Herzliche Grüße
kiss 33 Kuss
to kiss 95 küssen
kiwi 38 Kiwi
knowledge (no pl) 73 Wissen, Kenntnis(se)
kph (= kilometres per hour) 140 kmh (Stundenkilometer)

L

laboratory 124 Labor
the lads 160 die Jungs
lake 134 See
lamb 44 Lamm
lamp 118 Lampe
land 135 Land
to land 56 landen
to last 103 dauern

lawn 94 Rasen
lawyer 50 Rechtsanwalt, -anwältin
leaflet 151 Prospekt, Broschüre
league 161 Liga
legend 145 Legende
leisure (time) 107 Freizeit
lemonade 19 Limonade
length 108 Länge
to let (let, let) 53 lassen
library 50 Bibliothek, Bücherei
licence 111 Führerschein
to lie (lay, lain) 124 liegen
to lie down (lay, lain) 99 sich hinlegen
lift 111 Mitfahrgelegenheit
lift 172 Aufzug, Fahrstuhl
light 66 Licht
like 6 wie
lipstick 95 Lippenstift
liquid 169 Flüssigkeit
listener 179 Zuhörer(in)
loaf 11 Laib
local 146 örtlich, hiesig
locker 90 Schließfach, Spind
to log in 76 einloggen
to log on 74 sich anmelden, sich einwählen
login 76 Anmeldung
lonely 59 einsam
to look 34 hier: aussehen
to look after 28 sich kümmern um
to look for 60 suchen nach
to look forward to 36 sich freuen auf
to look up 81 nachschlagen
lord 175 Herr
lorry 28 Lastwagen
to lose (lost, lost) 158 verlieren
love at first sight 90 Liebe auf den ersten Blick
low 77 niedrig, tief
L-plate 111 Anfänger-Warnschild
lucky 143 glücklich
luggage 14 Gepäck
lunchtime 43 Mittagspause

M

machine gun 66 Maschinengewehr
magnetron 144 Magnetfeldröhre
magnificent 160 wunderbar, großartig
mailman (AE) 141 Briefträger, Postbote
main building 94 Hauptgebäude
main meal 38 Hauptmahlzeit
main verb 22 Vollverb
mainly 133 hauptsächlich
make 117 Marke
to make sure 158 sichergehen, dafür sorgen
(shopping) mall (AE) 90 Einkaufszentrum
to manage 122 (es) schaffen
to manufacture 122 herstellen, produzieren
manufacturing company 156 Herstellungsbetrieb
market 144 Markt
market research 34 Marktforschung
mast 164 Mast
mathematics 166 Mathematik
maths 25 Mathe
maximum 169 Maximal-, maximal
may (might) 36 dürfen, können
Me too. 78 Ich auch.
meal 25 Mahlzeit, Essen
meaning 27 Bedeutung
means 58 Mittel
meanwhile 129 zwischenzeitlich, unterdessen
mechanic 28 Mechaniker(in)
mechanics 80 Mechanik
medicine 150 Medizin, Medikament
medium 40 mittel
meeting point 6 Treffpunkt
to melt 144 schmelzen
member 52 Mitglied
membership number 53 Mitgliedsnummer
menu 39 Speisekarte
message 30 Nachricht
metal 142 Metall
method 73 Methode
method 129 hier: Zubereitung
microphone 66 Mikrofon
microscope 144 Mikroskop
microwave 144 Mikrowelle
midday 23 Mittag
midnight 47 Mitternacht
military 73 Militär
millimetre 109 Millimeter
minority 102 Minderheit
mirror 138 Spiegel
to miss 130 fehlen, verpassen
missing 15 fehlend
to mix 129 (ver)mischen
mixed 38 gemischt
mixture 129 Mischung
mobile (phone) 30 Mobiltelefon, Handy
model 167 Modell
modern 19 modern
modest 164 bescheiden
monitor 14 Bildschirm, Monitor
moon 71 Mond
Moscow 64 Moskau
(the) most 53 (die) meisten
mostly 58 hauptsächlich, meistens
MOT test 139 etwa: TÜV-Prüfung
mother tongue 167 Muttersprache
motor cycle 122 Motorrad
motor racing 163 Autorennsport
motorway 60 Autobahn
mountain 31 Berg
mouse (pl mice) 51 Maus
to move 98 (sich) bewegen, umziehen
movie (AE) 46 (Kino)Film
multicultural 56 multikulturell
multi-storey car park 59 Parkhaus
Munich 15 München
museum 68 Museum
mushroom 44 Pilz
musician 27 Musiker(in)
myself 84 mich/mir (selbst)
myth 142 Mythos

N

nacelle 154 Motorengehäuse
to name 44 (be)nennen
national 133 national, National-
national league 26 etwa: Bundesliga
National Vocational Qualification 166 etwa: nationale berufsbezogene Qualifikation
nationality 100 Nationalität, Staatsangehörigkeit
Native American 55 amerikanische(r) Ureinwohner(in)
natural 114 natürlich
to navigate 77 lenken, navigieren
nearby 132 in der Nähe
nearly 53 fast, beinahe
necessary 93 nötig, notwendig
negative 24 hier: Verneinung
neighbour 48 Nachbar(in)
nervous 82 nervös
Netherlands 115 Holland, Niederlande
New Zealand 174 Neuseeland
New Zealander 41 Neuseeländer(in)
nil 160 Null

no entry 169 Zutritt verboten
no one 113 niemand
No way! 113 Auf keinen Fall
nobody 124 niemand
noodle 44 Nudel
north 48 Norden
North America 102 Nordamerika
north pole 153 Nordpol
north-east 84 Nordosten
northern 57 nördlich
north-west 49 Nordwesten
north-western 57 nordwestlich
nose 98 Nase
not quite 84 nicht ganz
note 37 Notiz
to note down 52 notieren
to notice 105 bemerken, wahrnehmen
notice board 52 schwarzes Brett
noun 105 Hauptwort, Substantiv
nowadays 176 heutzutage
nurse 28 Krankenschwester
nursery 80 Kindergarten, Hort
nursery school 96 Kindergarten
nursing 78 Krankenpflege
nut 41 Nuss

O

object pronoun 93 Pronomen im Akkusativ
occupation 34 Beruf
of one's own 13 eigen
offer 97 Angebot
to offer 96 (an)bieten
office clerk 114 Bürokaufmann, -frau
Oh dear! 53 Du meine Güte!
oil 58 Öl
olive oil 129 Olivenöl
on the left 48 links
on the right 56 rechts
on the set 47 am Drehort
onion 40 Zwiebel
onto 144 auf
opening hours 117 Öffnungszeiten
opinion 107 Meinung, Ansicht
opportunity 177 Gelegenheit, Chance
opposite 27 entgegengesetzt
opposite 95 Gegenteil
order 14 Ordnung, Reihenfolge
order 119 hier: Bestellung
to order 118 bestellen
ordinary 113 normal, gewöhnlich
organisation 151 Organisation
to organise 77 einrichten, ordnen
organiser 84 Organisator(in), Veranstalter(in)
originally 39 ursprünglich
out 152 hinaus
outback 57 Busch, Hinterland
outside 54 außen, außerhalb, im Freien, draußen
oven 127 Backofen
over 73 (her)über
over there 9 dort drüben
overall 168 Arbeitskittel, -mantel
overnight 47 über Nacht
overweight 42 übergewichtig
own 83 eigene(r, s)
oxygen 150 Sauerstoff

P

Pacific 174 Pazifik
package 74 Paket
packaging 149 Verpackungsmaterial
paint 77 Farbe, Lack
to paint 115 malen, anstreichen
painter and decorator 114 Maler und Tapezierer
pants (pl) (AE) 172 Hose
parachute 140 Fallschirm
paragraph 124 Absatz, Abschnitt
parents (pl) 34 Eltern
part 38 Teil, Rolle
particularly 120 besonders
part-time job 24 Teilzeitstelle
to pass 111 hier: bestehen
to pass back 152 hier: zurückstrahlen
passive 151 Passiv
passport control 6 Passkontrolle
past 60 vorbei/vorüber an
past continuous 91 Verlaufsform der Vergangenheit
past perfect 121 Plusquamperfekt, Vorvergangenheit
patrol 141 Patrouille, Polizeistreife
payment 74 (Be)zahlung
pea 38 Erbse
to peel 129 schälen
pepper 128 Pfeffer
per 41 pro
per cent 41 Prozent
percentage 106 Prozentsatz
personal 52 persönlich
personality 95 Persönlichkeit
personnel 126 Personal
petrol 111 Benzin
pharmacy (AE) 150 Apotheke
to phone 87 anrufen
phone call 37 Telefonanruf
photographer 112 Fotograf(in)
phrase 6 Ausdruck, (Rede)wendung
physicist 124 Physiker(in)
to pick up 141 abnehmen
pie chart 42 Kuchendiagramm
piece of equipment 144 Ausrüstungsgegenstand
piece of paper 63 Blatt Papier
pine tree 140 Kiefer, Pinie
pipe 108 Rohr
plan 78 Plan
to plan 109 planen, anlegen
plant 51 Pflanze
plaster 99 Pflaster
plastic 108 Plastik, Kunststoff
platform 136 Gleis
player 67 Spieler
Pleased to meet you. 84 Es freut mich, dich/Sie kennen zu lernen.
plumber 28 Klempner(in)
plus 110 plus
pocket 145 Tasche
pocket calculator 71 Taschenrechner
point 106 hier: Komma
Poland 78 Polen
polar bear 131 Eisbär
police officer 28 Polizeibeamte(r)
police station 141 Polizeiwache
polite 97 höflich
popular 38 beliebt
population 54 Bevölkerung
pork 44 Schwein(efleisch)
port 132 Hafen
portable 124 tragbar
portion 40 Teil, Portion
possibility 173 Möglichkeit
post code 52 Postleitzahl
postcard 30 Postkarte
postman 26 Briefträger, Postbote
postperson 74 Postbote (-botin)
pot 124 Topf
potato (pl -es) 41 Kartoffel
to pour 172 eingießen, einschenken
power 162 Kraft
power station 154 Kraftwerk
practical 171 praktisch
to practise 36 üben
prairie 135 Prärie
to prefer 39 vorziehen, lieber mögen
prejudice 104 Vorurteil

to prepare 26 vorbereiten
preposition 81 Präposition
present 14 Geschenk
present continuous 30 Verlaufsform der Gegenwart
present perfect 55 Perfekt
president 70 Präsident(in)
press conference 165 Pressekonferenz
pretty 58 ziemlich
pretty 94 hübsch
primary school 99 Grundschule
printer 50 Drucker(in), Drucker
prison 56 Gefängnis
private 112 privat
prize 110 Preis, Gewinn
probable 143 wahrscheinlich
probably 65 wahrscheinlich
process 157 Verfahren, Vorgang
to produce 50 produzieren, herstellen
producer 135 Erzeuger, Hersteller
product 28 Produkt
production 153 Produktion, Herstellung
professional 104 Berufstätige(r) mit qualifizierter Ausbildung
professional 162 hier: Profi
profile 115 Profil
program 167 Programm
to program 28 programmieren
programme 101 Programm
programming language 50 Programmiersprache
to prohibit 169 verbieten
to promise 122 versprechen
proper 124 richtig, echt, ordentlich
to prosecute 173 strafrechtlich verfolgen
to protect 28 (be)schützen
protection 169 Schutz
protective clothes 168 Arbeitsschutzkleidung
to provide 174 liefern, bereitstellen
province 133 Gebiet, Provinz
pub 128 Kneipe, Lokal
public 132 öffentlich
to pull off 144 abziehen, entfernen
pullover 99 Pullover
purchasing manager 148 Einkaufsleiter
pure 173 rein, pur
to put on 66 anziehen, aufsetzen
to put through 68 durchstellen, verbinden
pyramid 64 Pyramide

Q

qualification 166 Qualifikation
qualified 104 qualifiziert, kompetent
quality 127 Qualität, Eigenschaft
quality control 156 Qualitätssicherung
quantity 119 Anzahl, Menge
to quarrel 31 streiten, zanken
quarter (past/to) 23 Viertel (nach/vor)
question 6 Frage
quiet 72 leise, ruhig

R

race 103 Rasse
radar 144 Radar, Funkmesstechnik
radiator 52 Heizkörper
railway 60 Bahn(hof)
railway station 60 Bahnhof
raindrop 94 Regentropfen
rainforest 56 Regenwald
raw material 156 Rohstoff
to reach 65 erreichen
to react (to) 114 reagieren (auf)
to read through 82 durchlesen
ready 109 fertig, bereit
real 46 echt, wirklich
rear light 138 Rücklicht
reason 83 Grund
recent 148 kürzlich, neulich
receptionist 18 Empfangsmitarbeiter(in)
recipe 43 (Koch)Rezept
record 52 Aufzeichnung
record 164 hier: Rekord
to recycle 158 recyceln, wieder verwerten
Red Cross 166 Rotes Kreuz
to reduce 152 reduzieren, vermindern
reduction 116 Preisnachlass, Rabatt
refrigerator 144 Kühlschrank
regular 40 regelmäßig, normal
relative clause 171 Relativsatz
relatively 155 relativ
release 26 hier: Veröffentlichung
to release 49 veröffentlichen
relevant 143 relevant, entsprechend
repair 174 Reparatur
to repair 28 reparieren
to repeat 37 wiederholen
to replace 139 ersetzen
reply 126 Antwort
to reply 127 antworten
report 83 Bericht
to report 161 berichten
reported speech 161 indirekte Rede
reporter 17 Reporter(in)
request 97 Bitte, Wunsch
research 156 Forschung
residence 46 Wohnsitz, Wohnung
to respect 175 respektieren, achten
to rest 99 (sich) ausruhen
restaurant car 135 Speisewagen
to restore 171 restaurieren
result 67 Ergebnis
retail 176 Einzelhandel
retailer 148 Einzelhändler
return ticket 136 Rückfahrkarte
revolution 50 Revolution
the Rhine 93 der Rhein
rice 44 Reis
to ride (rode, ridden) 72 fahren; reiten
right now 30 im Augenblick
ring 40 Ring
to ring (rang, rung) 92 klingeln
to ring (rang, rung) 147 hier: anrufen
ringtone 72 Klingelton
road train 57 Lastzug
robot 74 Roboter
rock 56 Fels, Stein
rock climber 65 Kletterer(in)
rock climbing 65 Klettern, Klettersport
to role-play 97 Rollenspiel spielen
Romania 171 Rumänien
romantic 95 romantisch
roof 159 Dach
rotor blade 154 Rotorblatt
round 58 rund
round 83 um … herum
roundabout 60 Kreisel, Kreisverkehr
rubbish 159 Müll
ruler 11 Lineal
Russia 17 Russland
Russian 17 Russe, Russin; russisch

S

sadly 104 traurigerweise, leider
safe 73 sicher
safety 168 Sicherheit
sail 164 Segel
to sail 164 segeln
sailing 164 Segeln
sailor 164 Segler(in)

salad 38 Salat
sale 116 hier: Schlussverkauf
sales 86 Verkauf, Vertrieb
sales assistant 117 Verkäufer(in)
sales representative 28 Handelsvertreter(in)
salesman 46 Händler, Verkäufer
salt 128 Salz
salted 129 gesalzen
sample 149 Muster
sand 58 Sand
sauce 44 Soße
sausage 38 Wurst, Würstchen
to save 53 hier: speichern
to save 64 hier: sparen
to save 151 hier: retten
scene 66 Szene
sceptical 115 skeptisch
science 144 (Natur)wissenschaft
scientist 46 Wissenschaftler(in)
scissors (pl) 73 Schere
scooter 108 Roller
score 160 Spielstand
to score 160 erzielen, schießen
Scotland 149 Schottland
Scottish 149 schottisch
screen 14 Leinwand, Bildschirm
screen name 33 Codename
to search 72 suchen
search engine 77 Suchmaschine
secondary school 54 etwa: weiterführende Schule
secure socket layer 74 SSL-Verbindung
security camera 127 Überwachungskamera
security check 14 Sicherheitskontrolle
See you soon. 33 Bis bald.
separate 52 einzeln, gesondert
to separate 48 (sich) trennen
serious 85 ernst(haft)
seriously 78 im Ernst
to serve 81 servieren, bedienen
to serve 129 hier: reichen für
service 139 hier: Inspektion
to service 66 pflegen, warten
sexist 95 sexistisch
shaft 154 hier: Welle
to shake (shook, shaken) 66 schütteln
to share 105 teilen
shed 122 Schuppen
sheet of paper 52 Blatt Papier
shirt 99 Hemd
shortened 171 gekürzt, verkürzt
shortly 149 in Kürze, bald
shoulder 98 Schulter
to shout 66 schreien
shower 86 Dusche
shy 50 schüchtern, scheu
sign 6 Zeichen, (Verkehrs)schild
silly 95 albern, dumm
to simmer 128 köcheln lassen
simple 73 einfach
simple past 47 einfache Vergangenheit
simple present 16 einfache Gegenwart
since 54 seit
to sing (sang, sung) 100 singen
singer 27 Sänger(in)
single room 36 Einzelzimmer
singular 73 Singular, Einzahl
to sit down 90 sich (hin)setzen
to sit up straight 179 gerade sitzen
site 72 hier: Seite
size 34 Größe
skateboarding 67 Skateboardfahren
ski 109 Schi
to ski 31 Ski laufen/fahren
skill 166 Fähigkeit, Fertigkeit
skirt 99 Rock
skydiving 67 Fallschirmspringen
slim 95 schlank, schmal, dünn
to slump 179 zusammensacken
smart 82 elegant
to smell 98 riechen
smile 47 Lächeln
to smile 32 lächeln
to smoke 107 rauchen
snowy 31 verschneit
so far 143 so weit, bisher
soap 123 Seife
social worker 28 Sozialarbeiter(in)
society 102 Gesellschaft
soda (drink) (AE) 42 Limonade
soft 128 weich
soft 142 hier: leise
solar energy 154 Solarenergie
solar panel 157 Sonnenkollektor
solo 49 solo; Solo-
someone 14 jemand
something 25 etwas
sometimes 22 manchmal
somewhere 64 irgendwo
song 49 Lied
songwriter 49 Komponist(in)
sort 116 Typ, Art, Sorte
to sound 116 klingen
soup 44 Suppe
south 57 Süden
South America 102 Südamerika
south-east 53 Südosten
south-eastern 57 südöstlich
southern 57 südlich
space 152 Weltraum
Spain 70 Spanien
spark plug 139 Zündkerze
speaker 69 Sprecher(in)
speaker 94 hier: Lautsprecher
special 27 besondere(r,s)
special offer 74 Sonderangebot
species (pl species) 150 Spezies, Art
spectacles (pl) 73 Brille
speed 122 Geschwindigkeit
speedometer 138 Tachometer
to spell 35 buchstabieren
spelling mistake 81 Rechtschreibfehler
spellings 24 Schreibweise
to spend (spent, spent) 31 verbringen, ausgeben
sportsman/-woman 160 Sportler(in)
sporty 95 sportlich
spring 31 Frühling
square kilometre 150 Quadratkilometer
squishy 76 matschig
staff 14 Mitarbeiter, Personal
stage 63 Bühne
stage 74 hier: Arbeitsgang, Phase
stall 100 (Verkaufs)stand
stamina 162 Ausdauer
to stamp 94 stampfen
to star 47 eine Hauptrolle spielen
star sign 46 Sternzeichen
start date 52 Starttermin
state 76 Staat
statement 24 Aussage(satz)
the States 30 die (Vereinigten) Staaten
stay 141 Aufenthalt
to stay 31 bleiben, übernachten
to stay in touch 30 in Kontakt bleiben
to steal (stole, stolen) 74 stehlen
steel 155 Stahl
steering wheel 138 Lenkrad
stereotype 126 Stereotyp, Klischee
to stick (stuck, stuck) 144 kleben (bleiben)
still 120 (immer) noch, noch immer
still 179 still

to stir 129 rühren
stock 81 Lager(bestand)
stomach 98 Magen, Bauch
store 75 Laden, Geschäft
storm 153 Sturm
straight 60 gerade
straight away 85 sofort
strange 41 sonderbar
strawberry 38 Erdbeere
stressful 113 stressig
strict 79 streng
strong 115 stark
stuff (informal) 76 Zeug
stupid 82 dumm, blöd
subject 101 (Schul)fach
subject 148 hier: Betreff
subway (AE) 172 U-Bahn
to succeed 105 Erfolg haben
success 113 Erfolg
successful 47 erfolgreich
sugar 42 Zucker
to suggest 124 vorschlagen
suggestion 82 Vorschlag
summary 29 Zusammenfassung
sun cream 110 Sonnenkrem
sunglasses (pl) 172 Sonnenbrille
sunny 31 sonnig
superlative 40 Superlativ
supper 23 Abendessen
to support 114 unterstützen
to surf 71 surfen
surfing 67 Surfen
surprise 49 Überraschung
surprised 105 überrascht
surprising 131 überraschend
survey 34 Untersuchung, Umfrage
to survive 140 überleben
survivor 153 Überlebende(r)
Sweden 8 Schweden
Swedish 68 schwedisch
sweet 41 süß
swimmer 162 Schwimmer(in)
swimming 99 Schwimmen
Swiss 41 Schweizer(in); schweizerisch
to switch on/off 158 an-/ausschalten
Switzerland 73 die Schweiz
system 73 System

T

tablespoon 129 Esslöffel
tablet 99 Tablette
to take a break 110 eine Pause einlegen
to take a seat 97 Platz nehmen
to take it in turns 7 sich abwechseln
to take off 111 entfernen, abnehmen
to take on 135 hier: aufnehmen, laden
to take part (in) 162 teilnehmen (an)
to take photos 34 Fotos machen
to take place 100 stattfinden
talk 50 Gespräch, Vortrag
to taste 173 schmecken
tasty 128 schmackhaft, lecker
to teach (taught, taught) 99 lehren, unterrichten
teaspoon 129 Teelöffel
technical 73 technisch, technologisch
technician 28 Techniker(in)
technology 71 Technik
telecoms 118 Fernmeldewesen
temperature 54 Temperatur
tense 56 Tempus, Zeitform
term 133 Schuljahresabschnitt
terrified 65 erschreckt
terrifying 62 erschreckend, Furcht einflößend
to test 20 prüfen, testen
to text 92 eine SMS-Nachricht senden, simsen
text message 34 SMS
Thanks very much. 17 Vielen Dank.
That's it. 34 Das war's.
theory 111 Theorie
thick 129 dick
thief (pl thieves) 173 Dieb
to think of 35 hier: sich überlegen
This is ... 87 hier: Hier spricht ...
This is me. 29 Das bin ich.
though 24 aber, dennoch
to tidy 22 aufräumen
tie 99 Krawatte
tin 11 Büchse, Dose
tinned 129 konserviert, in Dosen
tiny 144 winzig
tip 11 Rat(schlag), Tipp
tissue 10 Papiertaschentuch
title 65 Titel
toe 98 Zeh(e)
together 39 zusammen, gemeinsam
tonne 58 metrische Tonne
too 29 hier: zu
tooth (pl teeth) 42 Zahn
top 65 Spitze, Gipfel
topic 107 Thema
total 119 Summe
total cost 139 Gesamtkosten
total distance 164 Gesamtstrecke
total number 155 Gesamtzahl
totally 163 völlig, total
tourism 80 Tourismus
to tow away 173 abschleppen
towards 94 in Richtung (auf)
tower 154 Turm
toy 77 Spielzeug
track 58 Spur, Feldweg
track 73 hier: Titel
trade discount 148 Handelsrabatt
trade fair 86 Messe
trade journal 149 Fachblatt, Fachzeitschrift
traditional 114 traditionell, herkömmlich
traffic 82 Verkehr
traffic light 60 Ampel
trainee 17 Praktikant(in)
traineeship 166 Ausbildungsplatz
training course 84 Kurs, Lehrgang, Schulung
to translate 41 übersetzen
to transport 153 transportieren
transport 159 hier: Verkehrsmittel
to trap 152 einschließen
travel 80 Reise
travel agent 80 Reisebüro-kaufmann/-frau
trip 33 Ausflug, Reise, Fahrt
trolley 74 Einkaufswagen
truck 57 Lastwagen
trunk (AE) 138 hier: Kofferraum
truth 42 Wahrheit
tummy 98 Bauch
turbine 154 Turbine
Turkey 8 Türkei
turkey 44 Pute
to turn 60 sich drehen, abbiegen
to turn round 93 (sich) umdrehen
twin 46 Zwilling
to twist one's ankle 98 mit dem Fuß umknicken
type 149 Typ, Art, Sorte
to type in 74 eintippen
tyre 77 Reifen

U

UK (= United Kingdom) 30 Vereinigtes Königreich
unbelievable 140 unglaublich
unconscious 140 bewusstlos

uncountable 11 unzählbar
underground garage 50 Tiefgarage
to underline 25 unterstreichen
unfortunately 93 leider
unhappy 143 unglücklich
unhealthy 42 ungesund
uniform 81 Uniform
university 49 Universität
unlucky 143 unglücklich
unmarried 85 ledig, unverheiratet
unusual 62 unüblich, ungewöhnlich
up 60 hinauf
up 140 hier: weiter oben
up to 116 bis (zu)
urban 142 städtisch, urban
useless 113 nutzlos
usual 48 gewöhnlich, üblich, normal

V

vacation (AE) 172 Urlaub, Ferien
vacuum cleaner 46 Staubsauger
vanilla 39 Vanille
to vary 104 sich ändern, sich unterscheiden
vegetable 38 Gemüse
Velcro 144 Klettverschluss
version 50 Version, Ausgabe
vet (AE) 46 Tierarzt
Vienna 8 Wien
visit 84 Besuch
visitor 44 Besucher(in)
vocational college 30 etwa: Berufsschule
vocational school 54 etwa: Berufsschule
voluntary 173 freiwillig
volunteer 171 Freiwillige(r), Ehrenamtliche(r)

W

wages (pl) 81 Arbeitslohn
to wake up (woke, woken) 140 aufwecken, aufwachen
walk 144 Spaziergang
war 74 Krieg
to warm 152 (er)wärmen
warming 152 Erwärmung
to warn 143 warnen
warning 169 Warnung
waste bin 118 Abfalleimer
watch 83 Armbanduhr
to water 81 gießen
water pipe 28 Wasserleitung
wave 144 Welle
way 82 Art und Weise
weak 144 schwach
to weigh 58 wiegen
weight 53 Gewicht
west 57 Westen
western 57 westlich
wet 94 nass
whale 164 Wal
What about ...? 44 Was ist mit ...?, Wie wäre es mit ...?
whatever 66 was (auch immer)
wheat 135 Weizen
wheel 58 Rad
wheelchair 162 Rollstuhl
while 91 während, als
whipped cream 44 Schlagsahne
whole 49 ganz
wide 108 breit, weit
width 108 Breite, Weite
wild 49 wild
to win (won, won) 47 gewinnen
wind 154 Wind
window 52 Fenster
windscreen 138 Windschutzscheibe
wizard 123 hier: Genie
wood 123 Holz
wood 142 hier: Wald
worker 28 Arbeiter(in)
working hours 81 Geschäftszeiten
workplace 169 Arbeitsplatz, Arbeitsstelle
works 44 Werkanlage
workshop 82 Werkstatt
worldwide 68 weltweit, global
to worry 82 sich Sorgen machen
wound 99 Wunde
to write down 53 aufschreiben
to write out sth in full 32 etwa: ausformulieren
writer 148 Autor(in), Verfasser(in)

Y

yacht 164 Jacht
yard (AE) 172 Garten
You're welcome. 17 Gern geschehen.
Yours faithfully/sincerely 148 Mit freundlichen Grüßen
yourself 20 dich; dir
youth hostel 31 Jugendherberge

Abbildungsnachweis

Titel: ZEFA (Kruesselmann), Düsseldorf; Corbis (Tom Grill), Düsseldorf; Avenue Images GmbH (medio images), Hamburg; Corbis (Terry Vine), Düsseldorf • S. 6: Flughafen Düsseldorf GmbH (Andreas Wiese), Düsseldorf; Flughafen Köln/Bonn, Köln • S. 7: Avenue Images GmbH (Corbis RF), Hamburg; Avenue Images GmbH (Brand X Pictures), Hamburg • S. 8: Fotosearch RF (Image 100), Waukesha, WI; Avenue Images GmbH (Digital Vision RF), Hamburg; MEV, Augsburg; Imageshop RF (RF), Düsseldorf; Alamy Images RM (RF), Abingdon, Oxon; Avenue Images GmbH (Rubberball RF), Hamburg; Avenue Images GmbH (Digital Vision), Hamburg; Avenue Images GmbH (Comstock), Hamburg • S. 10: Avenue Images GmbH (Creatas RF), Hamburg • S. 12: iStockphoto (luba), Calgary, Alberta • S. 13: Imageshop RF (RF), Düsseldorf • S. 14: Getty Images (Photodisc), München; Flughafen Düsseldorf GmbH (A. Wiese), Düsseldorf; Deutsche Lufthansa AG, Frankfurt • S. 16: Inmagine (Dynamicgraphics RF), Houston TX; MEV, Augsburg • S. 17: Visum (Fotofinder/Duddek), Hamburg; Deutsche Lufthansa AG, Frankfurt • S. 18: Avenue Images GmbH (Comstock), Hamburg; STOCK4B (Fotofinder/König), München • S. 19: Avenue Images GmbH (Brand X Pictures), Hamburg • S. 21: Fotosearch RF (Stockbyte), Waukesha, WI; Ingram Publishing (RF), Tattenhall Chester; obs, Hamburg; MEV, Augsburg; creativ collection, Freiburg; ullstein bild (ddp), Berlin; Avenue Images GmbH (imageshop), Hamburg; Getty Images, München • S. 22: Fotofinder (plainpicture/AMI), Berlin; iStockphoto (RF), Calgary, Alberta; Avenue Images GmbH (imageshop), Hamburg; Bananastock RF, Watlington/Oxon; Avenue Images GmbH (Corbis RF), Hamburg; Avenue Images GmbH (Stockbyte RF), Hamburg • S. 24: Avenue Images GmbH (Digital Vision), Hamburg • S. 26: Ingram Publishing, Tattenhall Chester; Fotosearch RF (RF), Waukesha, WI • S. 28: iStockphoto (RF), Calgary, Alberta; Fotofinder (imageS.de/Schulten), Berlin • S. 29: Avenue Images GmbH (Index Stock/McGuire), Hamburg • S. 30: Getty Images (taxi/Andreas Pollok), München; Avenue Images GmbH (Corbis RF), Hamburg • S. 31: Fotosearch RF (Maps Resources), Waukesha, WI; Corbis (Bill Ross), Düsseldorf; Fotofinder (f1-online/PBY), Berlin • S. 32: Fotofinder (Vario Press), Berlin; Fotofinder (Vision Photo), Berlin; Avenue Images GmbH (Image Source RF), Hamburg; Fotosearch RF (Brand X Pictures), Waukesha, WI; Avenue Images GmbH (Banana Stock RF), Hamburg • S. 33: Fotosearch RF (Stockbyte), Waukesha, WI • S. 34: Getty Images (Image Bank/Yellow Dog Prod.), München • S. 35: iStockphoto (RF Bobbie Osborne), Calgary, Alberta; Getty Images (taxi/Stickler), München • S. 36: Fotofinder (Keystone/Zick), Berlin • S. 37: Fotosearch RF (Banana Stock), Waukesha, WI • S. 38: ZEFA (Grace), Düsseldorf; Fotofinder (Mediacolors/Firofoto), Berlin; Fotofinder (Caro/Hoffmann), Berlin; MEV, Augsburg; iStockphoto (RF Mika Hakkonen), Calgary, Alberta; iStockphoto (RF/Maartje van Caspel), Calgary, Alberta; iStockphoto (RF Jostein Hauge), Calgary, Alberta; iStockphoto (RF/Samantha Grandy), Calgary, Alberta; iStockphoto (Andrzej Tokarski), Calgary, Alberta; iStockphoto (RF/Edyta Pawlonska), Calgary, Alberta; iStockphoto (RF Suzannah Skelton), Calgary, Alberta; iStockphoto (RF), Calgary, Alberta; iStockphoto (RF/Jorge Sa), Calgary, Alberta; iStockphoto (RF/Sang Ngyen), Calgary, Alberta; iStockphoto (RF/Greg Nocholas), Calgary, Alberta; iStockphoto (RF Dawn Hudson), Calgary, Alberta; Klett-Archiv (Steinle), Stuttgart • S. 39: Getty Images (stone/Bobbe), München • S. 41: iStockphoto (Grafissimo), Calgary, Alberta • S. 42: Stockfood Photo Stock Agency (Maximilian Stock), München; Corbis (Jim Graigmyle), Düsseldorf • S. 43: Fotofinder (Axel Hess), Berlin • S. 44: Fotofinder (Bilderbox), Berlin • S. 46: Corbis (Reuters/Fred Prouser), Düsseldorf • S. 47: Avenue Images GmbH (Goodshoot), Hamburg • S. 48: Getty Images (Photodisc), München • S. 49: ullstein bild (ddp), Berlin • S. 50: Picture-Alliance (Jochen Siegle), Frankfurt; Corbis (Reuters/Bobante), Düsseldorf • S. 52: Fotosearch RF (Banana Stock), Waukesha, WI • S. 53: DigitalVision, Maintal-Dörnigheim • S. 54: Corbis (RF), Düsseldorf; MEV, Augsburg; Corel Corporation, Unterschleissheim; ZEFA (M. Pedone), Düsseldorf; iStockphoto (RF/Brian Sheldon), Calgary, Alberta; Alamy (Stock Connection: Rob Crandall) • S. 55: creativ collection, Freiburg • S. 56: Alamy Images RM (Penny Tweedie), Abingdon, Oxon; Alamy Images RM (Photo Network), Abingdon, Oxon; Corbis (Swim Ink 2), Düsseldorf; Corbis (Walter Hodges), Düsseldorf • S. 57: Avenue Images GmbH (Index Stock), Hamburg • S. 58: Corbis (Bob Rowan; Progressive Image), Düsseldorf • S. 60: MEV, Augsburg • S. 62: Getty Images (Image Bank/Terje Rakke), München • S. 63: Fotosearch RF (RF), Waukesha, WI; Getty Images (Jo Hale), München • S. 64: Avenue Images GmbH (Banana Stock RF), Hamburg • S. 65: iStockphoto (RF), Calgary, Alberta; Onsight Photography (Simon Carter), Blackheath • S. 66: PhotoAlto (RF), Paris • S. 67: Corbis (RF), Düsseldorf • S. 68: Getty Images (PHotodisc), München; MEV, Augsburg • S. 70: Alamy Images RM (Ange), Abingdon, Oxon • S. 71: Avenue Images GmbH (thinkstock), Hamburg; NASA, Washington , D.C. • S. 72: EasyJet, Bedfordshire; Amazon.de GmbH, München; Google Inc., Mountain View, CA 94043; H+BEDV Datentechnik GmbH, Tettnang; Apple Computer, Feldkirchen; handy.de/Corelations, Hamburg; Bananastock RF (Banana Stock), Watlington/Oxon • S. 73: Getty Images (AFP/Avikaimen), München • S. 76: Getty Images RF (PhotoDisc), München • S. 77: MEV, Augsburg • S. 78: Avenue Images GmbH (Design Pics), Hamburg • S. 79:Corbis (Tom Stewart), Düsseldorf • S. 80: Imageshop RF (Imageshop), Düsseldorf; Corbis (RF), Düsseldorf; Alamy Images RM (RF/BananaStock), Abingdon, Oxon; Robert Bosch GmbH, Stuttgart; Bananastock RF, Watlington/Oxon; Avenue Images GmbH (Brand X Pictures), Hamburg; Alamy Images RM (Photofusion/Solloway), Abingdon, Oxon; Roberto Degli Innocenti, Pistoia • S. 81: Corbis (Tom Stewart), Düsseldorf • S. 82: Avenue Images GmbH (Brand X Pictures), Hamburg; Getty Images (PhotoDisc), München • S. 84: Avenue Images GmbH (Corbis RF), Hamburg • S. 85: MEV, Augsburg; Inmagine (Dynamicgraphics RF), Houston TX • S. 86: Alamy Images RF (RF/Justin Kase), Abingdon, Oxon • S. 87: Getty Images (PhotoDisc), München • S. 88: iStockphoto (RF), Calgary, Alberta; Alamy Images RM (Photofusion/Stadtler), Abingdon, Oxon • S. 89: Fotosearch RF, Waukesha, WI; iStockphoto (RF), Calgary, Alberta • S. 90: Avenue Images GmbH (Corbis RF), Hamburg; Avenue Images GmbH (Banana Stock), Hamburg; DigitalVision (Digital Vision), Maintal-Dörnigheim; Avenue Images GmbH (comstock RF), Hamburg • S. 91: Avenue Images GmbH (Image Source RF), Hamburg • S. 93: Alamy Images RF (RF), Abingdon, Oxon • S. 94: Imageshop RF, Düsseldorf • S. 96: Visum (Fotofinder/Euler), Hamburg; Argum (Fotofinder/Einberger), München; Avenue Images GmbH (imageshop), Hamburg • S. 97: Getty Images RF (Digital Vision), München • S. 98: Alamy Images RM (Dan Atkin), Abingdon, Oxon; Bananastock RF, Watlington/Oxon • S. 99: DigitalVision, Maintal-Dörnigheim • S. 100: John Birdsall Photography, Nottingham • S. 101: Bananastock RF, Watlington/Oxon; John Birdsall Photography, Nottingham • S. 102: Avenue Images GmbH (imageshop), Hamburg; Fotosearch RF (PhotoDisc), Waukesha, WI; Avenue Images GmbH (Image Source/RF), Hamburg • S. 103: Alamy Images RM (Molly Cooper/Photofusion), Abingdon, Oxon • S. 104: John Birdsall Photography, Nottingham; Corbis (Hulton Deutsch), Düsseldorf • S. 109: Van Cleave, Ted/www.totallyaburd., Los Angeles CA 90068 • S. 110: Bananastock RF, Watlington/Oxon • S. 111: Avenue Images GmbH (Corbis RF), Hamburg • S. 113: iStockphoto, Calgary, Alberta • S. 114: Robert Bosch GmbH, Stuttgart • S. 115: Corbis (Sohber), Düsseldorf • S. 116: MEV, Augsburg; Bananastock RF, Watlington/Oxon • S. 117: MEV, Augsburg; Fotosearch RF (PhotoDisc), Waukesha, WI • S. 118: iStockphoto, Calgary, Alberta; Otto Versand, Hamburg • S. 120: Ben & Jerry's Homemade, Inc., South Burlington, VT 05403-6828 • S. 121: Corbis (Craig Aurness), Düsseldorf • S. 122: Fotofinder (R. Jahns), Berlin • S. 123: Nokia, Espoo; Apple Computer, Feldkirchen; The Body Shop Deutschland & Österre, Neuss • S. 124: Getty Images (AFP), München; SONY, Köln • S. 126: Fotosearch RF (Banana Stock), Waukesha, WI • S. 128: obs, Hamburg • S. 129: iStockphoto (James Wooten), Calgary, Alberta; Fotofinder (Stockfood), Berlin • S. 130: Corbis (Larry Williams), Düsseldorf • S. 131: Fotosearch RF (Digital Vision), Waukesha, WI; iStockphoto (Sang Nguyen), Calgary, Alberta; PhotoDisc, Seattle, WA • S. 132: Avenue Images GmbH (Index Stock), Hamburg; iStockphoto (Monika Wisniewska), Calgary, Alberta • S. 133: Alamy Images RM (Popperfoto), Abingdon, Oxon • S. 134: VIA Rail Canada; MEV, Augsburg • S. 136: Getty Images (Image Bank), München; Alamy Images RF (RF), Abingdon, Oxon • S. 137: Getty Images (Image Bank), München • S. 138: Ron Kimball Stock, Mt. View • S. 139: Getty Images (Photodisc), München • S. 140: Avenue Images GmbH (Corbis RF), Hamburg • S. 141: iStockphoto (Joshua Blake), Calgary, Alberta; iStockphoto (Mark Evans), Calgary, Alberta • S. 144: 3M Deutschland GmbH, Neuss; iStockphoto (RF), Calgary, Alberta; Raytheon Company, Waltham, MA • S. 146: Avenue Images GmbH (Digital Vision), Hamburg • S. 148: MEV, Augsburg • S. 150: Avenue Images GmbH (thinkstock RF), Hamburg • S. 151: MEV, Augsburg • S. 152: Getty Images PhotoDisc, Hamburg; MEV, Augsburg • S. 153: Cinetext, Frankfurt • S. 154: GE Energy, Atlanta, GA; www.nordex-online.com • S. 155: Image Source (Imagesource), Köln • S. 156: Corbis (Mark M. Lawrence), Düsseldorf • S. 157: MEV, Augsburg • S. 158: MEV, Augsburg; Widmann, Peter, Tutzing; Getty Images (Photodisc), München; Caro Fotoagentur (Fotofinder/Hoffmann), Berlin; iStockphoto (RF), Calgary, Alberta • S. 159: Alamy Images RM (Janine Wiedel), Abingdon, Oxon • S. 160: Fotosearch RF (PhotoDisc), Waukesha, WI; Getty Images (PhotoDisc), München; Corbis (David Madison), Düsseldorf • S. 161: Getty Images (Photodisc), München • S. 162: Fotosearch RF (image 100), Waukesha, WI; Getty Images RF (Photodisc), München • S. 163: Avenue Images GmbH (Brand X Pictures), Hamburg; Fotosearch RF (PhotoDisc), Waukesha, WI; Getty Images (PhotoDisc), München; Corbis (RF), Düsseldorf; Bananastock RF, Watlington/Oxon • S. 164: Corbis (Reuters), Düsseldorf; Corbis (Reuters/S. Hird), Düsseldorf • S. 166: Bananastock RF, Watlington/Oxon • S. 168: Corbis (Ted Horowitz), Düsseldorf; Corel Corporation, Unterschleissheim; Corbis (Michael Keller), Düsseldorf • S. 170: Fotosearch RF (Design Pics), Waukesha, WI • S. 171: Getty Images (Photodisc), München • S. 172: Mauritius (Superstock), Mittenwald • S. 173: iStockphoto (RF), Calgary, Alberta • S. 174: Camp Walt Whitman, Piermont, NH; iStockphoto (RF/Eldad Yitzhak), Calgary, Alberta • S. 176: MEV, Augsburg • S. 178: Fotosearch RF (PhotoDisc), Waukesha, WI; Joker (David Ausserhofer), Bonn • S. 179: www.canarypete.be • S. 180: Imageshop RF (Imageshop), Düsseldorf • S. 181: Alamy (Phil Talbot) • S. 182: Avenue Images GmbH (Corbis RF), Hamburg • Klappumschlag C: Highways Agency, London; • Klappumschlag F: Corbis (RF), Düsseldorf